P9-CNF-588

Dreamweaver® MX
e-Learning Toolkit

Dreamweaver® MX
e-Learning Toolkit:
Building Web-Based
Training with
CourseBuilder®

Michael Doyle

Wiley Publishing, Inc.

Dreamweaver® MX e-Learning Toolkit: Building Web-Based Training with CourseBuilder®

Published by
Wiley Publishing, Inc.
909 Third Avenue
New York, NY 10022
www.wiley.com

Copyright © 2003 by Wiley Publishing, Inc., Indianapolis, Indiana

Library of Congress Control Number: 2002114849

ISBN: 0-7645-2605-7

Manufactured in the United States of America

10 9 8 7 6 5 4 3 2 1

1B/QX/QT/QT/IN

Published by Wiley Publishing, Inc., Indianapolis, Indiana
Published simultaneously in Canada

No part of this publication may be reproduced, stored in a retrieval system or transmitted in any form or by any means, electronic, mechanical, photocopying, recording, scanning or otherwise, except as permitted under Sections 107 or 108 of the 1976 United States Copyright Act, without either the prior written permission of the Publisher, or authorization through payment of the appropriate per-copy fee to the Copyright Clearance Center, 222 Rosewood Drive, Danvers, MA 01923, (978) 750-8400, fax (978) 646-8700. Requests to the Publisher for permission should be addressed to the Legal Department, Wiley Publishing, Inc., 10475 Crosspoint Blvd., Indianapolis, IN 46256, (317) 572-3447, fax (317) 572-4447, E-Mail: permcoordinator@wiley.com.

LIMIT OF LIABILITY/DISCLAIMER OF WARRANTY: WHILE THE PUBLISHER AND AUTHOR HAVE USED THEIR BEST EFFORTS IN PREPARING THIS BOOK, THEY MAKE NO REPRESENTATIONS OR WARRANTIES WITH RESPECT TO THE ACCURACY OR COMPLETENESS OF THE CONTENTS OF THIS BOOK AND SPECIFICALLY DISCLAIM ANY IMPLIED WARRANTIES OF MERCHANTABILITY OR FITNESS FOR A PARTICULAR PURPOSE. NO WARRANTY MAY BE CREATED OR EXTENDED BY SALES REPRESENTATIVES OR WRITTEN SALES MATERIALS. THE ADVICE AND STRATEGIES CONTAINED HEREIN MAY NOT BE SUITABLE FOR YOUR SITUATION. YOU SHOULD CONSULT WITH A PROFESSIONAL WHERE APPROPRIATE. NEITHER THE PUBLISHER NOR AUTHOR SHALL BE LIABLE FOR ANY LOSS OF PROFIT OR ANY OTHER COMMERCIAL DAMAGES, INCLUDING BUT NOT LIMITED TO SPECIAL, INCIDENTAL, CONSEQUENTIAL, OR OTHER DAMAGES.

For general information on our other products and services or to obtain technical support, please contact our Customer Care Department within the U.S. at 800-762-2974, outside the U.S. at 317-572-3993 or fax 317-572-4002.

Wiley also publishes its books in a variety of electronic formats. Some content that appears in print may not be available in electronic books.

Trademarks: Wiley, the Wiley Publishing logo and related trade dress are trademarks or registered trademarks of Wiley Publishing, Inc., in the United States and other countries, and may not be used without written permission. CourseBuilder is a trademark or registered trademark of CCI Learning Solutions, Inc. Dreamweaver is a trademark or registered trademark of Macromedia, Inc. All other trademarks are the property of their respective owners. Wiley Publishing, Inc., is not associated with any product or vendor mentioned in this book.

 WILEY is a trademark of Wiley Publishing, Inc.

Credits

EXECUTIVE EDITOR
Chris Webb

PROJECT EDITOR
Sharon Nash

TECHNICAL EDITOR
Dan DeRose

COPY EDITOR
Maryann Steinhart

EDITORIAL MANAGER
Mary Beth Wakefield

VICE PRESIDENT AND EXECUTIVE GROUP PUBLISHER
Richard Swadley

VICE PRESIDENT AND EXECUTIVE PUBLISHER
Bob Ipsen

EXECUTIVE EDITORIAL DIRECTOR
Mary Bednarek

PROJECT COORDINATOR
Dale White

GRAPHICS AND PRODUCTION SPECIALISTS
Beth Brooks, Jennifer Click,
Heather Pope, Jeremey Unger

QUALITY CONTROL TECHNICIANS
John Tyler Connoley,
John Greenough

PROOFREADING AND INDEXING
TECHBOOKS Production Services

About the Author

Mike Doyle has been in the technical publishing industry for 20 years as writer, manager, and teacher, having worked on technologies ranging from operating systems to APIs for image and transaction processing systems to office systems.

Mike has been working in the Web development world since 1995, having built two successful companies in that time: PUBSNET, a training company specializing in publishing tool, technology, and process training; and The Editors, a design firm transformed into a Web development group. You can get additional information about Mike and his companies at www.web-graduate.com.

He has taught and presented on many Web tools and technologies, including HTML, XML, Macromedia Dreamweaver, Microsoft FrontPage, Adobe GoLive, HTML Transit. In addition to his technical and tools training, Mike was the senior lecturer in the University of Massachusetts–Lowell Technical Communications Certificate program for 15 years. He frequently presents at regional and national conferences on technical communications and Web technologies.

A Karaoke addict, Mike lives in Massachusetts with his wife, Julia; daughter Genevieve; and son Joseph.

For Julia, the source of everything good.

Preface

Did you know that

- Dreamweaver is the leading Web development tool in the world? Second to none?

- Dreamweaver MX is the version of Dreamweaver *after* Version 4?

- CourseBuilder and Learning Site are free extensions (add-ons) to Dreamweaver MX that were developed by Macromedia?

- Combined, you have everything you need to create a fully-functioning Web-Based Training course that includes highly interactive content, tests, and the ability to track and record student performance?

- The Dreamweaver exchange at Macromedia provides literally hundreds of other free extensions (add-ons) that enable you to create the most powerful and engaging Web sites without expensive additional tools?

This book is for people that want to create Web-Based Training (WBT) *without* substantial investment. Maybe you already use Dreamweaver and want to build WBT capabilities into your existing information set. Or maybe you are an instructor teaching about WBT and want to use a book that provides hands-on experiences. Or maybe you've never used Dreamweaver MX or created WBT but just want to try it out!

Everything you need is in this book and on this CD-ROM. You don't even need Dreamweaver MX to begin, because all of the software (including Dreamweaver MX, Learning Site, and CourseBuilder) is available on the CD-ROM as a fully-functioning 30-day trial.

Who Should Read This Book?

You should. How can I be so sure? If you're reading this, your curiosity has been piqued, probably because you have used tools to create Web pages or want to understand more about e-Learning.

If you've created Web pages with Dreamweaver (or even with some other tool), or wanted to create e-Learning and have a good command of software tools, you can follow this book.

If you don't understanding anything about computers and Web pages, then I am wrong. You shouldn't read this book.

What Hardware and Software Do You Need?

Dreamweaver MX is available for both Windows and Macintosh systems. The following requirements are specified by Macromedia for Dreamweaver MX.

Windows

◆ Windows 98, Windows ME, Windows NT4 (with SP 4 or later), or Windows 2000/XP:

◆ Intel Pentium II processor or equivalent 300+ MHz

◆ 96MB of available RAM (128MB recommended)

◆ Netscape Navigator or Internet Explorer 4.0 or greater

◆ 275MB available disk space

◆ 256-color monitor capable of 800x600 resolution (1024x768, millions of colors, recommended)

◆ A CD-ROM drive

As of the writing of this book, the Learning Site extension does not run on Windows 98 or Windows ME (check www.macromedia.com/exchange/ for the latest information). You can, however, use Dreamweaver MX and CourseBuilder on Windows 98 and Windows ME systems.

Macintosh

◆ Power Mac G3 or better

◆ Mac OS 9.1 or higher, or Mac OS X 10.1 or higher

◆ Netscape Navigator or Internet Explorer 4.0 or later

◆ 96MB of RAM (128MB recommended)

◆ 275MB available disk space

◆ 256-color monitor capable of 800x600 resolution (1024x768, millions of colors, recommended. Thousands of colors required for OS X.)

How this Book is Organized

When I proposed this book, I envisioned a book that combined process information with tool information. When I started learning CourseBuilder and Learning Site,

I found it difficult to follow the process *and* difficult to understand the concepts (since both the extensions and the process for developing e-Learning were both new to me at the time).

Now, after having used CourseBuilder and Learning Site extensively, I believe the processes and concepts were just poorly communicated because they focused on software functions instead of tasks. This book focuses on tasks, solutions, and processes, and provides many tools and samples for you to follow.

The book itself is organized as a process – and CourseBuilder and Learning Site are unbelievably good!

Part 1: Laying the Foundation

The goal of the first part of the book is to set the groundwork for the book. By the end of Part I, you should have an understanding of the basic concepts and processes for CourseBuilder and Learning Site. Part I also serves to bring up to speed anyone who is new to teaching and e-Learning concepts – or anyone who needs to understand the basics of Dreamweaver MX.

Goal: When you complete Part I, you should have a paper prototype of your course *and* a Learning Site structure for your course within a Dreamweaver MX site.

Part II: Test and Activity

CourseBuilder has five different types of test and activity interactions that you can use to assess student knowledge. Chapter 8 provides an overview of CourseBuilder interactions. Each of the remaining chapters in Part II describes a different type of CourseBuilder interaction:

◆ Chapter 9 describes True/False and Multiple-Choice interactions, which enable you to define a set of choices from which students select an answer (or answers). Multiple-choice questions test a student's ability to recognize a correct answer or answers.

◆ Chapter 10 discusses Text-Entry (fill-in-the-blank) interactions, which let students type an answer. Text-entry questions test a student's ability to recall a correct answer or answers.

◆ Chapter 11 explains Drag-and-Drop (match-up) interactions, which let students match text or objects from one group to another group. Drag-and-drop interactions test a student's ability to understand relationships.

◆ Chapter 12 discusses Explore (hot-area) interactions, which let students click on different areas of a graphic to answer a test question or to explore for learning. Explore interactions test a student's ability to understand components.

◆ Chapter 13 describes Slider (ranges) interactions, which let students slide an object along a track to answer a test question or to select options. Slider interactions test a student's ability to understand ranges.

Each chapter provides multiple application examples showing the step-by-step process for creating each type of test.

Goal: When you complete Part II, you should have all of your tests and activities developed.

Part III: Controlling and Processing Interactions

CourseBuilder controls enable you to manage interactivity between students and course content, and to build highly complex testing scenarios and processing rules. Chapter 14 provides an overview of controls and processing within CourseBuilder. The remaining chapters in Part III describe CourseBuilder controls and the Action Manager:

- ◆ Chapter 15 describes the use of buttons, which can be used to initiate the processing and evaluation of one or multiple test questions.

- ◆ Chapter 16 discusses the use of timers, which can be used to limit the amount of time a student is allotted for a test, a test question, or an activity.

- ◆ Chapter 17 explains the use of the Action Manager, the component within CourseBuilder that defines all of the processing rules and logic for tests and activities, including scoring of single-page tests as well as tests that span across multiple pages.

Each chapter provides application examples.

Goal: When you complete Part III, you should have all the knowledge necessary to develop a course using every test available within CourseBuilder, scoring student performance without using a database, and presenting those results to students at the end of the course or exam.

Part IV: Tracking Results

Learning Site comes with a complete tracking system using a pre-built Microsoft Access Database. Chapter 18 describes in detail how to use the Microsoft Access Database within your organization to manage students and courses. Because the database and scripts are developed, you *do not need to be a programmer* to set up tracking to the database.

Chapter 19 explains how to set up CourseBuilder to communicate with another Learning Management System if you already use an LMS in your organization. CourseBuilder can communicate with any AICC-compliant LMS.

Goal: When you complete Part IV, you should be able to set up and use the "out of the box" Microsoft Access database that ships with Learning Site, or understand the rules for getting CourseBuilder to communicate with your LMS.

Part V: Appendixes

There are four appendixes:

- ◆ Appendix A describes the contents of the CD-ROM.

- ◆ Appendix B explains how to install the Learning Site templates (and associated Cascading Style Sheets) that ship with the CD-ROM, and how to create custom Learning Site templates so that you can fully customize the look and feel of your courses.

- ◆ Appendix C discusses how to create custom CourseBuilder interactions.

- ◆ Appendix D describes how to change your CourseBuilder preferences.

Conventions Used in This Book

This book uses some (but not many) conventions.

Menu Selections

You will periodically see references to menu selections, such as Choose File → Learning Site → Create Learning Site. This convention is a path showing you how to navigate a menu structure.

The first part of the selection is the option on a program's main menu (in this case, you would look for the File option). When you select the File option, the menu that opens displays the next option (in this case, the Learning Site option); finally, when you select the Learning Site option, the menu that pops up displays the final option (in this case, Create Learning Site).

Mouse

The term *click* means a single mouse click, and *double-click* means two mouse clicks in quick succession.

You will sometimes see the word *select*, which is an abbreviation for "move the mouse pointer over the item and click."

Monospace Font

You will see a `monospace font` used throughout this book to indicate JavaScript code, HTML tags, variables, Web addresses, filenames, and other "verbatim" types of information.

Acknowledgments

In addition to requiring a tremendous amount of "figuring out" of tools that have minimal information available (Learning Site and CourseBuilder), this book also required a tremendous amount of work because of the robust nature of the samples, templates, planners, and other materials that ship with the CD-ROM. Luckily, I have three very talented individuals who work for me at The Editors (`www.theeditors.com`), and who have contributed greatly to this work.

First, I cannot begin to tell you how important Dan DeRose (of The Editors) has been to the successful completion of this book. His uncanny ability to solve every problem that I couldn't made a tremendous difference in the timely delivery of this book (which I guess is why Dan scored higher on Macromedia's Dreamweaver certification exam than I did!).

Next in line for great thanks is my daughter, Genevieve Doyle, who is a graphics artist with The Editors. She came through many times when I needed hand-drawn art (for example, her wonderful illustrations of Vannevar Bush and Tim Berners-Lee in the *HTML Basics* course), Learning Site templates, and other visual elements.

My appreciation also goes to Peter Grant of The Editors, who, along with Dan and Genevieve, developed many of the Learning Site templates.

Aside from the folks who work for me at The Editors, the biggest help in the original ideas and design for the book come from a lot of communications with Chris Webb, Executive Editor at Wiley Publishing. It was Chris who came up with the idea for the toolkit, which I think turned a good book into a great solution!

Finally, many thanks to Sharon Nash for driving the project through all phases (and many departments!) within Wiley, and Maryann Steinhart for many insightful editing suggestions.

Contents at a Glance

Contents

Part I

Laying the Foundation

Chapter 1

Using the Dreamweaver MX e-Learning Toolkit

- ◆ Looking at what this book can help you do

- ◆ Exploring the toolkit

- ◆ Finding additional help and support

So YOUR REQUEST for a $2 million budget for e-Learning this year got a response of, "Here's 45 bucks. Buy Doyle's book and do what you can!" Of course, the next logical question is, "OK, Doyle, here's my 45 bucks — what can I do?"

First, thank you for the money. I take my fiduciary responsibilities very seriously, so I expect your return on this investment to be one of the most profitable ventures you've ever undertaken! In exchange for your investment, I will teach you how to

- ◆ Use Learning Site to build course navigational shells that include pre-programmed page-turners and an automatically assembled menu.

- ◆ Integrate many different types of tests within your course using CourseBuilder, including multiple-choice, fill-in-the-blank, and match-up tests and activities.

- ◆ Choose from 17 pre-designed templates for navigation to jump-start the development of your course.

- ◆ Track your student performance data using the pre-built Microsoft Access database that ships with Learning Site LMS.

Another good question is, "Why bank my e-Learning on Dreamweaver MX?" When you use Dreamweaver MX to create your Web-Based Training (WBT), you are using *the* most widely-used and highly-regarded Web publishing tool in the world — second to none, with literally millions *and* millions of users throughout the world. When any software program has millions of users, you can trust the software to be both highly tested *and* supported.

You can try the demo version on this book's CD-ROM and, if you decide to invest in Dreamweaver MX as the solution, your total cash outlay for the software license *and* this book is around $400, with nothing else required!

What You Do and Don't Need to Know

Anyone who is reasonably proficient with computers and understands how to create Web pages can be successful using this book.

Maybe you've used earlier versions of Dreamweaver, or Microsoft FrontPage, or Adobe GoLive. . . or maybe you've hand-coded HTML. I've taught all of these tools and technologies, so I make this statement with the background to do so: if you know the basics of developing Web pages, *you can* follow this book!

To make the book inclusive rather than exclusive, I've included chapters to help bridge common gaps:

- Don't know the basics of Web-Based Training? Chapter 2 provides an overview of e-Learning concepts.

- Don't know how to use Dreamweaver MX? Chapter 3 provides an introduction to the tool.

- Don't understand the basics of creating tests? Chapter 5 describes general principles for developing effective tests.

What's in the Toolkit?

Trying to take my publisher's challenge of building a toolkit rather than just writing a book, I've gathered or developed and documented everything you need to build a complete Web-Based Training (WBT) course, including

- 11 planning documents.

- 17 pre-built Learning Site Templates (12 available *only* with this book).

- Trial version of Dreamweaver MX software.

- Learning Site and CourseBuilder software, which are free extensions available to Dreamweaver MX users.

- A Microsoft Access Database built by Learning Site to track student performance (requires Microsoft Access 97 or later).

- A dozen samples.

And all with easy-to-follow, step-by-step instructions for designing, developing, and implementing your own WBT course!

Planning

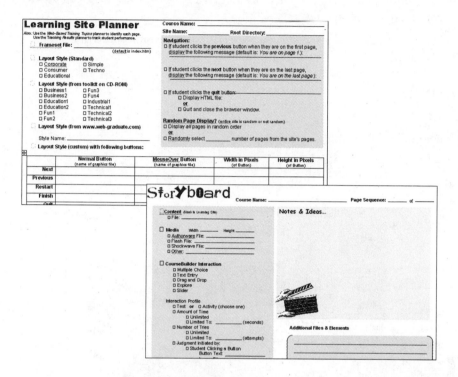

This book is as much about the process for developing Web-based training with Dreamweaver MX as it is about using the tool. Toward that end, the toolkit contains 11 planning documents that will help you through the entire process of developing your course, from taking inventory of current content to storyboarding a prototype of your course.

These documents are not meant to act like a bureaucracy. Instead, use them wherever they help *your* process:

- ◆ Content and media inventory planners help you take stock of current content.

- ◆ WBT topic, topic weight, and question planners help you organize your new course.

- ◆ Learning objectives planner helps you identify *know* and *do* content in the course.

◆ Storyboards and page sequencers help you organize content.

◆ Condition planner for interactions and element properties help you create the logic for evaluating tests.

◆ Learning Site planner helps you focus on the decisions you will need to make when creating your Learning Site.

Learning

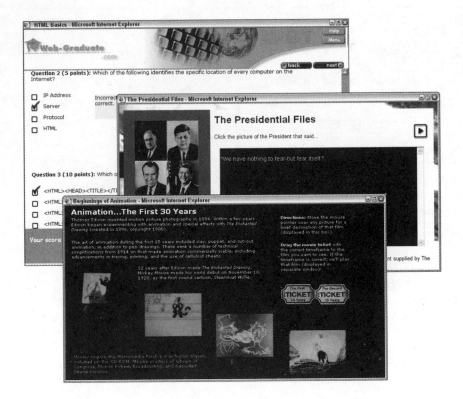

Having been a technology teacher for many years, I've found that people learn best by seeing *and* doing, so I've included many samples on the CD-ROM to show you how to use CourseBuilder and Learning Site to build engaging content and performance evaluation, and to let you practice, practice, practice!

Want a feel for the capabilities of CourseBuilder and Learning Site? I'd highly recommend you start with the *HTML Basics* course, which is a complete course—including a timed and graded final examination!

Table 1-1 lists some of the samples on the CD-ROM.

TABLE 1-1 SELECTED SAMPLES ON THE CD-ROM

Folder	Open this File
HTML Basics	index.html
Beginnings of Animation	animation.htm
GUI	gui-learn.htm
Cloze Test	vocabulary.htm
Kindergarten	my-house.htm
Multiple Pages Scoring	exam-directions-frameset.htm
Presidents	presidents1.htm
Speed Limits	driving-test.htm
The Mesozoic Era	dinosaur-info1.htm

Implementing

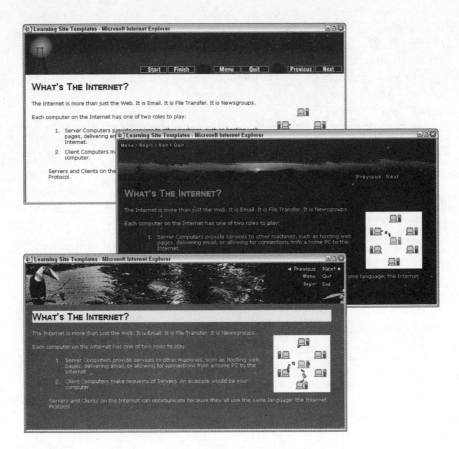

Once you have learned how to create Web-based training with CourseBuilder and Learning Site, you can use any of the 17 templates included with this kit to take the same content and present it in many different ways! Five templates ship with Learning Site — the additional 12 templates were specially developed for this book and are available only on this book's CD-ROM.

Use the templates in combination with Cascading Style Sheets to develop visually engaging sites. (You can, of course, create your own design, if you are so inclined.)

In addition to the Learning Site templates, CourseBuilder provides 20 test templates that let you easily create tests that evaluate and provide feedback to your online students. These tests include

◆ Six different true/false and multiple-choice templates

◆ Seven different drag-and-drop (match-ups) templates

- Two different text-entry (fill-in-the-blanks) templates
- Three different explore (graphical hot areas) templates
- Two different slider (ranges) templates

Ongoing Help and Support

Of course, the most valuable part of your investment in this book is your time and effort. Nobody wants to invest time and effort in developing Web-based training, only to find themselves on an island whenever they need help. By choosing the number one Web-development tool in the world (Dreamweaver) to create your Web-based training, you'll find plenty of resources for assistance—all you need to do is ask for help!

There are a number of online sources you can use for help and support, all available through the Web—and all responsive to requests for help.

The most useful resource specifically for CourseBuilder and Learning Site support is the Dreamweaver Attain (original name of CourseBuilder) discussion list, which you can find at `http://ls.kuleuven.ac.be/archives/dwa.html`.

This list is highly responsive, and contains a searchable archive of four years' worth of discussion about CourseBuilder and Learning Site. The list continues to be highly active, and is the best resource for helping you resolve issues specific to CourseBuilder and Learning Site.

Macromedia maintains many different support forums. In particular, I highly recommend the Dreamweaver product forum, and the Dreamweaver Extensions forum (CourseBuilder and Learning Site are Dreamweaver extensions), both available at `www.macromedia.com/support/forums/`.

Macromedia also publishes a CourseBuilder and Learning Site support page, a searchable database of TechNotes and tips, at `www.macromedia.com/support/coursebuilder/`.

I use the following site to post updates, tidbits, errata, URL changes, and other types of important information related to this book: `www.web-graduate.com`.

Finally, when you *do* get that $2 million dollar budget approved, please—give me a call!

Summary

This chapter provided a taste of what you get when you purchase this toolkit. The remainder of the book shows you how to use this toolkit to create e-Learning *solutions*.

Chapter 2

What is e-Learning All About?

IN THIS CHAPTER

- ◆ Understanding learning
- ◆ Examining Bloom's taxonomy for learning
- ◆ Defining your learning objectives
- ◆ Understanding distance learning and e-learning
- ◆ Understanding the WBT development process
- ◆ Exploring the *HTML Basics* course

THE EDUCATION MARKET, from public and private schools and universities to corporate training, is an enormous part of the U.S. economy. At $815 billion in the year 2000, the education market represented 9% of the nation's Gross National Product (GNP)[1], second only to healthcare expenditures.

Education is no longer limited – or even primarily limited – to the 21-and-under crowd. We've become a nation of lifelong learners. Skilled jobs in 1950 represented approximately 20% of all jobs in the United States[2]; in 50 years time, that percentage has grown to approximately 85%[3]. To maintain those skills, approximately 77 million adults are enrolled in some level of postsecondary training – compare that number to the approximately 47 million students in grades K–12[4].

Although analyst estimates for the e-Learning share of the education market in the United States have been vastly disparate, most analysts see annual growth levels of 50–100% throughout most of the first decade of this century. According to authors of *The Knowledge Web*, the e-Learning market in 2000 for K–12 was $1.6 billion, growing to $6.9 billion by 2003.

---

1 Cappelli, Gregory, Scott Wilson, and Michael Husman, e-Learning: Power for the Knowledge Economy (2000: Credit Suisse First Boston Corporation), page 127.

2 Moe, Michael and Henry Blodgett. The Knowledge Web. (2000: Merrill Lynch & Co., Global Securities Research & Economics Group, Global Fundamental Equity Research Department), page 173.

3 Meister, Jeanne, Corporate University Xchange, Inc. Testimony to the Web-based Education Commission, September 15, 2000.

4 Levine, Arthur. The Remaking of the American University. Presentation made at The Blackboard Summit. Washington, DC, March 20, 2000.

Connectivity levels are very high in the public schools. According to the Department of Education, 98% of public schools had computers with Internet access for instructional purposes (excluding administrative computers) in the year 2000. Furthermore, the ratio of students to computers for instructional purposes throughout the United States was 5 students to 1 computer, a level considered reasonable by the President's Committee of Advisors on Science and Technology.

The authors of *The Knowledge Web* also estimated the e-Learning market in 2000 for post-secondary students to be at $1.2 billion, growing to $7 billion by 2003. In the post-secondary education market in 1998, 58% of degree-granting colleges and universities offered distance learning; by 2002, that percentage rose to 84%, according to the American Society for Training and Development (ASTD).

All of these figures point to one fact: explosive growth in the use of the Internet, and particularly the Web, for delivering education and training.

Whenever growth in a technology increases at a rapid pace, a fair amount of confusion, particularly about concepts and terminology, ensues. This chapter is designed to provide the background terms and concepts for understanding the context of education within the technology of the Internet and, more specifically, the World Wide Web.

What is Learning?

Human skills fall into three domains:

- *Cognitive skills*, which drive our intellectual judgment.

- *Psychomotor skills*, which drive our physical judgment.

- *Affective skills*, which drive our social and behavioral judgment.

Learning is any person's (organism's?) ability to assimilate information from the external world to create a "new and improved" set of skills.

Teaching is the driving – *and* guiding – force behind learning. In the classroom, that force is the teacher. In distance learning, that force is typically the students themselves.

Education is the entire process of bringing learning and teaching together.

In the late 1940s through the early 1950s, Benjamin Bloom, a professor at the University of Chicago, headed a group of educational psychologists developing a classification for learning. In 1956, he published a book, *Taxonomy of Educational Objectives,* in which he outlined a model of cognitive learning that is still in high use today.

Bloom's model categorizes cognitive learning into six levels, with students using information in more complex ways at each subsequent level. The model sits as a background structure for our work because e-Learning is generally considered appropriate mainly for cognitive learning. Table 2-1 outlines Bloom's taxonomy of cognitive learning.

TABLE 2-1 BLOOM'S TAXONOMY OF COGNITIVE LEARNING

Cognitive Level	Student Uses Information To	Test Students By Asking Them To
Knowledge	Understand facts	Choose the correct fact.
		Answers are correct or incorrect.
Comprehension	Grasp meaning	Choose the correct summary, description, analogy, outcome.
		Answers are correct or incorrect.
Application	Solve problems with absolute right/wrong answers	Choose the correct solution, classification, calculation.
		Answers are correct or incorrect.
Analysis	Categorize information into components and patterns	Choose the best explanation, classification, comparison, inference....
		Answers are judgment.
Synthesis	Generalize and predict	Choose the best plan, generalization, "what if?", modification.
		Answers are judgment.
Evaluation	Make judgments	Choose the best ranking, order, conclusion, decision.
		Answers are judgment.

Although the first three levels (knowledge, comprehension, and application) are easiest to convey and test in Web-Based Training, you can also convey and test for student analysis, synthesis, and evaluation. For example, a multiple-choice question might require students to synthesize and evaluate information from a case study *before* they can reasonably select a correct answer, as in the following example:

You've just read the case summary of *State of Massachusetts v Clyde*. Given the facts of the case, select the best course of action for Clyde's attorney:
1. Continue to the trial and let Clyde testify.
2. Continue to the trial but do not let Clyde testify.
3. Recommend Clyde accept the plea bargain offered by the prosecution.
4. Hold your decision until Wilhelm testifies, even though waiting removes the plea offer.

Since these higher levels are levels of judgment and not black-and-white answers, they are often tested with multiple-choice questions that ask students to select the *best* choice. Ultimately, a "best choice" is a matter of judgment, and the underlying objective is to guide students to develop higher levels of thinking.

For the system of "best choice" to be accepted by students, experts must provide the logic and justification for grading such questions of judgment as correct or incorrect. An example of such an expert response in grading might be similar to the following:

Given the facts of the case, choice 3 is not the best answer because....

The best answer is choice 1 because....

What is Distance Learning?

Distance learning is by no means a new concept. In fact, it is older than electronic communications (a technological era launched by Samuel F.B. Morse's invention of the telegraph in 1840).

In the late 1830s Sir Isaac Pitman developed a system of phonetic-based short-hand that is still in wide use today. With the availability of the penny post in England, Pitman began teaching his shorthand courses through the mail, launching the era of distance learning.

The concept of distance learning took off in the late 19th and early 20th centuries in the United States. In 1883, the State of New York authorized the completion of degrees by correspondence at the Chautauqua Institute (Sunday school teachers trained at the institute during the summer, and then completed their training during the winter using mail correspondence.)

In 1890, Thomas J. Foster, a newspaperman, developed a correspondence program to enable motivated coal miners to train for jobs as supervisors and foremen. He founded the company International Correspondence School (ICS) to foster distance education. The program was an immediate success, enrolling more than 250,000 students in the first 10 years. By the early 1920s, ICS had trained nearly 2.5 million people worldwide in various home study courses.

Distance education through correspondence became a key vehicle for inexpensively delivering training to millions of adults who wanted to advance in their careers.

ICS is still in existence today, having recently become part of Thomson Education Direct. It's on the Web at www.educationdirect.com.

Distance learning based on correspondence schools continues through today, although such organizations (for example, ICS) are mainly moving toward Web-Based Training rather than United States Postal Service for closing the distance between student and teacher.

What is e-Learning?

Any learning experience that involves electronic technology as the key enabling factor is e-Learning. e-Learning could be delivered in many different ways:

◆ CD/DVD/Cassette

◆ Video

◆ Telephone

◆ Interactive television

◆ Internet

Of course, the explosion in e-Learning is largely due to the explosion of a specific delivery vehicle on the Internet: the World Wide Web, which allows for a high level of interactivity between the student and the e-teacher.

According to a report published by the U.S. Department of Education, 7.6% of college students participated in some sort of e-Learning during 1999–2000. Of those that participated, 37.3% participated in live TV/audio events; 39.3% participated in prerecorded TV/audio events; and 60.1% participated in Internet-based e-Learning.

What is Web-Based Training?

In its strictest definition, Web-Based Training (WBT) is e-Learning specifically delivered through the World Wide Web. However, in practical use it has come to encompass e-Learning that blends many different Internet-based technologies.

Web-Based Training is primarily divided into two main categories that are distinguished by time and participants:

◆ *Synchronous* learning (people focused), where students and instructors participate at a specific time to interact with each other using Internet technologies. Synchronous learning follows the traditional classroom model, where training is an event.

◆ *Asynchronous* learning (computer focused), where students primarily interact with a computer at their convenience using Internet technologies. Asynchronous learning typically follows the model of self-paced learning.

In many cases, Web-Based Training blends characteristics of both asynchronous and synchronous learning models. Some of the more common enabling Internet technologies used for Web-Based Training include the following:

◆ Chat (synchronous)

◆ Real-time audio and videoconferencing (synchronous)

- ◆ Whiteboard/presentation technologies (synchronous)
- ◆ World Wide Web (asynchronous)
- ◆ E-mail (asynchronous)
- ◆ File Transfer Protocol (asynchronous)
- ◆ Newsgroups and bulletin boards (asynchronous)

Following the instructional design model

Although the delivery vehicle and development tools for creating Web-Based Training are markedly different from traditional classroom materials, the overall instructional design process is similar.

The purpose of the instructional design process is to guide the development of a learning tool (paper course, online course, instructor guide, and so forth) so that the tool best meets the learning objectives. This process, which generally follows the standard model for any type of large-scale development, has five steps (see Figure 2-1), as follows:

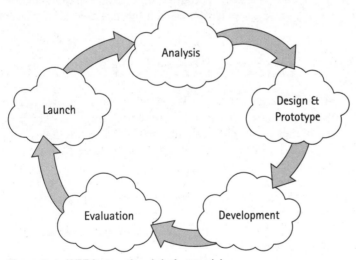

Figure 2-1: WBT instructional design model.

1. *Analysis* determines who needs to be trained, what they need to be trained in, and under what conditions the training will occur. The result of such analysis is a list of learning objectives used to drive the design of the course.

2. *Design and Prototype* creates the user interface (design) for the course, as well as a prototype that shows the layout for each screen and the flow of the entire course.

3. *Development* creates the content and interactions, and pulls together all pieces of the course.

4. *Evaluation* provides extensive testing of the course before launching.

5. *Launch* makes the final course available to all members of the intended audience.

The material covered in this book focuses on the second (design and prototype) and third (development) steps:

Defining learning objectives

A learning objective is a goal to create a targeted, measurable, and positive change in the performance of a skill; for WBT, a positive change in cognitive skills as a result of cognitive learning. When you state your learning objectives, you must state the following:

- Expected change in cognition. What can the student do differently?

- Conditions of learning. Under what conditions and support will students achieve this change in cognitive skill?

- Standards for measurement. Will you test students? Will they demonstrate the change in some other way?

Learning objectives typically fall into one of two categories: *know* or *do (the intellectual side of do, not to be confused with psychomotor skills)*. Both categories of objectives, however, are usually stated as action verbs. Table 2-2 shows examples of action verbs that could be used in stating learning objectives.

The learning objective for the *HTML Basics* course, for example, is:

Students who complete the course will be able to *read and write the HTML code* for:

- HTML file segments

- Paragraphs, formatted text, and headers

- Unnumbered, numbered, and glossary lists

- Tables (including headers, captions, and cell layout)

- Images and hyperlinks

- Attaching External Cascading Style Sheets

In addition, you will be able to identify:

- Internet protocols, servers, IP addresses

- Source and destination anchors in a hyperlink

TABLE 2-2 EXAMPLES OF ACTION VERBS FOR LEARNING OBJECTIVES

Adjust	Find	Recover
Assemble	Identify	Repair
Build	Install	Replace
Calculate	List	Resolve
Change	Maintain	Solve
Construct	Match	Standardize
Debate	Operate	Troubleshoot
Detect	Organize	Validate
Disassemble	Rebuild	
Explain	Record	

Notice that the learning objective uses the action verbs *read, write,* and *identify* to specify the learning objective.

In many ways, learning objectives also serve to motivate students. In the marketing world, benefits statements motivate potential buyers by answering, "What can I do with the product or service?" In the education world, learning objectives answer, "What can I do with what I learn?"

The toolkit includes a Learning Objectives Planner that helps you keep track of specific objectives for your WBT course.

Understanding technical issues for WBT

Because of the nature of the technologies used in Web-Based Training, there are four questions that you need to consider as you make decisions about your course:

- ◆ Which browsers do I target?
- ◆ Which screen resolutions do I target?
- ◆ Which plug-ins do I require?
- ◆ What network speed do I target?

Let's take a look at each of these considerations.

WHICH BROWSERS DO I TARGET?

The reason this question is so troublesome is that there are many functions within CourseBuilder that don't work (or don't work well) with various versions of Netscape Navigator. For example, drag-and-drop and explore interactions do not work at all with Netscape Navigator 4.x, and have troubles through Netscape Navigator 7.0 (the latest version of Netscape Navigator as of this writing).

The answer to the question, however, is becoming less relevant because of usage statistics. Table 2-3 shows the browser version usage statistics for September 2002, based on browser identifications logged for site visits by `thecounter.com`. (TheCounter.Com measures an array of Web statistics for many different Internet sites, and tallies those numbers into global Web statistics each month). Notice that Internet Explorer (4x–6x) accounts for 92% of the identified browsers.

TABLE **2-3 BROWSER VERSIONS IN USE**

Browser	Percentage Using
Internet Explorer 5.x	48%
Internet Explorer 6.x	42%
Netscape Navigator 4.x	2%
Internet Explorer 4.x	2%
All Others	6%

Toward the end of 2002, Internet Explorer's complete dominance of the browser market has been reflected in numerous Internet surveys.

WHICH SCREEN RESOLUTIONS DO I TARGET?

Screen resolution determines the grid size that is used to illuminate a computer monitor. Smaller screen resolutions mean that screens hold less information, and larger screen resolutions mean that screens hold more information.

Figure 2-2 shows a screen capture from the *HTML Basics* course at 800x600 resolution.

Figure 2-3 shows that same screen capture from the *HTML Basics* course at 1024x768.

Screen resolution is a setting that students can change, regardless of their monitor size. A student with a 21-inch monitor could set a screen resolution of 1024x768, and so could a student with a 13-inch monitor. Overlaying the same 1024x768 grid on a smaller size monitor, however, creates much smaller text and images.

Figure 2-2: A screen from the HTML Basics course at 800x600 screen resolution.

Figure 2-3: A screen from the HTML Basics course at 1024x764 screen resolution.

Table 2-4 shows the screen resolutions logged for site visits by thecounter.com. Notice that the single most popular resolution is 800x600, with almost half the people using the Web preferring that setting. With such high numbers for that resolution, I highly recommend that you test your WBT course on an 800x600 resolution to make sure everything looks OK.

Table 2-4 SCREEN RESOLUTIONS IN USE

Screen Resolution	Percentage Using
640x480	2%
800x600	48%
1024x768	38%
1152x864	3%
1280x1024	4%
All Others	5%

Statistics become quickly out of date. To check the latest statistics on browser usage and resolution settings, go to www.thecounter.com.

WHICH PLUG-INS DO I REQUIRE?

Plug-ins annoy users. That being said, there are a few plug-ins that are both popular and freely available to help you bring rich media content to your WBT course. Table 2-5 outlines the top seven plug-ins in the summer of 2002, according to research from the NPD Group (www.npd.com).

If you decide to use content that requires a plug-in, I strongly suggest that you

◆ Do not use the plug-in for critical content or navigation, since students may not want to download and install the plug-in.

◆ Include a statement in the course requirements about the need for the plug-in.

◆ Include a link to the plug-in so that students can easily find and download the plug-in if they so choose.

TABLE 2-5 TOP 7 BROWSER PLUG-INS

Plug-In	Percentage of Browsers Using
Macromedia Flash Player	98%
Java	90%
Adobe Acrobat Reader	77%
Macromedia Shockwave Player	70%
Windows Media Player	64%
Real Player	55%
QuickTime Player	39%

WHAT NETWORK SPEED DO I TARGET?

Have you heard of the term nanosecond? It used to be a unit of measurement for computer processing. Today, it measures student patience while waiting for downloads.

Imagine, if you will, a conversation with another person at a lively party. If the "give and take" in the conversation is moving along, very likely both people are engaged in the topic and in the interactivity of the conversation. Now, imagine that same conversation with 30-second gaps between each sentence. No matter how engaging the topic, the conversation would die quickly!

The same is true with any information delivered on the Web. Although many people have high-speed access, many more do not. The consensus of a number of research organizations puts the number of U.S. households with high-speed access at approximately 25% of online households in 2002. Furthermore, by 2007 that percentage is expected to only rise to just over 40%.

The connection speed of corporate networks is substantially better, and the result is more people accessing the Internet, and specifically the Web, from work. According to Nielsen NetRatings, the number of American office workers accessing the Web from work was 46 million, with an average access time of more than 29 hours per month.

Although Internet connection speeds are getting faster, there are significant numbers of folks (particularly in the home markets) with slower connections. Unless you know for sure that your students have high-speed access, I recommend you maintain tight control on the size of content for the foreseeable future.

The HTML Basics Course

The *HTML Basics* course is included in the toolkit to demonstrate a complete course developed using Dreamweaver MX, CourseBuilder, and Learning Site.

I highly recommend you take the course, which takes about three hours in total (there are eight course segments, making it easy to leave and return to the course at your convenience). *HTML Basics* is a complete Web-Based Training course that includes

- ◆ More than 125 pages

- ◆ Examples of all CourseBuilder interactions

- ◆ 18 graded CourseBuilder tests, including student evaluations for each

- ◆ Site structure built using Learning Site

Navigation within the course is easy. The Next and Previous buttons act as page-turners, moving you through the course one page at a time. The course also has a Menu button that launches a list of topics (see Figure 2-4).

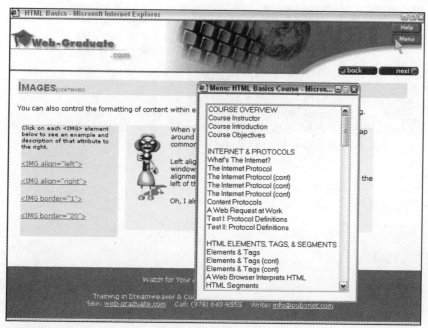

Figure 2-4: The menu window for the HTML Basics course.

You can click on any page in the menu and "jump into" the course at that location. If you only want to view the tests, for example, you can jump to each test by using the menu.

The course is highly interactive, using different tools to engage the learner into activities. For example, the course contains many blackboard exercises (see Figure 2-5), where students can try coding HTML on a blackboard and viewing the results in a browser.

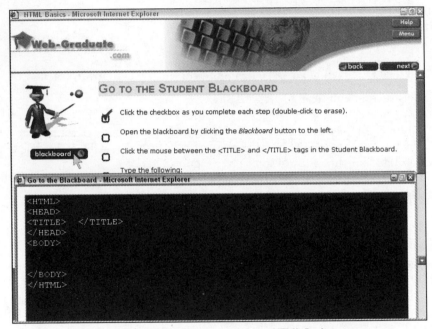

Figure 2-5: One of many blackboard exercises in the HTML Basics course.

Because the *HTML Basics* course uses every capability of CourseBuilder and Learning Site, it is by far the most comprehensive example on the CD-ROM.

Summary

This chapter provided an overview of the e-Learning market and opportunities, as well as grounding in e-Learning terminology, including

- ◆ The basics of learning, e-Learning, and Web-Based Training
- ◆ Defining learning objectives
- ◆ The key technical issues of Web-Based Training that affect your WBT design decisions

For further reading on Web design, I highly recommend two books considered to be WBT classics:

- ◆ William Horton's *Designing Web-Based Training* (Wiley, ISBN 0-471-35614-X).

- ◆ Margaret Driscoll's *Web-Based Training: Creating e-Learning Experiences* (Jossey-Bass/Pfeiffer, ISBN 0-7879-5619-8).

The next chapter provides a crash course on Dreamweaver MX. If you already know Dreamweaver MX, skip to Chapter 4.

Chapter 3

A Crash Course on Dreamweaver MX

IN THIS CHAPTER

- ◆ Understanding the Dreamweaver MX Workspace

- ◆ Designing page layout using layout tables

- ◆ Managing reusable content using library items

- ◆ Designing content style using external Cascading Style Sheets (CSS)

- ◆ Developing interactive pages, including rollovers, navigation bars, jump menus, and other object behaviors

- ◆ Working with layers

MACROMEDIA DREAMWEAVER IS THE most popular Web authoring tool on the market today. The latest version, Dreamweaver MX, combines multiple previous tools (Dreamweaver 4, Dreamweaver UltraDev 4, and HomeSite code editing) into a single, extraordinarily powerful Web authoring tool. But, alas, as with most things in the software world, with such power comes complexity.

This chapter provides an overview of Dreamweaver MX for people who are familiar with Web authoring, but not necessarily with Dreamweaver. It includes many abbreviated examples that help experienced Web authors quickly understand the Dreamweaver MX interface.

- ◆ Already familiar with Dreamweaver MX? Skip ahead to Chapter 4.

- ◆ Familiar with Dreamweaver 4 but want to understand the new interface? Skim this chapter.

- ◆ Want the definitive source for anything and everything about Dreamweaver MX? Read Joseph Lowery's *Dreamweaver MX Bible* (Wiley, ISBN 0-7645-4931-6).

Let's get started!

Understanding the Dreamweaver MX Workspace

The Dreamweaver MX Workspace has been refined to such a point that much of the tool's power is within a single click of the main screen. To launch Dreamweaver MX, choose Start → All Programs → Macromedia → Macromedia Dreamweaver MX.

If this is your first time running the program, Dreamweaver MX displays the Workspace Setup dialog box, shown in Figure 3-1.

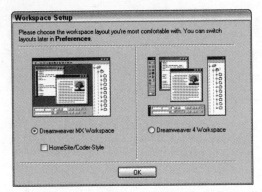

Figure 3-1: Dreamweaver MX Workspace Setup dialog box.

Select Dreamweaver MX Workspace, and then click OK.

Dreamweaver MX displays an Untitled Document in the document window surrounded by a series of toolbars and panels, similar to Figure 3-2. If this is your first time launching the tool, Dreamweaver MX also displays the Welcome window, where you can access tips on Workspace setup and information on new features. (Close the Welcome window now; you can read it later by choosing Help → Welcome.)

Insert   Common   Document
panel   objects tab   toolbar

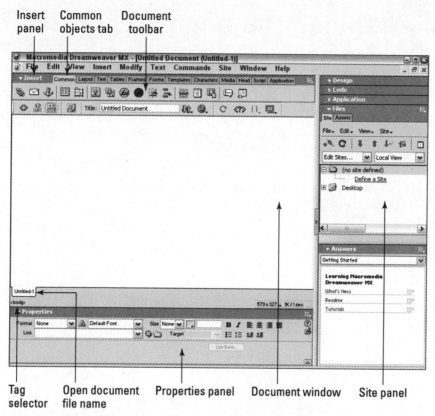

Tag   Open document   Properties panel   Document window   Site panel
selector   file name

Figure 3-2: Dreamweaver MX Untitled Document window.

Creating a site

In Dreamweaver MX, the term *site* refers to the collection of folders, subfolders, and files that make up a single Web site. Every site has a file hierarchy. Even sites that are contained within a single folder have a simple hierarchy of the folder and the files within that folder.

More common, however, are sites that categorize files and objects into subfolders, similar to the hierarchy shown in Figure 3-3.

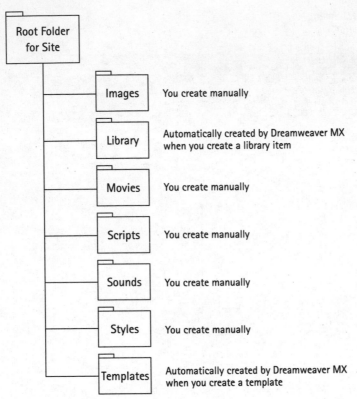

Figure 3-3: Common site hierarchy.

Before you create content, you need to create a container to hold that content. In Dreamweaver MX, the top-level folder that contains the site content is called the root folder. It is important to remember this term because, as you use Dreamweaver MX on a regular basis, you are often prompted about moving files and objects into the root folder.

To define your Dreamweaver MX site, choose Site → New Site from either the main menu bar or the Site panel. Dreamweaver MX displays the first screen of the Site Definition wizard, shown in Figure 3-4.

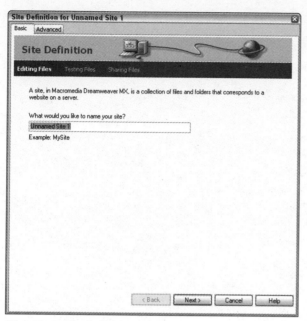

Figure 3-4: Site Definition wizard.

To create a Dreamweaver MX site, you need a minimum of two pieces of information on the Advanced tab:

◆ **Site Name:** A name used only within Dreamweaver MX to refer to all of the folders, subfolders, and files for a site as a single collection. The site name is only visible within Dreamweaver MX.

◆ **Local Root Folder:** The top-level folder for the Web site. Click the folder icon next to the Local Root Folder to browse to the folder that will contain the newly-created site. Dreamweaver MX displays the Choose Local Root Folder dialog box. (If you haven't already created the folder, you can create a new folder by clicking the Create New Folder button on the Choose Local Root Folder dialog box.)

Once you enter the Site Name and Local Root Folder fields, click OK to create the site.

Dreamweaver MX displays the hierarchy of folders, subfolders, and files in the Site panel. Figure 3-5 shows a populated site in the Site panel.

Local Root Folder

Site name   Site panel menu

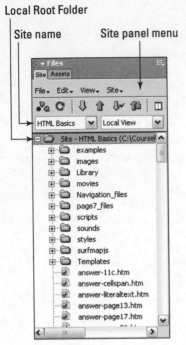

Figure 3-5: Site panel.

Editing a site

If you decide later that you want to change a site's settings (for example, you didn't initially enter FTP information and now you want to), choose Site → Edit Sites from either the main menu bar or the Site panel. Dreamweaver MX displays the Edit Sites dialog box listing all Dreamweaver MX sites that you created, as shown in Figure 3-6.

Figure 3-6: Edit Sites dialog box.

From the list of sites you've created in Dreamweaver, click to highlight the one you want to change and then click the Edit button. Dreamweaver MX displays the Site Definition dialog box (shown in Figure 3-4), including any settings you previously defined for that site.

 If you remove a Dreamweaver MX site in the Edit Sites dialog box, you are simply removing the *reference* to the site from within Dreamweaver MX — the files and folders that make up that site are *not* deleted. The concept is similar to deleting a Windows shortcut, where the shortcut is deleted but the folder or file referenced by that shortcut is not deleted.

Once you define your Dreamweaver MX site, you can work with files and objects in that site using the Site panel, as discussed later in this chapter.

Creating a document

Dreamweaver MX allows you to create many different types of documents, such as HTML pages, templates, library items, framesets, and so forth. To create a new document, choose File→New from the main menu bar. Dreamweaver MX displays the New Document dialog box, as shown in Figure 3-7.

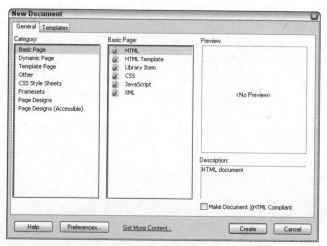

Figure 3-7: New Document dialog box.

Dreamweaver defaults to creating a basic HTML page. Once you select the category and page, click the Create button, and Dreamweaver MX opens an untitled document of the type you specified.

Previewing a document in your browser

While you're working in Dreamweaver, you'll often want to preview your document in your default Web browser to see how it looks. Because you'll frequently preview your pages, I want to point out a shortcut key: F12.

Press the F12 key at any time to preview your document in your defaultWeb browser. Dreamweaver MX previews your Web page by creating a temporary copy of the open document and previewing that temporary copy in the browser. (By using temporary copies, you don't need to save changes to your document to preview it; Dreamweaver MX doesn't actually save or update your document until you end your editing session or manually save the document using File → Save or File → Save As from the main menu bar.)

To add different browsers, change your default browser for preview, or eliminate the use of temporary copies for previewing documents, choose Edit → Preferences → Preview in Browser from the main menu bar.

Using the document toolbar

The Document Toolbar, shown previously in Figure 3-2, is located just above the document window.

To familiarize yourself with the Document Toolbar, click on each option described in Table 3-1 to see what happens. If you are an experienced Web author, most of the concepts should be recognizable, even though the interface is not.

TABLE 3-1 DOCUMENT TOOLBAR OPTIONS

Option	Name	Result
	Show Code View	Displays document in HTML code view.
	Show Code and Design Views	Displays document as split screen editor (HTML and WYSIWYG).
	Show Design View	Displays document in WYSIWYG view.
	Live Data View	Retrieves dynamic data, such as ASP and ColdFusion pages (does not work unless the document has calls to dynamic data).
	Document Title	Inserts your text as the page title (used by browser for window title, tracking history, marking favorites, and so forth).

Option	Name	Result
	File Management	Moves documents between local and remote site (you define the remote site and login information when you create or edit the site).
	Preview/Debug in Browser	Previews document, lets you select browser, debugs JavaScript code.
	Refresh Design View	Refreshes the WYSIWYG view after HTML editing (when editing in split view).
	Reference	Displays quick reference info for HTML, CSS, JavaScript, and more.
	Code Navigation	Navigates and edits JavaScript code included in your HTML file.
	View Options	Displays visual aids such as rulers and grids (visual aids are only visible to help you edit the document in Dreamweaver MX; visual aids do not affect the HTML code).

Identifying invisible elements

As you insert content into Dreamweaver MX documents, some of that content is invisible in the WYSIWYG view because it is invisible to the viewer of the web page. Examples of invisible content include named anchors, comments, line breaks, JavaScript, and so forth.

Although Dreamweaver MX does not display the invisible content in the design (WYSIWYG) view, it does display a symbol representing that content, so that you know of its existence within the HTML file. Figure 3-8 shows a Dreamweaver MX document showing symbols representing invisible content.

Different types of invisible content have different symbols. You can easily determine the content of a symbol by clicking on that symbol and reviewing the properties in the Properties panel (or clicking the Show Code View button on the Document Toolbar, which highlights the content represented by the symbol).

Internal anchor symbol

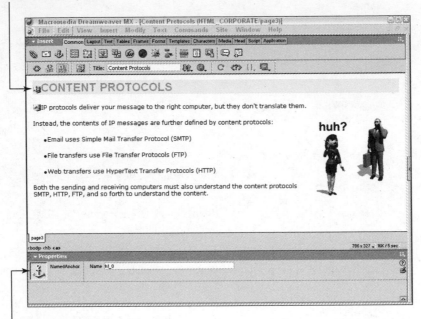

Internal anchor properties
when anchor is selected

Figure 3-8: Invisible content represented by symbols in WYSIWYG view.

Do not delete the invisible symbols in the WYSIWYG view unless you want to delete the invisible content they represent. If you don't want some or all of the symbols displayed in the WYSIWYG view, change your viewing preferences by choosing Edit → Preferences → Invisible Elements.

Working with panels

Much of the new interface for Dreamweaver MX uses expandable/collapsible panels that surround the document window. You control whether a panel is hidden or visible by selecting or deselecting that panel from the Window menu, as shown in Figure 3-9.

To hide a visible panel, select the panel name from the Window menu. To show an invisible panel, again select the panel name from the Window menu. Selecting panels in the Window menu simply toggles between visible and invisible.

Window	Help	
✔ Insert	Ctrl+F2	
✔ Properties	Ctrl+F3	
✔ Answers	Alt+F1	
CSS Styles	Shift+F11	
HTML Styles	Ctrl+F11	
Behaviors	Shift+F3	
Tag Inspector	F9	
Snippets	Shift+F9	
Reference	Shift+F1	
Databases	Ctrl+Shift+F10	
Bindings	Ctrl+F10	
Server Behaviors	Ctrl+F9	
Components	Ctrl+F7	
Site	F8	
Assets	F11	
Results		▶
Others		▶
Arrange Panels		
Hide Panels	F4	
Cascade		
Tile Horizontally		
Tile Vertically		
Untitled-2		

Figure 3-9: Window menu controls visibility of panels.

Each visible panel has three icons for controlling that panel (see Figure 3-10):

◆ **Expander arrow:** This toggles between expanding and collapsing the panel with each mouse click.

◆ **Options menu:** This displays a menu of options specific to the context of each panel.

◆ **Gripper icon:** This lets you undock a panel and move it to wherever you want on your screen.

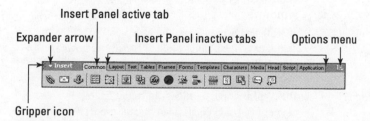

Figure 3-10: The Insert panel with the Common tab active.

Let's look at four important Dreamweaver MX panels in detail. . . .

INSERT PANEL

The Insert panel enables you to insert many different types of objects, including images, tables, forms, hyperlinks, and so forth, into your Dreamweaver MX document. When you launch Dreamweaver MX, the Insert panel automatically makes the Common tab active, as Figure 3-10 shows.

There are initially 12 tabs in the Insert panel, but the installation of Dreamweaver MX extensions (add-ons) may add to this number. For example, when you install the CourseBuilder extension, Dreamweaver MX adds a tab titled Learning. To see how these tabs work:

1. Click inside the document window and type a few words.

2. Click the Text tab to make it active (see Figure 3-11). Notice that the options on the Insert Bar change. Clicking each tab simply changes the insert options that are available to the same document.

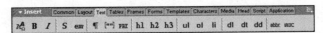

Figure 3-11: The Insert panel with the Text tab active.

If you are familiar with Web authoring tools, you are likely already familiar with many of the options on the Common tab, although the interface may be different. Table 3-2 defines the commonly used objects available from the Insert panel.

TABLE 3-2 INSERT PANEL OPTIONS (COMMON TAB)

Option	Name	Result
	Hyperlink	Creates a text hyperlink by prompting you for the clickable text and the URL for the hyperlink (if the text already exists, highlight the text and type the URL for the hyperlink in the Properties panel).
	Email Link	Creates an e-mail hyperlink based on the text you highlight; if you don't highlight text, Dreamweaver MX prompts you for it.
	Named Anchor	Creates an internal anchor (a target for other hyperlinks), and displays an anchor graphic visible only within Dreamweaver MX.

Option	Name	Result
	Insert Table	Inserts a table, prompting you for number of rows, number of columns, table width, border width, and cell padding/spacing values (in pixels). Once the table is created, you can resize the table, columns, and rows in the WYSIWYG view by clicking and holding the mouse pointer on any border and dragging.
	Draw Layer	Inserts a layer based on either the HTML <DIV> or <SPAN> elements (defined in Edit → Preferences → Layers). Layers are discussed in the "Working with layers" section later in this chapter.
	Image	Inserts an image file, or inserts an image defined in a data source such as a database.
	Image Placeholder	Inserts a placeholder for a graphic. The placeholder enables you to continue designing the layout of a page until you have the image available (once the image is available, double-click the placeholder to replace it with the final image).
	Fireworks HTML	Inserts HTML code generated from an image that was sliced and hyperlinked within Macromedia Fireworks.
	Flash	Inserts a Macromedia Flash movie file (.SWF), or inserts a Flash movie defined in a data source such as a database.
	Rollover Image	Inserts a rollover image. Rollover images contain an "off" version of an image as well as the JavaScript to replace that image with an "on" version when the mouse pointer moves over it. Rollover images are discussed more fully in the "Rollovers" section later in this chapter.
	Navigation Bar	Inserts a group of rollover images either horizontally or vertically (typically used as navigation bars). Navigation bars are discussed more fully in the "Navigation bars" section later in this chapter.

Continued

TABLE 3-2 INSERT PANEL OPTIONS (COMMON TAB) *(Continued)*

Option	Name	Result
▤	Horizontal Rule	Inserts a horizontal rule (the HTML `<HR>` element).
▦	Date	Inserts the current day, date, and time (note that this is simply inserted as text, *not* as a dynamically updated time stamp).
▨	Tabular Data	Inserts tabular data, which typically comes from databases or spreadsheets. Before you include the tabular data, you need to know how it is delimited (are fields separated by tabs? Commas? Other punctuation?).
▨	Comment	Inserts a comment into the HTML code, and displays a comment placeholder in the WYSIWYG view. The comment is not visible when the file is viewed in a browser window.
▨	Tag Chooser	Inserts a tag from Dreamweaver MX tag libraries, including ColdFusion and ASP tags.

PROPERTIES PANEL

The Properties panel, shown in Figure 3-12, is located near the bottom of the Dreamweaver MX workspace. Use this panel to define the properties of text and objects within the Dreamweaver MX document. Examples of text properties are attributes that further define text such as paragraphs, headings, and lists; examples of object properties are attributes further defining objects such as width, height, and source filename.

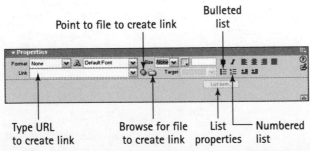

Figure 3-12: Properties panel, assuming text is selected (active) in the document window.

The Properties panel options are entirely context sensitive; that is, the options Dreamweaver MX displays in the Properties panel depend on whether text or an object is active in the document window.

To make text active, click and drag the cursor across the text; Dreamweaver MX highlights the selected text, making it active.

Click on objects to make them active. Dreamweaver MX displays an active object by drawing a rectangular border around the object, and including resize handles.

SITE PANEL

Once you've created your Dreamweaver MX site, you can manage its folders and files from within the Sites panel (shown previously in Figure 3-5).

To create a new folder, for example, choose New Folder from the Site panel's File menu, as shown in Figure 3-13.

▾ Files	
Site	Assets

File▾ Edit▾ View▾ Site▾	
New File	Ctrl+Shift+N
New Folder	Ctrl+Alt+Shift+N
Open	
Save Site Map...	
Rename	F2
Delete	Del
Turn Off Read Only	
Preview in Browser	▸
Check Links	Shift+F8
Design Notes...	
Exit	Ctrl+Q

Figure 3-13: Site panel's File menu.

Dreamweaver MX creates a new, untitled folder in the Site panel, ready for you to name.

TIP Be sure to think about your site architecture before creating folders and subfolders. Consider design questions such as should you put all your HTML files in the root folder? In subfolders based on categories? If so, what are the categories? Should you categorize assets? Once you identify the structure, use the Site panel to create the folders and subfolders beneath your root folder.

Now, here's the real power of Dreamweaver MX site management. Assume you've created a graphics file titled logo.gif in the root folder, and you've included that graphics file in 10 Web documents.

Later, you decide you want to create a subfolder called images and move all graphics to the new folder. When you move the graphics file to the new subfolder images, Dreamweaver MX asks if you want to update the paths in the 10 Web documents. As long as you move files and objects *within the Dreamweaver MX Site panel,* Dreamweaver MX keeps track of all references to files and folders, eliminating the problem of broken links when you change the location of documents and objects within your site.

ASSETS PANEL

The Assets panel catalogs select categories of assets within the site, as shown in Figure 3-14.

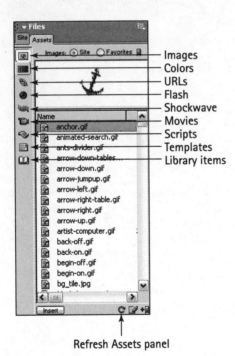

Refresh Assets panel

Figure 3-14: Assets panel.

Anytime you add a new object (in the specified categories) to your site, Dreamweaver MX automatically catalogs that object in the Assets panel. Those objects are then automatically listed on the Assets panel the next time the Assets panel is refreshed (either when you restart Dreamweaver MX or when you click the Assets panel Refresh button).

Once an asset is catalogued on the Assets panel, you can easily insert objects into other documents within your site in one of two ways:

- ◆ Drag the object from the Assets panel and drop it into the document.

- ◆ Click the cursor in the desired location within the document, highlight the asset in the Asset panel, and click the Insert button on the Asset panel.

Creating links

Through all the flash, glitz, and hype since its invention by Tim Berners-Lee in 1989, the core attraction to the Web continues to be the ability to interweave relationships between text and objects. Yet, the creation and maintenance of links within Dreamweaver MX is elegantly simple.

Links consist of two components: the text or object that students click on (called the "source anchor"), and the Web page or other URL that loads into the browser *after* the source anchor is clicked (called the "destination anchor").

To create your links from the Properties panel, first select the text or object in your document window that you want as your clickable source anchor. Then, on the Properties panel, define the destination anchor in one of three ways (see Figure 3-13 to refer back to the Properties panel):

- ◆ Type the URL in the Link field. This option is typically used to define links outside your site. For example, if you were creating a link to Web-Graduate. Com, you'd type the full URL here (http://www.web-graduate.com).

- ◆ Click and drag the Point to File icon and move your mouse pointer to the destination anchor (any Web page or object) in the Site panel and then release the mouse button. This option can only be used to define links within your site.

- ◆ Click the Browse for File icon and browse to the file you want as your destination anchor. This option is typically used to select any Web page or object anywhere on your computer or your computer's network. When you select a Web page or object outside of your site's root folder, Dreamweaver MX will ask you if you want to copy the file into your root folder, helping to ensure that you don't publish Web sites that point to inaccessible resources.

Web pages also allow you to define destination anchors that reside within the *same* Web page as the source anchor, which is useful for easily navigating to different locations within a long Web page. When a destination anchor is in the same page as the source anchor, the destination anchor is called a "named anchor" because you need to create an internally-referenced name for that location in the page. Once you create a named anchor, you can link to it from a source anchor and allow students to instantly jump to that specific location within the Web page.

Getting Context-Sensitive Help

The Dreamweaver MX online help system is very . . . helpful!

Dreamweaver MX provides context-sensitive help throughout the interface. As you work through the many dialog boxes in Dreamweaver MX, you will undoubtedly find many occasions where you want a quick description of a dialog box or panel options. Instead of choosing Help → Using Dreamweaver (which brings you to the main help screen), you can direct Dreamweaver MX to provide specific help based on the context within which you are working.

To obtain help specific to your context, simply click the Help button on the dialog box, or select Help from the drop-down menu on a panel or panel group.

To insert a named anchor, move your cursor to the desired location within the Web page and click the Named Anchor icon on the Insert panel's Common tab. Dreamweaver MX prompts you for a name. Enter any text you want for the name, but names must consist only of letters and numbers, and may not contain spaces. When Dreamweaver MX inserts your named anchor, it displays an invisible element showing an anchor, so that you know of the anchor's existence (remember, anchors are for internal reference only and are completely invisible to students).

Once you create the named anchor, you can define source anchors that link to it. To create a link between your source anchor and the named anchor, first select the text or object in your document window that you want as your source anchor. Then type the name you selected for the named anchor in the Link field, preceded by the # symbol.

For example, if your named anchor is "Question2" then the link for your source anchor would be "#Question2".

You can also use the Point to File icon to link a source anchor to a named anchor. Simply highlight the source anchor text or object and click and drag the Point to File icon to the invisible element representing the named anchor.

Designing Page Layout Using Layout Tables

HTML was *not* initially designed to include style or layout capabilities. But early in the language's development, tables were introduced; and shortly after the introduction of tables, Web designers began using tables as tools for page layout — although primitive in comparison to desktop publishing systems' layout capabilities, tables were initially the *only* option for page layout.

To make the use of tables for layout purposes easier, Dreamweaver MX created a layout view for tables that lets you visually draw a table and, more impressively, visually draw rectangular content areas (cells) that can easily be resized and dragged to any location within the table.

Because layout tables are used to manage the layout of content, the defaults for layout tables are differ from regular tables. For example, borders, cell padding, and cell spacing are all set to 0 to allow exact alignment of content within cells.

You create layout tables from the Layout tab on the Insert panel. The Layout tab provides two different views of tables: Standard View (active by default) and Layout View. Figure 3-15 shows a sample layout table with three layout cells drawn inside it (autostretch is discussed in section "Understanding layout table and cell widths", later in this chapter).

Fixed width columns specify exact width of column, in pixels

Autostretch columns take up remaining width of browser window

Column markers delineate each table column, whether or not it contains layout cells

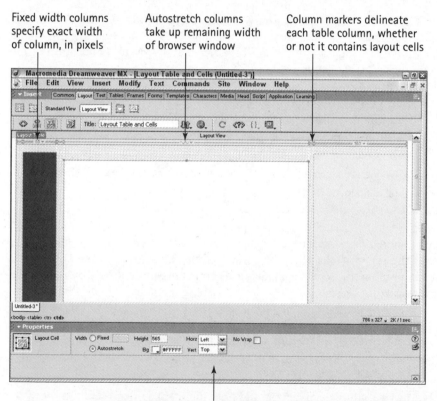

Properties panel defines properties for selected cell

Figure 3-15: A layout table with three layout cells drawn inside it. Notice that the Properties panel reflects the properties of the selected cell.

When you create layout tables and cells, Dreamweaver MX inserts comments inside the HTML code to identify them as layout tables whenever you edit the table within Dreamweaver MX.

You can toggle between views by clicking the Standard View and Layout View buttons; however, keep in mind that these are two views of the *same* HTML table code. As you do, notice that there are important differences between those views:

- Active and disabled buttons change depending on the view you select. When you select Standard View, the buttons to the left (Insert Table, Draw Layer) become active and other buttons are disabled. Conversely, when you select Layout View, the buttons to the right (Draw Layout Table, Draw Layout Cell) become active and other buttons are disabled.

- Properties panel options change depending on the view you select.

- Columns in Layout View show the pixel widths for each column, and provide a drop-down menu with further options.

Drawing layout tables and layout cells

To draw a layout table, click the Draw Layout Table button on the Layout tab. Notice that your mouse pointer turns into crosshairs. Click and hold the crosshairs at the location of the upper-left corner of the table, and drag to the location of the lower-right corner of the table.

To draw layout tables and layout cells with precise guidelines, you can display horizontal and vertical rulers. The rulers are a visual aid only; they do not write anything to the HTML. To display rulers (and to select from three measurement units: pixels, inches, and centimeters), choose View → Rulers from the main menu bar.

You can subdivide a layout table into different layout cells. To create a layout cell within the layout table, click the Draw Layout Cell button on the Layout tab. Notice that your mouse pointer again turns into crosshairs. You now have two options for drawing cells:

- **To draw a single cell:** Click and hold the crosshairs at the location of the upper-left corner of the cell, and drag to the location of the lower-right corner of the cell. When you draw single cells, you must click the Layout Cell button for each layout cell you draw.

- **To draw multiple cells:** Press and hold the Ctrl key (for Windows) or Command key (for Macintosh). Then click and hold the crosshairs at the location of the upper-left corner of the cell, and to the location of the lower-right corner of the cell. As long as you continue to hold the Ctrl/ Command key, you can draw as many cells as you want without clicking the Layout Cell button each time.

Once your layout table and layout cells are drawn, you can change to the Standard View and populate them with content, and regulate the display of that content through the Properties panel.

Understanding layout table and cell widths

You can specify the width of tables in several ways:

- In Layout View, specify a value for the table width in pixels.

- In Standard View, specify a value for the table width in pixels or as a percentage of the browser window

As you draw layout cells, however, notice that you can also specify the width of each column (in pixels) by selecting any cell within the column and changing the width of that cell in the Properties panel. When you change the width of a column (either in layout or standard views), Dreamweaver MX automatically adjusts the other columns to fit within the confines of the defined table width, if possible.

In addition to specifying pixel widths for columns, Dreamweaver MX enables you to select a single column in layout view to autostretch. To specify a column for autostretch, select the Make Column Autostretch option from that column's drop-down menu, as shown in Figure 3-16.

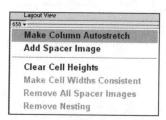

Figure 3-16: Selecting the Make Column Autostretch option
from a column's drop-down menu in layout view.

When you select a column for autostretch, Dreamweaver MX (and subsequently, the browser) grants that single column 100% of the remaining browser width. If, for example, you have two columns, the first set to 100 pixels wide and the second set to autostretch, the second column automatically stretches to fill the remaining browser window width.

Typically, you use the autostretch feature for the main column in a layout table. If you use one column for navigation and one for content, for instance, you would likely want to specify a value for the navigation column width, and let the content column use the remaining window space.

When you select a column to autostretch, Dreamweaver MX inserts a transparent spacer image to the other columns (sized to their pixel widths) to ensure each column maintains the specified width when viewed in the browser window.

Managing Reusable Content with Library Items

Whenever you have content that you reuse in different areas of your site, the best way to manage that content is through the use of library items (the last set of objects on your Assets panel). A library item consists of any text or object, or any combination of text and objects, collected as a single unit.

Common uses for library items would be navigation panels, legal notices, and other types of repeating content. Once you create a library item, you can drag that item from the Assets panel to as many pages as you want. When you drag the library item into Web pages, you create a copy of that content that maintains a connection to the original library item.

When you make changes to the original library item stored in the Library, Dreamweaver MX asks whether you want to make those changes to every copy of the library item in the site, so that it is extraordinarily easy to update copied library items throughout a site. So, for example, if you created a legal notice library item that was included on every page in your site, you could change the copyright date each year, for example, and have Dreamweaver MX ripple that change to every copy of the library item in the site. Figure 3-17 shows the concept of a library item.

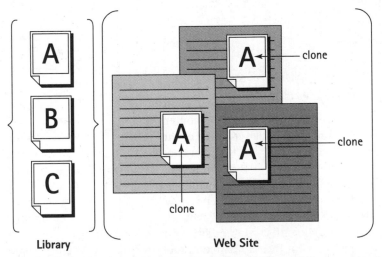

Library   Web Site

Figure 3-17: Library items hold modules of content that can be reused in multiple pages.

When you create a library item (which we discuss in the next section), Dreamweaver MX collects the content and stores it as a separate item in a folder called Library within your site.

To begin working with library items, be sure the Library category is selected in your Assets panel, as shown in Figure 3-18.

Library item category

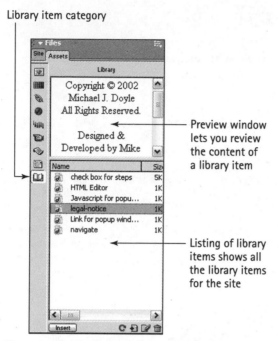

Preview window lets you review the content of a library item

Listing of library items shows all the library items for the site

Figure 3-18: Library items in the Assets panel.

Creating library items from content

To create a library item, you simply need to select part or all of the content in the document window and click and drag that content to the Library preview window in the Assets panel. Dreamweaver MX copies that content into a library item. The upper window of the Assets panel displays the content you are inserting into the library item; the lower window displays the name of the library item, which defaults to Untitled (you can then type whatever name you choose for the library item).

Dreamweaver MX does not impose a limit on the amount or type of content you can insert into a single library item. You can include text, images, JavaScript, Flash movies, or whatever else you want. Keep in mind, however, that the *context* from a page is not automatically copied into a library item. If you copy text, for example, it won't carry external or embedded CSS styles; if you copy a JavaScript, it won't carry variables that might be defined elsewhere in that file. Also, you will need to change pointers to any dependent files (such as included images, movies, and so forth) *if* you insert a library item into a document stored in a different folder from the original content, and that original content uses relative paths.

Also, when you create a library item, Dreamweaver MX copies the content from the document into a library item; that original content does *not* maintain a connection to the newly-created library item. If you want that original content to be the first copy of the library item, you must delete the content and add it as a library item.

Adding library items to content

If you thought creating library items was easy (and it was, wasn't it?), you'll really be impressed with the ease of adding library items to content.

As with other assets, you can add a library item to your content in one of two ways:

◆ Click and drag the library item from the Assets panel and drop it into the document.

◆ Click the cursor in the desired location within the document, click to highlight the library item in the Asset panel, and then click the Insert button at the bottom of the Asset panel.

When you add a library item to your document, the content is highlighted to indicate that it is a library item, as Figure 3-19 shows. The highlighting is only displayed in Dreamweaver MX; there is no visible difference to the content when viewed in a browser window.

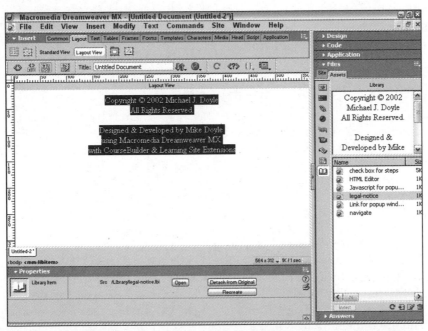

Figure 3-19: Library items are highlighted when editing a document to show that the content is derived from a library item. The highlighting is not displayed when the page is viewed in a Web browser.

Detaching library items

Copies of library items inserted into documents maintain their attachment to the original library item unless you manually detach them. To detach a copy of a library item from the original, select the copy in the document to make it active. The Properties panel at the bottom of the document window changes to show the properties of this copy of the library item.

To detach the copy from the original library item, click the Detach from Original button on the Properties panel. You are not prompted to confirm, so if you accidentally detach a library item, you can undo the action by choosing Edit→Undo Break Library Link, provided you choose it before your next edit to that document (otherwise, you need to delete the detached content and add the library item again).

 If you detach a copy of a library item, the Recreate button on the Properties panel replaces the original library item in the Library with the current copy of that library item. If you choose to recreate your library item, *you will overwrite the original library item.*

Editing library items

You can edit an original library item stored in the Library in one of two ways:

◆ Double-click the library item in the Assets panel.

◆ Highlight a copy in any open document and select Open from Properties panel. This second option enables you to edit the original library item, *not* the copy.

Once you save your changes to the original library item, Dreamweaver MX prompts to see whether you want to update all documents containing copies of that library item.

Designing Content Using External Cascading Style Sheets (CSS)

HTML was originally intended solely to identify content by structural elements only (paragraphs, headings, list items, and so forth); style and presentation characteristics were left to the browser.

As the language developed, new elements were added to enable Web authors to define style and presentation characteristics within each file. In Dreamweaver MX, these new elements show themselves in the Properties panel when you edit content.

For example, if you highlight a Heading 1 and use the Properties panel to change the font for that heading to Arial font face, color red, Dreamweaver MX writes the HTML for that change into the content, as follows:

```
<h1><font color="#FF0000" face="Arial, Helvetica, sans-serif">
Heading Text</font></h1>
```

You've obviously changed the style of that heading to the desired font and color, so what's the problem? The problem, of course, is that you are creating a maintenance nightmare one click at a time. What if, somewhere down the road, you want to change the color or font for Heading 1? You'll need to make those changes one at a time as well, which is a significant task when you have sites consisting of hundreds or thousands of pages.

To address this issue, the World Wide Web consortium (www.w3.org), the organization chartered with defining Web specifications including HTML, recommended the use of Cascading Style Sheets in HTML.

The reason style sheets are called cascading is that you can use three different levels of CSS:

- ◆ **External CSS:** The style definitions are kept in a completely separate file (with a file type .CSS) and linked to as many documents as you'd like. This book mainly discusses external CSS because they completely separate style from content pages.

- ◆ **Embedded CSS:** The style definitions are written at the top of a specific HTML document between <STYLE> and </STYLE> tags. Those definitions are available only to that document.

- ◆ **Inline CSS:** The style definitions are wrapped around specific content within an HTML document. Those definitions are available only to that specific content within that one document (such as the change to the font and color of the Heading 1 discussed earlier).

With so many levels of style sheets, all potentially defining styles for the same content, what are the rules for mediating conflicts? Style definitions for content are always inherited from higher levels; style definitions closest to the content generally trump inherited style definitions from higher levels wherever there is a conflict. For example, here are three style definitions:

- ◆ External CSS:

```
p {font-family: "Times New Roman", Times, serif;
    font-size: large;
    color: red;}
```

◆ Embedded CSS:

```
p {font-size: medium;
   color: blue;}
```

◆ Inline CSS:

```
p {font-size: small;}
```

A paragraph inheriting all three levels of style definitions would be defined as:

```
p {font-family: "Times New Roman", Times, serif;
   font-size: small;
   color: blue;}
```

The paragraph inherits the font-family from the external CSS because the embedded or inline style definitions do not trump it; it inherits the font color blue because the embedded style trumps the external style; and it must use the small font size because the inline style, which trumps both of the other styles, specifies font-size: small.

External Cascading Style Sheets (CSS files) enable Web authors to separate content from style and presentation by inserting style information in a separate file. The style and presentation characteristics of a CSS file are applied to an HTML file when the HTML file is read by the browser.

Because the style definitions are stored in a separate CSS file, you can attach the same CSS file to as many documents as you like. This design enables you to change style and presentation characteristics in a single CSS file rather than opening up each HTML document.

Step 1: Creating a style sheet

To create an *external* CSS file that you will later attach to documents in your site, choose File → New. Dreamweaver MX displays the New Document dialog box, shown in Figure 3-20. Select the Basic Page category CSS, and click the Create button.

Figure 3-20: Select the Basic Page category, and then choose CSS in the New Document dialog box.

Dreamweaver MX opens an untitled CSS file, with the following label at the top of the file

```
/* CSS Document */
```

Note that Dreamweaver MX disables all of the panels and tabs except for the CSS Styles panel, shown in Figure 3-21.

New CSS Style icon adds a style definition.

Attach Style Sheet button attaches an external CSS to an opened document.

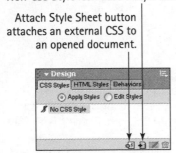

Figure 3-21: CSS Styles panel.

Step 2: Entering style definitions

Every style definition consists of two components:

◆ **Selector:** This is the name of the style. For example, a selector could be an HTML element such as P or H1 or LI; or it could be a custom class selector, discussed later in this chapter.

◆ **Declarations:** These are the style characteristics for a specific selector. For example, a declaration might be for a specific font, font color, or background color.

You can include as few or as many style definitions in a single external CSS as you want. As you create each style definition, you do so using a series of dialog boxes.

To define styles, click on the New CSS Style button at the bottom of the CSS Styles tab on the Design panel. Dreamweaver MX displays the New CSS Style dialog box, shown in Figure 3-22.

Before you begin entering style definitions, be sure the Define In field on the New CSS Style dialog box is set for This Document Only when you enter your first style definition. This ensures that the style definitions you create are inserted into the CSS file you just created.

Figure 3-22: New CSS Style dialog box.

There are three types of selectors that you can define in your style sheet:

◆ Redefine HTML Tag, which lets you specify declarations for a specific HTML tag.

◆ Use CSS Selector, which lets you specify declarations for a group of HTML tags at once (if you want the group of HTML elements to share the same declaration).

◆ Make Custom Style (class), which lets you specify declarations that you manually apply to content when editing a document in Dreamweaver MX, regardless of the HTML tag that defines the content.

When you choose a type of selector, the name of, and options in, the first drop-down menu change. For example, when you select the Redefine HTML Tag type, the name of the drop-down menu becomes Tag, and the drop-down menu displays all HTML tags. When you select Use CSS Selector type, the name of the drop-down menu becomes Selector, and so forth.

The following sections briefly discuss the concept behind each type of selector. Once you decide on a selector, you then specify the declarations for that selector using the CSS Style Definition dialog box (the process for specifying declarations is the same for all three selector types).

TIP
To work effectively with style sheets, you need to understand the underlying HTML tags. Dreamweaver MX includes a reference library describing each tag, which you can access from the Code panel by selecting the Reference tab. To display the Code panel (if it is not already displayed), select Window → Reference from the main menu bar.

SELECTOR: REDEFINE HTML TAG

Choose Redefine HTML Tag, and the Tag drop-down menu displays the entire set of HTML tags, as shown in Figure 3-23.

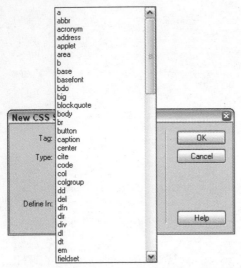

Figure 3-23: Redefine HTML Tag type showing the menu
of HTML tags available in the Tag drop-down menu.

When you create style definitions that redefine an HTML tag, you are simply telling Dreamweaver MX (and ultimately the browser that displays your page) to apply your style definition to all content that is marked-up by that tag.

For example, if you create a style definition for the P tag as Arial medium navy blue font, Dreamweaver MX and browsers will display all content identified as paragraphs (marked up with the P tag) with the new style definitions.

To redefine the style of an HTML tag, select that tag from the drop-down menu.

Click OK, and Dreamweaver MX displays the CSS Style Definition dialog box, where you specify the declarations for your selector.

SELECTOR: USE CSS SELECTOR

Choose Use CSS Selector, and the Selector drop-down menu displays the four different states of hyperlinks.

You can redefine any of the four hyperlink states, of course. But the real power for this type of selector is that you can create declarations for a group of HTML tags at once, provided you want those tags to share the same exact declaration.

Again assume you redefine the style for the P tag to Arial, medium, navy blue font. Although all paragraphs will carry that style, other content that you might assume are paragraphs won't. For example, the text in lists won't carry the paragraph style definitions because text in lists are marked-up by the LI tag; and the text in table cells won't carry the paragraph style definitions because text in table cells are marked-up by the TD tag.

To define a group of selectors at once, enter them into the Selector field separated by commas. For example, Figure 3-24 shows a group of selectors for paragraphs, list items, and text in table cells.

Figure 3-24: Use CSS Selector type used to define a group of selectors at once.

Click OK, and Dreamweaver MX displays the CSS Style Definition dialog box, where you specify the declarations for your selector.

Then, enter your style definitions once for the entire group of selectors.

SELECTOR: MAKE CUSTOM STYLE (CLASS)

Choose Make Custom Style (class), and the Name field displays an unnamed class, as shown in Figure 3-25.

Figure 3-25: Make Custom Style (class) type showing a custom class created for .highlight.

The real power of CSS is that you can create and apply your own custom styles, called *classes*. For example, the *HTML Basics* course included on this book's CD-ROM contains a CSS class named .highlight, which creates a yellow background for certain text, giving that text the appearance of highlighting (similar to how students highlight a textbook).

Because a class is not related to a specific HTML element, it is not automatically applied, but rather can be applied manually to whatever content you choose. For example, if you create a custom class called highlight you can apply the .highlight class to any text, including paragraphs, table cells, list items, headings, and so forth.

To create a custom class, be sure Make Custom Style is selected, and enter a name for your new style (begin the name with a period; if you don't, Dreamweaver MX will add it anyway).

Click OK, and Dreamweaver MX displays the CSS Style Definition dialog box, where you specify the declarations for your selector.

DECLARATION: CSS STYLE DEFINITIONS

Regardless of the selector you choose to define, the process for specifying the style declarations for any selector is the same. After you choose your selector and click OK, Dreamweaver MX displays the CSS Style Definition dialog box, as shown in Figure 3-26.

First, you select style properties in this CSS Style definition box.

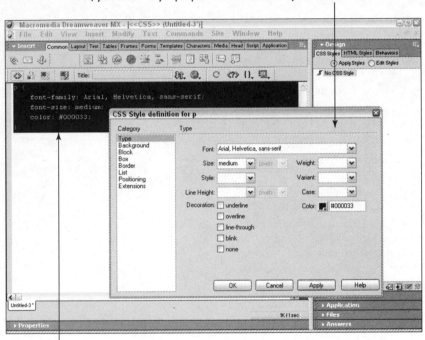

Second, Dreamweaver MX writes style definitions in the CSS document when you click OK or Apply.

Figure 3-26: CSS Style Definition dialog box.

You can define as few or as many declarations as you want for your selector by choosing any (or all!) of the eight categories of style declarations. It is relatively easy to specify your declarations because most fields consist of drop-down menus that let you choose valid options. For example, the Font drop-down menu contains the fonts you can choose; the Color field contains a color-picker with an eyedrop selection tool; and so forth.

When you finish specifying your declarations, click OK to write those declarations into the external CSS file you are creating. Dreamweaver MX writes the syntax for CSS style definitions into the CSS file, so you do not need to be familiar with syntax.

Dreamweaver MX offers eight different categories of style declarations. Although the description of each category is beyond the scope of this book, you can easily get context-sensitive help by highlighting any of the categories on the CSS Style Definition dialog box and clicking the Help button. Dreamweaver MX displays a description of all options for the specific category you highlighted.

Step 3: Saving your style sheet

Once you complete all of your definitions, click OK to return to the CSS file. Then save that file by choosing File → Save As from the main menu bar. Be sure to select the file type *Style Sheets (*.css)* in the Save As dialog box to ensure that Dreamweaver MX saves it as a CSS file.

 It is generally good practice to keep all of the style sheets for a specific site in a folder named Styles.

Step 4: Attaching style sheets and applying styles

Now that you've created an external CSS (or if you have another style sheet from a different source), you can attach it to as many documents as you want. To attach a style sheet to any document opened in Dreamweaver MX, click on the Attach File Sheet option at the bottom of the CSS Styles panel. Dreamweaver MX displays the Link External Style Sheet dialog box, shown in Figure 3-27.

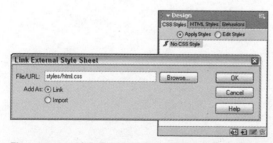

Figure 3-27: Link External Style Sheet dialog box, where you can browse to select an external CSS to attach to your document. The example shows an external style sheet named html.css (stored in a folder named styles) being attached to the opened document.

How Do You Apply Custom Style in Dreamweaver MX?

Since custom styles can be independent of specific tags, how do they get applied to content after you define them in the external CSS? The answer is: you apply them manually to whatever content you want within your Dreamweaver MX document.

Whenever you attach an external CSS with custom styles, those custom styles are displayed on the Styles tab, as shown in Figure 3-28. To apply the custom style to specific content, highlight the content in the document window and then click on the custom style on the Styles tab. It's that easy in Dreamweaver MX!

Browse to the name of the CSS file you want to use. Before you click OK, be sure that you Add As: Link is selected, which works in all versions of browsers.

One you attach a style sheet, all of the style definitions are automatically applied with the exception of custom styles (classes). Since custom styles aren't related to HTML tags, you must (and obviously would want to) manually apply those styles to content.

First, select the content to which you want to apply your custom style (class).

Second, select the custom style (class) you want to apply.

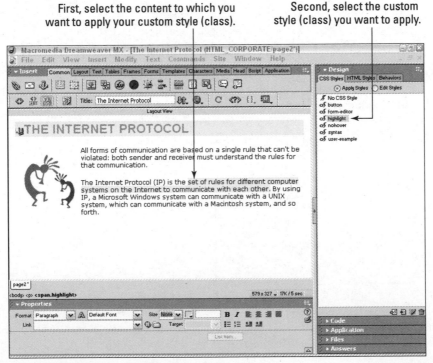

Figure 3-28: Applying a custom class to content.

Editing your style sheet

Once you've created an external CSS, you can easily edit the style definitions by opening the CSS file as you would any other document in Dreamweaver MX, choosing File → Open.

Browse to the CSS file you want to edit, then choose the Edit Styles option on the CSS Styles tab. Dreamweaver MX displays the entire list of selectors defined in that style sheet, as shown in Figure 3-29. You can then change the declarations for an existing style definition by double-clicking on it. You can also add additional style definitions by clicking the New CSS Style icon, as described earlier in this chapter.

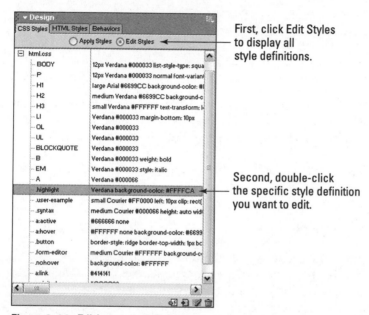

Figure 3-29: Editing style definitions.

Developing Interactive Pages

Do you remember the days of TV before cable? Before big-screen, surround-sound TV? Before VCRs and DVDs? Remember how exciting it was to navigate through channels, hunched over the tube turning knobs one channel at a time (one for VHF channels, one for UHF channels), and rotating the antenna to get a clear enough picture to judge whether or not you were interested in watching the program on your fuzzy black-and-white screen?

Of course, when you had to go through all of that work for each channel, you did far less "surfing" and were much quicker to settle for "I guess I'll watch this."

Then the remote control was invented, and cable lines started bringing in hundreds of channels accessible through that remote; then came interactive programming guides and pay-per-view, and suddenly you had the epiphany of interactive television.

Okay, perhaps that was a little dramatic, but if you haven't experienced creating content with Dreamweaver MX behaviors, be prepared for another such epiphany!

Interactive navigation

Dreamweaver has many tools to spice up interactivity and navigation. Three in particular are very easy to understand and implement:

◆ Rollovers

◆ Navigation bars

◆ Jump menus

ROLLOVERS

A rollover (often called a "mouseover") consists of two separate image files that swap when the student moves the mouse pointer over the image are, and swap again when the student moves the mouse pointer out of the image area:

◆ **Original Image ("off" version):** The browser displays this when the mouse pointer *is not* over the image area.

◆ **Rollover Image ("on" version):** The browser displays this when the mouse pointer *is* over the image area.

The difference between the two images does not need to be dramatic to foster an interactive feel to the navigation: you can make simple changes like highlighting or shadowing the rollover image. You'll need to create your images in a graphics program before you create the rollover in your Dreamweaver MX Web page.

To insert a rollover image, select the Rollover Image option on the Insert panel's Common tab. Dreamweaver MX displays the Insert Rollover Image dialog box, as shown in Figure 3-30.

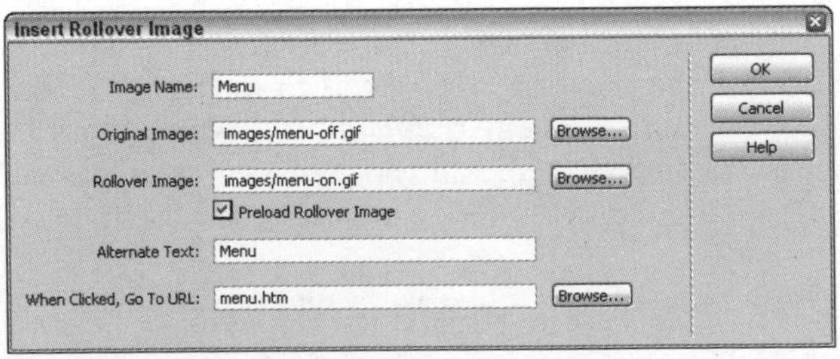

Figure 3-30: Insert Rollover Image dialog box.

Dreamweaver MX defines a default image name, which is used internally for reference only.

Select the Original Image (off version) and the Rollover Image (on version) by browsing to each file.

 When you create rollover images, be sure that both images are sized exactly the same. Otherwise, the images will be distorted.

Since rollover images are typically used as navigation buttons, you can also enter a Web page (or other URL) that will be loaded into the browser window when the student clicks on the button.

NAVIGATION BARS

A navigation bar is simply a collection of rollover images that Dreamweaver MX arranges either horizontally or vertically. Dreamweaver MX only allows one navigation bar in a document.

To insert a navigation bar, select the Navigation Bar option on the Common tab. Dreamweaver MX displays the Navigation Bar dialog box, as shown in Figure 3-31.

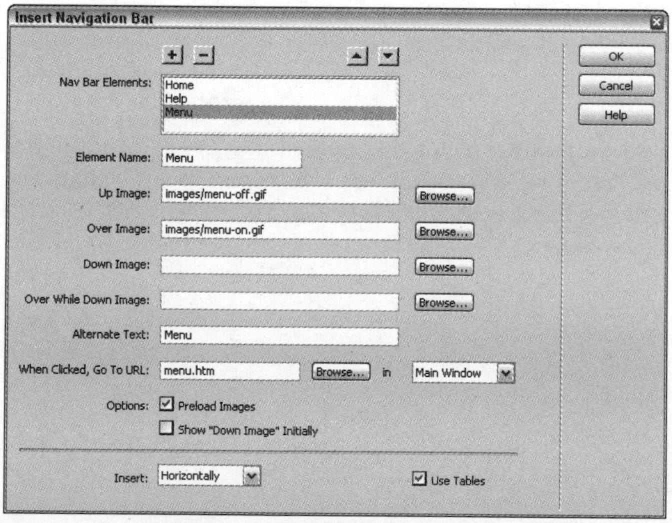

Figure 3-31: Navigation Bar dialog box.

You can add or subtract Nav Bar Elements by clicking the add or subtract icons at the upper left of the Navigation Bar dialog box. Dreamweaver MX defines a default element name, which is used internally for reference only.

Each element on the navigation bar can have up to four different image states (although many Web developers just specify two states, similar to the rollover image, and leave the others blank):

◆ **Original Image ("off" version):** The browser displays this when the mouse pointer *is not* over the image area.

◆ **Over Image ("on" version):** The browser displays this when the mouse pointer *is* over the image area.

◆ **Down Image:** The browser displays this when the student clicks on the image area.

◆ **Over While Down Image:** The browser displays this after the student clicks on an image, moves the mouse pointer away from the image area, and then returns to the image area.

You can rearrange the order of your navigation bar elements by highlighting an element and using the up arrow and down arrow icons in the upper right of the Navigation Bar dialog box.

TIP To edit a navigation bar already in the document, you can click the Navigation Bar icon regardless of where your cursor is because there can only be one navigation bar in a document.

JUMP MENUS

A jump menu is a standard drop-down menu that only shows one item until you click the drop-down arrow. Use jump menus wherever you want to insert multiple navigation options for students in a limited amount of space. Figure 3-32 shows a jump menu collapsed and expanded.

Collapsed   Expanded

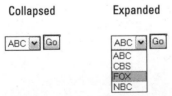

Figure 3-32: Collapsed (left) and expanded (right) jump menu.

To insert a jump menu, select the Jump Menu option on the Insert panel's Forms tab. Dreamweaver MX displays the Insert Jump Menu dialog box (see Figure 3-33).

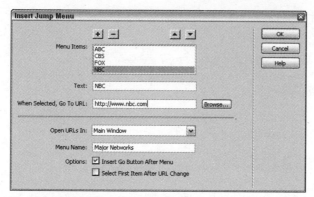

Figure 3-33: Insert Jump Menu dialog box.

There are three key definitions in the dialog box:

◆ **Text:** The text selected by students from the jump menu.

◆ **Go To URL:** The Web page (or other URL) that is loaded when the student selects the option from the jump menu.

◆ **Open URLs In:** The destination window *or* frame for the loading content. If you insert a jump menu in a site using frames, you can choose to load the content in a frame *different from* the frame containing the jump menu. The Menu Name is used for internal reference only.

Once you've created a jump menu, you can easily edit that menu by selecting the jump menu and clicking List Values in the Properties panel. Note that Dreamweaver MX uses slightly different terms in List Values:

◆ Text is called *Item Label*.

◆ Go To URL is called *Value*.

When you create your jump menu, students are unable to select the first option unless you include a Go button. To insert a Go button, select the Insert Go Button After Menu option at the bottom of the Insert Jump Menu dialog box. If you choose not to insert a Go button, use instructional text such as "Select an Option" for the Initially Selected option.

Specifying behaviors

A Dreamweaver MX behavior is a combination of a browser event and an action that triggers if the browser event occurs. Think of the processing logic as:

> *if* (event happens) *then* (action is taken)

For example:

> *if* (student clicks on image) *then* (go to a new URL)

> *if* (student moves mouse pointer over image) *then* (swap images)

> *if* (page loads in browser) *then* (run a JavaScript)

Sometimes, the processing logic can include branches, such as the following:

> *if* (browser is Netscape 4+) *then* (go to URL-A)
> > *else if* (browser is Netscape 3 or earlier) *then* (go to URL-B)
> > *else if* (browser is IE 4+) *then* (go to URL-C)
> > *else if* (browser is IE 3 or earlier) *then* (go to URL-D)

The good news is that you apply behaviors by selecting options; Dreamweaver MX handles all of the coding!

HOW ARE BEHAVIORS PROCESSED?

All browsers constantly test for events within the browser window. Where is the mouse pointer? Was it clicked? Double-clicked? Is the student dragging a layer? Where is the layer? Is the student pressing a key in a form field?

It is important to understand that Dreamweaver MX does not insert code to test for events; only browsers do the testing.

Once a Web page loads into the browser window, the browser constantly checks for events. Different browsers (and different versions of browsers) test for different events. Earlier versions of browsers test for far fewer events than current browsers.

Figure 3-34 shows an overview of the processing of a behavior.

When you create a behavior, Dreamweaver MX embeds JavaScript code into the Web page. In a nutshell, the code asks the browser to execute the action (JavaScript code) *if or when* it detects a specific event.

ATTACHING BEHAVIORS

You can attach behaviors to any object (images, movies, layers, forms, and so forth) or hyperlink, or the loading or unloading of a Web page. You *cannot,* however, attach behaviors to text, because browsers do not look for events within text.

To begin working with behaviors, first be sure that the Behaviors panel is visible by choosing Windows → Behaviors. Dreamweaver MX displays the Design Panel Group, with the Behaviors panel active, as shown in Figure 3-35 (figure shows a behavior already inserted).

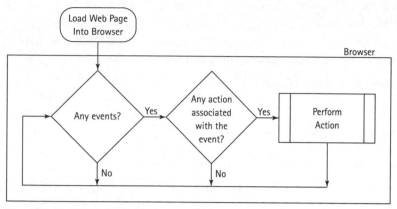

Figure 3-34: How behaviors are processed.

Figure 3-35: Behaviors panel lets you specify events and the actions they trigger.

Generally, the process for attaching a behavior to an object or hyperlink is as follows:

1. Select the object, hyperlinked text, or the BODY tag (using the Tag selector) within your open Web page to which you want to attach a behavior.

2. Click the Actions button (plus sign) on the Behaviors panel to display a pop-up list of actions that you can attach to the selected object.

3. Choose Show Events For (near the botton of the list) to select your target browser.

4. Click the Actions button again to display a pop-up list of behaviors specifically available to the browser version you selected.

5. Select the action you want to apply to the object from the drop-down list.

TIP Different browsers (and versions of browsers) test for different events, so the list of actions will differ depending on the browser version you target. Web developers most often select the 4.0 and Later Browsers option for Web pages designed for the general Internet community. Because the capabilities of browsers are evolving, later browsers have more capabilities, and thus allow for a greater selection of actions. Refer to Chapter 2 for guidance on choosing a target browser.

Dreamweaver MX selects a default event to trigger the action. To change the event that triggers the action, click on the Behavior and then click the drop-down arrow to the right of the event to display the list of events available, as shown in Figure 3-36.

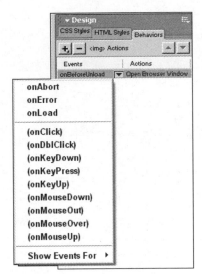

Figure 3-36: Events menu.

Dreamweaver MX actions

Table 3-3 shows the complete list of actions that ship with Dreamweaver MX. Although this list may seem overwhelming at first, you can use the table as an ongoing source of reference.

If you can read JavaScript and want to review the code for actions available with Dreamweaver MX, the scripts for each action are stored in (for Windows systems; on MacIntosh, they would be on the hard disk):

```
C:\Program Files\Macromedia\Dreamweaver MX\Configuration\Behaviors\Actions
```

TABLE 3-3 DREAMWEAVER MX ACTIONS

Action	Lets You . . .
Call JavaScript	Specify a JavaScript function or line of code to be executed.
Change Property	Change the value of an object's property (you can determine an object's properties in the Properties panel).
Check Browser	Check the browser type and version, and send control to different URLs for different browsers.
Check Plugin	Check for the existence of a specific plugin on the student's system (such Flash, Shockwave, LiveAudio, QuickTime, or Windows Media Player), and send control to a specific Web page (or other URL) if the plugin exists, or to an alternate Web page (or other URL) if the plugin does not exist.
Control Shockwave or Flash	Play (from beginning or specific frame), stop, or rewind a Shockwave or Flash movie.
Drag Layer	Specify parameters for allowing students to drag a layer. (This behavior is also used by CourseBuilder for drag-and-drop exercises.)
Go to URL	Load a different Web page (or other URL) into a browser window or frame.
Hide Pop-Up Menu	Hide a pop-up menu (secondary navigation menu, typically created with Macromedia Fireworks MX).
Jump Menu	Not typically used anymore since Dreamweaver MX includes the ability to insert a Jump Menu from the Forms tab on the Insert panel.
Jump Menu Go	Not typically used anymore.
Open Browser Window	Open a new browser window with the URL you specify. You can also specify window dimensions, and attributes of that window (whether to display toolbars or allow scrolling, for example).
Play Sound	Play a sound file. Different sound file types require different players on different systems, frequently causing plugin error messages. Unless you know the browsers your students will use, I recommend avoiding this action.

Continued

TABLE 3-3 DREAMWEAVER MX ACTIONS *(Continued)*

Action	Lets You . . .
Popup Message	Display a pop-up message similar to system and application pop-up messages.
Preload Images	Preload images into student's browser even if they aren't immediately displayed (such as the "on" versions of mouseovers).
Set Nav Bar Image	Define different images for different mouse pointer actions (no mouse, mouse over, mouse click), and send control to a Web page (or other URL) when clicked, and so forth.
Set Text	Define text for display in a specific layer, frame, or text field, or on the status bar of the browser window.
Show Pop-Up Menu	Show a pop-up menu (secondary navigation menu, typically created with Macromedia Fireworks MX).
Show-Hide Layers	Set a layer (and the content in that layer) to visible or invisible. This is very powerful because you can control the display and removal of content from the screen.
Swap Image	Replace one image with another. (Be sure both images are same height and width to avoid image distortion.)
Swap Image Restore	Return a swapped image to the original image. Valid only after you swap an image.
Timeline	Play (from beginning or specific frame) or stop a timeline. Timelines let you animate objects without using plugins.
Validate Form	Perform rudimentary data validation, such as requiring a field to be filled out; requiring a field to be numeric; requiring a numeric field to fall within a certain range; and checking for proper e-mail format.

Browser events that can trigger Dreamweaver MX actions

Table 3-4 shows the browser events available for 4.0+ browsers (both Netscape and Internet Explorer). Remember, different browsers check for different events; if the browser finds an event and you've inserted a behavior for that event, the browser automatically processes any actions associated with the event.

If you can read HTML and want to review the events checked for different browser versions, the scripts for each action are stored in (for Windows systems; on MacIntosh, they would be on the hard disk):

```
C:\Program Files\Macromedia\Dreamweaver MX\Configuration\Behaviors\Events
```

 When you attach a behavior to an image, most events appear in parentheses. The parentheses indicate that Dreamweaver displays a null (no destination anchor) hyperlink of "JavaScript:;" in the Properties panel (that is the only way the behavior can be attached). The hyperlink does not click to anywhere. Although you can insert a destination anchor, *if you remove the hyperlink entirely you will remove the behavior from that object.*

TABLE 3-4 BROWSER EVENTS (4.0 + BROWSERS)

Event	Commonly Applied To	Tests For . . .
onAbort	Images	If the loading of an image into the browser is aborted, the browser triggers the action.
onBlur	Body page in browser window, framesets, and form inputs (buttons, checkboxes, files, passwords, selection area, text areas, and text fields)	A click outside of a specified area. For example, if you test an onBlur event for a text field in a form, and the student clicks outside of that text field.
onChange	Form inputs (file, password, text field, selection area, text area)	A change in the contents of a specified area. For example, if a student changes the text in a text field.
onClick	Form inputs (buttons, checkboxes)	A click on an object or in an area. For example, if a student clicks on an image.
onDblClick	Hyperlinks (including image areas in an image map, linked images, and linked text)	A double-clicks on a hyperlink. For example, if a student double-clicks on a linked image.
onError	Body page in browser window, images	If the browser detects an error while loading, it triggers the action.

Continued

TABLE **3-4 BROWSER EVENTS (4.0 + BROWSERS)** *(Continued)*

Event	Commonly Applied To	Tests For . . .
onFocus	Body page in browser window, framesets, form inputs (buttons, files, password, text fields, selection areas, text areas)	A click into a region, making that region active, or "in focus". For example, if a student clicks in a text field that has an onFocus event.
onKeyDown	Hyperlinks (including image areas in an image map, linked images, and linked text), form inputs (files, password, text fields, text areas)	Any keyboard key press, including alphanumeric, function, and arrow keys.
onKeyPress	Hyperlinks (including image areas in an image map, linked images, and linked text), form inputs (files, password, text fields, text areas)	A press and release on any alphanumeric key.
onKeyUp	Hyperlinks (including image areas in an image map, linked images, and linked text), form inputs (files, password, text fields, text areas)	The release of any keyboard key previously depressed.
onLoad	Body page in browser window, framesets, images	When a page, frameset, or image completes loading into the browser window.
onMouseDown	Hyperlinks (including image areas in an image map, linked images, and linked text), form buttons	The mouse pointer moving down.
onMouseOut	Hyperlinks (including image areas in an image map, linked images, and linked text), image areas in an image map	The mouse pointer moving outside of the object's area.
onMouseOver	Hyperlinks (including image areas in an image map, linked images, and linked text), image areas in an image map	The mouse pointer moving inside an object's area.

Event	Commonly Applied To	Tests For . . .
onMouseUp	Hyperlinks (including image areas in an image map, linked images, and linked text), form buttons	The release of a mouse button.
onReset	Forms.	The click of a Reset button in a form,.
onResize	Body page in browser window, framesets	User resizing of a browser window or frameset.
onSelect	Form inputs (text, text areas)	Selection of a text field or text area.
onSubmit	Forms	A click on a Submit button in a form.
onUnload	Body page in browser window, framesets	If a user leaves a browser or frameset, the browser triggers the action.

Working with layers

Although layout tables offer a great deal of assistance in page layout for a Web browser, there are still limitations in using tables as layout tools. Here's where layers come in.

Layers are rectangular containers that you can place within a browser window with exact positioning. Based on standard HTML code (<DIV> or <SPAN> tags), layers can contain the same kind of content that any Web page contains, including text, images, scripts, movies, and so forth.

Layers are powerful because you can

- ◆ Have as many layers as you want on a single page.

- ◆ Make layers visible or invisible, and change visibility based on events.

- ◆ Animate layers using a timeline.

- ◆ Dynamically change the content of layers.

- ◆ Nest layers within other layers.

- ◆ Overlap layers and define their stacking order.

As you'll see when you begin using CourseBuilder, layers are used extensively for CourseBuilder interactions such as drag-and-drop and explore.

To insert a layer into your document, select the Draw Layer option from the Insert panel's Common tab. Dreamweaver MX turns the mouse pointer into crosshairs.

To draw the layer, click and hold the crosshairs where you want the upper-left corner, and drag to where you want the lower-right corner of the layer. (Don't worry about exact positioning, you can easily move and resize the layer after it is drawn.)

Figure 3-37 shows an inserted and selected layer; notice that the Properties panel displays properties relevant to layers. Although you see a border around the layer as it is drawn in Dreamweaver MX, the border is not visible when the browser displays the layer; only the content is visible.

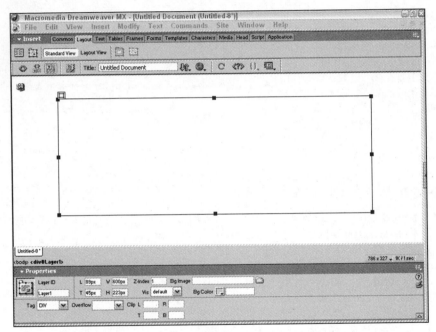

Figure 3-37: Drawn layer ready for content.

You can type text, insert images, and include whatever content you want in the layer. The Properties panel changes context according to the content you insert, defaulting to text properties.

To define the properties of a layer, click the selection handle in the upper-left corner (or, for that matter, anywhere on the layer's border). Dreamweaver MX makes the layer active, and changes the options in the Properties panel to reflect that specific layer's properties, as shown in Figure 3-38.

Figure 3-38: Properties panel for layers.

You can reposition the layer anywhere on the page by clicking and holding the selection handle (or anywhere on the layer's border) and dragging the layer to the new location. You can resize the layer by clicking and dragging the sizing handles on the layer's border. You can also change any of the properties on the Properties panel. The properties for layers include:

- **Layer ID:** Specifies an internal name used to reference the layer for processing, such as behaviors that affect the layer.

- **L and T (left and top):** Specify the distance that the upper-left corner of the layer is from the left-top corner of the browser window, in pixels. Watch how these values change as you click and drag the layer to different locations. These values can be negative, enabling you to place a layer off-screen. This is useful, for example, if you want to animate a layer using timelines (moving the layer from off-screen to on-screen).

- **W and H (width and height):** Specify the width and height of the layer rectangle, in pixels.

- **Z-Index:** Specifies the stacking order of a layer (only relevant if you overlap layers). Higher-numbered layers are displayed in front of lower-numbered layers.

- **Bg Image/Color:** Specifies the background color or background image for the layer.

- **Vis (Visibility):** Specifies the visibility of the layer, which can be: visible, invisible, default (to the browser settings), or inherit (where a layer nested inside a parent layer inherits the visibility setting from the parent layer).

- **Tag:** Specifies the HTML tag used to define the layer (stay with the default DIV unless you have good reason to change).

- **Overflow:** Specifies how the browser should handle content that is too large for the layer. Values are

  - Visible (layer automatically stretches to accommodate content)

  - Hidden (overflow content is simply not displayed)

  - Scroll (scrollbars are included automatically)

  - Auto (scrollbars are included only if there is overflow)

- **Clip (L and T, R and B):** Specifies the coordinates for a rectangular clipping region that is a portion of the layer, with the left and top corner of layer being 0,0 on the coordinate system. Regardless of how much content is in the layer, the browser only displays content within the clipping region, if one is specified.

Summary

In this chapter you've learned how to

- ◆ Navigate the Dreamweaver MX interface.
- ◆ Use layout tables and cells to control page layout.
- ◆ Store and retrieve reusable content in library items.
- ◆ Create external Cascading Style Sheets that define style for HTML tags, groups of HTML tags, and custom classes.
- ◆ Create interactive navigation with jump menus, rollovers, and navigation bars.
- ◆ Add behaviors to objects to make pages more action-oriented.
- ◆ Use layers to further control content layout.

To further your knowledge about Dreamweaver MX, use

- ◆ Joseph Lowery's *Dreamweaver MX Bible* (Wiley, ISBN 0-7645-4931-6).
- ◆ Context-sensitive online help in Dreamweaver MX.

The next chapter provides an overview of Learning Site and CourseBuilder, two freely available extensions that provide the tools necessary for building Web-Based Training with Dreamweaver MX.

Chapter 4

Introduction to Learning Site and CourseBuilder

IN THIS CHAPTER

◆ Using the Macromedia Extension Manager to install Learning Site and CourseBuilder

◆ Understanding how Learning Site designs and assembles courses

◆ Understanding how CourseBuilder builds interactions (activities) into Web pages

DREAMWEAVER MX has many extensions that are freely available. An extension is additional software that can be installed into Dreamweaver MX to provide supplementary capabilities. Extensions integrate themselves directly into the Dreamweaver MX interface, and operate as if they were part of Dreamweaver (for example, an extension may add a tab to the Insert panel, or additional options to a drop-down menu).

While Macromedia creates some extensions, most are created by outside developers. Regardless of the source, most extensions have versions for both Microsoft Windows and Macintosh platforms. Two extensions created by Macromedia to integrate WBT development capabilities into Dreamweaver MX are Learning Site and CourseBuilder.

Many Macromedia products (such as Flash MX, Fireworks MX, and Dreamweaver MX) use extensions. Regardless of the product, extensions are installed using a separate, freely-available program called the Macromedia Extension Manager. Although extensions such as Learning Site and CourseBuilder are installed directly *into* Dreamweaver MX (and used only within Dreamweaver MX), they are installed *from* the Macromedia Extension Manager. Figure 4-1 shows the required order of installation for these different programs.

To install the Macromedia Extension Manager on either a Windows or Macintosh system (assuming you've already installed Dreamweaver MX), double-click the appropriate installer and follow the standard installation dialog for your system.

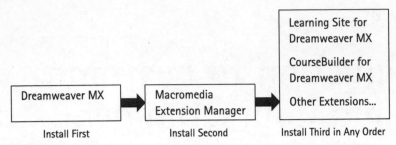

Install First   Install Second   Install Third in Any Order

Figure 4–1: Install Dreamweaver MX first, followed by the Extension Manager, and then extensions such as Learning Site and CourseBuilder.

 The CD-ROM contains the installers for both Windows (em_install.exe) and Macintosh (em_install.hqx) systems.

Once the Extension Manager is installed, you are ready to install Dreamweaver MX extensions, in any order you choose.

Installing the Learning Site and CourseBuilder Extensions

To install your CourseBuilder and Learning Site extensions, launch the Extension Manager by choosing Start → All Programs → Macromedia → Macromedia Extension Manager.

Because the Extension Manager is used to install extensions into different Macromedia programs, select Dreamweaver MX from the drop-down menu if it is not already selected, as shown in Figure 4-2. (The list of programs that displays in the drop-down menu reflects the Macromedia products installed on your system.)

At this point, assuming you have not yet installed extensions, your Extension Manager window is empty.

 The CD-ROM also contains the CourseBuilder (MX515130_CourseBuilder 4211.mxp) and Learning Site (MX515130_LearningSite118.mxp) Macromedia extension packages.

Install New Extension button

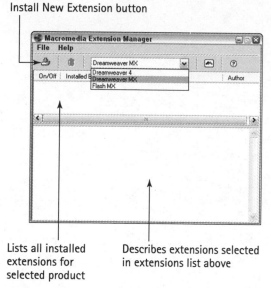

Lists all installed
extensions for
selected product

Describes extensions selected
in extensions list above

Figure 4–2: Selecting Dreamweaver MX from the
Macromedia Extension Manager.

Follow these steps to install the Learning Site extension into Dreamweaver MX:

1. Close all applications (including Dreamweaver MX) **except** the Extension
   Manager.

2. Click the Install New Extension button on the Extension Manager.

   The Extension Manager displays the Select Extension to Install dialog box.

3. Browse to and select the Learning Site extension –
   MX515130_LearningSite118.mxp – on your CD-ROM.

   The Extension Manager installs the Learning Site extension into
   Dreamweaver MX, and Learning Site is now listed in the Extension
   Manager.

To verify the installation of Learning Site, launch Dreamweaver MX and select
Site. Dreamweaver MX displays the new Learning Site option integrated into the
Site menu, as shown in Figure 4-3.

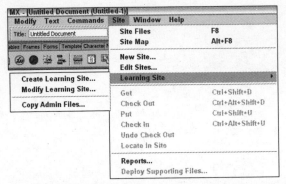

Figure 4-3: Once the Learning Site extension is installed,
it's available through the Dreamweaver MX Site menu.

Close Dreamweaver MX to install the CourseBuilder extension. Repeat the steps you followed to install the Learning Site extension, except browse to and select the CourseBuilder extension — MX515130_CourseBuilder4211.mxp — on your CD-ROM:

To verify the installation of CourseBuilder, launch Dreamweaver MX. Notice that Dreamweaver MX displays an additional tab, the Learning tab, on the Insert panel (see Figure 4-4).

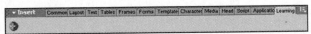

Figure 4-4: CourseBuilder adds a Learning tab, which includes the Insert
CourseBuilder Interaction icon, to Dreamweaver's Insert panel.

Close the Extension Manager now. You won't need it again unless you decide to install other extensions.

You can find many additional free extensions and various levels of support (including online discussion forums) at the Macromedia Exchange, http://exchange.macromedia.com.

What is Learning Site?

Learning Site lets you set up the entire structure for your course. It creates the frameset that contains your course, the navigation and menu system, the buttons and layout for your navigation, and so forth.

Once you create a paper prototype for your course, you are ready to begin laying the foundation for that course with Learning Site. The beauty of Learning Site is that you can build your structure without knowing the tenants (so to speak). Learning Site lets you define the structure *and* assemble the key pieces for that course even before you create your content. Figure 4-5 shows the process of building your course architecture with Learning Site.

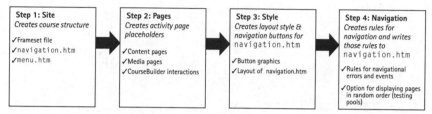

Figure 4–5: The process for building the architecture of a course with Learning Site.

Before you create a Learning Site, you must first create a Dreamweaver MX site to contain it (Learning Site modifies an existing Dreamweaver MX site into a Learning Site, so you must have created a Dreamweaver MX site first). See Chapter 3 for information about creating a Dreamweaver MX site.

Creating a Learning Site with the dialog box

Before you create a Learning Site, you must first create a Dreamweaver MX site to contain it (Learning Site modifies an existing Dreamweaver MX site into a Learning Site, so you must have created a Dreamweaver MX site first). See Chapter 3 for information about creating a Dreamweaver MX site. You create and modify a Learning Site through a single dialog box, which Learning Site displays when you select Site → Learning Site → Create Learning Site from the main menu bar. Figure 4-6 shows the Learning Site dialog box with the Pages tab active.

You define your Learning Site by using the various tabs on the Learning Site dialog box. For example, you assemble the page names and titles for the course on the Pages tab, and you select the style for you navigation elements on the Style tab.

Normally, you use the Learning Site dialog box once to create the site architecture, and then again each time you want to add or subtract pages from the course. Chapter 7 fully describes how to create a Learning Site in detail.

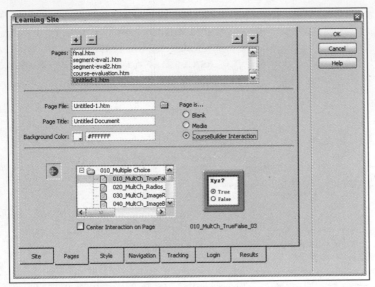

Figure 4-6: The Learning Site dialog box showing the Site, Pages, Style, and Navigation tabs.

Understanding the Learning Site files

Learning Site creates the following files within an existing Dreamweaver MX site:

- A course frameset consisting of two frames: navFrame, the top frame used for navigation, and mainFrame, the larger frame used for course content.

- A navigation file (navigation.htm) and the navigation buttons using the graphics from the style you select on the Styles tab of the Learning Site dialog box. The navigation.htm file also contains internal tables of all pages and page titles in the course, which the file uses to understand the sequence of pages used in that course. The navigation.htm file always remains resident in the top frame of the frameset to maintain navigational context.

- A menu file (menu.htm) that dynamically builds a pop-up menu for each page in the entire course. The menu is built based on the table of pages and page titles contained within the navigation.htm file, and is displayed when students click the Menu button.

- Activity pages (course content), which include the following:

  Blank pages (placeholder pages for content).

  Media pages (include Authorware, Flash, or Shockwave movies).

  CourseBuilder pages (include specific interaction placeholders).

Figure 4-7 shows an example of a frameset created by Learning Site and opened up in Dreamweaver MX. Note the JavaScript code in the `mainFrame` frame that loads the first page listed in the `navigation.htm` page table.

navFrame
Contents of this frame is the file, which remains resident in this frame.

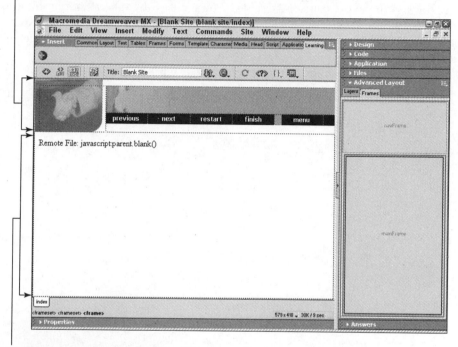

mainFrame
Contents of this frame determined by the table of pages in navigation.htm, along with current page context.

When the frameset is loaded, the navigation.htm file finds the first page listed in the page tables and loads that page into this frame.

Figure 4-7: Learning Site creates a frameset consisting of a navigation frame (`navFrame`) at the top and a content frame (`mainFrame`) below.

Understanding how navigation works

The workhorse file is the `navigation.htm` file. This file contains all of the navigational buttons that allow students to

- Page backward and forward one page at a time.
- Move to the beginning or end of the course with a single click.

◆ Select topics from a menu (automatically built by the `navigation.htm` file) of clickable titles for all pages in the course.

◆ Quit the course.

All of these navigational buttons work because Learning Site builds two tables within the `navigation.htm` file that list, in sequence, all of the files and associated page titles in the entire course; the table of files is used by the navigation buttons to understand the course sequence; the table of titles is used to build the menu for the course. In addition, `navigation.htm` stores the settings for the course, such as the navigation rules defined in Learning Site.

Figure 4-8 shows a snippet of the table of pages in the `navigation.htm` file for the *HTML Basics* course on the CD-ROM.

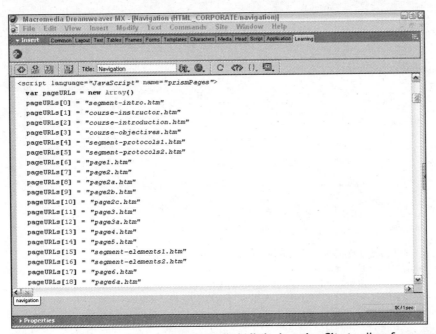

Figure 4–8: The table of files is automatically built by Learning Site to allow for course navigation. This table is stored in the `navigation.htm` file, which remains resident in the top frame of the course.

Notice that the files in Figure 4-7 are sequenced, beginning with `pageURLs[0]`. When the course is loaded, the `navigation.htm` file looks at the table of pages for the first URL, finds that URL (`segment-intro.htm`), and loads that page into the `mainFrame` frame. Now that page context has been established (the location in the array), it is easy for the scripts in navigation.htm to know how to process the navigation buttons Next, Previous, and so forth.

What is CourseBuilder?

While Learning Site is used to maintain course structure and style, CourseBuilder is used to integrate tests and activities within each Web page of the course. CourseBuilder is a robust set of templates, tools, and scripts that let you easily integrate interactions (tests and activities) within a Web page.

You can use CourseBuilder interactions to develop activities or perform and grade tests. You can also track the results of student tests and store those results in a database.

To insert a CourseBuilder interaction into a Web page, first open that page in Dreamweaver MX (the page may have content or be a blank page). Position the cursor at the location on the Web page where you want the CourseBuilder interaction inserted. Click the Insert CourseBuilder Interaction button on the Dreamweaver MX Insert panel's Learning tab (see Figure 4-4) to display the CourseBuilder Interaction dialog box.

The CourseBuilder Interaction dialog box initially shows a single tab, named Gallery. The categories displayed in the Gallery depend on whether you target your course to work with 3.0 browsers or 4.0+ browsers (since 4.0+ browsers offer more capabilities, CourseBuilder offers many more interactions):

◆ For 3.0 browsers, three categories display: Multiple Choice, Text Entry, and Action Manager.

◆ For 4.0+ browsers, all categories display: Multiple Choice, Text Entry, Drag and Drop, Explore, Button, Slider, Timer, and Action Manager.

Once you select an interaction category, CourseBuilder displays a collection of CourseBuilder templates for it, as shown in Figure 4-9.

Unless you know that your students will be using extraordinarily old browsers, it is safe to select interactions that work with 4.0+ browsers.

Click on a template in the Gallery to insert that type of interaction (test or activity) into the Web page. The CourseBuilder Interaction dialog box will display additional tabs to help you further define student options and processing rules for the interaction. For example, Figure 4-10 shows the `Multch_Radios` (Multiple Choice, Radio Buttons) template selected.

CourseBuilder templates

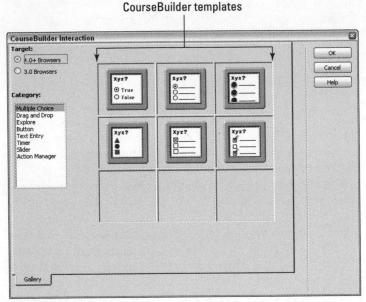

Figure 4-9: CourseBuilder Interaction dialog box with Multiple Choice category selected. The Multiple Choice category contains six templates, represented by the icons to the right of the category list.

As you make changes in the CourseBuilder Interaction dialog box, CourseBuilder updates the template inserted into the Web page. You can make a change to an interaction on your page at any time by simply selecting the CourseBuilder invisible element (the red icon inserted with each interaction). When you select the CourseBuilder invisible element, the Properties panel displays the properties for that CourseBuilder interaction; you can then click the Edit button on the Properties panel to launch the CourseBuilder Interaction dialog box, where you can edit the definitions for that interaction.

Because CourseBuilder has so many templates — a total of 25 spread over eight categories — it is very easy to lose sight of the overall process. Exactly what are you defining each step of the way? Figure 4-11 shows a high-level overview of this process. (This diagram only illustrates the overall process and is not a description of every option.)

CourseBuilder interaction inserted into the web page

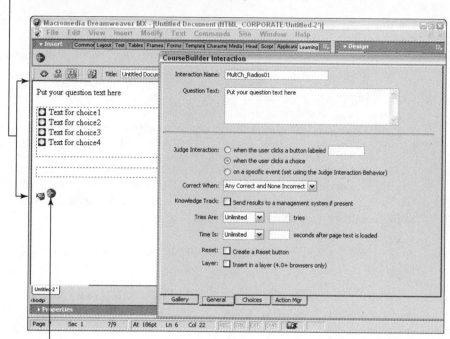

CourseBuilder element representing this interaction. When selected, you can edit the interaction from the Properties panel.

Figure 4-10: CourseBuilder interaction selected and inserted into the Web page.

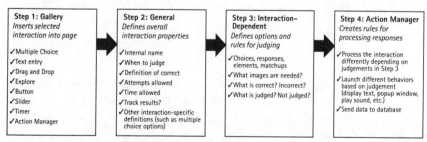

Figure 4-11: The process for defining a CourseBuilder interaction.

CourseBuilder interactions are typically used in one of three ways:

- **Testing a student.** When you test students, students expect both an evaluation and a response. CourseBuilder interactions that are used to test are designed to identify correct and incorrect answers and provide feedback to the student.

- **Developing interactive exercises.** CourseBuilder interactions can be used as vehicles for interactivity without evaluating answers. For example, you can use a drag-and-drop exercise to demonstrate a point (drag-and-drop is used to demonstrate points several times in the *HTML Basics* course).

- **Controlling events.** Some CourseBuilder interactions are meant only to control and spawn other events. For example, you can use a timer interaction to time a test, or a button interaction to provide a graphical button to launch another interaction.

Table 4-1 shows the eight categories of CourseBuilder interactions, and what each one does.

TABLE 4–1 COURSEBUILDER INTERACTIONS

Interaction	Typical Uses	Description
Multiple Choice	Testing	True/false and multiple choice, where students click one or multiple choices.
Text Entry	Testing	Text field where students type answer.
Drag and Drop	Testing, interactive exercises	Matchups consisting of two parts: items that students drag, and targets on which the students drop them.
Explore	Testing, interactive exercises	Hot areas of an image that students click (similar to image maps).
Button	Control	Button students click to trigger an event, such as the judgment (processing) of a test.
Slider	Testing, control	Slider used to make a selection in a range of choices.
Timer	Control	Timer displayed to limit time for completion of activity.
Action Manager	Control	Controls all of the processing for interactions (what to do if answer is correct or if incorrect or if time runs out, for example).

Summary

In this chapter you've learned how to:

- Install and use the Extension Manager.

- Install the Learning Site and CourseBuilder extensions into Dreamweaver MX.

- Follow the process for using Learning Site to build a learning site structure.

- Follow the process for using CourseBuilder to insert activity pages into a Dreamweaver MX Web page.

The next chapter provides the tools and processes for creating a paper prototype of your course.

Chapter 5

Developing Effective Tests

IN THIS CHAPTER

- Understanding the different types of tests available
- Minimizing the impact of student guessing
- Increasing the effectiveness of test distractors
- Understanding automatic scoring

WE ADMINISTER TESTS for only two reasons: to bolster learning, and to measure performance distinctions among students.

Tests bolster learning by

- Reinforcing what the student already knows.
- Identifying problem areas, giving motivated students the ability to focus future learning on those areas.
- Motivating students to study and focus.

Tests are also the key tool for measuring performance distinctions among students by

- Asking test questions that all students have equal opportunity to answer (either the same questions or questions from the same test pool).
- Ranking students according to performance based solely on test results.

The purpose of a test does not always have to be stated or obvious to students. I recall a test from my high school years that made me learn to pay a bit more attention to directions.

The teacher distributed the test and said, "Write your name at the top, and then read *all* of the questions before you begin writing." The test must have been several pages of questions, and I was pretty eager to start answering them. Like almost everybody else in the class, I pretended to do a quick read of the pages and then flipped back to the first page, furiously answering whatever I could. I made it to the final question of the final page. . . and there it was:

If you hand this paper in without a single mark on it except for your name, you get an automatic A for following directions.

Hoodwinked. Bamboozled. Very few students received the automatic A. The purpose of the test was never to test our knowledge of the subject, but rather to test our ability to listen to and follow directions. It was effective both as a teaching tool and as a measurement of the performance of students in following directions, and none of the students had a clue as to the real purpose of the test until it was over.

 The topic of test validity (does a test measure what it says it measures?) and reliability (is the test consistently valid?) are beyond the scope of this book. The classic document in testing is *The Standards for Educational and Psychological Testing*, jointly developed by the American Educational Research Association (www.AERA.net), the American Psychological Association (www.APA.org), and the National Council on Measurement in Education (www.NCME.org).

Developing Effective Questions

As a teacher (albeit it an online one), your goal for testing students is to develop questions that reinforce learning *and* distinguish performance among students. Although online testing has added new dimensions to testing, the types of testing available are the standard forms that have been used for many years in classroom settings:

- ◆ True/false
- ◆ Multiple choice
- ◆ Drag and drop (match-ups)
- ◆ Text entry (fill-in-the-blank)
- ◆ Essay

The first three types are all variations of multiple-choice questions, which test students more for recognition than recall. Students know that the right answer is among the choices — if they can just recognize it!

Text-entry questions test students for recall, typically at the fact or knowledge level. Students can guess, but their guesses are statistically far less significant than in multiple-choice because students are not choosing from a limited pool of options (they have to pull the answers from their brain without a menu to choose from).

Essay questions test students for their depth of knowledge about a subject, and provide them with the opportunity to fully demonstrate cognitive mastery of the subject, from comprehension through evaluation in Bloom's taxonomy.

Table 5-1 shows my subjective rating of each type of question. Based on a number of factors, the table shows why I most like to use multiple-choice and drag and drop (matchup) questions, and least like to use essay for online tests. Use the ratings as another source of consideration when you are creating questions for your online test.

TABLE 5-1 RATING OF DIFFERENT QUESTION TYPES

	Easy to Develop	Easy to Score	Breadth of Topic Coverage	Depth of Topic Coverage	Ranking for Online Testing*
True/False	High	High	High	Low	4
Multiple Choice	Medium	High	High	Medium	1
Drag and Drop	Medium	High	High	Medium	1
Text Entry	High	Medium	High	Low	3
Essay	High	Low	Low	High	5

*1 is the most desirable and 5 is the least desirable.

Making test questions valid

All test questions must be *valid*. A test question is valid when students who "have the learning", so to speak, can answer that test question correctly. For example, read and answer the following test question:

President Lyndon Baines Johnson served two terms in office. True? False?

What is your answer? Because of the imprecise wording, you could make an argument that the question is true because Johnson did have two terms in office, just not two *full* terms. You could also make the argument that the question is false because the first term was not considered a term by the Constitution (if a President fulfills more than half of an elected President's term, that President is only eligible to serve one additional term, not two). A better rewrite would be:

President Lyndon Baines Johnson served two full terms in office. True? False?

In addition to the problem of imprecise wording, another common problem with multiple-choice questions is multiple interpretations of key words. Read and answer the following test question:

George W. Bush won the U.S. presidential election in 2000. True? False?

Of course, Republicans see this question as a true/false question, and Democrats see it as a trick question. We heard the arguments from both sides, and both sides had good arguments. A better rewrite would be:

Although he clearly did not win the presidential election in 2000, a Republican-controlled Supreme Court declared George W. Bush the winner of the 2000 presidential election.

Okay, just kidding. A better rewrite would be:

George W. Bush was eventually declared winner of the presidential election in 2000 after the U.S. Supreme court disallowed Florida's statewide hand recount. True? False?

Test questions should be designed to test the full range of a student's cognitive learning (knowledge, comprehension, application, and so forth) about a topic. If test questions have reasonable arguments for more than one answer, well, that's just not good test design. Test questions *must* reside in the land of absolutes!

Reducing the odds of guessing in multiple choice

Multiple-choice questions consist of the following:

- The *stem,* which is the question or introduction.
- *Correct choice or choices.**
- *Distractors,* which are incorrect choices designed to make it tougher for students to select the right answer. *
  Typically, correct choices and distractors together are referred to as options.

The purpose of a test is to evaluate students on what they have learned, and not how well they can guess. One of the challenges of using multiple-choice questions is to cut down the odds of a student simply guessing the correct answer. Since the purpose of the test is to evaluate student knowledge, having multiple-choice questions that are easier to guess ultimately impacts the validity of a test score.

There are two important steps you can take to reduce the impact of student guessing in multiple-choice questions:

- Increase the total number of options or increase the number of correct choices.
- Increase the effectiveness of distractors.

DECREASING THE CHANCES OF GUESSING CORRECTLY

The chances of a student guessing the answer to a multiple-choice question are determined by a simple formula:

1 / {number of possible combinations of correct choices}

To decrease the chances of a student guessing correctly, you can either increase the total number of options or you can increase the total number of correct choices (to a point, as we'll discuss in a moment).

When you construct a multiple-choice question with four options, the chance of a student guessing the correct choice is 25%. To decrease the chances of a student guessing correctly, you could:

◆ Increase the options. Increasing the number of options to six, for example, decreases the student's chances of guessing the correct answer to 16.67%.

◆ Keep the same number of options, but increase the number of correct choices. For example, if you make *two* of the four options correct choices (where the student must select *both* correct choices), you also decrease the student's chances of guessing the correct answer to 16.67%.

Table 5-2 shows example calculations of student chances for guessing correctly based on varying numbers of correct choices for 4-, 6-, and 8-option multiple-choice questions.

TABLE 5-2 CALCULATIONS OF STUDENT CHANCES FOR CORRECTLY GUESSING
MULTIPLE-CHOICE ANSWERS

Total Number of Options	Number of Correct Choices	Number of Possible Combinations of Correct Choices	Chance of Students Guessing All Choices Correctly
4	1	4	25.00%
6	1	6	16.67%
8	1	8	12.50%
4	2	6	16.67%
6	2	15	06.67%
8	2	28	03.57%
4	3	4	25.00%
6	3	20	05.00%
8	3	56	01.79%

Table 5-2 demonstrates the dramatic decrease in student chances of guessing correctly by simply adding more correct options to a multiple-choice question (again, assuming that students must guess *all* of the correct choices).

When you pick a number of correct choices, the chances of students guessing all correctly decrease through the midway mark, and then begin increasing. Table 5-3 illustrates this point.

TABLE 5-3 EFFECT OF ADDITIONAL CORRECT CHOICES TO MULTIPLE-CHOICE TEST

Total Number of Options	Number of Correct Choices	Chances of Students Guessing All Choices Correctly
6 options	1 correct choice	16.67%
6 options	2 correct choices	06.67%
6 options	3 correct choices	05.00%
6 options	4 correct choices	06.67%
6 options	5 correct choices	16.67%
6 options	6 correct choices	100.00%

Notice that the odds of a student correctly guessing a multiple-choice question with 1 correct choice are the same as the odds of them correctly guessing a multiple-choice question with 5 correct choices. More options decrease the odds of students correctly guessing until the mid-point, after which the law of diminishing returns takes over.

INCREASING THE EFFECTIVENESS OF DISTRACTORS

If distractors do their job, they ensure that the chances of students guessing correct answers to multiple-choice questions are minimal. There are also, however, a number of cues that test creators unwittingly provide when developing test questions, and these cues *increase* the chances of students guessing correctly. These cues include the following:

1. Selecting the third choice ("C" or "3") as the correct choice more often than any other choice in a multiple-choice question.

2. Selecting the "true" choice more often than the "false" choice as the correct choice in a true/false question.

3. Adding more detail to the correct choice than is added to distractors.

4. Making grammatical errors in connecting the stem to options.

5. Making more grammatical errors and typos in distractors than in correct choices.

6. Using trite distractors.

Avoiding cues 1 and 2 are easy: truly randomize the order of options. Too often test creators try to outthink students by focusing on the placement of correct choices. If you construct a multiple-choice question, roll the dice (or a die) for the placement of each option. If you use true/false questions, make as many false statements as true ones.

Avoiding cue 3 involves writing distractors that are approximately the same length and detail as correct choices. For example, read the following multiple-choice question:

The boiling point of water is
   1. 100 degrees Fahrenheit
   2. 100 degrees Celsius (at sea level)
   3. 100 degrees Kelvin

The creators of the question were so focused on making sure that the question was valid (which is a good thing), they added specifics that weren't there for distractors (which is not a good thing). Put the same level of details for all options:

The boiling point of water (at sea level) is
   1. 100 degrees Fahrenheit
   2. 100 degrees Celsius
   3. 100 degrees Kelvin

Avoiding cues 4 and 5 requires you to pay attention to your grammar. Read the following multiple-choice question:

A dinosaur that is part of the armored herbivores (Thyreophora suborder) is an
   1. Ankylosaurus
   2. Wannanosaurus
   3. Styracosaurus
   4. Brachiosaurus

What is the answer? Even if you do not know the subject area, you might pick up on the fact that the correct choice for this question is the first choice, Ankylosaurus. Why? Because that is the only dinosaur name that grammatically matches the introductory article "an". The easiest solution to this particular example is to place the appropriate article with each choice:

A dinosaur that is part of the armored herbivores (Thyreophora suborder) is
   1. an Ankylosaurus
   2. a Wannanosaurus
   3. a Styracosaurus
   4. a Brachiosaurus

Automated Scoring of Essays?

Part of the resistance to computer scoring of essays is our focus on the question, "Can computers understand and appreciate the nuances of an essay?" Of course it seems like we're really asking, "Can a computer carry these uniquely human capabilities?" The focus of the question associates uniquely human capabilities with that gray electronic box sitting underneath our desks; so, of course, our answer is a resounding, "No!"

What if the question were posed in a slightly different way? What if we instead asked, "Given enough time and resources, could a *human being* map out all of the rules and decisions that go into evaluating an essay?"

Both questions are, for all practical purposes, the same question. Yet I find the second question a little more palatable. Don't you?

Educational Testing Systems (ETS) is the organization that creates and administers many of the standard tests — such as the SAT, TOEFL, and CMAT — used by educational institutions throughout the United States.

The GMAT (Graduate Management Admissions Test) is used as a standardized test for applicants of more than 2,000 MBA programs. Part of the GMAT test includes an essay. Until 1999, each essay was independently judged and scored by two judges. If there were differences in the judging (beyond a particular threshold), the deadlock would be broken by a third judge. Then came e-rater.

E-rater is a software program that uses artificial intelligence to evaluate essays. In a nutshell, the e-rater software is fed significant numbers of previously graded essays to "learn" to grade a specific essay. E-rater is able to understand and apply evaluations based on a variety of complex language criteria including structure, organization, and content.

Since 1999, each GMAT essay has been judged by a single human judge and by e-rater. Again, if there are differences in the judging, the deadlock is broken by a third judge. In 98% of the cases, there is independent agreement of scoring between the human judge and e-rater.

A number of companies have products that evaluate essays, including the following:

Educational Testing Systems Technologies (www.etstechnologies.com)

Knowledge Analysis Technologies (www.knowledge-technologies.com)

Vantage Learning (www.vantagelearning.com)

Each of these three companies has a demo and papers explaining each evaluation system.

TIP When you proofread your multiple-choice questions, read the stem with each option to make sure they flow.

Trite distractors (cue 6) simply increase the student's odds of guessing correctly. For example, read the following multiple-choice question:

The inventor of the World Wide Web is
1. Vannevar Bush
2. Tim Berners-Lee
3. Al Gore
4. Ted Nelson

Obviously, it isn't Al Gore, so the elimination of that distractor increased the student's chances of guessing correctly to 33%. If you are having trouble creating distractors, use completely unknown distractors instead of obviously false distractors. For example, you could use a generic name such as Robert Stevens instead of Al Gore, for instance (with my apologies to anyone named Robert Stevens who doesn't feel generic).

Automating scoring

There are two general types of tests in CourseBuilder:

◆ Recognition tests, where students only need to recognize the correct answer or answers. CourseBuilder interactions that fall into this category are Multiple Choice, Drag and Drop, Slider, and Explore tests and activities.

◆ Recall tests, where students must recall a word or phrase and type their answers. CourseBuilder interactions that fall into this category are Text Entry tests.

Just as in the "paper test" world, tests of recognition are easily automated because the student is not contributing variable content to the process, but rather is simply selecting from content the test creator developed. Answers are absolutely correct or absolutely incorrect.

Tests of recall, however, provide students with the opportunity to contribute individualized content to the process. In the "paper test" world, this individualized content is typically evaluated by teachers who decide "gray area" rules for evaluation: Does spelling count? Do partial answers count? Do transposed words count?

There are a few considerations around automatic scoring in CourseBuilder for tests of recall (text entry, or "fill-in-the-blank" questions). With text-entry tests, the processing of answers is a little more complex, particularly if the "blank" involves a phrase rather than a single word. For text-entry tests you can define rules that judge the following:

♦ Uppercase and lowercase student responses as the same. For example, if the correct answer is *APPLE* and the student types *apple* or *Apple* or *ApPLe*, all three answers are judged to be true (to match).

♦ Uppercase and lowercase student responses as different. For example, if the correct answer is *APPLE* and the student types *apple* or *Apple* or *ApPLe*, all three answers are judged to be false (not a match).

♦ Exact matches as required (including spacing, wording, and punctuation). For example, if the correct answer is *apples are red* and the student types *red apples*, the answer is judged to be false (not a match).

♦ Exact matches as not required. For example, if the correct answer is *apples* and the student types *red apples* or the *color of apples is red*, the answer is judged to be true (to match).

Unlike the recognition tests, you'll need to be substantially more diligent about identifying all acceptable variations for correct answers when you use text entry tests and activities.

Summary

This chapter described how to create effective test questions. We discussed

♦ Developing test questions that mitigate the impact of student guessing on the final score.

♦ Using the Topic Weight Planner and Question Developer to develop questions that focus on the important topics in your course.

♦ Some of the issues and directions of automated scoring.

The next chapter shows you how to create your course prototype.

Chapter 6

Creating a Course Prototype

IN THIS CHAPTER

- ◆ Making design decisions for multiple-choice, text-entry, drag-and-drop, and explore interactions

- ◆ Controlling CourseBuilder interactions with buttons, sliders, and timers

- ◆ Choosing responses to student interactions

- ◆ Understanding browser version limitations on design

- ◆ Creating a storyboard (a paper prototype) of your course

IN THE REAL WORLD, when teachers give tests, students expect to respond to various types of questions – multiple-choice, fill-in-the-blank, true/false, and essay, for example.

Students expect that some questions carry more weight than other questions (for example, "this question is worth 5 points, and that question is worth 2 points"); students further expect to know those weights when the test is administered.

Students expect their test responses to be evaluated by the teacher. Depending on the type of question, that evaluation might be objective (responses are correct or incorrect), or subjective (how well the student covered the salient points in an essay, based solely on the teacher's judgment).

Students also expect to receive a score on test, with the scale typically being 0–100.

To reinforce the learning experience, teachers also construct nongraded activities such as unannounced pop-quizzes or hands-on activities. Whatever the approach, students do *not* expect to receive a score on such activities (at least not a score that is "recorded"). Teachers use such activities to coach rather than correct student responses.

When designing tests and activities for the classroom, teachers typically focus on the wording of questions, the selection of a question type (multiple-choice, essay, and so forth), and the weight of each question (if scored).

In some cases, the only differences between tests and activities in the classroom are the presence of scoring and the stress-level!

CourseBuilder enables you to build student interactions that mimic much of the real world (in fact the word interaction is intended to convey the interaction between student and teacher). You can use CourseBuilder interactions (one or many interactions) for both tests *and* activities. For example, you might have students drag pictures and drop them on corresponding target pictures (match-ups). If that interaction is scored, it's a test, and if it isn't scored, it's an activity.

There are many decisions that you need to make for each CourseBuilder interaction, and they fall into one of two categories: design or processing.

Design choices answer questions such as

- What kind of CourseBuilder interaction will I use?

- Will I use text only? Graphics? Animated graphics?

- What kind of distractors (incorrect choices making the test or activity a little tougher) will I create?

- Can the student try to answer more than once?

- Is the student's time for completion limited?

- What does the student do (select a choice? click a button? drop a layer?) to initiate processing of the interaction?

- How do I construct valid tests? (Making sure *all* possible correct or incorrect responses are identified as such.)

- Is the interaction scored?

- If the interaction is scored, is each interaction weighted equally?

Processing choices answer questions such as

- What are the rules for evaluating responses?

- What answers should be considered correct? Incorrect?

- How should the course respond to correct answers? Incorrect answers?

- Should I send the results to a database?

 These questions (and other series of questions throughout this chapter) are carefully constructed to relate to fields and other options in the CourseBuilder dialog boxes, so please give each question careful consideration.

After you define the learning objectives (see Chapter 2) for your course and are ready to begin design, the first step in the design process is to develop a paper prototype (such as a storyboard) of your course. Paper prototypes help you visually organize the flow of content (including tests and activities) for your entire course *before* you create it electronically, making it easier to arrange and rearrange the flow of your course.

When you create your paper prototype, you only need to know your options for *designing* CourseBuilder interactions to create your paper prototype; most of the rest of the book deals with *processing* the interactions. Let's look at the design options now.

Choosing CourseBuilder Interactions

CourseBuilder interactions let you create tests and activities that provide students with interactive feedback and responses. These interactions include

- ◆ Multiple choice (including true/false)
- ◆ Text entry
- ◆ Drag and drop
- ◆ Explore

CourseBuilder interactions are inserted into a Web page with a default template (layout and design for an interaction), but you have substantial control over the final look and feel of the interaction.

To understand this point, first take a look at Figure 6-1, which shows the default look of an Explore interaction when it's inserted into a Web page.

The template in Figure 6-1 was modified for the *HTML Basics* course; Figure 6-2 shows the final look.

Notice how different the pages in Figures 6-1 and 6-2 look. This is an example of how you can change the look of an interaction to work best in your page. The visual design of your interactions should be driven by the overall design of your Learning Site, and not by the "look and feel" of CourseBuilder interactions. If you pay too much attention to the CourseBuilder templates (the initial design of CourseBuilder interactions in the CourseBuilder Gallery), they will begin driving the design of your interactions. You want to maintain control of your own design plan.

ON THE CD The CD-ROM contains examples of each CourseBuilder interaction so that you can observe how they work interactively. I recommend that you look at the samples of each interaction before reading about its design. Keep in mind that the examples only convey *a* specific design approach, not *the* design approach.

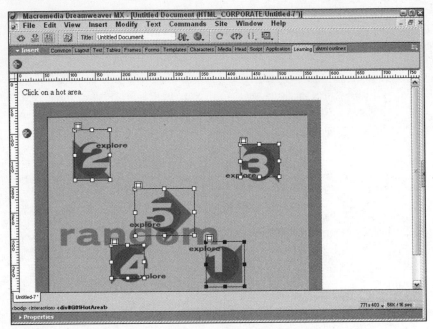

Figure 6-1: An Explore interaction as it is initially inserted into a Web page

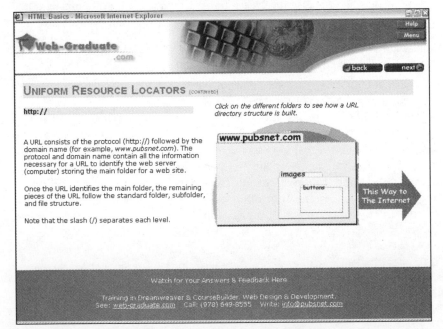

Figure 6-2: The Explore interaction modified for the HTML Basics course

Multiple choice interactions (including true/false)

Multiple-choice interactions provide students with two or more options from which to select one (or more) correct answers. For example, the interaction shown in Figure 6-3 has a button in the upper-right corner *of each choice* and initiates processing of the interaction as soon as the student clicks one of the buttons.

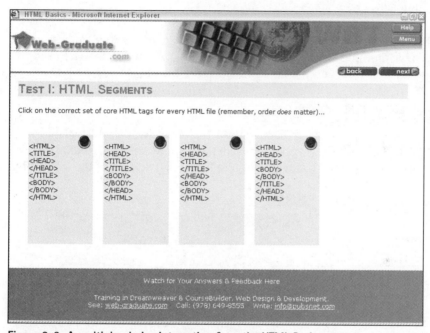

Figure 6-3: A multiple-choice interaction from the HTML Basics course

Other interactions allow the student to select one or more choices and ask him to click a button to initiate processing (in the *HTML Basics* course, for example, some interactions require students to click a Grade It button to initiate processing).

To create a multiple-choice interaction in CourseBuilder, you need to make the following design decisions:

- ◆ What is the wording of the question or instructions that introduce the choices?

- ◆ How many correct choices are there? What is the wording of correct choices?

- ◆ How many incorrect choices are there? What is the wording of incorrect choices?

- ◆ What does the student click to select a choice?

◆ What initiates processing of the interaction?

    a. Is the choice automatically processed as soon as the student clicks it?

    b. Do students click a choice (or choices) and then use a CourseBuilder control (such as a button) to initiate processing?

◆ What is the wording of feedback about correct and incorrect choices?

◆ How is feedback delivered?

Multiple choice interactions are fully described in Chapter 9. You can also see an example of a multiple choice test using image buttons in the folder Presidents, under the Samples folder on the CD-ROM (open the file named `presidents1.htm`).

Text-entry interactions

Text-entry questions provide students with a text field within which they type a response. Figure 6-4 shows a text-entry example in which students would type their response and then click the Grade It button to initiate processing of the interaction.

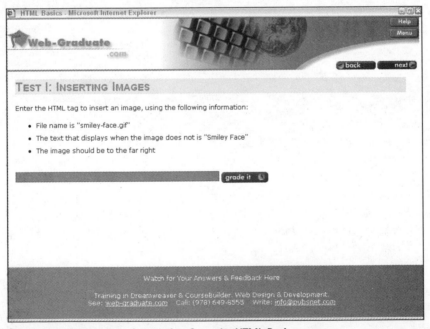

Figure 6-4: A text-entry interaction from the HTML Basics course

As a general design rule, use text-entry questions only for single-word or exact-phrase (such as syntax statements where there is little room for variance) answers.

As a teacher in a classroom you can evaluate an entry on a fill-in-the-blank and say "Oh, that's close enough!" or "She misspelled Machiavelli but I'm going to give her the points because she knew the name". You can't program such leeway into the evaluation of a CourseBuilder interaction (although you can make responses case insensitive and only look for key phrases in the response).

To create a text-entry question in CourseBuilder, you need to make the following design decisions:

◆ What is the wording of the question or instructions that introduce the choices?

◆ Is there initial text in the field?

◆ What initiates processing of the interaction?

    a. Is the text entry automatically processed as soon as the student tabs or clicks out of the text-entry box?

    b. Do students click a CourseBuilder control (such as a button) to initiate processing?

◆ What is the wording of feedback about correct and incorrect choices?

◆ How is feedback delivered?

The text field can be a single line allowing a maximum number of characters, or it can be a multiline text field.

TIP You can create custom styles for any HTML element, including form elements. Text-entry fields are standard form elements. In the *HTML Basics* course, for example, text boxes are all colored blue to fit the course color theme. You can style text entry boxes however you want; see Chapter 3 for information on creating custom styles.

Text entry interactions are fully described in Chapter 10. You can also see an example of a text entry test in the folder Cloze Test, under the Samples folder on the CD-ROM (open the file named `vocabulary.htm`).

Drag-and-drop interactions (including true/false)

Drag-and-drop interactions provide students with two sets of elements: drag elements and target elements. A drag-and-drop interaction (in the paper test world called a "match-up") enables students to drag objects (text or images) from one set and place them over corresponding target objects (text or images).

Figure 6-5 shows a simple drag-and-drop interaction, in which students are provided terms (drag elements) and are expected to drag and drop those terms onto the corresponding definitions (target elements). Students then initiate processing by clicking the Grade It button.

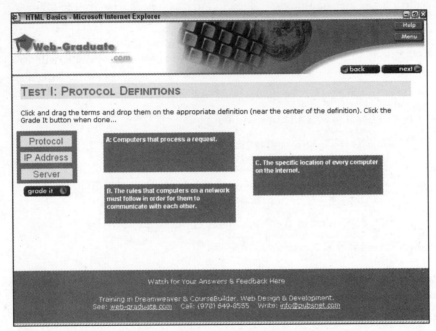

Figure 6-5: A drag–and–drop interaction from the HTML Basics course

To create a drag-and-drop interaction in CourseBuilder, you need to make the following design decisions:

◆ What is the wording of the instructions that introduce the drag-and-drop interaction?

◆ How many drag elements are there? Are they text? Images?

◆ How many target elements are there? Are they text? Images? Empty?

◆ What are the correct pairs, or matches?

◆ What initiates processing of the interaction?

   a. Is the drag-and-drop automatically processed as soon as the student drops a drag element?

   b. Do students move all drag elements to corresponding target elements and then use a CourseBuilder control (such as a button) to initiate processing?

◆ If students drop a drag element and it is not on any target, is that incorrect? Or do you want the drag element to snap back to the original position and *only* allow it to be dropped over a target element?

◆ What is the wording of feedback about correct and incorrect choices?

◆ How is feedback delivered?

Although there are seven template options in the CourseBuilder Gallery, some of the differences between templates fall into processing rules (for example, will you only allow students to move drag elements to target elements, or can students also move target elements to drag elements?). Table 6-1 shows the four different designs for drag-and-drop exercises.

TABLE 6-1 DRAG-AND-DROP COMBINATIONS

Number of Drag Elements	Number of Target Elements	Description
1	1	Drag a single element to a single target. Typically used for activities rather than tests.
1	2 or more	Drag a single element to one correct target blended into a group of distractors (incorrect targets).
2 or more	2 or more	Pair up drag elements with corresponding target elements (have as many elements as you want, but the number of drag elements equals the number of target elements). Each drag element matches only one target element.
1	2 or more	Move a single drag element multiple times, dropping it on different target elements in a specific order. Typically used to teach steps, procedures, and other content where sequence is important. Students usually receive feedback after each drop to reinforce the interaction (if the interaction is for a test, the feedback could be something like, "Step 1 selection recorded. Proceed to Step 2.").

Drag-and-drop interactions are fully described in Chapter 11. You can also see an example of a drag-and-drop test in the folder Kindergarten, under the Samples folder on the CD-ROM (open the file named `my-house.htm`).

Explore interactions

Standard HTML allows you to create "hot spots" on an image, with each hot spot clicking to a different Web page (or other URL). Such HTML constructions are called image maps.

Explore interactions use a similar construction by designating different rectangular areas of an image as "hot" areas. The difference, however, is that Explore interactions can be set up as a mechanism for creating test questions or activities that are processed by CourseBuilder.

Imagine the Possibilities...

If you've got the images (graphics and photographs), you can create some powerful drag-and-drop activities and tests. For example, you could create drag-and-drop activities that test a student's ability to identify different parts of a whole object. Students would drag text labels or images to different parts of another image. Such applications might include

◆ Labeling the parts of a computer or parts of any anatomy by dragging text labels to their appropriate locations on an image.

◆ Matching illustrations of world explorers to the locations of their discoveries on a world map.

◆ Placing figures representing historical events at their appropriate locations on a timeline.

Although drag-and-drop exercises can only match a drag element with a target element, there is a trick you can use to make it seem like students are dropping elements on part of an image. It involves inserting an additional layer in the background, and moving empty target layers on top of the background layer.

To design these tests, you actually need fewer images than a traditional drag-and-drop. (In fact, you can create this entire exercise with one background layer and using text layers for the labels.)

Figure 6-6 shows the setup of such a drag-and-drop exercise. The rectangular layer drawn around the ejection seats shows one of the empty target layers.

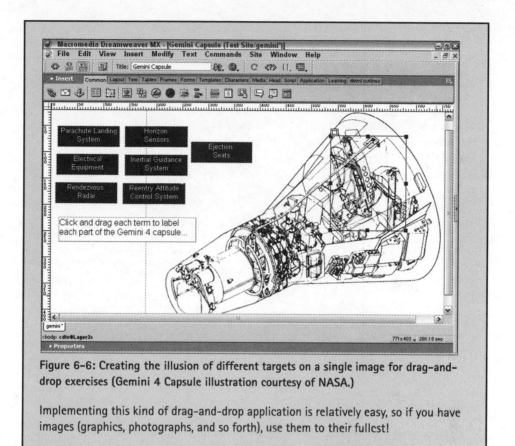

Figure 6-6: Creating the illusion of different targets on a single image for drag-and-drop exercises (Gemini 4 Capsule illustration courtesy of NASA.)

Implementing this kind of drag-and-drop application is relatively easy, so if you have images (graphics, photographs, and so forth), use them to their fullest!

Figure 6-7 shows an example of an Explore interaction. When the student clicks on a label, a description box provides more information about that area.

Explore is a very powerful tool for using different areas of a graphic for different purposes, such as displaying additional information or launching other interactions (including tests). Figure 6-8 shows an Explore interaction set up to quiz students at each hot area.

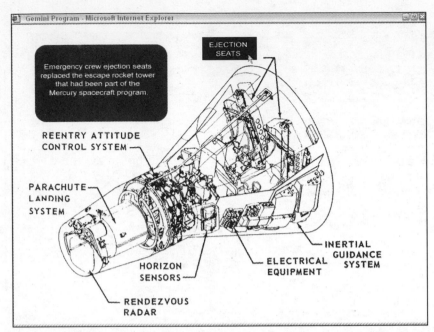

Figure 6–7: An Explore interaction that enables students to learn more as they navigate around the Gemini 4 space capsule image (Gemini 4 capsule illustration courtesy of NASA.)

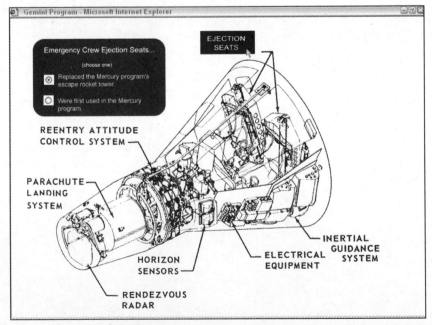

Figure 6–8: An Explore interaction that tests students as they navigate around the Gemini 4 space capsule image (Gemini 4 capsule illustration courtesy of NASA.)

To set up tests that use Explore interactions as the mechanism for answering, you need to launch a different interaction for each hot area, which is easily done. See Chapter 12 for an explanation and detailed example.

To create an Explore interaction in CourseBuilder, you need to make the following design decisions:

- ◆ What is the wording of the instructions that introduce the explore interaction?

- ◆ What serves as the background image, the "backdrop" to the entire interaction?

- ◆ How many hot areas are there?

- ◆ What will each hot area contain? Text? Images? Be empty?

- ◆ What does each hot area do when the student clicks it? Pop up a description? Test the student? Play a movie?

- ◆ What initiates processing of the interaction? Is the hot area automatically processed as soon as the student clicks? (Almost always the case.)

- ◆ What is the wording of feedback about correct and incorrect choices if used as a test?

- ◆ How is feedback delivered?

Explore interactions are fully described in Chapter 12. You can also see an example of an Explore test in the folder GUI, under the Samples folder on the CD-ROM (open the file named gui-learn.htm).

Controlling CourseBuilder Interactions

CourseBuilder controls enable students to interact with tests and activities in different ways—and *you* decide those ways! CourseBuilder provides three types of controls: buttons, sliders, and timers. You can, for example, set up buttons and sliders to initiate judgment of interactions, to select options, or to launch Dreamweaver MX actions, or set up timers to give students a visual cue as to how much time remains for a test or activity. You could use a

- ◆ Button that submits test interactions for processing (such as the Grade It button in the *HTML Basics* course).

- ◆ Button that enables students start the timer on an activity, rather than having the timer start when the page loads.

◆ Slider to select values in a range (such as Test II in the Images section of the *HTML Basics* course).

◆ Slider to select different dates on a timeline for different test questions.

Button interactions

Button interactions enable students to click buttons to initiate CourseBuilder inter-actions or other Dreamweaver MX actions (Table 6-5 in the "Creativity with the Action Manager" section later in the chapter lists the available Dreamweaver MX actions).

CourseBuilder ships with 11 different button sets. Each set consists of one button in seven different states, as follows (the asterisk is a wildcard that represents the button name in Table 6-2):

◆ Default: `*.gif`

◆ Highlighted (mouseover): `*_hlt.gif`

◆ Selected (clicked on): `*_sel.gif`

◆ Disabled (can't be clicked): `*_dis.gif`

◆ Selected (previously clicked on) and highlighted (mouseover): `*_sel_hlt.gif`

◆ Selected (previously clicked on) and disabled (can't be clicked): `*_sel_dis.gif`

◆ Thumbnail (representation only for the CourseBuilder Gallery): `*_tnail.gif`

For example, the button name `checkbox_red` in Table 6-2 would have the following seven files (one for each state):

```
Checkbox_red.gif
Checkbox_red_hlt.gif
Checkbox_red_sel.gif
Checkbox_red_dis.gif
Checkbox_red_sel_hlt.gif
Checkbox_red_sel_dis.gif
Checkbox_red_tnail.gif
```

Table 6-2 shows the button sets available with CourseBuilder. You can also easily create custom buttons, using your own graphics for two or more states (discussed in Chapter 15).

TABLE 6-2 DEFAULT AND SELECTED STATES OF COURSEBUILDER BUTTON SETS

Button Name	Default State	Selected State
checkbox_red		
dial_ridge		
emboss		
lighted		
lighted_mini		
round_red		
sphere_blue		
square_gray		
switch_gray		
switch_slot		
switch_zero_one		

To create a button interaction in CourseBuilder, you need to make the following design decisions:

◆ Will you use an existing image set or create custom buttons?

◆ Will the button work like a push button (pops back to its original state after being pressed)? Or will it work like a toggle button (stays in its switched state until clicked again)? You can choose push or toggle for *any* button.

◆ Is the button initially enabled (students can click it) or disabled (students can't click it)? Initially disabling a button usually is done with the idea that you will enable the button upon some event or action. For example, you may have multiple interactions on a page and want enable a button only after the preceding interaction is completed.

◆ Is the button initially in the default state or the selected (clicked-on) state?

◆ What action is launched when the student clicks the button? (Table 6-5, later in the chapter, provides a complete listing of actions available.)

Button interactions are fully described in Chapter 15. You can also see an example of different button states in the folder Button States, under the Samples folder on the CD-ROM (open the file named button-states.htm).

Slider interactions

Slider interactions are unique because they can be used as either a test or activity interaction *or* a control interaction. Slider interactions provide students with a slider that they can move through a range of numbers and select an answer. The example in Figure 6-9 shows the slider being used as a test interaction to select numbers in a range of 0–300, with only the numbers 72–96 being correct.

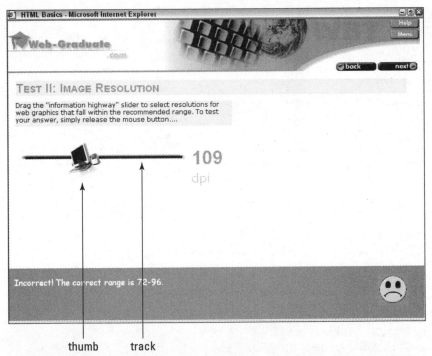

thumb   track

Figure 6-9: A slider test from the HTML Basics course, using a custom "information highway" graphic for the slider thumb

Sliders are a good choice for tests that involve any scale, range, or series of objects such as timelines and sequenced procedures. They are also good as controls for sliding through many options in a small amount of space.

To create a slider in CourseBuilder, you need to make the following design decisions:

- What is the wording of the question, if any?

- What is the entire range (can be any range of numbers, including negative numbers)?

- What is the number of ranges that are correct, if any? (You can have multiple correct ranges on the slider.)

- Will you show or hide the text box showing the exact location on the range? (To hide the text box, put it in a layer and use the Properties panel to hide that layer.)

- How will the ranges be represented to the student?

  a. Will they be represented as numbers?

  b. Will they be represented by some other label type? (For example, each range could equate to a different President's name.)

- What initiates judgment of the test? (Typically, slider tests are initiated by a student releasing the mouse button on the slider thumb after dragging it to the desired location.)

- What is the wording for feedback about correct and incorrect choices?

- How is feedback delivered?

Table 6-3 shows the various types of sliders included with CourseBuilder. You can also easily create custom sliders, using your own graphics for the thumb or track, or both! For example, if you were creating a test about baseball, you could use a baseball player for the thumb, and draw a track that consisted of a white chalk line connecting two bases. If you opt to use sliders for tests, be creative with the imagery — everyone loves to move sliders!

TABLE 6-3 COURSEBUILDER'S SLIDER CHOICES

Slider Name	Thumb	Track
black_h_penta		
black_v_penta		
blue_ball		

Continued

TABLE 6-3 COURSEBUILDER'S SLIDER CHOICES *(Continued)*

Slider Name	Thumb	Track
blue_h_dmnd_arrow		
blue_h_dmnd		
blue_h_dmnd_notch		
blue_v_dmnd_notch		
blue_v_dmnd		
blue_vert		
gray_horiz		
gray_vert		
green_horiz		
green_vert		
red_horiz		
red_vert		
umber_vert		
violet_horiz		
violet_vert		

Slider interactions are fully described in Chapter 13. You can also see an example of a Slider test in the folder The Mesozoic Era, under the Samples folder on the CD-ROM (open the file named dinosaur-info1.htm).

Timer interactions

Timers enable you to place time limits on student tests and activities. In addition to setting the time limit, you can set one or more triggers that are activated at specific times while the clock is ticking (so to speak). For example, you might give a student one minute to complete an interaction (set the timer for one minute), add a trigger to display a warning when the student has 15 seconds remaining, and then disable the interaction if the student has not answered when the minute is up.

Triggers are not limited to simply displaying warnings. A trigger can spawn any of the actions outlined in Table 6-5 (in the "Creativity with the Action Manager" section later in this chapter). For example, you might play a movie – a video of a teacher saying, "You have 30 seconds remaining" – when there are 30 seconds left to give students the feeling that there is a human monitoring the test.

By default, timers begin timing when the page loads into the browser window, but you can set other interactions (such as buttons) to start a timer, giving control for the start of timing to the student.

 A timer doesn't track the amount of time it takes a student to complete an activity, but simply limits the time allotted for it. You can, however, track the amount of time students use to answer questions. See Chapter 19.

To create a timer in CourseBuilder, you need to make the following design decisions:

- What will be the graphical representation of the timer (see Table 6-4)?

- What should be the timer's total length of time (in seconds)?

- Will triggers be needed within the timer? To what number of seconds into timing should they fire?

- What action will each trigger initiate?

- What initiates the timer?

- What is the wording for trigger warnings?

- How is feedback delivered?

Timers are represented graphically. You can either specify one of the six pre-designed timers that ship with CourseBuilder (shown in Table 6-4), or build custom timers. (Custom timers can be time-consuming to create, since you need to create a separate graphic for each time interval. Creating custom timers is covered in Chapter 16.)

TABLE 6-4 COURSEBUILDER TIMER CHOICES

Timer Name	When Timer Starts	When Timer Ends
Clapboard		
Gradient		
Hourglass		
Rising_Bars		
Small_Gradient		
Small_Rising_Bars		

Timer interactions are fully described in Chapter 16. You can also see an example of a Timer test in the folder Speed Limits, under the Samples folder on the CD-ROM (open the file named driving-test.htm).

Creativity with the Action Manager

The Action Manager is the program within CourseBuilder that lets you choose processing rules for a CourseBuilder interaction.

 As you use CourseBuilder more, you'll notice the word "judge" in reference to interactions. In CourseBuilder terms, judging refers to processing the interaction through CourseBuilder, and not simply testing for correct or incorrect. Even buttons and sliders ("We were just standing there, your honor...") are judged!

We cover how to choose processing rules later in this book, but for design purposes, you should know that you can set up the CourseBuilder Action Manager to respond to conditions within a CourseBuilder interaction. Table 6-5 shows the responses you can select with the Action Manager.

TABLE 6-5 COURSEBUILDER ACTION MANAGER RESPONSES

Response	Description
Set Text	
Set Text of Frame	Changes the contents of a specific frame (within the current frameset) to your new text. For example, the *HTML Basics* course writes responses to tests in the bottom frame. To define this response, you must open the entire frameset in Dreamweaver MX.
Set Text of Layer	Changes the contents of a specific layer (within the same page) to your new text. The Explore example shown earlier in this chapter writes different text to the same layer depending on which folder image the student clicks.
Set Text of Status Bar	Writes the text you specify to the status bar of the browser window (usually lower-left corner of browser's border). I don't recommend using this much, because most people don't look there for messages.
Set Text of Text Field	Changes the text of a specific text box (within the same page) to your new text. For example, when a student enters text in a text box, you can process that text and then write a message into the same text box.
Main (Dreamweaver MX Actions)	
Call JavaScript	CourseBuilder can also call any
Change Property	Dreamweaver MX actions described in
Check Browser	Table 3-3 in Chapter 3. You can call these
Check Plugin	actions as easily as any other within
Control Shockwave or Flash	CourseBuilder.
Drag Layer	
Go to URL	

Continued

TABLE 6-5 COURSEBUILDER ACTION MANAGER RESPONSES *(Continued)*

Response	Description
Hide Pop-Up Menu	
Jump Menu	
Jump Menu Go	
Open Browser Window	
Play Sound	
Popup Message	
Preload Images	
Set Nav Bar Image	
Set Text	
Show Pop-Up Menu	
Show-Hide Layers	
Swap Image	
Swap Image Restore	
Timeline	
Validate Form	

CourseBuilder Actions

Judge Interaction	Processes an interaction. For example, you can choose processing rules that automatically judge the next interaction in a sequence if the current interaction meets specific criteria (see the "A Word About Judging and Design" section later in this chapter).
Set Interaction Properties	Changes the properties of an interaction. For example, you can disable an interaction if the time allowed expires. (The list of properties is covered in Chapter 17.)
Reset Interaction	Returns all values for an interaction to the original state. For example, you can reset an interaction when the student presses a Reset button.

Response Tracking	Description
Send CoreData Send ExitAU GetParam Interaction Info Send Lesson Status Send Lesson Time Send Objective Info Send Score	CourseBuilder allows the Action Manager to communicate with a Learning Management System, following a set of standards defined by the Aviation Industry CBT Committee (AICC, the reigning standards board in this area). You can get more information on these standards at www.aicc.org. Communications between CourseBuilder and a Learning Management System are covered in Chapter 19.

You can set the Action Manager to respond to standard conditions, such as the following:

◆ Did the student submit a correct answer? If so, Set Text of Frame.

◆ Did the student submit an incorrect answer? If so, Set Text of Frame and Reset Interaction.

◆ Did the student submit without answering? If so, Popup Message and Reset Interaction.

◆ Did time expire? If so, Go to URL and Set Interaction Properties to disabled.

◆ Has the number of attempts allowed been met? If so, Go to URL and Set Interaction Properties to disabled.

You can also set up CourseBuilder interactions to respond to conditions that are specific to your interaction (further refining your responses), such as the following:

◆ Did the student choose number 1 *and* number 3? If so, Set Text of Layer.

◆ Did the student drag label 2 to target 3? If so, Show Layer.

◆ Did the student put the steps in the order 1-2-4-3 instead of 1-2-3-4 on the drag-and-drop sequence? If so, Swap Image and Set Text of Frame.

Finally, you can set up CourseBuilder controls to perform actions without responding to any other condition except for the control. Here are two examples:

- Did the student press the Reset button? If so `Reset Interaction`

- Did the student slide the slider to range 80–100? If so, `Control Flash or Shockwave`.

It is important for you understand that interactions do not need to be "correct" or "incorrect" in order for the Action Manager to respond.

Keep in mind that the level of response is up to you. If you only choose to display a single response for correct answers, and a single response for incorrect answers, that's fine!

A WORD ABOUT JUDGING AND DESIGN

One of the key capabilities about the judgment of interactions is that you can choose automatic judgment based on certain events happening. For example, look at Test II: HTML Segments (see Figure 6-10) of the *HTML Basics* course. The test consists of nine different interactions (eight text-entry boxes and the Grade It button, which submits the test to the Action Manager for processing).

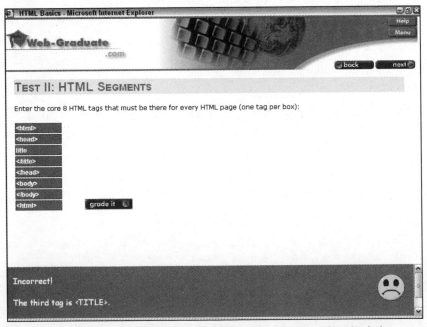

Figure 6-10: A series of interactions with automatic judgment using the Judge Interaction action

When the Grade It button is clicked, the Action Manager begins processing:

1. Evaluate the first text box interaction:

   a. Correct? Then `Judge Interaction` #2.

   b. Incorrect? Then `Set Text of Frame` telling the student that his answer for the first text box is incorrect; end judgment of the test.

2. Evaluate the second text box interaction:

   a. Correct? Then `Judge Interaction` #3.

   b. Incorrect? Then `Set Text of Frame` telling the student that his answer for the second text box is incorrect; end judgment of the test.

3. Evaluate the third text box interaction:

   a. Correct? Then `Judge Interaction` #4.

   b. Incorrect? Then `Set Text of Frame` telling the student that his answer for the third text box is incorrect; end judgment of the test.

As the example test is judged, the entries in the first two text boxes are judged as correct. The third text box, however, is judged incorrect (no angle brackets around the TITLE tag) and the Action Manager displays a message in the bottom frame specifically identifying the incorrect entry.

Using `Judge Interaction` relieves students from having to click a button for each interaction. Remember this important design consideration as you construct more complex interactions.

SOME IDEAS FOR RESPONSES

To further stoke your creative fires, consider these ideas for setting up responses:

- Use drag-and-drop as a selection list. For example, say you have a group of Flash movies from which students select one to play. Students could drag a picture representing a movie (a different drag element for each movie) onto a picture of a movie camera (a target element) and set up the interaction to automatically launch that particular movie `Control Shockwave or Flash`.

- Use `Show-Hide Layers` and `Set Text of Layers` for feedback. You can initially set a layer to hidden in Dreamweaver MX (on the Properties panel), and then show the hidden layer `Show-Hide Layers` and write specific text to that layer using `Set Text of Layers` based on different conditions. This approach enables you to create a feedback area without adding an additional frame to your course. You can write different messages based on different conditions, for example:

- Message #1 if the student is correct.

- Message #2 if the student is incorrect.

- Message #3 if the student runs out of time.

- Message #4 if the student uses up the number of attempts allowed.

◆ Use Explore as a tool for teaching about software. For example, say you have a software screen that you want students to learn about. Capture that screen into an image file, and make each area of the screen a different hotspot that launches a separate browser window (Open Browser Window) with a detailed description of that area.

Once you understand the power of the Action Manager, you can use it to prototype many different designs and responses.

Creating a Storyboard

Creating a storyboard (paper prototype) of your Web course is the best choice for quick and inexpensive design of Web-Based Training. The instructions in this section along with the planning tools on the CD-ROM will give you enough direction to complete the storyboard.

A storyboard consists of a screen-by-screen visual layout of your course. Creating your storyboard is a three-step process (see Figure 6-11):

1. **Take inventory of your existing materials** (if any). The CD-ROM includes two forms (Content Inventory and Media Inventory) to help you gather this information.

2. **Select a Learning Site style.** The CD-ROM includes storyboard templates for the five styles that ship with Learning Site plus the additional styles that ship with this toolkit. If you are creating a custom style, you should do so *before* you begin the storyboard process.

3. **Develop your storyboard.** The CD-ROM includes a storyboard for each of the 17 Learning Site styles, as well as a Storyboard Planner to help you identify information about the content for each screen in your course (one planner per screen). Use this planner in conjunction with each storyboard to make the transition to implementation easier.

Taking inventory of your existing materials

Before you begin developing new materials for your course, you want to take stock of what you already have. Although most of the materials probably aren't appropriate for WBT use (printed materials typically have far too many words to be effective in a Web course), you can often find nuggets of information as well as media to use.

1. Take inventory of your existing materials.   2. Select a Learning Site style.   3. Develop your storyboard.

Figure 6-11: The process for creating your storyboard

The toolkit on the CD-ROM includes two documents to guide you in taking stock of and organizing your materials.

The Content Inventory (see Figure 6-12) planner helps you keep track of your various content sources such as HTML files, Web addresses, white papers, e-mail messages — anything that might contain valuable content for your course.

Sample Content Inventory - Microsoft Word

File Edit View Insert Format Tools Table Window Help Acrobat

Course Name: __HTML Basics__   Pages: __1__ of __5__

CONTENT INVENTORY

File Type	File Name	Brief Description
☐ HTML ☐ Text ☐ MS Word X Other (PDF)	HTML4.PDF	☐ Free to Use X Copyright Restrictions The full HTML 4.0 specification (Note: copyrighted by W3)
☐ HTML X Text ☐ MS Word ☐ Other	Images.txt	X Free to Use ☐ Copyright Restrictions Email from Kathy Doyle describing some creative uses for the <IMG> element fully, including parameters.
X HTML ☐ Text ☐ MS Word ☐ Other	Internal-links.htm	X Free to Use ☐ Copyright Restrictions HTML file created to show how internal links work from course predecessor. I own the copyright.
☐ HTML ☐ Text X MS Word ☐ Other	Internet-protocols.doc	X Free to Use ☐ Copyright Restrictions Overview description I created for class that explains high-level internet concepts. I own the copyright.
☐ HTML ☐ Text X MS Word ☐ Other	Internet-topology.doc	☐ Free to Use X Copyright Restrictions A white paper describing different topologies. Use for reference only.
☐ HTML		☐ Free to Use ☐ Copyright Restrictions

Page 1   Sec 1   1/1   At 36pt   Ln 1   Col 1

Figure 6-12: The Content Inventory planner helps you keep track of all sources for content and content ideas.

The Media Inventory (see Figure 6-13) planner helps you keeps track of your various media sources such as images (graphics, photographs, animations), movies (Flash, Shockwave, Quicktime, and so forth) and sounds.

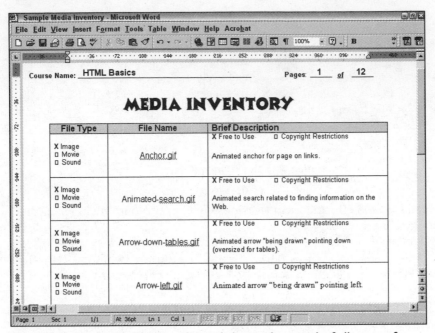

Figure 6-13: The Media Inventory planner helps you keep track of all sources for media, such as images, movies, and sounds.

These planning documents are included both as Microsoft Word documents (which you can edit), or PDF documents (which you can print). I recommend using the Microsoft Word documents to maintain your inventory lists electronically so that you can easily sort and search your lists.

Selecting a Learning Site style

Before you can develop a storyboard and course prototype, you need to make decisions about the look and feel of your course navigation. You can either select a pre-designed style or design your own style (creating custom Learning Site styles is covered in Chapter 7).

The CD-ROM contains a storyboard for each of the five Learning Site styles that ship with Learning Site, as well as the additional twelve additional Learning Site styles that are exclusively available with this toolkit. They are located within the Planning Documents folder.

Once you select your style, you can print copies of the storyboard for that style to begin creating storyboards.

Developing your storyboard

Storyboards are graphical depictions of a sequence of images that tell a story. Used for many years in the motion picture industry, storyboards allow for inexpensive changes before production. They have exactly the same benefits for designing a WBT course, so we've set up the toolkit to help you use this same process for designing your course.

After you've collected your inventory and selected a Learning Site style, create a storyboard for every page in your course. **Do not shortchange this process.** By designing your storyboard, you are getting a full picture of your production before you spend valuable time developing each page (it takes *substantially* more time to develop and test a page than it does to design it). Also, by using storyboards, you can more easily identify

◆ Design flaws and issues. For example, you might find that you need additional navigation buttons, or that you need a better way to convey feedback to users because of limited screen space.

◆ Areas that raise consistency issues. For example, you might identify areas that use similar elements and decide to create Dreamweaver MX library items for those elements.

◆ Areas to resequence. For example, you might find that certain modules or pages flow better in a different arrangement.

◆ Gaps in information. You'll spot these more easily as you try to make information flow.

TIP Keep lots of pencils and erasers on hand. They are *the* "tool of choice" for storyboards since they allow you to easily erase and modify paper storyboards.

Figure 6-14 shows a sample storyboard from the *HTML Basics* course. It is quite evident from the example that you do not need to be an artist to develop storyboards.

Regardless of the type of page (content, media, CourseBuilder interaction), each page should have a storyboard representing the material on that page. In addition, each storyboard should have a Storyboard Planner (usually stapled to the storyboard so they don't get separated).

The Storyboard Planner helps you collect information about each storyboard, information that is particularly important when it comes to developing the Web page. Figure 6-15 shows a Storyboard Planner for the storyboard shown in Figure 6-16.

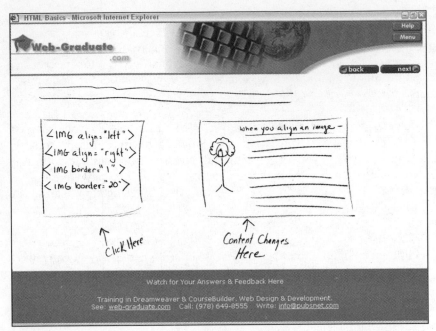

Figure 6-14: A storyboard from the HTML Basics class showing the design of the page about images

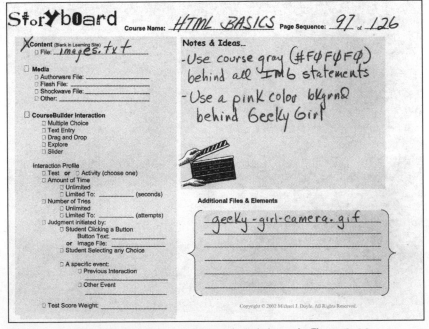

Figure 6-15: Storyboard Planner for the storyboard shown in Figure 6-14

When it's time to develop each page, you can use the design of the storyboard along with the details in the Storyboard Planner to develop the final page. Figure 6-16 shows the page developed using the storyboard and Storyboard Planner from the preceding two figures.

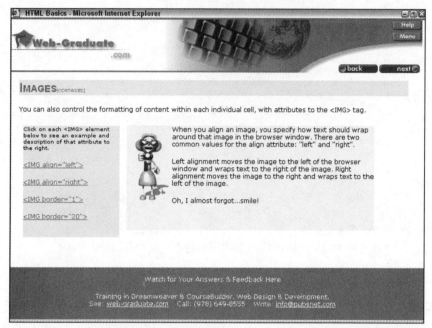

Figure 6-16: Finished page in the HTML Basics course based on the storyboard (Figure 6-14) and Storyboard Planner (Figure 6-15)

The Storyboard Planner was carefully designed to help you make the necessary decisions for building a CourseBuilder interaction. For example, Figure 6-17 shows the storyboard for a test in the *HTML Basics* course (you saw the finished page in Figure 6-3).

Figure 6-18 shows the Storyboard Planner for the CourseBuilder interaction storyboard in Figure 6-17.

Figure 6-17: Storyboard for a CourseBuilder interaction from the HTML Basics course

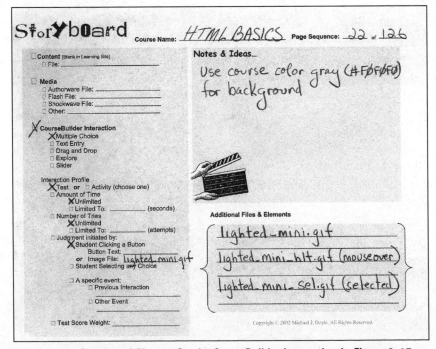

Figure 6-18: Storyboard Planner for the CourseBuilder interaction in Figure 6-17

By looking at the Storyboard Planner, you can get a quick profile of the CourseBuilder interaction:

- It is a multiple-choice test.

- The student is allowed unlimited time and an unlimited number of tries for this test.

- The student initiates judgment (sending the test to the Action Manager for evaluation) by clicking a button.

- The button is a CourseBuilder button called `lighted_mini.gif` (refer to Table 6-2 for button samples).

- The background for each choice will be set to color #F0F0F0, which is a very light gray.

- The page is the 22nd page in a course that consists of 126 total pages.

Continue the storyboard process until you have a complete paper prototype of your course. When you are happy with it, you are ready to move from prototype to development.

Summary

You now have enough information to create your course prototype. Use the planning documents on the CD-ROM to keep your project organized — you'll be amazed how many different pieces (documents, images, style sheets, and so on) even small projects amass!

This chapter described how to:

- Check your current inventory of information using the Content Inventory and Media Inventory planners.

- Select a Learning Site style from the CD-ROM, or create your own custom style. Whichever path you choose, you need to create an example without content to use as a storyboard.

- Develop your storyboards. Be creative with your use of interactions. And spend as much time as you can looking for consistency issues — they are least costly to fix in the design stage!

One you've finished the storyboard for your course, you are ready to begin implementation. The next chapter shows you how to set up the structure for your course using Learning Site.

Chapter 7

Creating Your Learning Site

IN THIS CHAPTER

- ◆ Using the Learning Site planner
- ◆ Selecting your layout style
- ◆ Creating your Learning Site structure
- ◆ Adding the sequence of content and interaction placeholder pages, and media pages
- ◆ Customizing your frameset, navigation, and menu files

TO CREATE YOUR Learning Site structure, you simply need to have determined (as best you can) the sequence of pages and page titles; you can always add and subtract pages in the future.

 The capability of Learning Site to track results in a database is covered at the end of this book, in Part IV, "Tracking Results." Also, Chapter 4 covers important base concepts in understanding Learning Site. I highly recommend you read Chapter 4 before you read this chapter to understand the structure of a Learning Site.

Planning Your Learning Site

Before you jump into creating your Learning Site, you need to

- ◆ Create the Dreamweaver MX site to contain the Learning Site.
- ◆ Complete the Learning Site planner to decide key design decisions.

Creating your Dreamweaver MX site

A Learning Site is a structure built within an existing Dreamweaver MX site. You must create a Dreamweaver MX site *before* you create your Learning Site. Learning Site inserts files and folders specific to your course, and stores those files and folders in the Dreamweaver MX site.

Chapter 3 provides details about creating a Dreamweaver MX site.

Using your Learning Site planner

Once you've created your paper prototype (Chapter 6), you are ready to build the structure for it. First, you need to make a few decisions about how the course will be implemented. Those decisions include the following:

- ◆ What is the name of the frameset file that will contain the contents and navigation for your course?

- ◆ Will you use the same layout style that you selected for your paper prototype? Select a new layout style? Create a custom style?

- ◆ What happens when a student quits the course? Do you display a specific HTML page, or just close the browser window?

- ◆ What message do you want to display if the student presses the Previous button and he's on the first page? If the student presses the Next button and she's on the last page?

- ◆ Do you want your site to display in random order? You would select this option *only* if you are creating a Learning Site that is exclusively a pool of questions for a test, and not a WBT course.

- ◆ Will you track student performance? (Tracking is covered in Part IV of this book.)

Use the Learning Site planner included in the toolkit to keep track of your decisions. Figure 7-1 shows a sample of the Learning Site planner for the *HTML Basics* course.

The next 5 sections provide the details for helping you make these design and implementation decisions.

Naming your frameset file

Frames are a method of subdividing a single browser window into multiple content areas, with each area capable of loading and displaying a different file. A *frameset* is a single HTML file that defines how the browser window is subdivided into frames, specifies the dimensions for each frame, and identifies the files you want initially loaded into each frame.

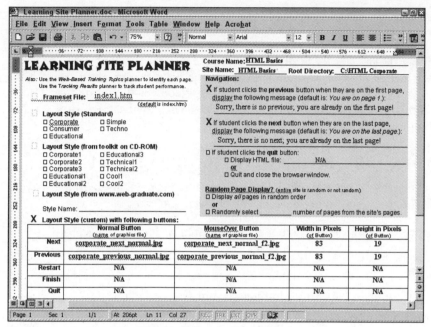

Figure 7-1: The Learning Site planner for the HTML Basics course

When you create your Learning Site structure, Learning Site creates a frameset with two frames:

- navFrame, which is the top frame, contains the navigation for the course. When the frameset is loaded into the browser window, this frame is loaded with the file navigation.htm, which is the navigation file created by Learning Site. The navigation.htm file always remains resident in this frame.

- mainframe, which is the bottom frame, contains the content for the course. When the frameset loads into the browser window, this frame is initially loaded with the first file in the sequence of pages for the course.

To build your course, Learning Site prompts you for the name of the frameset file, which defines the frames for the course. The *HTML Basics* course, for example, initially consisted of two frames (navigation.htm and segment-intro.htm) that were defined in the frameset file index1.html as follows:

```
<frameset rows="100,*" framespacing="0" frameborder="0" border="0">
<frame name="navFrame" src="navigation.htm" frameborder="0"
    scrolling="no" noresize marginwidth="0" marginheight="0">
<frame name="mainFrame" frameborder="0" src="segment-intro.htm">
</frameset>
```

Even if you don't fully understand the HTML code, you can see that the frameset file does not contain content, but rather the definitions and sources for each frame.

I recommend that you select a name for the frameset that is different from the name of your home page (typically the home page is named index.html). As you'll read later in this chapter, by reserving the home page for an entry page to the frameset, you can open the frameset in a browser window without browser buttons, address fields, and other unnecessary browser elements, giving the course window as much of the screen as possible.

Choosing your layout style for navigation

The layout style determines the look and feel for the navigation frame in your Learning Site frameset. To define your layout style, you can

◆ Select one of the five layout styles that ship with Learning Site.

◆ Select one of the twelve additional layout styles that ship with this book's toolkit.

◆ Select one of the many additional layout styles available at www.web-graduate.com.

◆ Create a custom layout style using graphics and buttons you create.

Each layout style, by default, has six standard navigation buttons: Next, Previous, Restart, Finish, Quit, and Menu. (These buttons are discussed more fully later in this chapter.)

The style you choose can give similar content a completely different look. Furthermore, you can easily modify the pre-designed file to give it a custom look. For example, Figure 7-2 shows a page from the *HTML Basics* course.

And Figure 7-3 shows the same content presented with a different layout style, using the default set of buttons with that new style.

You can change layout styles at any point—even after your course is fully developed, if you change your mind! However, if you've customized your Learning Site navigation, you will need to reapply those customizations to the newly created navigation.htm file. (Learning Site recreates the navigation.htm file each time you modify the course.) For example, notice the customizations that were made to the *HTML Basics* course (see Figure 7-3):

◆ A third frame, for feedback to the student, was added to the bottom of the frameset.

◆ The Restart, Finish, and Quit button functions were deleted.

◆ A Help button was added.

◆ A logo and other background graphics were added.

The customizations can easily be added again. You just need to be aware of the issue.

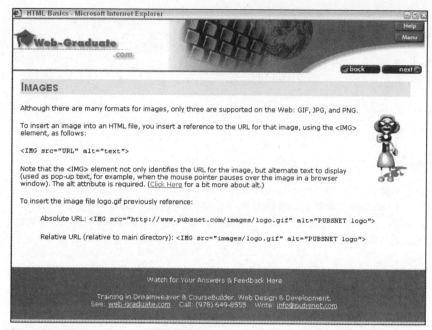

Figure 7-2: A page from the HTML Basics course using the custom layout style developed for that course

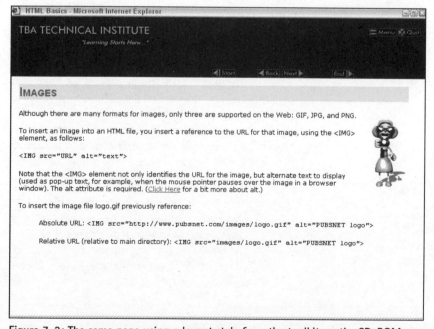

Figure 7-3: The same page using a layout style from the toolkit on the CD-ROM

Planning and naming the sequence of pages

Before you create your Learning Site structure, you also need to organize the sequence of pages for your course. You'll recall from your Storyboard Planner that there are three types of pages available:

- ◆ Content (called Blank in the Learning Site dialog box)
- ◆ Media
- ◆ CourseBuilder Interaction

To add the sequence of pages and page titles to Learning Site, organize all of your topics into their final sequence and identify the file name (even if the file doesn't exist yet) for each page in the course. Table 7-1 describes each type of page you can add to your Learning Site.

TABLE 7-1 TYPES OF PAGES

Learning Site Category	Description
Blank (Content)	For any of the following HTML pages: ◆ HTML pages that don't yet exist (placeholders). Learning Site creates a blank HTML page using the file name and page title you specify. ◆ HTML pages that do exist. You can browse to existing pages by clicking the folder icon and browsing to the HTML file you want to include. If the HTML file is outside of your Dreamweaver MX site's root folder, Learning Site moves a copy of it to the root folder. Learning Site also automatically uses that HTML page title. Note that when Learning Site copies the HTML file to your root folder, it does not copy inserted objects such as images, movies, style sheets, and other files that are outside of the HTML file. You will need to collect and move those objects manually.

Learning Site Category	Description
Media	For any of the following media types: ◆ Authorware files (.aam) ◆ Flash files (.swf) ◆ Shockwave files (.dcr) You can browse to existing media files by clicking the folder icon and browsing to the file you want to include. If the media file is outside of your Dreamweaver MX site's root folder, Learning Site moves a copy of that file to the root folder.
CourseBuilder Interaction	For any of the following CourseBuilder interaction types: ◆ Multiple Choice ◆ Drag and Drop ◆ Explore ◆ Text Entry ◆ Button ◆ Timer ◆ Slider ◆ Action Manager You don't actually enter any of the CourseBuilder interaction definitions at this point; Learning Site just inserts the default template for the type of interaction you select. You can edit that interaction later in Dreamweaver MX.

Figure 7-4 shows the Sequence of Pages planner that helps you organize all pages in the Learning Site. The example shows the sequence of pages for the *HTML Basics* course. Use the planner to put your pages in sequence and, just as importantly, to identify the page titles and segments for your course (read the next section, "Understanding the importance of page titles and segments pages," before completing your Sequence of Pages planner).

142   Part 1: Laying the Foundation

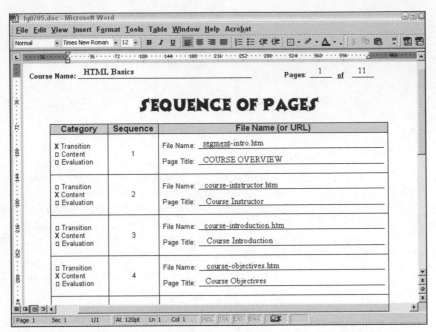

Figure 7-4: The Sequence of Pages planner helps you organize all of the file names and page titles used in your course.

Understanding the importance of page titles and segments pages

In addition to inserting a file name for each page, you must insert a page title for each page. The page title is important because it becomes the clickable text that Learning Site uses for the menu.

As you enter file names and page titles for each page in Learning Site, they are stored in the `navigation.htm` file (described more fully in Chapter 4). To generate the menu, Learning Site creates an additional file called `menu.htm`, which includes scripts that build the menu dynamically by reading the page titles from `navigation.htm` and generating a menu similar to the one shown in Figure 7-5.

The menu is difficult to use because it isn't segmented – all the page titles are lumped together.

The structure that you want for your menu is similar to the one shown in Figure 7-6.

Because the menu is built dynamically, you cannot manually insert blank lines or segments. So how do you create segments? You can force blank lines in the menu by inserting a page without a title before each segment. The *HTML Basics* course, for example, uses a page without a title *before* each segment's introductory page. The page includes a single line of text, as follows:

This Next Segment Takes Approximately 15 Minutes to Complete.

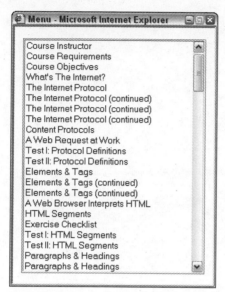

Figure 7-5: The menu for the HTML Basics course, which is built dynamically by scripts in the menu.htm file

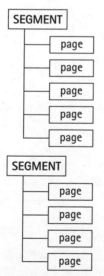

Figure 7-6: The structure for course menus should delineate each segment or module.

Figure 7-7 shows the *HTML Basics* course menu that uses untitled pages to separate the segments. To further enhance menu segmentation, the title for each segment's introductory page (a flash movie introducing the segment) is inserted using all capital letters.

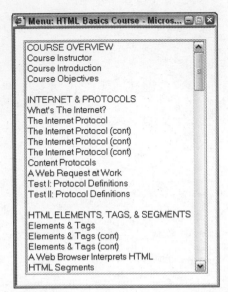

Figure 7-7: The menu for the HTML Basics course
using pages without titles to segment the menu

As you'll see later in this chapter, you can also change the style characteristics of the menu.

Using random page display to create test pools

Learning Site gives you the option to display the pages of a Learning Site in random order for sites that are *only* being used to administer tests. Some applications of random page display include

◆ Selecting random test questions out of a testing pool.

◆ Creating games such as trivia games where the activities, topics, or questions are selected randomly.

◆ Presenting random tips, notes, facts, quotes, and so forth.

When you choose to display a site using random pages, you can either randomly display all pages in that site, or select a specific number of pages from the site to display randomly. Figure 7-8 shows how random page display works for all pages in a site — all pages are presented to the student but in a random order each time the site is accessed.

Figure 7-9 shows how random page display works when selecting a specific number of pages from the pool. In this example, five pages are selected from the pool. A different five pages are chosen in random order each time the site is accessed.

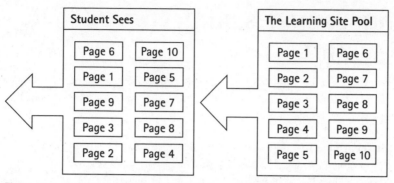

Figure 7-8: Random page display for all pages uses every page in the Learning Site, but displays those pages in an arbitrary order for each student.

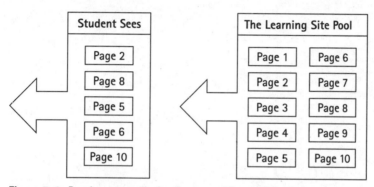

Figure 7-9: Random page display for a specific number of pages

Learning Site has a strict limitation on random page display: it's all or nothing. That is, the decision you are making is: "Should my entire Learning Site display in sequence or randomly?" You cannot have some sections of a Learning Site in sequence and other sections in random order.

You can, however, create two Learning Sites and connect them. For example, assume you want to create a course that includes content and activities until the very end of the course, at which point the student takes a test with questions randomly pulled from a pool of test questions. You can create one Learning Site with the content and activities and, at the very end of the course, include a page that links to the Learning Site with the random test pool.

The main issue with linking multiple Learning Sites is that the navigation and menu are not linked. When you jump from one site to another, you are using a completely new navigation system that doesn't include the context of the previous Learning Site in the navigational buttons or menu. Be sure that when you link to a different Learning Site, you open that different Learning Site in a new browser window (you can use the Dreamweaver MX Open Browser Window action, described in Chapter 3, to do this).

Creating Your Learning Site Structure

Once you've created your Learning Site and Sequence of Pages planners, you're ready to build the Learning Site structure. With your Dreamweaver MX site defined and opened, follow these steps:

1. Open the Learning Site dialog box by choosing Site → Learning Site → Create Learning Site. The Learning Site dialog box displays with the Site tab active, as shown in Figure 7-10.

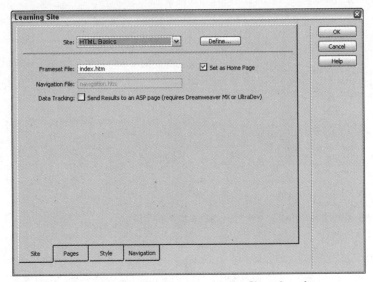

Figure 7-10: Learning Site dialog box, with the Site tab active

2. Make sure that the name of the site displayed is the name of the Dreamweaver MX site that will hold your Learning Site. (The example in Figure 7-11 shows the name of the site as HTML Basics.) A drop-down menu allows you to easily select any Dreamweaver MX site. If you want to create a new Dreamweaver MX site, click the Define button to set up that new site.

3. Enter the name of the frameset file from the Learning Site planner into the Frameset File field (Learning Site defaults to index.htm). For example, if the name of the frameset file is index1.html (as it is for the *HTML Basics* course), enter that name.

The Navigation File field specifies `navigation.htm` as the name of the navigation file. That field is inactive because you cannot change the name of the navigation file.

4. Select whether or not you want the file named in the Frameset File field to be your Learning Site home page. I recommend (for reasons stated elsewhere) that you do *not* make the Learning Site your home page.

5. Make sure that the Data Tracking field in unchecked (if you are tracking data, you need to read Part IV of this book before creating your Learning Site structure).

Learning Site does not write any files to the Dreamweaver MX site until you click the OK button in the dialog box. Wait until you complete all tabs (Site, Pages, Style, and Navigation) before you click OK.

If you click the Cancel button (regardless of how little or how much information you entered), Learning Site does not write anything to the Dreamweaver MX site. If you complete part of your definitions and want to continue at a later time, click OK, and then modify the Learning Site at when you're ready by choosing Site → Learning Site → Modify Learning Site.

Adding the sequence of pages

Now you can add all of the blank content, media, and CourseBuilder interaction pages to populate your Learning Site. Keep in mind that you can easily modify the sequence of pages in the future, so don't be overly concerned if you are undecided about a few pages.

Enter your pages from your Sequence of Pages planner. You may occasionally need to refer to the storyboards as well.

To begin, click the Pages tab (see Figure 7-11) in the Learning Site dialog box.

You can create your Learning Site structure with all, some, or none of your pages created ahead of time. Although you don't need to have your content developed, you do need to complete the Learning Site and Sequence of Pages planners before you create the Learning Site.

Adds or subtracts pages

Moves highlighted page
up or down in the sequence

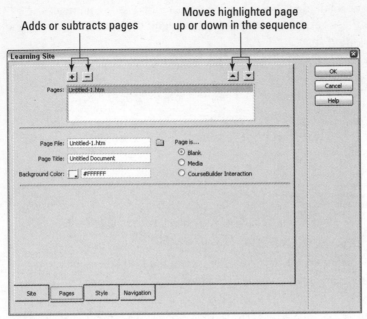

Figure 7-11: Learning Site dialog box with the Pages tab active

While you can re-sequence the pages afterward, the easiest approach is to initially enter pages in their correct sequence. So, for example, your pages might be sequenced as

Media
Blank
Blank
Blank
CourseBuilder Interaction
Blank
Blank

Enter them in that order. Trying to enter all the blank pages, then all the media pages, and then all CourseBuilder interactions will cost you quite a bit of time. Let's discuss the background color option, though, before you enter your pages.

CHOOSING A BACKGROUND COLOR

Learning Site requires that you choose a background color for each page, which gets written into the BODY element for that page. By default, Learning Site chooses the background color white (hex code #FFFFFF).

Normally, precedence for style definitions would be determined by proximity to content, meaning the definitions in the BODY element would take precedence over external Cascading Style Sheets (CSS). Because of the way rules of inheritance work with the BODY element, however, specifying a background color in an external CSS file actually takes precedence over the background color specified with the BODY element.

So what's the bottom line? Don't worry that Learning Site is writing the background color to the BODY element; you can always override that by specifying the background color to the BODY element in an external Cascading Style Sheet. See Chapter 3 for more information about creating and using external Cascading Style Sheets in Dreamweaver MX.

BLANK PAGES

To add blank (placeholder or existing HTML) pages to your Learning Site, follow these steps:

1. Click the Add Page (plus sign) button.

2. Select the Page is...Blank option on the Learning Site dialog box's Pages tab, if it is not already selected.

3. Enter the file name for the page in the Page File field if it doesn't already exist, or click the Browse to File folder icon to browse to an existing HTML file. If you select an existing file outside your Dreamweaver MX site root folder, Learning Site copies that HTML file into your root folder.

4. Enter the title of the page in the Page Title field (if you select an existing file in Step 2, Learning Site automatically uses the page title for that file and does not give you the option of changing it).

5. Select the background color for the page.

MEDIA PAGES

To add media pages to your Learning Site, follow these steps:

1. Click the Add Page (plus sign) button.

2. Select the Page is...Media option. The Pages tab displays with media pages active.

3. Enter the file name for the HTML page that will contain the media page in the Page File field. (Media pages are contained within—and launched from—HTML pages.)

4. Enter the title of that HTML page in the Page Title field.

5. Select the background color for that HTML page.

6. Select the type of media file (Authorware, Flash, or Shockwave) you are including.

7. Click the Browse to File folder icon next to the File field (below the Authorware, Flash, and Shockwave options) to browse to the file name for the media file. If you browse to a media file outside of your Dreamweaver MX site root folder, Learning Site copies that media file into your root folder.

8. Enter the width and height (in pixels) for the media. Since you cannot leave these fields blank, enter the width and height for the media when scaled to 100%. In Figure 7-12, for example, the media file used in the *HTML Basics* course is 600 pixels wide by 450 pixels high. If you aren't sure of the dimensions of the media, you can always insert the media file into a blank Dreamweaver MX page and check its dimensions in the Properties panel.

9. Select Center Media on Page if that page consists only of the media file. Learning Site centers the media file in the course content window when the student displays that page. (Learning Site places the media file in a one-row, one-column table sized to 100% width and 100% height, and then centers the interaction in that table.)

Figure 7-12 shows the Pages tab for adding a Flash movie into the *HTML Basics* course (the course uses a Flash movie to introduce each course segment).

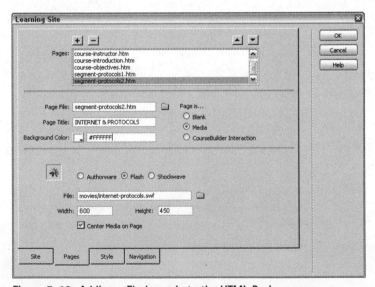

Figure 7-12: Adding a Flash movie to the HTML Basics course

COURSEBUILDER INTERACTION PAGES

To add CourseBuilder interaction pages to your Learning Site, follow these steps:

1. Click the Add Page (plus sign) button.

2. Select the Page is...CourseBuilder Interaction option. The Pages tab displays with CourseBuilder Interaction active.

3. Enter the file name for the HTML page that will contain the CourseBuilder interaction. (CourseBuilder interactions are contained within HTML files.)

4. Enter the title of that HTML page in the Page Title field.

5. Select the background color for that HTML page.

6. Select the type of CourseBuilder interaction you want to insert in the page. For example, if you want to insert a drag-and-drop interaction, select the appropriate drag-and-drop template.

7. Click the Center Interaction on Page if that page consists only of the CourseBuilder interaction. Learning Site centers the CourseBuilder interaction in the course content window when the student displays that page. (Learning Site places the interaction in a one-row, one-column table sized to 100% width and 100% height, and then centers the interaction in that table.)

Figure 7-13 shows the Pages tab for adding a drag-and-drop CourseBuilder interaction to the *HTML Basics* course.

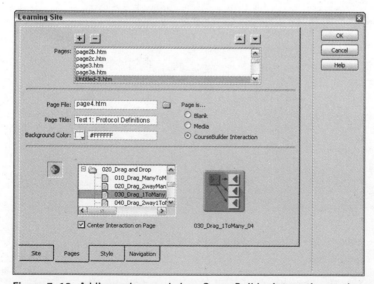

Figure 7-13: Adding a drag-and-drop CourseBuilder interaction to the HTML Basics course

ADDING, REMOVING, AND RE-SEQUENCING PAGES

You can easily add, remove, and re-sequence the order of the pages after you insert them (or anywhere down the road as well). To re-sequence a page, highlight that page in the Pages list and use the up or down arrow buttons to move the page to its proper location in the sequence.

To add a new page to the sequence of pages, click the add page (+) button. Learning Site always adds new pages to the end of the sequence of pages. Once you add the new page, you can re-sequence it.

To remove an existing page from the sequence of pages, highlight the page you want to remove and click the remove page (–) button. Learning Site removes the page from the sequence of pages. (If the page was an existing page added to the sequence of pages, Learning Site only removes the reference to that page – it does *not* delete the file.)

Selecting a pre-designed layout style for navigation

Once you've added the sequence of pages, you are ready to select your layout style for the navigation.htm file. To select your style, follow these steps:

1. Click the Style tab. The Learning Site dialog box displays with the Style tab active, as shown in Figure 7-14.

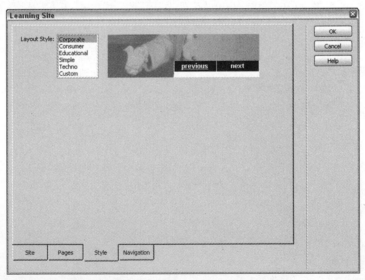

Figure 7-14: Learning Site dialog box with Style tab active

2. Select the style you want for your course from the Layout Style list. To preview each layout style, click any of the pre-designed layout styles.

Specifying a custom layout style for navigation

If you want to create a custom layout style for your course (as was done with the *HTML Basics* course, for example), you define the buttons in Learning Site and then make other modifications by editing the `navigation.htm` file in Dreamweaver MX.

By default, Learning Site has six navigational buttons that allow the student to move about the course. `navigation.htm` maintains a bookmark (so to speak) of the student's location within the sequence of pages for the course.

By knowing the student's location, the navigation file is able to process the six navigation buttons:

◆ **Next:** Loads the next content page into the `mainFrame` content frame.

◆ **Previous:** Loads the previous page into the `mainFrame` content frame.

◆ **Restart:** Loads the first page into the `mainFrame` content frame.

◆ **Finish:** Loads the last page into the `mainFrame` content frame.

◆ **Menu:** Displays the `menu.htm` file in a separate window. The menu is a clickable list of page titles that allows students to jump to any page in the course.

◆ **Quit:** Closes the browser window or displays a specific HTML file (or goes to a results page if you are tracking student performance), depending on what you choose.

To create a custom layout style, you need to create graphics for each button that you plan to use in your course. You can create custom buttons for these six standard navigational buttons and for other functions. For example, In the *HTML Basics* course, for example, three standard buttons (Restart, Finish, and Quit) have been removed and a new button (Help) has been added.

You make such customizations by editing the `navigation.htm` file in Dreamweaver MX after you define the navigation in the Learning Site.

When you select the custom layout style, enter the file name (or use the Browse to File option) for each custom button. Learning Site automatically inserts the height and width of custom buttons, as shown in Figure 7-15.

Although you can customize your `navigation.htm` file by editing it in Dreamweaver MX, you must *enter* your navigation buttons in Learning Site. Why? Because Learning Site attaches custom scripts to each button to enable it to process the navigation. Take a look at Figure 7-16, which shows a `navigation.htm` file open in Dreamweaver MX. Notice the custom script (the code is shown in Notepad) that is processed when the user clicks the Next button.

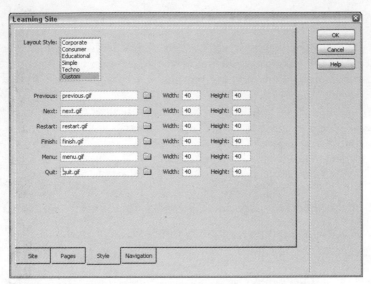

Figure 7-15: Selecting the custom layout style in Learning Site

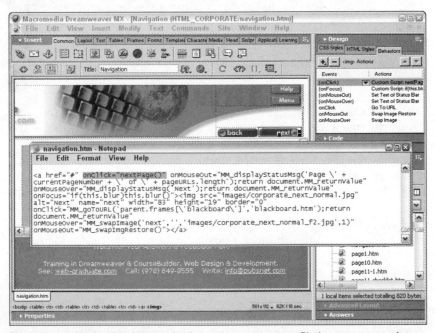

Figure 7-16: Navigation buttons in the `navigation.htm` file have custom scripts attached to them, enabling them to process the navigation.

Decide which of the buttons you are going to include in your custom navigation, and select the graphics file for each button. If you intend to use mouseover buttons, select the "off" or standard version of the button graphic; you will need to add the mouseover behaviors later when you edit `navigation.htm` in Dreamweaver MX.

Learning Site requires that you add all six buttons. It uses default buttons for those for which you do not enter image files. For example, when the buttons are added for the *HTML Basics* course, Learning Site adds default buttons for Restart, Finish, and Quit, as shown in Figure 7-17.

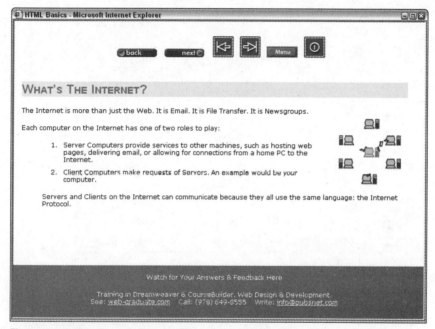

Figure 7-17: All six navigation buttons are required initially. You can then edit the navigation.htm file in Dreamweaver MX.

The navigation layout in Figure 7-17 is obviously not how you want your navigation designed. You modify the look of the `navigation.htm` file by editing the file in Dreamweaver MX.

TIP If you want to create a custom Learning Site template, you can avoid editing the custom layout of your `navigation.htm` file each time you change something in the Learning Site dialog box. See Appendix B for details.

Setting navigation messages and rules

Once you define your layout style, the final step is to set the messages and rules for navigation. To specify these messages and rules, follow these steps:

1. Click the Navigation tab. The Learning Site dialog box displays with the Navigation tab active, as shown in Figure 7-18.

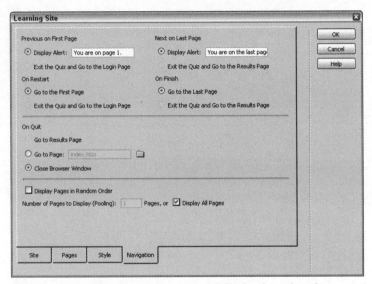

Figure 7-18: Learning Site dialog box with Navigation tab active

2. Enter the text message you want to display when the student clicks the Previous button on the first page. Figure 7-19 shows the message used by the *HTML Basics* course.

Figure 7-19: Message displayed when students click the Previous button when they are on the first page of HTML Basics

3. Type the text message you want to display when the student clicks the Next button on the last page.

4. Select what happens when the user clicks the Quit button: either the course displays a Quit page in the content frame (possibly a warning about the course ramifications of quitting), or the browser window just closes.

5. Decide whether or not to display pages in random order. If you choose to display pages in random order, decide whether to display all pages in random or choose the number of pages Learning Site should randomly select each time a student accesses the course.

Writing the Learning Site definitions

Now that you've entered your site definitions by completing the four tabs (Site, Pages, Style, and Navigation), click OK in the Learning Site dialog box to direct Learning Site to write the appropriate files to your Dreamweaver MX site. Assuming you started with an empty site and added one file, Untitled-1.htm, to the sequence of pages on the Pages tab, Learning Site writes the following files (shown in Figure 7-20):

◆ The *images* folder, which contains the graphics for the navigation.htm file (including buttons and other graphics)

◆ The *scripts* folder, which contains three scripts:

■ behCourseBuilder.js, which processes CourseBuilder functions

■ cmi.js, which processes the passing of data to a database or Learning Management System when using Tracking functions

■ navigation.js, which processes navigation and menu functions

◆ The frameset file (in this example, index.htm), which contains the frameset definitions

◆ The menu.htm file, which builds the menu from the pages and page titles defined in navigation.htm

◆ The navigation.htm file, which contains tables of pages and page titles used in the course

◆ Any other pages (blank, media, or CourseBuilder interaction) added in the Pages tab

Figure 7-20: The Dreamweaver MX directory after Learning Site writes its files

Customizing Your Learning Site

You can customize many aspects of your course relatively easily with Learning Site. Such customizations include

- Changing your frameset
- Changing your navigation frame
- Changing the style for your menu
- Adding, removing, and re-sequencing pages
- Customized your course browser window

Changing your frameset

When you create a frameset, you subdivide your browser window into two or more frames. As you saw earlier in the chapter, Learning Site creates a frameset with two frames (navFrame and mainFrame).

 Whatever modifications you make to frames, do not change the names of the two frames that Learning Site creates: navFrame and mainFrame. These frame names are used in numerous scripts, in documentation, and elsewhere.

Because each frame has a name, you can easily control the content of frames based on events, user actions, interaction results, and so forth. For example, as you'll see when you create CourseBuilder interactions, you can direct student feedback to a particular frame by specifying the name of the frame to receive feedback. Or, as you've seen with the navigation buttons, you can click on a button in one frame and affect the content of another frame. The name of each frame is important for controlling frame content.

SETTING YOUR WORKSPACE TO EFFICIENTLY WORK WITH FRAMES

To work with your frameset and frames, set the following (if they are not already set):

1. Choose View → Visual Aids → Frame Borders so that frame borders show in your document window.

2. Choose Window → Others → Frames so that the Frames panel for the frameset is visible.

3. Click the Frames tab in the Objects panel.

4. Expand the Properties panel so that you can see the settings for the frameset and frames.

Now that you've set up your Dreamweaver MX workspace, your screen should look similar to the one shown in Figure 7-21.

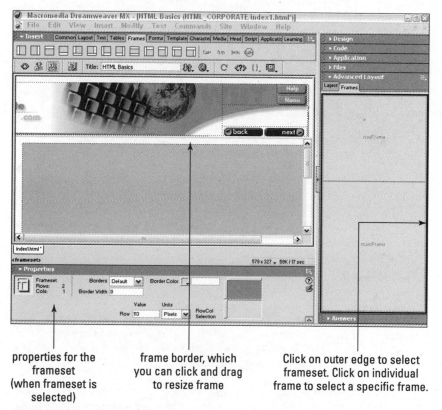

properties for the frameset (when frameset is selected)

frame border, which you can click and drag to resize frame

Click on outer edge to select frameset. Click on individual frame to select a specific frame.

Figure 7-21: Initial frameset with two frames (navFrame and mainFrame) in Dreamweaver MX

ADDING A FRAME

When you add a frame you are either splitting another frame or another frameset. In a Learning Site, you would split the mainFrame frame, as follows:

1. Select the `mainFrame` frame in the Frames panel to select it, as shown in Figure 7-22.

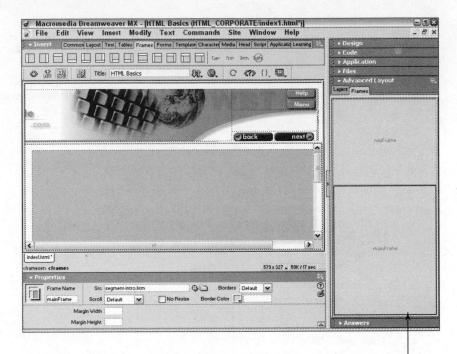

The mainFrame frame selected. Notice that the Properties
panel shows the properties for the selected frame.

Figure 7-22: Selecting the mainFrame frame in the Frames panel of
Dreamweaver MX

2. Click the Bottom Frame icon on the Frames tab on the Insert Panel.
   Dreamweaver MX splits the mainFrame into two separate frames, as
   shown in Figure 7-23. Notice that the bottom frame (named bottomFrame)
   defaults to loading an untitled file for contents.

3. Click to select the new frame (initially named bottomFrame) in the Frames
   panel to change the properties of that frame in the Properties panel. In the
   HTML Basics course, for example, the name of the frame is changed to
   blackboard, and the source file initially loaded into the frame is
   blackboard.htm (see Figure 7-24).

Click the Bottom Frame icon
to add an empty frame to the
bottom of the mainFrame frame.

Dreamweaver MX splits the
mainFrame frame and
inserts the new frame at the
bottom of the frameset.

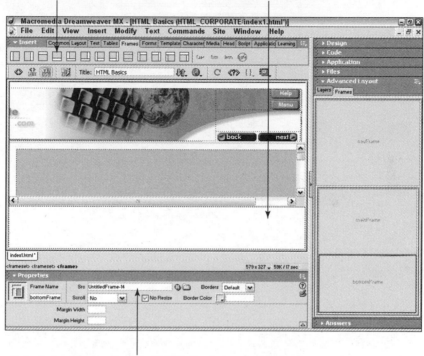

Defaults loading to an untitled HTML file. Select the HTML
file you want loaded into the new frame. In the HTML Basics
course, that file is `blackboard.htm`.

Figure 7-23: Splitting the mainFrame to add a new frame to the bottom of the
frameset

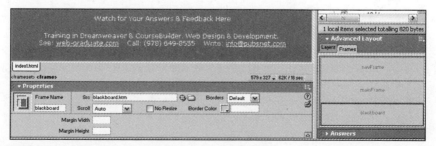

Figure 7-24: The Properties panel for the new frame

DELETING A FRAME

To delete a frame, click and drag the frame border to the edge of the document window, or to the border of the parent frame (if it is a nested frame), as shown in Figure 7-25.

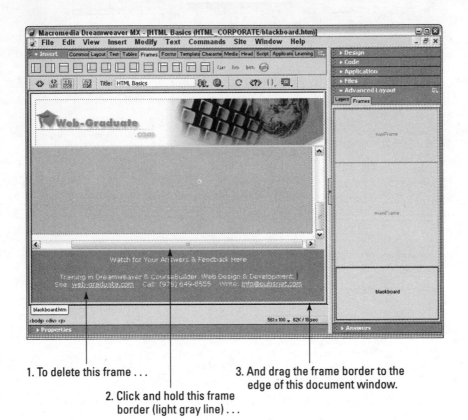

1. To delete this frame . . .

2. Click and hold this frame border (light gray line) . . .

3. And drag the frame border to the edge of this document window.

Figure 7-25: To delete the frame, drag the frame border to the edge of the document window.

Dreamweaver MX deletes the frame from the frameset. Remember that the frameset contains only the definitions for the frames, so any file you might have included into the deleted frame remains untouched and in its original location.

RESIZING YOUR FRAMESET

To resize a frame, follow these steps:

1. Click the outer edge of the Frames panel to select the frameset.
   Dreamweaver MX highlights the entire frameset, as shown in Figure 7-26.

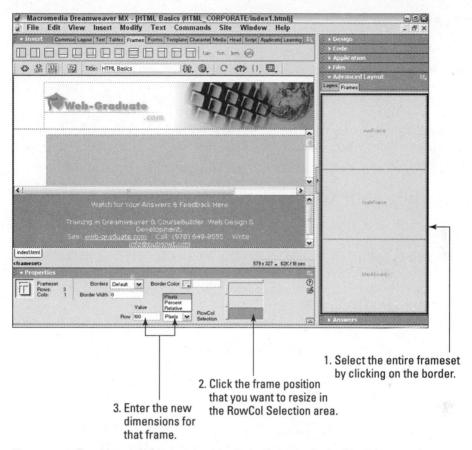

1. Select the entire frameset
   by clicking on the border.

2. Click the frame position
   that you want to resize in
   the RowCol Selection area.

3. Enter the new
   dimensions for
   that frame.

Figure 7-26: To resize each frame, select the entire frameset in the Frames panel, and then click on each frame in the Properties panel.

2. Click the representation of the frame you want to resize in the RowCol Selection area on the Properties panel (bottom right). Dreamweaver MX displays the current settings for the frame you select.

3. Decide the units of measurement that you want to specify:

   ■ Pixels, to specify number of pixels.

   ■ Percent, to specify a percentage of the browser window

   ■ Relative, to specify a frame to receive the remaining browser space available (set to a value of 1).

The *HTML Basics* course is sized as follows:

- ◆ navFrame is set to 100 pixels high

- ◆ mainFrame is set to 1 relative unit

- ◆ blackboard is set to 100 pixels high

Because the mainFrame frame is set to a relative value of 1, it takes all remaining browser window space after the navFrame and blackboard frames each reserve 100 pixels.

Changing your navigation frame

As you know, you have plenty of leeway in rearranging the layout of your navigation.htm file.

As stated earlier in this chapter, navigation buttons have custom scripts associated with them that allow the buttons to process navigation when they are clicked. Because these custom scripts are attached by Learning Site, you *must* add custom buttons within the Learning Site dialog box.

What you *can* do is

- ◆ Move the graphics around the navigation.htm file using click and drag.

- ◆ Delete any of the six standard navigation buttons you don't want. The Next, Previous, and Menu buttons, however, are core buttons that should *not* be deleted.

- ◆ Attach additional behaviors to any of the standard navigation buttons. For example, you can add mouseovers because you are not deleting any custom scripts by doing so.

- ◆ Change the graphics file used for any of the standard navigation buttons. Simply highlight the button you want to change and click the Browse to File folder icon next to the Src field of the Properties panel. Since you are modifying the graphics file associated with the button and *not* deleting the button, the custom scripts remain intact.

- ◆ Insert additional navigational buttons and other graphics. The *HTML Basics* course, for example, has a Help button. The Help button is set up with a behavior that when the student clicks the Help button (onClick), the browser opens a new browser window.

Changing the style for your menu

The menu created by menu.htm is relatively plain; with black text and white background, and doesn't offer much by way of "style".

You can change the style definitions for the two HTML elements used by the menu.htm file (refer to Chapter 3 for a refresher on CSS and style definitions):

◆ The SELECT element, which controls the style definition for the list of menu items.

◆ The BODY element, which controls the style definitions for the entire menu.htm file (typically used to change the background color).

Figure 7-27 shows what each element affects on the menu.

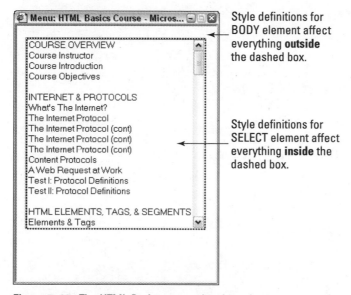

Style definitions for BODY element affect everything **outside** the dashed box.

Style definitions for SELECT element affect everything **inside** the dashed box.

Figure 7–27: The HTML Basics menu, showing what the BODY and SELECT HTML elements affect

Follow these steps to include the style definitions directly into your menu.htm file (not using an external CSS):

1. Choose File → Open and select the menu.htm file in Dreamweaver MX. Your screen should look similar to Figure 7-28. Notice the SELECT element in the CSS Styles panel (in the upper right of your screen).

2. Double-click the SELECT element in the CSS Styles panel. Dreamweaver MX displays the CSS Style Definition for Select dialog box.

3. Select a category from the Category list and then choose your style definitions for the SELECT element. Figure 7-29 shows the CSS Style Definition for Select dialog box with various style definitions selected.

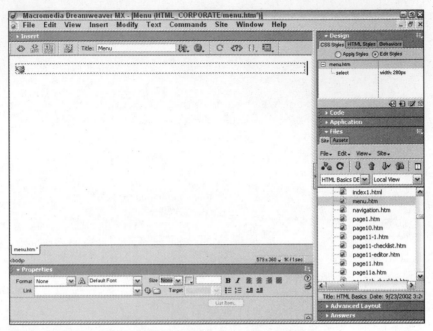

Figure 7-28: The menu.htm file opened in Dreamweaver MX

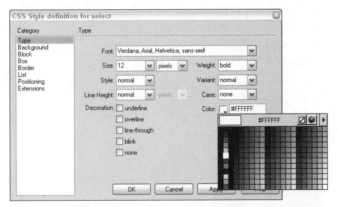

Figure 7-29: The CSS Style definition dialog box. Enter font and background color definitions to affect the style of the menu topics.

4. Click the OK button at the bottom of the dialog box when you've finished. Dreamweaver MX writes your new style definitions for the SELECT element into the menu.htm file.

5. Click the New CSS Style button on the CSS Styles panel, as shown in Figure 7-30.

Figure 7-30: The New CSS Style button
on the CSS Styles panel

Dreamweaver MX displays the New CSS Style dialog box.

6. Choose Redefine HTML Tag.

7. Select the BODY tag from the Tag drop-down menu.

8. Be sure This Document Only is selected, as shown in Figure 7-31.

Figure 7-31: Specifying the style definitions for
the BODY element

9. Click OK. Dreamweaver MX displays the CSS Style definition dialog box
   again, only this time you are entering style definitions for the BODY element.

10. Click OK when you have finished entering your style definitions for the
    BODY element.

11. Save and close your menu.htm file and test it out.

To make additional changes to the menu styles, simply repeat the process.

Adding, removing, and re-sequencing pages at any time

Now that you know how Learning Site adds and removes pages from the
navigation.htm file, you understand that simply adding or removing pages in your

Dreamweaver MX site does *not* update the navigation system. To add or remove pages from your course, follow these steps:

1. Choose Site → Learning Site → Modify Learning Site to open the Learning Site dialog box.

2. Click the Pages tab.

3. Add, remove, or re-sequence pages using the procedures you followed when you set up your Learning Site.

4. Click OK to write the changes to your Dreamweaver MX site. Learning Site creates an updated version of the `navigation.htm` file, reflecting the new sequence of pages for your course.

Customizing your course browser window

The *HTML Basics* course is launched within an Internet Explorer browser window that does not contain browser toolbars, buttons, menus, and so forth, giving a customized look at feel to the course.

When you open the *HTML Basics* course, the first page you see is the *Welcome to HTML Basics* page that contains a link to launch the course in a different browser window. The reason for launching the course in a separate window is that it affords the opportunity to create a link using the Dreamweaver MX action Open Browser Window, which is how we customize the look of the browser window.

To create a text link that launches your course in a different browser window:

1. Select the text you want students to click to launch your course.

2. Type the following in the Link field on the Properties panel:

   ```
   javascript:;
   ```

   Typing this text in the Link field turns the text into hyperlinked text, although the text does not click through to any URL. Creating this null hyperlink is necessary if you want to attach Dreamweaver MX behaviors to that text, since Dreamweaver MX cannot attach behaviors to regular text.

3. Choose the Open Browser Window option from the Behaviors panel (refer to Chapter 3 for details about adding Dreamweaver MX behaviors).

   Dreamweaver MX displays the Open Browser Window dialog box, as shown in Figure 7-32.

Figure 7-32: Using the Open Browser Window action to open your course in a browser window without browser buttons and menus

4. Type the name of your course's frameset file in the URL to Display field.

5. Check the Scrollbars as Needed and Resize Handles options.

6. Type a name for the new browser window in the Window Name field. This name cannot contain spaces, and is only used internally for reference.

7. Click the OK button.

When students click on the hyperlinked text, your frameset file opens in a new browser window without browser toolbars, menus, and buttons showing.

Summary

You've completed the first part of the book! In this chapter you

◆ Selected a layout style for your site (either pre-designed or your customized style).

◆ Built the frameset file that contains your course.

◆ Created the navigation.htm file, which contains the navigation and sequence of pages for your course.

◆ Created the menu.htm file, which builds your course menu.

◆ Added the content pages and placeholders to your Learning Site structure.

◆ Learned how to customize the navigation, menu, and frameset.

The next part of the book shows you how to create CourseBuilder interactions.

Part II

Test and Activity

Chapter 8

Getting Started with CourseBuilder

IN THIS CHAPTER

- ◆ Setting up your course to work with CourseBuilder
- ◆ Navigating the CourseBuilder Interaction dialog box
- ◆ Understanding how CourseBuilder interactions are processed in the Web browser
- ◆ Selecting CourseBuilder interactions from the CourseBuilder Gallery
- ◆ Defining the General tab properties

LEARNING SITE BUILDS the structure of your Web-Based Training course, and CourseBuilder creates specific activities and tests within a single HTML page. CourseBuilder interactions fall into three general categories:

- ◆ **Test and activity,** including true/false and multiple-choice, text-entry, drag-and-drop, explore, and sliders
- ◆ **Control,** including buttons, sliders, and timers
- ◆ **Processing,** including Action Manager

CourseBuilder and Learning Site are completely separate Dreamweaver MX extensions. That means that, if you so choose, you can use Learning Site without using CourseBuilder; conversely, you can use CourseBuilder without using Learning Site.

A Tale of Two Perspectives

CourseBuilder is, in a sense, a Web developer's WBT development kit. To understand how CourseBuilder works, the next two sections describe the same CourseBuilder interaction from the student's and course author's perspectives.

The *student's perspective* demonstrates how a CourseBuilder interaction works within a course using Internet Explorer. The *course author's* perspective demonstrates how to construct that same CourseBuilder interaction within Dreamweaver MX.

The student's perspective

To understand how interactions work from a student's perspective, take a look at a drag-and-drop interaction from the *HTML Basics* course. Figure 8-1 shows the first CourseBuilder interaction in the course, a test question on protocol definitions.

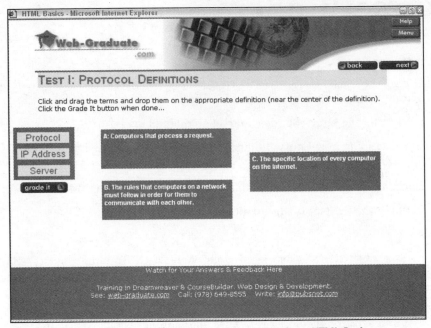

Figure 8–1: A CourseBuilder drag–and–drop interaction from HTML Basics

Notice that there are three drag items on the left (the terms Protocol, IP Address, and Server) and three target items on the right (definitions labeled A, B, and C).

The student is directed to click and drag the terms to the correct definitions, and to click the Grade It button when finished. When students click the Grade It button, they receive one of three possible feedback messages:

- ◆ Correct!

- ◆ Incorrect! (with further information about what exactly is incorrect)

- ◆ Please drag the terms to the definition before you click Grade It. (If the student clicked the Grade It button without moving any drag items.

Student feedback is delivered in the bottom frame, regardless of the feedback message, as shown in Figure 8-2.

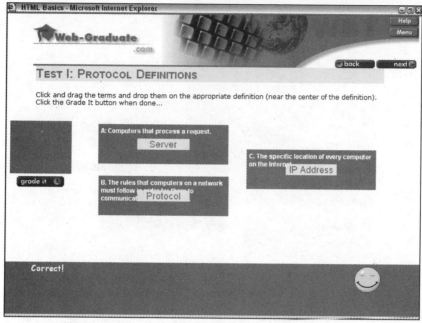

Figure 8-2: Student feedback is delivered in the bottom frame.

The course author's perspective

Let's look at the same CourseBuilder drag-and-drop interaction from the course author's perspective.

Editing your pages within a frameset

Quite frequently in CourseBuilder you will send control from one course frame to another. For example, the *HTML Basics* course contains interactions in the `mainFrame` frame, and yet all feedback messages are displayed in the `blackboard` frame.

To send control between frames, you need to edit Web pages *within their frameset*. To do so, open the frameset file (for example, `index.htm` in the *HTML Basics* course), click inside the frame that typically contains your Web page (`mainFrame`), and choose File → Open in Frame from the main menu bar. Then select the Web page you want to edit, and Dreamweaver MX opens that page within the frameset.

If you are creating a new page, you need to create that page using the Learning Site dialog box *before* you edit it in your Dreamweaver MX frameset. See Chapter 7 for information about adding new pages to your Learning Site.

Figure 8-3 shows the interaction opened in Dreamweaver MX, within the frameset file.

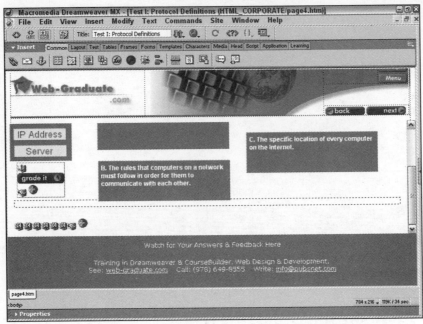

Figure 8-3: The CourseBuilder interaction open in Dreamweaver MX

There are actually two separate CourseBuilder interactions on the page: drop-and-drag and button. This type of drag-and-drop interaction is called `Drag_ManyToMany` because you have multiple drag elements (terms) and multiple target elements (definitions). It's an example of a test and activity interaction. The judgment of the drag-and-drop interaction is initiated by the student clicking the Grade It button, which is an example of a control interaction.

To create the drag-and-drop interaction, follow these steps:

1. Open a blank page within the `mainFrame` frame (see sidebar for instructions).

2. Click the Learning tab on the Insert panel. The Learning tab displays with one button, the Insert CourseBuilder Interaction button, as shown in Figure 8-4.

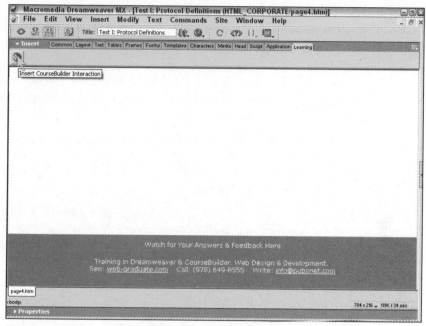

Figure 8-4: The Insert CourseBuilder Interaction button in Dreamweaver MX

3. Click the Insert CourseBuilder Interaction button.

The CourseBuilder Interaction dialog box displays, with the CourseBuilder Gallery active, as shown in Figure 8-5:

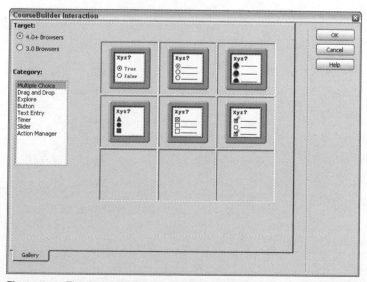

Figure 8-5: The CourseBuilder Interaction Gallery

The CourseBuilder Interaction Gallery contains 25 different interactions (18 test and activity interactions, and eight control and processing interactions).

4. Choose Drag and Drop from the Category list to display the seven drag-and-drop templates (see Figure 8-6). Each template is different in terms of the number of drag and target elements, the direction that elements can move, and whether a sequence is required.

   We want the student to move only drag items (drag terms to definitions), and because we have multiple drag and target elements, we want "many" drag elements and "many" target elements. Drag_ManyTo_Many is the template that best fits our needs.

5. Click the Drag_ManyToMany template. CourseBuilder inserts a working copy of the template into your Dreamweaver MX page, and activates additional tabs for that template (General, Elements, Pairs, and Action Manager tabs) in the dialog box, as shown in Figure 8-6.

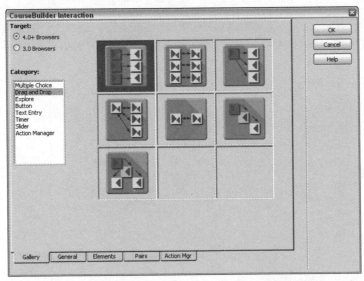

Figure 8-6: With the Drag_ManyTo_Many template selected, other tabs appear at bottom of the dialog box.

Three tabs are common to *all* CourseBuilder interactions: Gallery, General, and Action Manager. Most interactions use additional tabs (placed between the General tab and the Action Manager tab) to define options specific to those interactions.

6. Click the General tab to define the general properties for the interaction. Figure 8-7 shows the General tab for a drag-and-drop interaction.

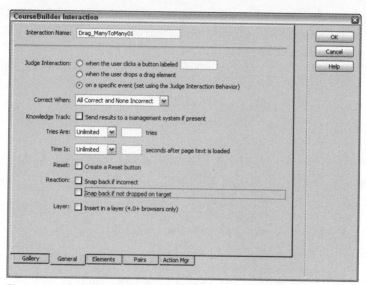

Figure 8-7: General tab for a drag-and-drop interaction. General tab options vary slightly among interactions.

Although there are some variances in terms of options on the General tab for each interaction, the following options are there for all of them:

- **Interaction Name.** All interactions are named so that they can be referenced in scripts. (CourseBuilder provides default names; you can change those names if you want.)

- **Judge Interaction.** Specifies when judgment of the test or activity will occur. In Figure 8-7, this is set to On a Specific Event. That "specific event" is a separate interaction named `Button_Push02`. With CourseBuilder, you can set up control interactions such as buttons and sliders to initiate judgment of test and activity interactions such as drag-and-drop and multiple choice.

- **Correct When.** Specify when a student's answer should be considered correct: when *all* are correct and none incorrect, or when *any* are correct and none incorrect.

- **Knowledge Track.** Specify whether to enable Knowledge Tracking (sending the results to a Learning Management System or database).

- **Tries Are.** Define the number of tries a student can make to complete the interaction.

- **Time Is.** Define the amount of time the student has to complete the interaction.

- **Reset.** All interactions except Button and Action Manager give you the option of including a Reset button that students can click to return that specific interaction to its original state (for example, if they started to drag elements in a drag-and-drop interaction, clicking the Reset button would return all elements to their starting positions).

- **Layer.** You can choose to include the entire interaction in a layer. Doing so lets you more easily control and manipulate the interaction using behaviors for layers.

7. Click the Elements tab, which is specific to the drag-and-drop interaction. Here you specify the elements (both drag and target) used by the interaction, as shown in Figure 8-8.

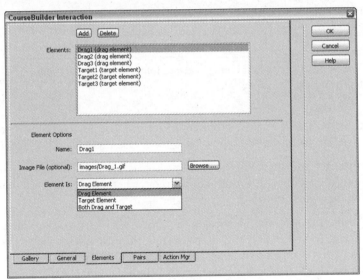

Figure 8-8: Elements tab for a drag-and-drop interaction. Specify the drag and target elements to be used in the interaction.

By default, CourseBuilder creates 3 drag and 3 target elements, and inserts a placeholder image for each element in a separate layer (allowing you to easily rearrange each element when you edit the interaction in Dreamweaver MX). You can select an image to replace each placeholder by selecting those images in the Image File field. If you use text, as this example does, you insert text into the layer when you edit the interaction in Dreamweaver MX.

If you want to add or subtract elements, you'd simply click the Add or Delete buttons above the list of elements.

8. Click the Pairs tab, which is specific to the drag-and-drop interaction. CourseBuilder automatically defines all possible pairings unless you add elements on the Elements tab. Specify the judgment of every potential pairing as correct, incorrect, or not judged by highlighting a pair and selecting Correct, Incorrect, or Not Judged in the Correct drop-down menu.

As the course author, you identify the correct pairings in the Pairs tab, as shown in Figure 8-9. All other pairings are judged incorrect.

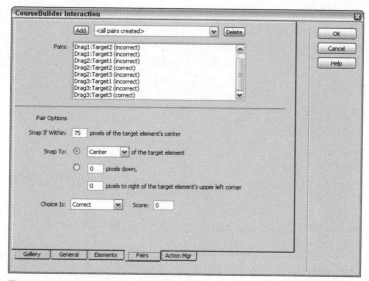

Figure 8-9: Set correct pairings of drag and target elements in the Pairs tab.

Now CourseBuilder needs to know what to do with all of this information – and that's where the Action Manager comes in!

9. Click the Action Manager (Action Mgr) tab, and specify the rules for processing the interaction. Figure 8-10 shows the processing rules being defined for our example interaction.

Processing responses can be quite complex, as you'll see in Chapter 17. For now, know that the Action Manager specifies different messages to write to the blackboard frame depending on whether the student's answer is judged correct, incorrect, or unknown (he clicked the Grade It button without moving any of the drag elements). Figure 8-11 also shows the dialog box where you specify the frame in which the feedback message will display.

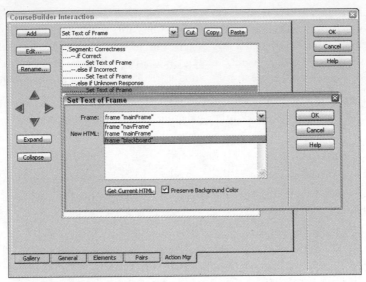

Figure 8-10: The Action Manager defines the rules for processing
interactions.

Keep in mind that the number of tabs between the General tab and the Action
Manager tab varies with each interaction. Table 8-1 gives you a general idea of the
different tabs and options within the CourseBuilder Interaction dialog box.

TABLE 8-1 UNIQUE TABS FOR EACH COURSEBUILDER INTERACTION

CourseBuilder Interaction	Unique Tab	Description
Multiple Choice	Choices	Lets you specify each choice available to students, and which choices are correct, incorrect, or not judged. You can have as few or as many choices as you want.
Drag and Drop	Elements	Lets you specify each element available to students, and whether an element is a drag element, a target element, or both (can be dragged to other targets, and can be a target for other elements). You can have as few or as many drag elements and target elements as you want.
Drag and Drop	Pairs	Lets you specify which pairs, or match-ups, of drag and target elements are correct, incorrect, or not judged. You can also define how close a student must drop a drag element to a target element.

CourseBuilder Interaction	Unique Tab	Description
Explore	Hot Areas	Lets you specify the different hot areas of a graphic, and whether those areas are correct, incorrect, or not judged. You can have as few or as many hot areas as you want.
Text Entry	Responses	Lets you specify which words or phrases that students enter are correct, incorrect, or not judged. You can specify how exact the word or phrase must be for a match. You can have as few or as many response evaluations as you want.
Timer	Triggers	Lets you specify how many triggers to signal warnings and the like, and how long into the activity those warnings should be signaled. You can have as few or as many triggers as you want.
Slider	Ranges	Lets you specify each range on the slider, and whether that range is correct, incorrect, or not judged. You can have as few or as many ranges as you want.

Using CourseBuilder

Before you begin exploring the complexities of CourseBuilder, there are some basics you need to know, including how to copy the support files to a Dreamweaver MX site to enable CourseBuilder interactions for that site, how to insert new and edit existing CourseBuilder interactions, and how to define the General tab properties for all interactions.

Setting up your Dreamweaver MX site to work with CourseBuilder

You set your Dreamweaver MX site up for CourseBuilder by copying the support files to that site. To do so, follow these steps:

Each Dreamweaver MX site that uses CourseBuilder needs to have the support files copied into its local root folder. Otherwise, the CourseBuilder interactions will not work.

1. Open any page in your Dreamweaver MX site.

2. Choose Modify → CourseBuilder → Copy Support Files. Dreamweaver MX displays a Copy Support Files confirmation box similar to the one shown in Figure 8-11.

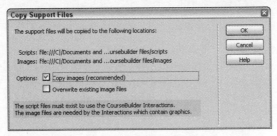

Figure 8-11: Copy Support Files confirmation box

CourseBuilder copies the support files to folders named images and scripts in your root folder. If the image and scripts folders already exist, CourseBuilder writes the files to them. (If you previously created a Learning Site in your Dreamweaver MX site, for example, these folders already exist in that Dreamweaver MX site.) If not, CourseBuilder automatically creates them.

3. Select the Copy Images option in the Copy Support Files confirmation box to copy all CourseBuilder files (both scripts and images).

4. Select (or don't – it *is* optional) the Overwrite Existing Image Files option to overwrite existing files if there is a naming conflict.

5. Click the OK button. CourseBuilder copies the necessary files to your Dreamweaver MX site's root folder.

Inserting and editing CourseBuilder interactions

To insert a CourseBuilder interaction into your Web page in Dreamweaver MX, follow these steps (refer to Figure 8-4):

1. Select the Learning tab in Dreamweaver MX.

2. Click your cursor at the location in your Web page where you want the CourseBuilder interaction inserted.

3. Click the Insert CourseBuilder Interaction button. Dreamweaver MX inserts the interaction at the exact location of your cursor in the Web page, and launches the CourseBuilder Interaction dialog box.

To edit an existing CourseBuilder interaction in Dreamweaver MX, follow these steps:

1. Click the CourseBuilder icon that represents the interaction you want to edit. Dreamweaver MX highlights the entire interaction, and the Properties panel changes to display the properties of that highlighted interaction, including its name (see Figure 8-12).

Figure 8-12: Selecting and editing an existing CourseBuilder interaction in Dreamweaver MX

2. Click the Edit button on the Properties panel. The CourseBuilder Interaction dialog box displays with the selections previously made for that specific CourseBuilder interaction. (Note that CourseBuilder does not display the Gallery tab because the interaction already exists.)

Defining the General Tab properties

Every CourseBuilder interaction includes the General tab. Figure 8-13 shows the General tab for an Explore interaction, although many of the options on the General tab are the same for all interactions.

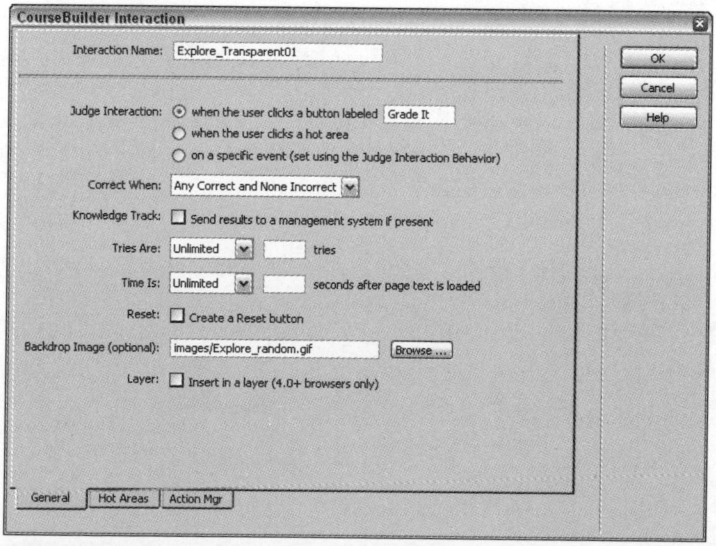

Figure 8-13: Many of the options on The General tab are the same options for all interactions.

Let's look at these common options.

INTERACTION NAME

Interaction names are used by CourseBuilder to reference each interaction for actions, controls, and processing (it is only used internally by CourseBuilder; students do not see the interaction name). By default, CourseBuilder names each interaction based on the name of the template selected from the CourseBuilder Gallery, and then numbered consecutively within a single Web page in case there are multiple interactions on a single page.

So, for example, if you insert the `Explore_Transparent` template, CourseBuilder names that interaction `Explore_Transparent01`. If you then insert a toggle button to judge the `Explore_Transparent01` interaction, that button is named `Button_Toggle02`.

The name for an interaction needs to be unique only on a specific page, not for the entire course. You can, of course, choose your own name for each interaction if you prefer custom names.

JUDGE INTERACTION

Judging an interaction means processing that interaction. Even interactions that are not judged as correct or incorrect are still judged. For example, a button interaction is judged (meaning the Action Manager tests for conditions and processes actions related to that button), yet a button is obviously a control that cannot logically be evaluated for correctness.

Every interaction needs a catalyst to initiate the judgment (processing) of that interaction. Except for Timer interactions, that catalyst is the student, either directly or indirectly. On the General tab, you have three options for initiating the judgment of an interaction:

◆ **When the user clicks a button labeled [button_name].** This option creates a standard HTML *form* button using the text you supply. Although you can apply CSS styles to form buttons, you do not have the same design flexibility as you would when creating an *image* button (for example, you cannot create mouseover effects with form buttons). If you type Grade It, for example, CourseBuilder creates a button similar to the following: `Grade It`

◆ **When the user clicks a hot area.** (The "hot area" phrase is specific to each interaction.) Select this option to instruct CourseBuilder to automatically judge the interaction immediately when a student performs any of the following:

■ Clicks a choice in a Multiple Choice interaction.

■ Drops a drag element in a Drag and Drop interaction.

■ Clicks a hot area in an Explore interaction.

■ Clicks or tabs out of a text field in a Text Entry interaction.

- Releases the thumb in a Slider interaction.

- Clicks a graphical button in a Button interaction.

Keep in mind that if you use this automatic initiation of judgment, it initiates judgment immediately for *each* student action. For example, if you have a drag-and-drop interaction, judgment is initiated when the student drops the first drag element, again when the student drops the second drag element, and so forth.

◆ **On a specific event (set using the Judge Interaction Behavior).** This option means that the interaction is judged only when *a different interaction or Dreamweaver MX behavior* initiates judgment. For example, many of the tests in the *HTML Basics* course are initiated by the Grade It button.

CourseBuilder interactions can initiate the processing of *other* interactions by inserting a Judge Interaction action in the Action Manager that specifies the interaction to judge. Figure 8-14 shows the Action Manager for a button interaction (the Grade It button) using the Judge Interaction action to initiate judgment of a drag-and-drop interaction named Drag_ManyToMany.

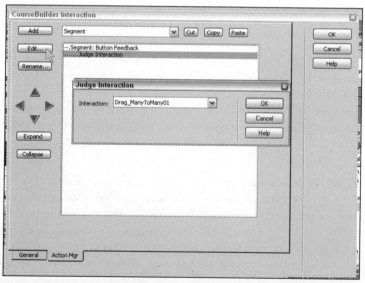

Figure 8-14: The Grade It button interaction from the HTML Basics course initiates judgment of the drag-and-drop interaction.

You can also initiate the Judge Interaction action from the Behaviors panel within Dreamweaver MX by adding the action CourseBuilder → Judge Interaction.

CORRECT WHEN

There are often multiple correct responses in CourseBuilder interactions. For example, the Protocol Definitions drag-and-drop interaction discussed earlier in this chapter has three correct answers (pairs). You have two options for assigning the value of "correct" to an interaction on the General tab:

◆ **Any Correct and None Incorrect.** The interaction is judged correct if the student selects *any* of the correct answers. Select this option if you want to provide a response to students if *any* of their answers are correct and none are incorrect (even though other correct answers are unanswered). This option is not frequently selected.

◆ **All Correct and None Incorrect.** The interaction is judged correct *only* if the student selects *all* of the correct answers. For example, the Protocol Definitions interaction requires three correct match-ups. If the student answers (matches) all three correctly, the Action Manager displays a "Correct!" message. If *any* answer is incorrect, the Action Manager displays an "Incorrect!" message to the student.

KNOWLEDGE TRACK

Select the Knowledge Track option if you are tracking student performance. Tracking student performance is covered in Part IV, "Tracking Results," of this book.

TRIES ARE

You have two options for the number of tries that you allow a student to attempt answering an interaction (a "try" is counted each time an interaction is judged):

◆ **Unlimited.** Students can try as many times as they want. Typically used when interactions are activities or ungraded tests. All of the tests in the *HTML Basics* course, for example, allow students to try as many times as they want.

◆ **Limited To [number of] tries.** A student is limited to a specific number of tries. Typically used when interactions are graded tests, and the student is allowed a single try for each interaction (similar to a graded classroom test). Whenever the student reaches the limit for the number of tries and still hasn't answered correctly, the Action Manager, by default, disables the interaction from further answers and displays the popup message, "You are out of tries."

Of course, you can change how the Action Manager processes and responds to reaching the tries limit by adding different actions (described in Chapter 17).

TIME IS

You have the option of putting a time limit on how long (in seconds) a student has to complete an interaction.

- ◆ **Unlimited.** A student can take as much time as he wants. Typically used when interactions are activities or ungraded tests. All of the tests in the *HTML Basics* course, for example, allow students to take as much time as they want.

- ◆ **Limited To [number of] seconds after page text is loaded.** A student is limited to a specific amount of time to answer. If the student reaches the time limit and still hasn't answered, the Action Manager, by default, disables the interaction from further answers and displays the message "You are out of time."

Again, you can change how the Action Manager processes and responds to reaching the time limit by adding different actions (described in Chapter 17).

RESET

CourseBuilder gives you the option to include a Reset button that, when clicked by the student, resets the CourseBuilder interaction to its original state when the page first loaded (including the reset of time and try counts). The button looks similar to the following: `Reset`

Because it is a standard form button, you can change its appearance using CSS style definitions. The Reset button does *not* reset Multiple Choice radio buttons because radio buttons only allow a single choice to be selected.

Note that Reset is not an option for the Button interaction (it wouldn't make sense to have a student click a button to reset another button).

LAYER

CourseBuilder gives you the option to insert an entire interaction into a layer (layers are only available in 4.0+ browsers). On interactions that already use layers (Drag and Drop, Explore, Sliders), CourseBuilder puts any text and buttons in the layer, but does not nest the existing layers.

Inserting interactions into layers provides you with far greater control over their display, because there are many behaviors that you can apply to layers. For example, you can move a layer on a timeline; or show and hide layers.

Figure 8-15 shows an example of a Multiple Choice interaction inserted into a layer. Notice that all of the text and images for that interaction are included in a single layer.

Figure 8-16 shows an example of an Explore interaction inserted into a layer. Only the text and buttons are included in the layer, since the interaction already uses layers for the background image and hot areas.

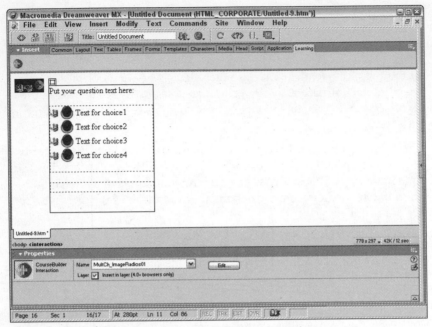

Figure 8-15: A Multiple Choice interaction inserted into a layer

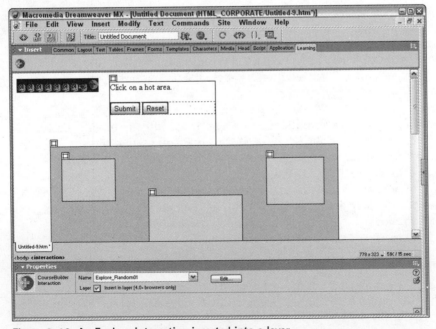

Figure 8-16: An Explore interaction inserted into a layer

The JavaScripts Behind CourseBuilder

Now that you understand the basics of CourseBuilder interactions, let's take a brief look at the JavaScript files that drive CourseBuilder processing.

CourseBuilder inserts interactions into an HTML page using a custom <INTERACTION> tag. Here's example code from a drag-and-drop interaction in the *HTML Basics* course:

```
<interaction name="Drag_ManyToMany01" object="G01" template="020_Drag and
   Drop/010_Drag_ManyToMany_04.agt"
   includesrc="interactionClass.js,elemDragClass.js,behDragLayer.js">
      .
      .
      .

<div name="G01Layer"> </div>
<div id="G01Drag1" style="position:absolute; left:15px; top:177px; width:100;
      height:20; visibility: visible; z-index: 2; overflow: visible;">
      .
      .
      .

<interaction>
```

The <INTERACTION> tag references three JavaScript files: interactionClass. js, elemDragClass.js, and behDragLayer.js. These are the JavaScript files necessary to process this specific drag-and-drop interaction. Different interactions require different JavaScript files.

When you copy the CourseBuilder support files to a Dreamweaver MX site, a good chunk of those support files are the JavaScript files necessary for processing interactions, all included in the scripts folder of that Dreamweaver MX site. Table 8-2 provides an overview of the JavaScript support files for CourseBuilder.

TABLE 8-2 JAVASCRIPTS INCLUDED IN COURSEBUILDER SUPPORT FILES

JavaScript File	Description
`behActions.js`	Processes the actions available in the Action Manager in the Main and Set Text categories: **Main** Call JavaScript Change Property Check Browser Check Plugin Control Shockwave or Flash Go to URL Open Browser Window Play Sound Popup Message Show-Hide Layers Swap Image Swap Image Restore Validate Form **Set Text** Set Text of Frame Set Text of Layer Set Text of Status Bar Set Text of Text Field
`behCourseBuilder.js`	Processes the actions available in the Action Manager in the CourseBuilder and Tracking categories: **CourseBuilder** Judge Interaction Reset Interaction Set Interaction Properties **Tracking** Send Core Data Send ExitAU Send GetParam Send Interaction Info Send Lesson Status Send Lesson Time Send Objective Info Send Score (Learning Site also copies this file into a Dreamweaver MX site.)

JavaScript File	Description
behDragLayer.js	Called by the Drag and Drop interaction to process the dragging of a layer.

behTimeline.js	Processes the actions available in the Action Manager in the Timeline category:
	
	Timeline
	  Go to Timeline Frame
	  Play Timeline
	  Stop Timeline

cmi.js	Contains the functions that track and send student performance data to a Learning Management System (LMS). Computer Managed Instruction (CMI) is the industry standard for tracking and sending information to an LMS. (Learning Site also copies this file into a Dreamweaver MX site.)
elemDragClass.js	Called by the Drag and Drop interaction to construct and process a drag-and-drop element.
elemHotaClass.js	Called by the Explore interaction to construct and process a hot-area element.
elemIbtnClass.js	Called by the Button interaction to construct and process an image button element.
elemInptClass.js	Called by the Multiple Choice interaction to construct and process a multiple-choice element.
elemSldrClass.js	Called by the Slider interaction to construct and process a slider element.
elemTextClass.js	Called by the Text Entry interaction to construct and process a text-entry element.
elemTimrClass.js	Called by the Timer interaction to construct and process a timer element.
interactionClass.js	Called by all interactions to manage interactions (initialize, reset, enable, disable interactions, set tries and time limits, and so forth).

If you move your Dreamweaver MX site, you must also move these scripts in the scripts folder, or your CourseBuilder interactions will not work.

Summary

This chapter provided an overview of CourseBuilder interactions, as well as some of the basics for using CourseBuilder. You learned

◆ How interactions work from a student's perspective.

◆ To create interactions in CourseBuilder.

◆ To navigate the CourseBuilder Interaction dialog box, and about the various tabs available in that dialog box.

◆ To make selections in the General tab in the CourseBuilder Interaction dialog box.

◆ About the JavaScript files in the `scripts` folder of your Dreamweaver MX site.

The next chapter describes how to create true/false and multiple-choice interactions.

Chapter 9

True/False and Multiple-Choice Interactions

IN THIS CHAPTER

- ◆ Understanding multiple-choice interactions from the student's and course author's perspective

- ◆ Choosing the appropriate multiple-choice template in the CourseBuilder Gallery

- ◆ Understanding the Choices tab, which is unique to multiple-choice interactions

- ◆ Viewing different applications of the multiple-choice interaction

MULTIPLE-CHOICE QUESTIONS (including true/false) provide students with one or more correct choices hidden among a number of distractors. Each choice consists of two separate pieces (a selector and content), as shown in Figure 9-1.

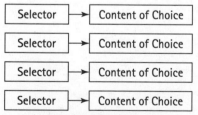

Figure 9-1: Each choice consists of a selector and question content.

Students click selectors to indicate their selection of specific content. In CourseBuilder multiple-choice questions, the selectors can be buttons, checkboxes, or clickable images (image buttons). The content can be any type: text, an image, a movie, and so forth.

One of the key challenges to developing effective multiple-choice questions is to reduce the impact of student guessing. Chapter 5 discusses student odds in multiple-choice questions, and offers various methods of significantly reducing the chances of a student guessing correctly (ensuring that the test is gauging a student's knowledge).

Understanding How Multiple-Choice Questions Work

To understand the concepts behind multiple-choice interactions, it is important that you comprehend the process for an interaction from the student's perspective (how it works) and a course author's perspective (how you create it).

This section describes both perspectives of multiple-choice interactions.

The student's perspective

To see how multiple-choice interactions work from a student's perspective, take a look at a multiple-choice interaction from the *HTML Basics* course. Figure 9-2 shows a sample multiple-choice test question on HTML lists.

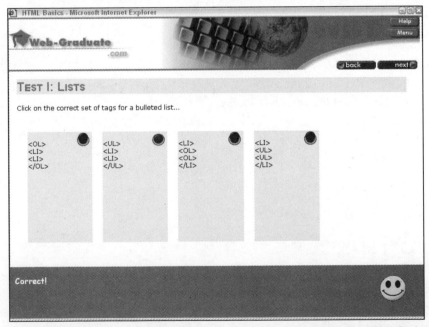

Figure 9-2: A multiple-choice question from the segment on lists in the HTML Basics course

This example has a total of four choices (sets of tags for the HTML list element) from which the student chooses the correct set. The second choice is correct, and all others are incorrect.

The student is directed to click on the button that represents the correct sequence of tags for a bulleted list. Although most of the tests and activities in the *HTML Basics* course instruct students to click a Grade It button, the multiple-choice tests are graded automatically, immediately after a student selects a choice. When the student makes a choice by clicking a button, the course delivers feedback (correct, incorrect, or unknown response) in the bottom frame.

 Good interface design requires consistency of function. Requiring a Grade It button in some instances and not in other instances may seem inconsistent, but that consistency is with expectations outside of this course. When we use software and select one choice (such as through a menu), we expect to click on one item and receive a reaction. When we use software and type something, move something, or select multiple items, we expect to click something else to indicate we're finished.

The course author's perspective

Let's look at the same multiple-choice interaction from the course author's perspective. Figure 9-3 shows the multiple-choice question open in Dreamweaver MX.

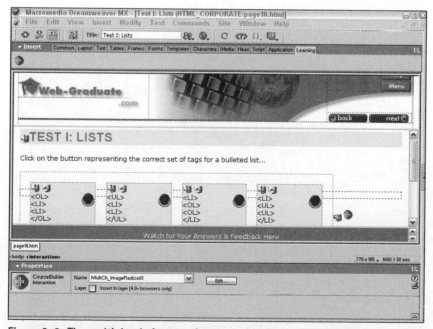

Figure 9-3: The multiple-choice question opened in Dreamweaver MX

The question consists of a multiple-choice interaction that offers four choices, one of which is correct. Students indicate their choice by clicking an image button (lighted_mini) that is part of CourseBuilder's standard set of buttons (in Chapter 6, Table 6-2 provides descriptions of the buttons available). This type of multiple-choice interaction is called MultCh_ImageRadios.

To create this multiple-choice interaction, follow these steps (assuming you've opened the file within the frameset):

1. Click the Insert CourseBuilder Interaction button on the Learning tab. The CourseBuilder Interaction dialog box displays, with the CourseBuilder Gallery active.

2. Choose the Multiple Choice category to display the six multiple-choice templates (see Figure 9-4). Each template is different in terms of the number of correct choices, number of distractors, and what the student clicks to indicate their selection.

   We want students to click on a button to indicate their choice without having to click on a separate Grade It button. Instead of standard form radio buttons, we use a button from the CourseBuilder's standard set of buttons (lighted_mini). We also want to limit students to a single choice. The template that fits these requirements is the MultCh_ImageRadios template.

3. Click the MultCh_ImageRadios template. CourseBuilder inserts a working copy of the template into your Dreamweaver MX page, and activates the additional tabs for that template (General, Choices, Action Mgr) in the CourseBuilder Interaction dialog box, as shown in Figure 9-4.

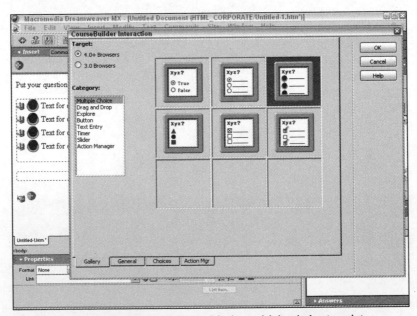

Figure 9-4: The CourseBuilder Gallery with the multiple-choice template MultCh_ImageRadios selected

4. Click the General tab to define the general properties for the interaction.

5. Type the text for the question in the Question Text field, as shown in Figure 9-5.

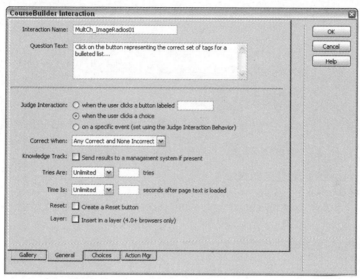

Figure 9-5: General tab for the MultCh_ImageRadios interaction. The options vary slightly between templates.

Chapter 8 describes the General tab in detail.

6. Click the Choices tab to define the choices (both correct and incorrect) for the interaction. By default, the MultCh_ImageRadios interaction includes four choices, with choice1 initially set as correct and the remaining choices set as incorrect, as shown in Figure 9-6.

 Roll a die to select the correct choice (rolling dice ensures a truly random selection for the correct choice). When I created this interaction, number 2 came up — making choice2 correct and all other choices incorrect (choice3 and choice4 are already incorrect and don't need to be changed).

7. Highlight choice1 and select Incorrect from the Choice Is field.

8. Highlight choice2 and select Correct from the Choice Is field. Your choices should now be set as shown in Figure 9-7.

9. Highlight each choice and enter the text content for each choice (the correct choice and three distractors). Figure 9-7 shows the text being entered for choice2 (the correct choice).

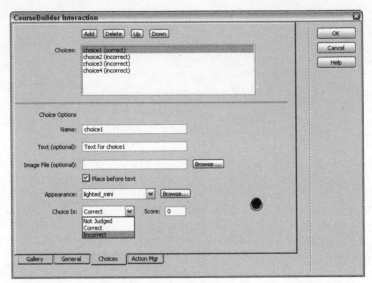

Figure 9-6: You define correct and incorrect choices on the Choices tab.

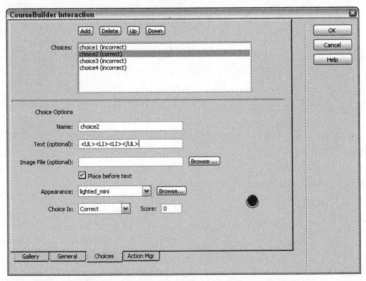

Figure 9-7: Enter the content for each choice in the Text field.

10. Be sure that each choice has lighted_mini selected in the Appearance field (it is the default for this interaction, and should already be selected). Figure 9-8 shows your options for button appearance (the options correspond to the CourseBuilder button options outlined in Table 6-2). You can easily select another button as a selector.

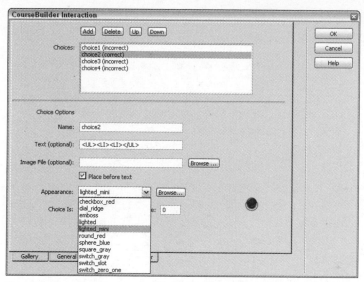

Figure 9-8: In the Appearance field, select the look of the choice button.

11. Click the Action Manager (Action Mgr) tab. CourseBuilder displays the default rules for processing this interaction, defining CourseBuilder actions for correct, incorrect, and unknown student responses.

    Since the design of the *HTML Basics* course sends student feedback to the bottom frame (named `blackboard`), we need to delete each Popup Message in the Action Manager, and insert a Set Text of Frame action instead (so that we can write text messages to the bottom frame).

12. Highlight the `Popup Message` action under the `if Correct` condition and click the Edit button, as shown in Figure 9-9. CourseBuilder displays the Popup Message dialog box.

13. Highlight each `Popup Message` action in the Action Manager tab and click the Cut button to delete it. (This must be done for each message; there's no way to cut all three actions at once.)

14. Click the `if Correct` condition in the Action Manager. Now that it is active (highlighted), any actions we add are added to that highlighted condition.

15. Select the Set Text of Frame action from the Action Manager pop-up menu, as shown in Figure 9-10, and then click the Add button.

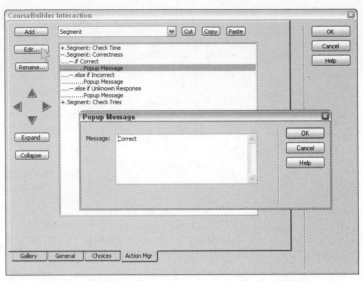

Figure 9-9: The Action Manager displays a pop-up message for each condition (correct, incorrect, and unknown response) by default.

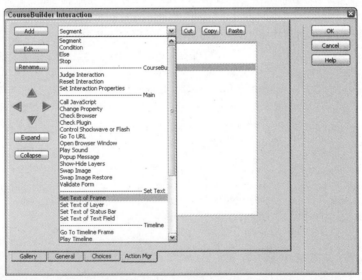

Figure 9-10: Select the Set Text of Frame action and apply it to the if Correct condition.

We want to send all student feedback to the frame named blackboard, and *not* the frame containing the multiple-choice interaction.

16. Select the blackboard frame from the Frame drop-down menu.

    CourseBuilder displays the Set Text of Frame dialog box.

17. Enter the text for the message that you want displayed in the blackboard frame when students answer correctly. You can enter simple text, or you can format that text with HTML tags, depending on the effect you want. The example in Figure 9-11 shows the HTML tags for the correct state of this interaction in the *HTML Basics* course.

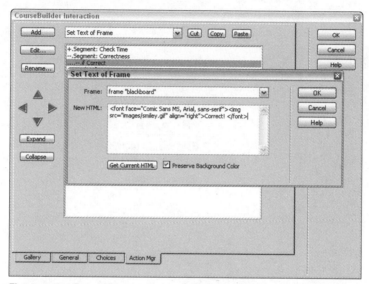

Figure 9-11: Enter the text for student feedback when the answer is correct (defined by the if Correct condition). This text is written to the frame named blackboard when the student answers correctly.

17. Repeat Steps 12-17 for the if Incorrect and if Unknown Response conditions as well, using text that is appropriate to each condition.

Figure 9-12 shows a flowchart that diagrams the decisions and actions taken by the Action Manager when processing this multiple-choice interaction.

18. Click OK when you've completed defining the rules in the Action Manager. CourseBuilder writes the processing rules into the HTML file, and displays the multiple-choice question in Dreamweaver MX, as Figure 9-13 shows.

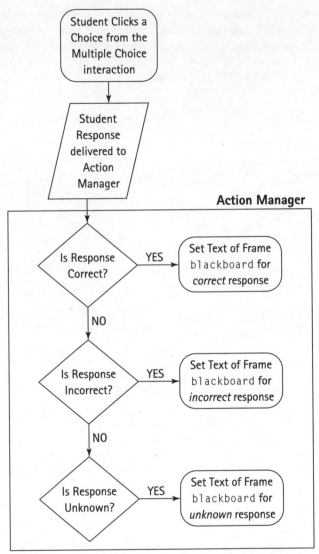

Figure 9-12: Processing of the multiple-choice interaction in
the Action Manager

Once the interaction is written into Dreamweaver MX, you can rearrange the layout by cutting and pasting (or highlighting and dragging) content. In the *HTML Basics* course, for example, the choices were formatted into a table with one row and four cells (one choice per table cell), as shown in Figure 9-14. By inserting each choice into a table cell, you have greater control over the display of the content for that choice. For example, in the example from the *HTML Basics* course, the background for each choice is shaded gray to distinguish one set of tags from another.

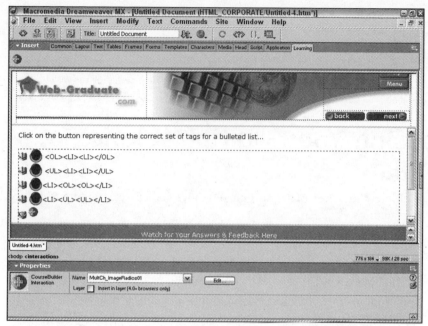

Figure 9-13: The multiple-choice interaction inserted into Dreamweaver MX

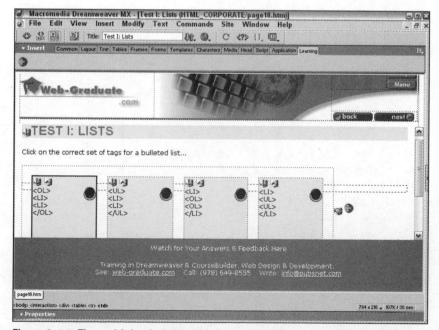

Figure 9-14: The multiple-choice interaction reformatted into a table

When you cut and paste (or select and drag) CourseBuilder buttons and other content within Dreamweaver MX, be sure that all of the behaviors attached to that button *remain with* the button by cutting and pasting any invisible elements (which represent the processing code for the interaction) as well.

Choosing Your Multiple-Choice Template

The six multiple-choice templates in CourseBuilder Gallery (see Figure 9-15) fall into three categories:

◆ One correct choice with one distractor (MultCh_TrueFalse).

◆ One correct choice with multiple distractors (MultCh_Radios, MultCh_ImageRadios, and MultCh_ImageButton).

◆ One *or more* correct choices with multiple distractors, also called "all that apply", MultCh_Checkboxes, and MultCh_ImageChkboxes).

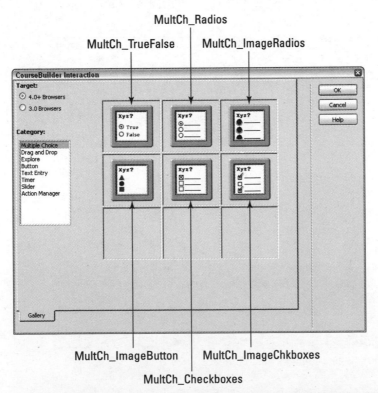

Figure 9-15: Multiple-choice templates available in the CourseBuilder Gallery

The next 6 sections describe each of the multiple-choice templates in detail.

Choosing true or false (MultCh_TrueFalse)

Use the `MultCh_TrueFalse` template when there are only two choices: one correct and one incorrect. Students use radio buttons for selectors (radio buttons are commonly used in standard Web forms to let the user select a single option from two or more options). By default, this interaction

◆ Judges an answer correct when the student selects *any* correct answer (General tab).

◆ Judges the interaction automatically when the student clicks *any* choice (General tab).

◆ Initially provides two choices (Choices tab).

◆ Lets you optionally select an image instead of text for the content of each choice. Don't confuse this with image buttons; students do not click on this image to select their choice. (Choices tab).

◆ Initially specifies `choice1` as correct and `choice2` as incorrect (Choices tab).

You can modify these defaults on the General and Choices tabs. Figure 9-16 shows the default layout for the `MultCh_TrueFalse` interaction after it is inserted into Dreamweaver MX.

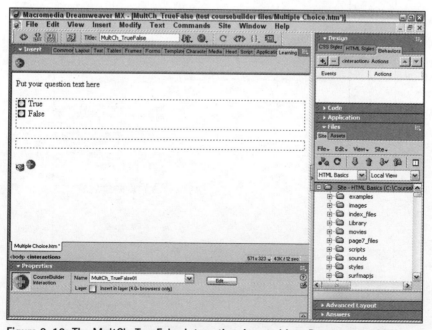

Figure 9-16: The MultCh_TrueFalse interaction, inserted into Dreamweaver MX

Choosing one from many with radio buttons (MultCh_Radios)

Use the `MultCh_Radios` template when there is only one correct choice among multiple distractors, and you want to use a standard radio button as a selector (radio buttons are commonly used in standard Web forms to let the user select a single option from many options). By default, this interaction

- ◆ Judges an answer correct when the student selects *any* correct answer (General tab).

- ◆ Judges the interaction automatically when the student clicks *any* choice (General tab).

- ◆ Initially provides four choices (Choices tab).

- ◆ Lets you optionally select an image instead of text for the content of each choice. Don't confuse this with image buttons; students do not click this image to select their choice (Choices tab).

- ◆ Initially specifies `choice1` as correct and all other choices incorrect (Choices tab).

You can modify these defaults on the General and Choices tabs. Figure 9-17 shows the default layout for the `MultCh_Radios` interaction after it is inserted into Dreamweaver MX.

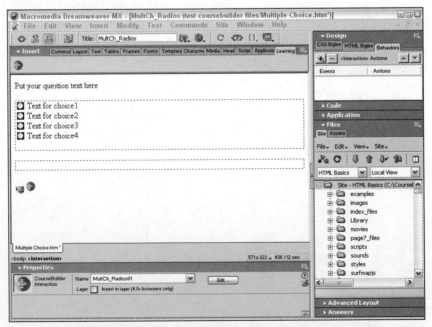

Figure 9-17: The MultCh_Radios interaction, inserted into Dreamweaver MX

Choosing one from many with image radio buttons (MultCh_ImageRadios)

Use the `MultCh_ImageRadios` template when there is only one correct choice among multiple distractors, and you want to use an image button as a selector (see Table 6-2 for a description of the buttons available; of course, you can also use custom buttons). By default, this interaction

- ◆ Judges an answer correct when the student selects *any* correct answer (General tab).

- ◆ Judges the interaction automatically when the student clicks *any* choice (General tab).

- ◆ Positions the button selector to the left of the text for each choice (Choices tab).

- ◆ Initially provides four choices (Choices tab).

- ◆ Lets you optionally select an image instead of text for the content of each choice. Don't confuse this with image buttons; students do not click on this image to select their choice (Choices tab).

- ◆ Initially specifies `choice1` as correct and all other choices incorrect (Choices tab).

You can modify these defaults on the General and Choices tabs. Figure 9-18 shows the default layout for the `MultCh_ImageRadios` interaction after it is inserted into Dreamweaver MX.

Choosing one from many with image buttons MultCh_ImageButton

Use the `MultCh_ImageButton` template when there is only one correct choice among multiple distractors, and you want to use a *custom* image button as a selector (for example, students click on photographs of presidents to indicate their choices in *The Presidential Files* sample on the CD-ROM). By default, this interaction

- ◆ Judges an answer correct when the student selects *any* correct answer (General tab).

- ◆ Judges the interaction automatically when the student clicks *any* choice (General tab).

- ◆ Positions the button selector to the left of the text for each choice (Choices tab).

- ◆ Initially provides four choices (Choices tab).

◆ Lets you optionally select an image instead of text for the content of each choice. Don't confuse this with image buttons; students do not click this image to select their choice (Choices tab).

◆ Initially specifies `choice1` as correct and all other choices incorrect (Choices tab).

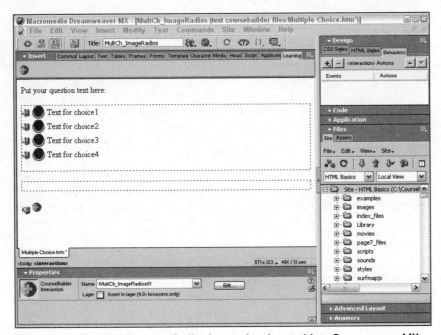

Figure 9-18: The MultCh_ImageRadios interaction, inserted into Dreamweaver MX

You can modify these defaults on the General and Choices tabs. Figure 9-19 shows the default layout for the `MultCh_ImageButton` interaction after it is inserted into Dreamweaver MX.

You can select the image for image buttons in the Choices tab by using the Appearance field's Browse button to browse to a file for each choice. Or, as shown in Figure 9-19, you can let CourseBuilder insert placeholder images into the Web page and change those images on the Properties panel in Dreamweaver MX.

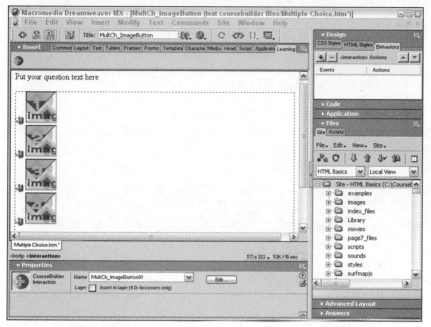

Figure 9-19: The MultCh_ImageButton interaction, inserted into Dreamweaver MX

Choosing all that apply with checkboxes (MultCh_Checkboxes)

Use the MultCh_Checkboxes template when there are one *or more* correct choices among multiple distractors. (Checkboxes are commonly used in standard Web forms to let the user select "all that apply" from a set of options.) By default, this interaction

- ◆ Judges an answer correct when the student selects *all* (not just *any*) correct answer (General tab).

- ◆ Judges the interaction when the student clicks a Submit button because the interaction often has more than one correct answer (General tab).

- ◆ Inserts a Reset button (General tab).

- ◆ Positions the checkbox selector to the left of the text for each choice (Choices tab).

- ◆ Initially provides four choices (Choices tab).

◆ Lets you optionally select an image instead of text for the content of each choice. Don't confuse this with image buttons; students do not click on this image to select their choice (Choices tab).

◆ Initially specifies `choice1` and `choice2` as correct, and `choice3` and `choice4` as incorrect (Choices tab).

You can modify these defaults on the General and Choices tabs. Figure 9-20 shows the default layout for the `MultCh_Checkboxes` interaction after it is inserted into Dreamweaver MX.

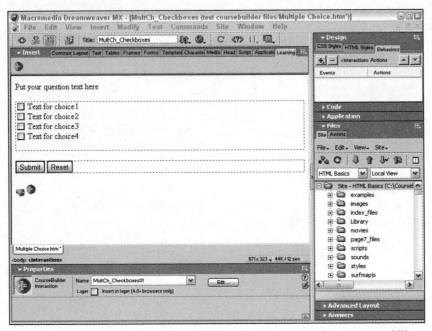

Figure 9-20: The MultCh_Checkboxes interaction, inserted into Dreamweaver MX

Choosing all that apply with image checkboxes (MultCh_ImageChkboxes)

Use the `MultCh_ImageChkboxes` template when there are one *or more* correct choices among multiple distractors, and you want to use an image button as a selector (see Table 6-2 for a description of the buttons available; you can also use custom buttons). By default, this interaction

◆ Judges an answer correct when the student selects *all* (not just *any*) correct answer. (General tab).

◆ Judges the interaction when the student clicks a Submit button because interaction often has more than one correct answer (General tab).

◆ Inserts a Reset button (General tab).

◆ Positions the checkbox selector to the left of the text for each choice (Choices tab).

◆ Initially provides four choices (Choices tab).

◆ Lets you optionally select an image instead of text for the content of each choice. (Don't confuse this with image buttons.)

◆ Initially specifies `choice1` and `choice2` as correct, with `choice3` and `choice4` as incorrect (Choices tab).

You can modify these defaults on the General and Choices tabs. Figure 9-21 shows the default layout for the `MultCh_ImageChkboxes` interaction after it is inserted into Dreamweaver MX.

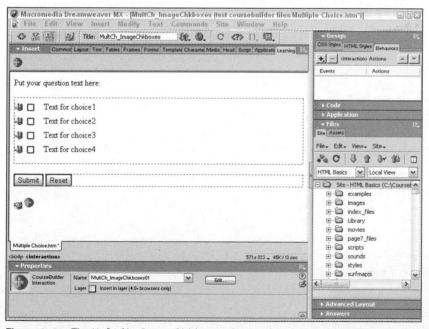

Figure 9-21: The `MultCh_ImageChkboxes` interaction, inserted into Dreamweaver MX

Defining the Choices Tab Properties

The Choices tab is unique to multiple-choice interactions. Figure 9-22 shows the Choices tab with the default settings for the MultCh_ImageChkboxes,

Adds a new choice or Deletes an existing choice in the Choices list.

Moves the order of a highlighted choice up or down the list.

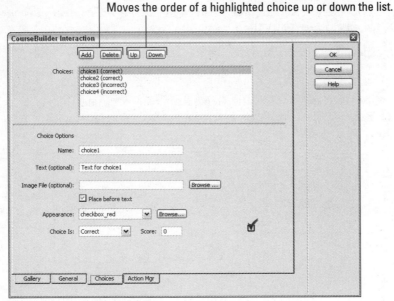

Figure 9-22: The Choices tab for the MultCh_ImageChkboxes multiple-choice interaction

On the Choices tab, you

◆ Define correct and incorrect choices by highlighting each choice in the Choices list, and selecting Correct or Incorrect from the Choice Is drop-down menu at the bottom of the Choices tab (define one at a time).

◆ Use the Add and Delete buttons to add new or delete existing choices.

◆ Rearrange the order of choices by highlighting a choice and clicking the Up or Down button to reposition the choice.

◆ Name for the choice, which is an internal name used for processing.

◆ Enter text for the content of the choice, which is optional. The text is initially placed to the right of buttons. If you rearrange the choice, remember to move *both* the selector button and the content for the choice.

◆ Select an image file for the content of the choice instead of text, which is optional. If you select an image file, students must still click the selector button initially positioned to the left of that image file.

◆ Choose an appearance for the image button, which inserts an image that students click to indicate their selection (the image *is both* the selector button and content). This option is available only for templates that use image buttons (`MultCh_ImageRadios`, `MultCh_ImageButton`, `MultCh_ImageChkboxes`).

◆ Identify whether each choice is Correct, Incorrect, or Not Judged by selecting a category from the Choice Is drop-down menu. The course author uses these categories to define correct choices and distractors, as well as any choices that are not judged (for example, if you are using checkboxes to track completed tasks on a list, those checkboxes would be set to Not Judged).

◆ Define the score for each choice. Scoring and tracking is covered in detail in Part IV of this book. Briefly, the score is the numeric value you put on each choice. Often, scorers put positive values on correct answers, and a zero value on incorrect answers.

Application Examples

Image buttons (`MultCh_ImageButton`) enable students to click on images rather than selectors next to the content for their choice. The CD-ROM contains a sample course called *The Presidential Files,* which displays famous presidential quotes and asks students to click on the picture of the president who made the quote. Figure 9-23 shows the first screen from *The Presidential Files* after the student correctly clicks President Roosevelt's picture.

Image buttons are selected on the Choices tab. Figure 9-24 shows the image button for `choice4` being selected. Remember, to select an image button, browse from the Appearance field and *not* the Image File (an image file is for content, it does *not* make an image button).

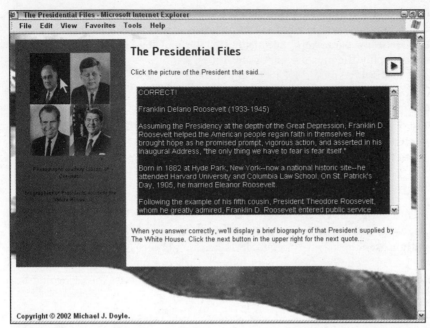

Figure 9-23: Initial screen from The Presidential Files, a multiple-choice course where students click on image buttons (MultCh_ImageButtons) to select answers

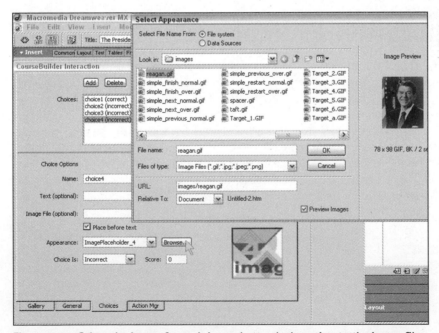

Figure 9-24: Select the image for each image button by browsing to the image file from the Appearance field on the Choices tab.

The first file in this course (presidents1.htm) is set up as a two-column table with a text area inserted in the second column (using Insert → Form Objects → Textarea in Dreamweaver MX to insert the text area). The text area is used for two purposes: to display the presidential quotes (in effect, the questions for the multiple choice) and to display student feedback for correct answers.

The CourseBuilder interaction is inserted into the first column after the creation of the text area (if you are using frames, layers, or text areas for student feedback, those areas must be created *before* you create your interaction). Figure 9-25 shows the file *before* the multiple-choice interaction is inserted into the table.

table column   table column   text area

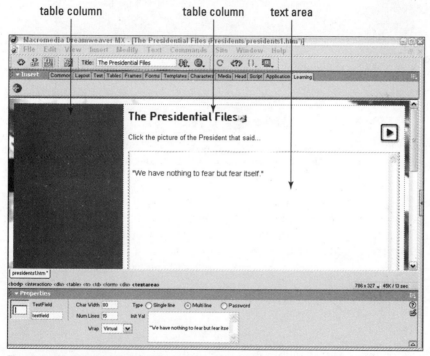

Figure 9-25: The Presidential Files is structured as a two-column table. Student feedback is sent to the text area in the second column.

Remember, the feedback area must be created before you define your rules for processing in the Action Manager.

The text area is "dressed up" by creating a CSS file that defines style properties for the HTML element textarea, as shown in Figure 9-26.

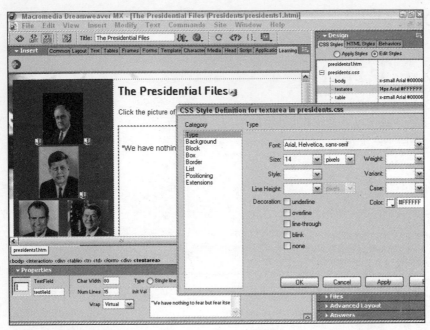

Figure 9-26: Use a CSS file to define style definitions for the textarea HTML element.

Since this multiple-choice interaction is similar in layout on all pages, you can create either a template or library item for the interaction and easily reproduce the page throughout the site. That way, you simply tweak each page (with new quotes, images, and correct choices) rather than recreating it.

Summary

In this chapter you learned how to use one of the most popular types of test question, the multiple-choice question. You learned

◆ The process for inserting and defining a multiple-choice interaction.

◆ How to choose the appropriate multiple-choice template based on your course needs.

◆ How to define correct and incorrect choices on the Choices tab.

◆ How to define the unique multiple-choice fields on the General tab.

You also looked at different applications of multiple-choice through various examples including the *HTML Basics* and *The Presidential Files* courses.

The next chapter describes how to create text entry ("fill in the blank") interactions.

Chapter 10

Text Entry (Fill-in-the-Blank) Interactions

IN THIS CHAPTER

◆ Understanding Text Entry interactions from the student's and course author's perspectives

◆ Choosing the appropriate text entry template in the CourseBuilder gallery

◆ Understanding the Responses tab, which is unique to Text Entry interactions

◆ Seeing an application of a fill-in-the-blank Cloze test.

TEXT-ENTRY QUESTIONS test students for total recall of a word or phrase, similar to the fill-in-the-blank tests that students take on paper, only students type their answers from the keyboard.

One of the key challenges to developing effective text-entry questions is to ensure that the "blank" students fill in has only *one* answer, or that you evaluate for every possible correct answer. For example here's a question:

The capital of the United States is [blank].

Which of the following answers are correct?

Washington
Washington DC
Washington, DC
Washington D.C.
Washington, D.C.
Washington, District of Columbia
Wash, DC
and so forth.

When grading such questions, a human teacher decides what are correct and incorrect responses. However, rarely would a teacher sit down and write, in advance, all of the possible correct combinations that students might enter as answers. If you use CourseBuilder for text-entry questions, you need to think of these possibilities in advance because you are not afforded the opportunity for teacher intervention and interpretation.

In CourseBuilder, use text-entry questions only in cases where the possible correct answers are very limited and have, by nature, an exactness to them. Good candidates for text-entry questions include

- ◆ Questions with numeric answers, such as
  - There are [blank] states in the United States.
  - The speed limit is [blank] miles per hour in a school zone.
  - The maximum weight of cargo on this van is [blank] pounds.

  To minimize confusion, you should always indicate the unit of measurement for the number (miles per hour, pounds, degrees, and so forth).

- ◆ Questions of terminology (definitions), such as
  - Fibrous tissues connecting bones or cartilage at a joint is called a [blank].
  - An [blank] is a ridge of coarse gravel deposited by a stream from glacial ice.
  - In a fraction, the expression written above the line is called the [blank].

  Be sure that the article introducing the term maintains proper grammar in the sentence. For example, the answer to the first example is ligament, which should be introduced with the indefinite article *a* (a ligament). On the other hand, the answer to the second example is esker, which should be introduced with the indefinite article *an* (an esker).

- ◆ Questions of symbols, such as
  - [blank] is the symbol for Iron on the Periodic Table.
  - Use the symbol [blank] to specify multiplication in an expression.

- ◆ Questions of syntax, such as markup and programming languages:
  - The HTML element and attribute for a 100% width table is [blank].
  - The [blank] statement writes the specified string to the file EMPLOYEE.DB.
  - The DOS command to change to your WINDOWS directory is [blank].

Understanding How Text-Entry Questions Work

To understand the concepts behind text-entry interactions, it is important that you comprehend the process for such an interaction from the student's perspective (how it works) and from the course author's perspective (how you create it).

This section describes both perspectives.

The student's perspective

To appreciate how text-entry interactions work from a student's perspective, take a look at a text-entry interaction from the *HTML Basics* course, a somewhat complex syntax statement with multiple attributes. Figure 10-1 shows a sample text-entry test question on inserting images into an HTML file, from the IMAGES module of the *HTML Basics* course.

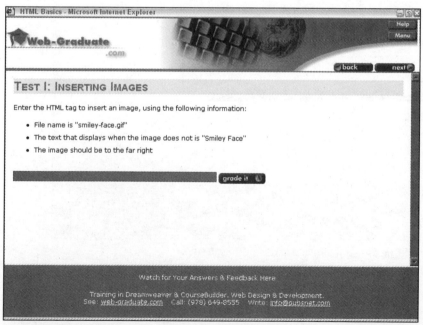

Figure 10-1: A text-entry question from the segment on images in the HTML Basics course

The student is directed to enter the HTML tag for an image element. To successfully answer the question, the student needs to recall

◆ The HTML element:

```
<IMG>
```

◆ The three attributes (including the values for each attribute):

```
src="smiley-face.gif"
alt="Smiley Face"
align="right"
```

◆ The syntax for correctly composing the entire HTML tag.

The student enters the syntax statement and then clicks the Grade It button to submit the answer for evaluation. Figure 10-2 shows one correct answer. As we'll see in the course author's perspective, there are many correct answers that you need to consider when judging this interaction.

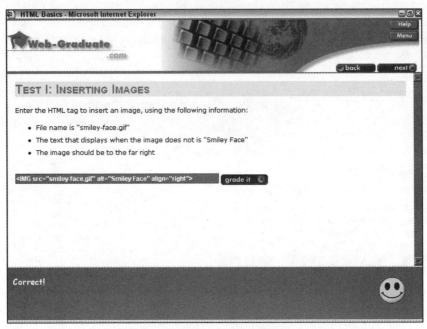

Figure 10-2: One of many correct answers to the question

When the student clicks the Grade It button, the course delivers student feedback in the bottom frame, regardless of what the feedback message is.

The course author's perspective

Let's look at the same text-entry interaction from the course author's perspective. Figure 10-3 shows the Text Entry question opened in Dreamweaver MX.

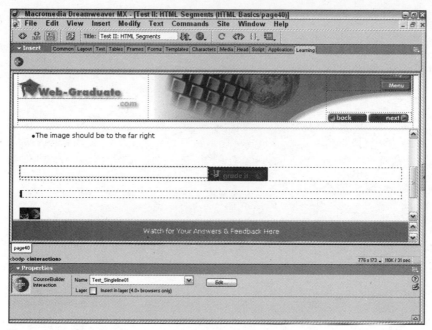

Figure 10-3: The text-entry question open in Dreamweaver MX

The question consists of a single-line text area interaction. This type of text-entry interaction is called Text_Singleline.

To create this interaction, follow these steps (assuming you've opened the file within the frameset):

1. Click the Insert CourseBuilder Interaction button on the Learning tab. The CourseBuilder Interaction dialog box displays, with the CourseBuilder Gallery active.

2. Choose the Text Entry category to display the two text-entry templates (see Figure 10-4). The templates are different in terms of the number of lines only (the first is a single-line text entry, the second is a multiline text entry).

   We want students to enter their answer in the text-entry field and then click the Grade It button to indicate they are finished. Since this is a fill-in-the-blank type interaction, a single-line text box is sufficient. The Text_Singleline template best meets these requirements.

3. Click the Text_Singleline template. CourseBuilder inserts a working copy of the template into your Dreamweaver MX page, and activates the additional tabs for that template (General, Responses, Action Mgr) in the dialog box, as shown in Figure 10-4.

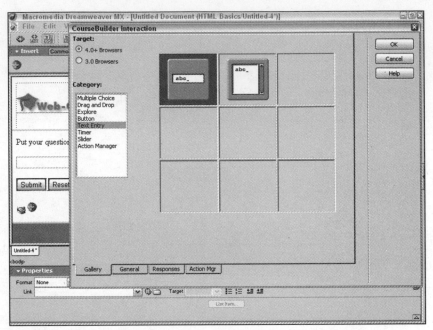

Figure 10-4: The CourseBuilder Gallery with the single line text-entry template Text_Singleline selected

4. Click the General tab to define the general properties for the interaction. Although there is a field for typing the text of a question, our question spans several lines, so we will type it in Dreamweaver MX instead.

5. Select the Judge Interaction option that specifies judgment on a specific event, as shown in Figure 10-5. We're going to use a separate button interaction to initiate judgment of the text-entry interaction, and this option tells CourseBuilder to hold judgment until a specific event (clicking the Grade It button, an event we define later) occurs.

6. Click the Responses tab to define the responses for the interaction. Because of the nature of what we are asking (syntax), we will define only the correct answers and judge every other answer as incorrect.

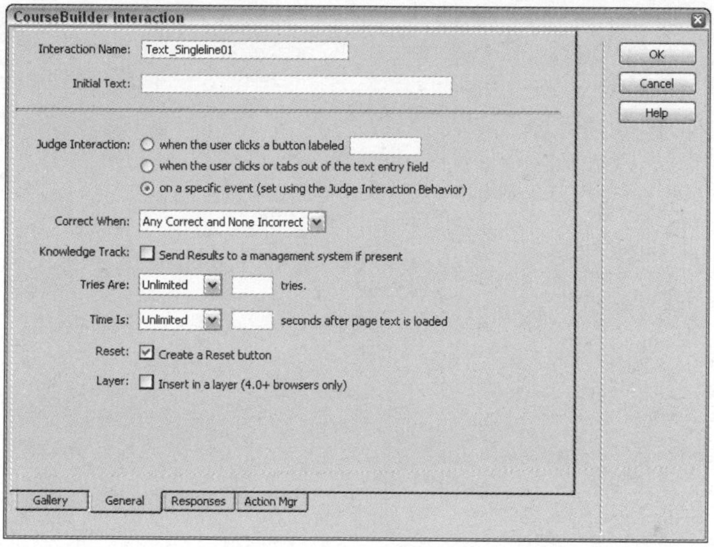

Figure 10-5: General tab for the Text_Singleline interaction. The options for Text_Singleline and Text_Multiline on the General tab are identical.

Before we define the various responses, we need to understand the rules for judging answers as correct or incorrect. To do that for this example, we need to know the HTML syntax rules, which include the following:

- Attributes can be in any order, separated by a space. Because there are three different attributes, there are six permutations of the order of attributes:`<img src="smiley-face.gif" alt="Smiley Face" align="right">`

```
<img src="smiley-face.gif" align="right" alt="Smiley Face">
<img align="right" src="smiley-face.gif" alt="Smiley Face">
<img align="right" alt="Smiley Face" src="smiley-face.gif">
<img alt="Smiley Face" align="right" src="smiley-face.gif">
<img alt="Smiley Face" src="smiley-face.gif" align="right">
```

- Attributes can include a space between the last attribute and the closing angle bracket. That means that the six permutations now double to
  12 permutations to include a blank space before each closing angle
  bracket. Those permutations are

```
<img src="smiley-face.gif" alt="Smiley Face" align="right">
<img src="smiley-face.gif" alt="Smiley Face" align="right" >
<img src="smiley-face.gif" align="right" alt="Smiley Face">
<img src="smiley-face.gif" align="right" alt="Smiley Face" >
<img align="right" src="smiley-face.gif" alt="Smiley Face">
<img align="right" src="smiley-face.gif" alt="Smiley Face" >
<img align="right" alt="Smiley Face" src="smiley-face.gif">
<img align="right" alt="Smiley Face" src="smiley-face.gif" >
<img alt="Smiley Face" align="right" src="smiley-face.gif">
<img alt="Smiley Face" align="right" src="smiley-face.gif" >
<img alt="Smiley Face" src="smiley-face.gif" align="right" >
<img alt="Smiley Face" src="smiley-face.gif" align="right">
```

- HTML elements and attributes are not case sensitive. That means any
  characters, including element and attribute names, can either be lowercase or uppercase, or a mixture of the two.

7. Add nine additional responses by highlighting `Response3` and clicking the
   Add button nine times. (We need to specify a total of 12 correct responses
   for this interaction; by default, CourseBuilder only inserts 3 responses.)
   CourseBuilder inserts them in the Possible Responses list, and we now
   have 12 responses (`Response1` through `Response3`, and `unnamed1` through
   `unnamed9`).

   Because of the nature of the text-entry interaction, we will define only the
   correct responses (there could literally be millions of incorrect responses),
   and judge all other responses as incorrect.

8. Highlight the response `unnamed1` and rename it `Response4` by typing
   Response4 in the Name field; CourseBuilder automatically makes the
   change as soon as you move the cursor to another field or select another
   response on the Possible Responses list. Repeat this step for all of the
   responses, so that you finish with `Response1` through `Response12`. Figure
   10-6 shows the response `unnamed9` about to be changed to `Response12`.

The purpose of this step is for consistent name conventions, and not to fulfill
any processing needs. Since the names of responses are internal only, you
could skip this step.

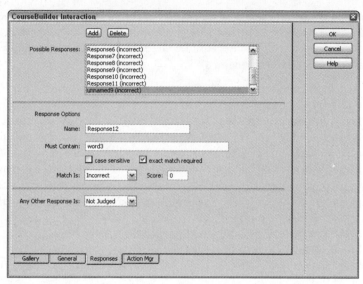

Figure 10-6: Changing the names of all responses so that they are named and numbered consistently on the Responses tab

9. Highlight each response and enter the text for a correct choice in the Must Contain field. Enter the text for each possible correct response in a separate response (Response1 through Response12, representing the 12 correct permutations). Figure 10-7 shows the Must Contain field for the first response (Response1) being changed to the first of the 12 permutations for correct responses.

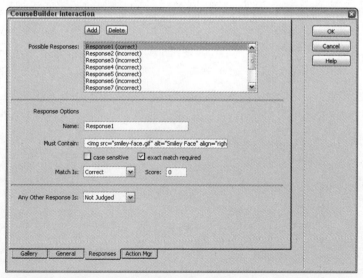

Figure 10-7: Changing the responses to reflect the 12 possible correct choices in the Must Contain field

By default, the case sensitive box is not checked, meaning that uppercase and lowercase letters of the alphabet are interpreted as the same character. Leave the box unchecked because HTML does not differentiate between uppercase and lowercase letters.

Enter all 12 permutations, once for each response, as follows:

```
<img src="smiley-face.gif" alt="Smiley Face" align="right">
<img src="smiley-face.gif" alt="Smiley Face" align="right" >
<img src="smiley-face.gif" align="right" alt="Smiley Face">
<img src="smiley-face.gif" align="right" alt="Smiley Face" >
<img align="right" src="smiley-face.gif" alt="Smiley Face">
<img align="right" src="smiley-face.gif" alt="Smiley Face" >
<img align="right" alt="Smiley Face" src="smiley-face.gif">
<img align="right" alt="Smiley Face" src="smiley-face.gif" >
<img alt="Smiley Face" align="right" src="smiley-face.gif">
<img alt="Smiley Face" align="right" src="smiley-face.gif" >
<img alt="Smiley Face" src="smiley-face.gif" align="right" >
<img alt="Smiley Face" src="smiley-face.gif" align="right">
```

10. Change each response so that the Match Is field is Correct for *each* response.

11. Set the Any Other Response Is field to Incorrect (you only need to set this once, regardless of the number of responses you have). The Responses tab should now look similar to the one shown in Figure 10-8.

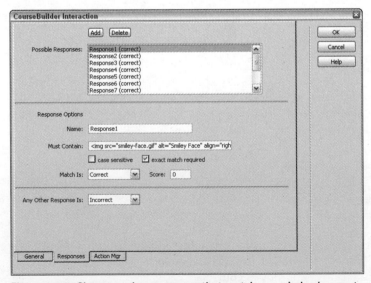

Figure 10-8: Change each response so that matches are judged correct and all other responses are judged incorrect.

12. Click the Action Manager (Action Mgr) tab. CourseBuilder displays the default rules for processing this interaction, defining CourseBuilder actions for correct, incorrect, and unknown student responses (see Figure 10-9).

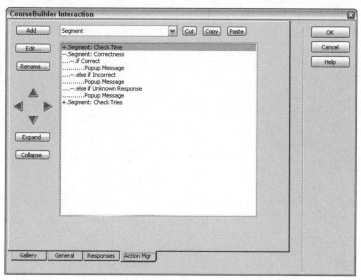

Figure 10-9: By default, the Action Manager displays a pop-up message for each condition (correct, incorrect, and unknown response).

13. Highlight each Popup Message action in the Action Manager tab and click the Cut button to delete it. Since the design of our course sends student feedback to the bottom frame (named blackboard), we need to delete each Popup Message in the Action Manager, and insert a Set Text of Frame action instead (so that we can write text messages to the bottom frame). To do this, you must do this separately for each message; there is no way to cut all three actions at once.

14. Click the if Correct condition in the Action Manager to highlight it. Now any actions we add are added to that highlighted condition.

15. Select the Set Text of Frame action from the Action Manager drop-down menu, as shown in Figure 10-10.

16. Click the Add button on the Action Manager tab to add the Set Text of Frame action to the if Correct condition. CourseBuilder displays the Set Text of Frame dialog box. You can enter simple text, or you can format that text with HTML tags, depending on the effect you want. The example in Figure 10-11 shows the HTML tags for the correct state of this interaction in the *HTML Basics* course.

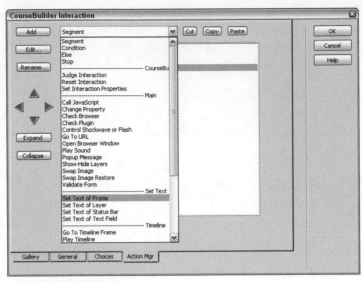

Figure 10-10: Select the Set Text of Frame action.

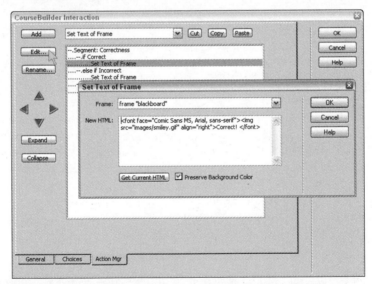

Figure 10-11: Enter the text for student feedback when they answer correctly (defined by the if Correct contition). This text is written to the frame named blackboard.

17. Repeat Steps 14-16 for the if Incorrect and if Unknown Response conditions as well.

Figure 10-12 shows a flowchart that diagrams the decisions and actions taken by the Action Manager when processing this single line text-entry interaction.

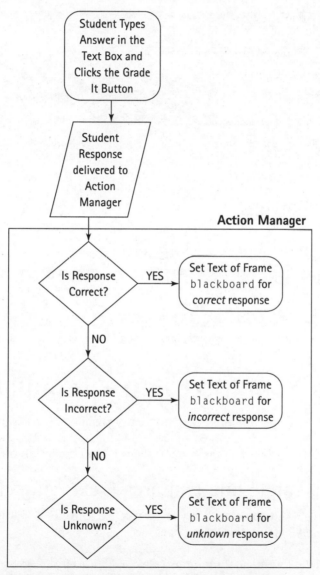

Figure 10–12: Processing of the single-line text-entry interaction in the Action Manager

18. Click OK when you've completed defining the rules in the Action Manager. CourseBuilder writes the processing rules into the HTML file, and displays text-entry question in Dreamweaver MX, similar to Figure 10-13.

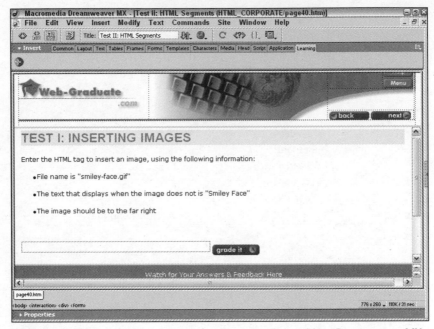

Figure 10-13: The single-line text-entry interaction inserted into Dreamweaver MX

Choosing Your Text Entry Template

The CourseBuilder Gallery contains two text-entry templates, as shown in Figure 10-14.

The significant different between the two templates is the number of lines.

Choosing single line text area (Text_Singleline)

Use the Text_Singleline template when you want a text-entry box that is a single line (or smaller). By default, this interaction

◆ Inserts a single-line standard form text field, with a width of 24 characters visible. You can easily change the size by selecting the text field in Dreamweaver MX and entering a different character width (Char Width field) on the Properties panel.

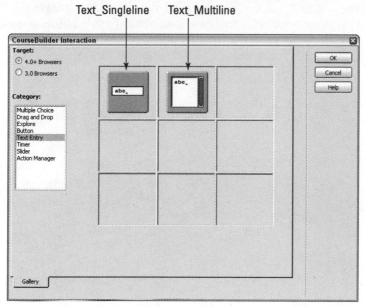

Figure 10-14: Text-entry templates available in the CourseBuilder Gallery

◆ Inserts and judges the interaction when students click a Submit button. You have the option for automatic judgment (when the student leaves the text field by clicking or tabbing elsewhere); or you can have the interaction judged by a specific event, such as a button or slider interaction (General tab).

◆ Judges an answer correct if any are correct (General tab).

◆ Inserts a Reset button to allow students to erase what they've typed and start over (General tab).

◆ Provides three choices — `Response1` is correct; `Response2` and `Response3` are incorrect (Responses tab).

◆ Requires an exact match. For answers to be judged correct, students' answers must be exactly the same as the answer in the Must Contain field, including punctuation and spacing, although capitalization may vary (Responses tab).

◆ Is not set case sensitive. Students may vary the capitalization of an answer and still have that answer judged as correct as long as it matches everything else in the answer in the Must Contain field. Thus, "Smiley Face", "smiley face", and "SMILEY FACE" would all be interpreted as the same answer (Responses tab).

◆ Does not judge any response that is not specified as correct or incorrect, meaning the response is an unknown response. In most applications you want to change any other response to be incorrect, so that answers that aren't specifically judged as correct or incorrect default to incorrect (Responses tab).

You can modify these defaults on the General and Responses tabs. Figure 10-15 shows the default layout for the Text_Singleline interaction after it is inserted into Dreamweaver MX.

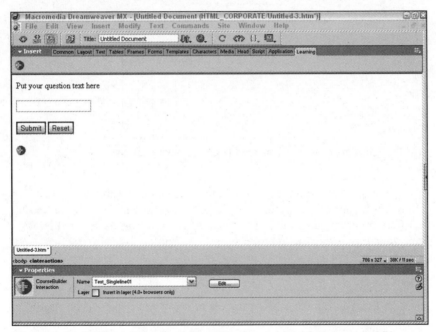

Figure 10-15: The Text_Singleline interaction, inserted into Dreamweaver MX

Choosing multiple-line text area (Text_Multiline)

Use the Text_Multiline template when you want a text-entry box that has multiple lines. By default, this interaction

◆ Inserts a multiple-line standard form text area field, with a width of 40 characters and a length of 4 lines visible. You can easily change the size by selecting the text field in Dreamweaver MX and entering a different character width or number of lines (Char Width and Num Lines fields) on the Properties panel.

◆ Inserts and judges the interaction when students click a Submit button. You have the option for automatic judgment (when the student leaves the text field by clicking or tabbing elsewhere); or you can have the interaction judged by a specific event, such as a button or slider interaction (General tab).

◆ Judges an answer correct if any are correct (General tab).

◆ Inserts a Reset button to allow students to erase what they've typed and start over (General tab).

◆ Provides three choices — `Response1` is correct; `Response2` and `Response3` are incorrect (Responses tab).

◆ Does *not* require an exact match. For answers to be judged correct, a student answer *must contain* the answer in the Must Contain field somewhere within it. However, the student's answer may contain additional text and still be judged as correct (Responses tab).

For example, assume the Must Contain field identifies a correct response as *farm,* and the student answer is *Old McDonald Had a Farm.* Because the word or phrase in the Must Contain field (the correct answer) is found within the student's answer, the student's answer is judged as correct (Responses tab).

◆ Is not set case sensitive. Students may vary the capitalization of an answer and still have that answer judged as correct as long as it matches everything else in the answer in the Must Contain field. Thus, "Smiley Face", "smiley face", and "SMILEY FACE" would all be interpreted as the same answer (Responses tab).

◆ Does not judge any response that is not specified as correct or incorrect, meaning the response is an unknown response. In most applications you want to change any other response to be incorrect, so that answers that aren't specifically judged as correct or incorrect default to incorrect (Responses tab).

You can modify these defaults on the General and Responses tabs. Figure 10-16 shows the default layout for the `Text_Multiline` interaction after it is inserted into Dreamweaver MX.

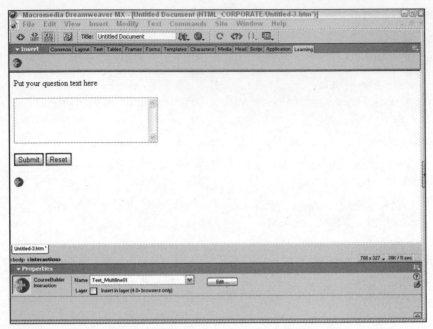

Figure 10–16: The Text_Multiline interaction inserted into Dreamweaver MX

TIP Generally speaking, you'll find very little use for this interaction. There are too many lines to make it an effective fill-in-the-blank test. If you are looking for a mechanism for allowing an essay response that is not automatically graded, I would suggest using a similar Text Area box within a form, and having the results e-mailed to a human evaluator.

Defining the Responses Tab Properties

The Responses tab is unique to text entry interactions. Figure 10-17 shows the Responses tab with the default settings for the Text_Singleline interaction.

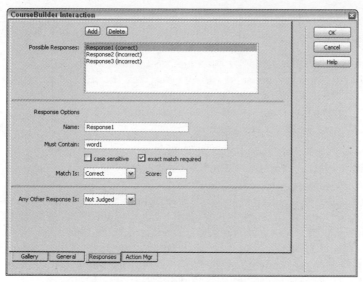

Figure 10-17: The Responses tab for the Text_Singleline interaction

On the Responses tab, you:

- ◆ Define each correct and incorrect response (normally, you would define incorrect responses only if you wanted to give feedback for a specific incorrect response). To define a response as correct or incorrect, highlight each response in the Possible Responses list, and select Correct or Incorrect from the Match Is drop-down menu (define one at a time for each response).

- ◆ Add or delete a possible response. Add new responses by clicking the Add button, or delete existing responses by highlighting an existing response and clicking the Delete button.

- ◆ Specify a name for each response, which is an internal name used for processing.

- ◆ Define the content of each response in the Must Contain field. The Must Contain field identifies the text that a student response must contain to be declared a match. Once a match is found, it is up to the Match Is field to determine whether a match constitutes a correct, incorrect, or not-judged response.

- ◆ Choose whether case sensitivity matters in determining the match. If check case sensitive, the case of the letter (uppercase or lowercase) must also match. For example, if case sensitive is checked, "HTML" and "html" are different responses; if case sensitive is *not* checked, "HTML" and "html" are seen as the same response.

- Choose whether an exact match is required. If checked, a student answer must exactly match the answer in the Must Contain field to be a match. If unchecked, a student answer must contain the possible response, but can contain additional text as well. For example, assume the Must Contain field identifies a correct response as *the first day,* and the student answer is *Today is the first day of the rest of my life.* Because the word or phrase in the Must Contain field (the correct answer) is found within the student's answer, the student's answer is judged as correct.

- Specify whether each response should be judged as Correct, Incorrect, or Not Judged by selecting from the Match Is drop-down menu. This field determines the evaluation for a match. If the student response matches a response in the list of Possible Responses, does a match mean correct, incorrect, or not judged? Normally you would judge a match as correct; however, there may be times where a match means incorrect or not judged. For example, you may include specific incorrect responses that, when matched with the student's response, give you the opportunity to explain to the student exactly why the student's response is incorrect. Assume the question is "How many fluid ounces in a quart?" You would make a student answer of 32 a match for the correct answer. You might also make a student answer of 128 a match for an incorrect answer, and have the Action Manager display a message such as, "Incorrect. There are 128 fluid ounces in a gallon, not a quart."

- Define the score for each choice. Scoring and tracking is covered in detail in Part IV of this book. Briefly, the score is the numeric value you put on each choice. You'd usually set positive values for correct answers, and leave incorrect answers blank. You can, however, using negative scores for incorrect choices to deduct points for wrong answers.

- Choose whether student answers that are *not* on the Possible Responses list should be judged as Correct, Incorrect, or Not Judged by selecting from the Any Other Response Is drop-down menu. When CourseBuilder matches the student response against the list of Possible Responses, what happens if there no match is found? This field specifies how to handle those cases. Normally, any other response would be set to Incorrect.

Application Example

Let's examine an example that is designed to give you ideas about how to use text-entry interactions to judge a series of fill-in-the-blank tests. The files for this example are contained on the CD-ROM that shipped with this book.

Devised by journalist Wilson Taylor in the early 1950s, Cloze procedures were designed to measure the readability of text. As they were originally designed, Cloze procedures called for every n*th* word (every 5th; every 10th; or some other number) to be deleted and replaced with a blank. Readers were then asked to fill in the missing words.

The theory of the Cloze procedure was that a higher percentage of correct fill-ins meant the material was easier to read (0–49% meant the material was very difficult; 40–60% meant the material was moderately difficult; 60–100% meant the material was easy).

Since the 1950s, the Cloze procedure has been redesigned as a method of testing the understanding of vocabulary in context. There are many variations of Cloze procedures for testing (you can find many books about it at Amazon.Com and elsewhere). The example of the Cloze test we're discussing here can be used as a model for any fill-in-the-blank test.

Selecting the passage

To develop this test, we used the following excerpt from *A History of Science* (Henry Smith Williams, Volume I). The words in bold are omitted from the test, and the student is asked to type in the missing word by selecting from a list of omitted words:

Primitive man must have conceived that the earth is flat and of **limitless** extent. By this it is not meant to imply that he had a distinct **conception** of infinity, but, for that matter, it cannot be said that any one today has a conception of infinity that could be called definite. But, reasoning from **experience** and the reports of travellers, there was nothing to suggest to early man the limit of the earth. He did, indeed, find in his **wanderings**, that changed climatic conditions barred him from farther progress; but beyond the farthest reaches of his **migrations**, the seemingly flat land-surfaces and water-surfaces stretched away unbroken and, to all appearances, without end. It would require a reach of the philosophical **imagination** to conceive a limit to the earth, and while such imaginings may have been current in the prehistoric period, we can have no proof of them, and we may well postpone consideration of man's early dreamings as to the shape of the earth until we enter the historical epoch where we stand on firm ground.

The student's perspective

Before we discuss the coding of the Cloze test, let's take a look at the example from the student's perspective. Figure 10-18 shows an example of the Cloze test in Internet Explorer.

Once the student answers, each response is judged as a separate interaction, giving specific feedback for any incorrect answer, as shown in Figure 10-19.

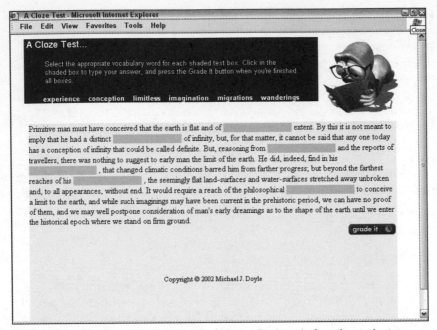

Figure 10-18: Example of a Cloze test in Internet Explorer before the student answers.

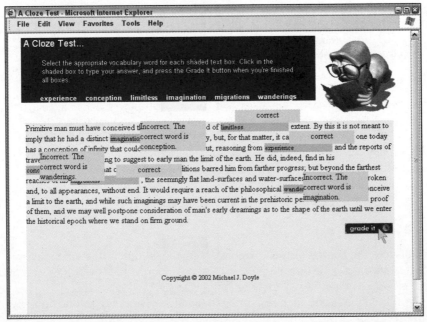

Figure 10-19: Example of test after the student answers and clicks the Grade It button

The course author's perspective

This interaction required the following elements:

- ◆ A layer at the top of the page that contains an introduction.

- ◆ A layer containing the decorative image of the bookworm.

- ◆ A layer containing the passage of text.

- ◆ Six single-line text-entry interactions, one for each text-entry box.

- ◆ Six hidden layers placed near each text-entry box for delivering the feedback (correct and incorrect messages).

- ◆ One button interaction (the Grade It button), which initiates judgment of the text-entry interactions.

The key to the design of this interaction is controlling the placement of the text passage, the text-entry boxes, and the layers for feedback on each text-entry interaction. To begin, set up the file as shown in Figure 10-20, with three layers: one for the introduction, one containing the bookworm, and one containing the passage of text.

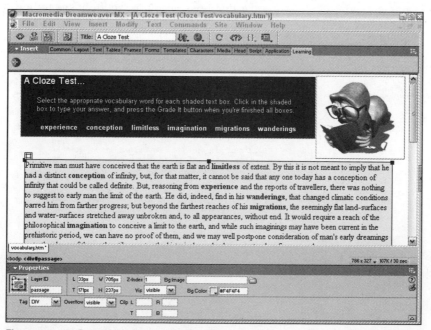

Figure 10-20: Set up three layers in the file.

After the file is set up, insert the first text-entry interaction for the vocabulary term *limitless* (the first bolded term in the text passage) by following these steps:

1. Click the Insert CourseBuilder Interaction button on the Learning tab.

2. Choose the Text Entry category from the Category list.

3. Select the `Text_Singleline` template.

4. Select the Judge Interaction on a specific event option. The judgment of the first text-entry interaction will be initiated by students clicking the Grade It button; judgment of each successive text-entry interaction will be initiated in the Action Manager by the previous text-entry interaction.

5. Deselect the Create a Reset button field on the General tab.

6. Highlight and delete `Response2` and `Response3` from the Responses tab.

7. Highlight `Response1` and enter the following settings:

   - Must Contain field should be limitless (the correct word for the blank)

   - Exact match required should be checked

   - Match Is: Correct

   - Any Other Response Is: Incorrect.

8. Rearrange the text as you insert each text-entry box into the file. For example, Figure 10-21 shows the first text-entry interaction inserted into Dreamweaver MX.

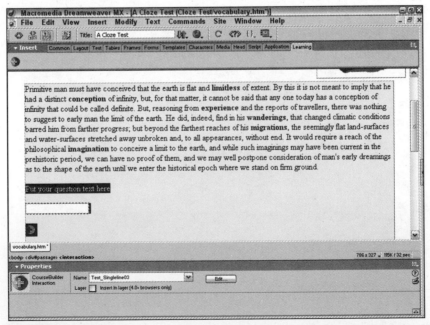

Figure 10-21: The first text-entry interaction, named Text_Singleline01, inserted into Dreamweaver MX.

Click and drag the text-entry box to the location of the word *limitless* in the text passage, and delete the word limitless. Also, delete the additional instructions inserted by the interaction ("Put your question text here").

9. Draw a layer (click the Draw Layer icon on the Common tab of the Objects panel) near the text-entry box. This layer will be used as a container for feedback to the student. By inserting the original text passage into a layer and using layers for feedback, you can be sure that the feedback layers will remain next to the appropriate text-entry box.

10. Select the layer and set the following properties for that layer in the Properties panel:

- Rename the Layer ID to limitless (easier to remember later).

- Change Overflow to visible, so that the layer resizes itself automatically for various levels of feedback.

- Change Vis to hidden, so that the layer is initially hidden when the page displays in the browser window.

- Set the Bg Color to yellow to make the layer stand out from surrounding text.

After you insert the first text-entry box, your screen should look similar to Figure 10-22.

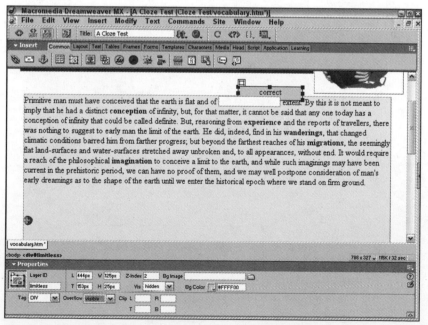

Figure 10-22: The first text-entry interaction, Text_Singleline01, moved to its proper location in the text passage, and the feedback layer drawn next to it

11. Repeat the preceding steps for each text-entry box (Text_Singleline02 through Text_Singleline06).

Once you have all text-entry boxes inserted, you can insert the button interaction that launches judgment of the first text-entry box, as follows:

1. Click the Insert CourseBuilder Interaction button on the Learning tab. CourseBuilder displays the CourseBuilder Gallery.

2. Select the Button category to display the button templates.

3. Click the Button_Push template to insert a push-button. We'll use the default push button for this exercise; to use a custom button like the Grade It button in the example, refer to Chapter 15.

4. Click the Action Manager (Action Mgr) tab.

5. Highlight the Button Feedback segment.

6. Select Judge Interaction from the drop-down menu.

7. Click the Add button to add the Judge Interaction to the Button Feedback segment. CourseBuilder displays the Judge Interaction dialog box, as shown in Figure 10-23.

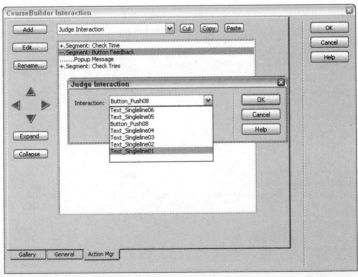

Figure 10-23: Inserting a Judge Interaction into the Action Manager for a button interaction

8. Select Text_Singleline01 and click OK.

9. Highlight and delete the `Popup Message` action in the Button Feedback segment.

10. Click OK to return to Dreamweaver MX.

Now you've included a button that, when clicked, is directed by the button's Action Manager to Judge Interaction `Text_Singleline01`. We still need to define the Action Manager instructions for each text-entry box (`Text_Singleline01` through `Text_Singleline06`).

To edit `Text_Singleline01`, highlight the CourseBuilder icon for that interaction in the document window and click the Edit button on the Properties Panel. The CourseBuilder Interaction dialog box opens. Click on the Action Manager tab, and CourseBuilder displays the Action Manager with the default actions for `Text_Singleline01`.

Change the `if Correct` condition so that it

◆ Shows the layer named `limitless` (remember that we typed the word Correct in each layer, so we don't need to change the text if the student's answer is judged as correct).

◆ Judges the next interaction in the sequence (`Text_Singleline02`, as shown in Figure 10-24).

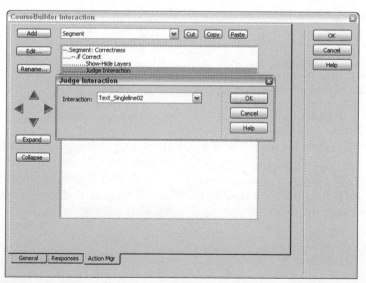

Figure 10-24: The Action Manager for Text_Singleline01 launching the judgment of interaction Text_Singleline02

Change the `if Incorrect` condition so that it

◆ Shows the layer named `limitless`.

◆ Sets the text of the layer named `limitless` so that it changes the text from the default message ("Correct") to a specific incorrect answer, as shown in Figure 10-25.

◆ Judges the next interaction in the sequence (`Text_Singleline02`).

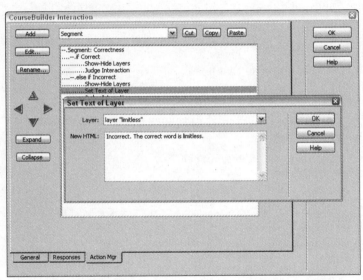

Figure 10-25: Defining the message in the layer named limitless for incorrect answers

Repeat this process for the rest of the text-entry interactions (except for the final text entry interaction), making sure that each text-entry interaction initiates the judgment of the next text-entry interaction in the Action Manager. Since the final text entry interaction does not need to initiate judgment of another interaction, *do not* insert a Judge Interaction in the `Text_Singleline06` conditions.

Summary

In this chapter you learned

- ◆ To choose single-line or multiple-line text-entry interactions, depending on requirements.

- ◆ How text-entry interactions work from both the student and course author's perspectives.

- ◆ To define each field on the Responses tab, which is unique to text-entry interactions.

- ◆ To create a Cloze test, which strings the processing of numerous text-entry interactions together.

The next chapter describes how to create Drag and Drop (match-up) interactions.

Chapter 11

Drag-and-Drop (Match-up) Interactions

IN THIS CHAPTER

◆ Understanding Drag and Drop interactions from the student's and course author's perspectives

◆ Choosing the appropriate drag-and-drop template in the CourseBuilder gallery

◆ Defining options on the Elements and Pairs tabs, which are unique to Drag and Drop interactions

◆ Understanding snaps

◆ Seeing two different applications of the Drag and Drop interaction

DRAG-AND-DROP INTERACTIONS are variations on traditional match-up tests, and require students to recognize associations – or relationships – between elements (text and/or pictures). On paper tests, students typically are asked to draw lines between matching elements, similar to Figure 11-1.

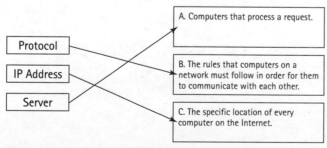

Figure 11-1: A traditional paper-based match-up test

With CourseBuilder drag-and-drop interactions, students drag elements (text or pictures) and drop them on matching target elements, indicating an association or relationship between the elements.

Understanding How Drag-and-Drop Interactions Work

To grasp the concepts behind drag-and-drop interactions, it is important that you understand the interaction's process from both the student's perspective (how it works) and a course author's perspective (how you create it). Let's examine the student's perspective first.

The student's perspective

To see how drag-and-drop interactions work from a student's perspective, take a look at a drag-and-drop interaction from the *HTML Basics* course. Figure 11-2 shows an example.

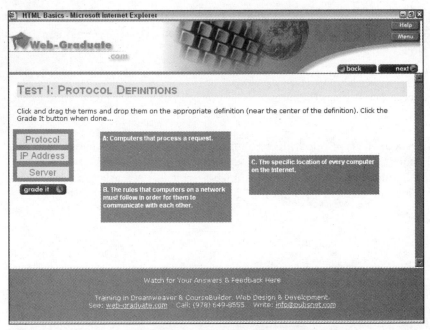

Figure 11-2: A drag-and-drop question from the HTML Basics course

The example question provides three drag elements (the terms Protocol, IP Address, and Server) and three target elements (definitions labeled A, B, and C).

The student is directed to click and drag the terms (drag elements) and drop them on the appropriate definitions (target elements), and to click the Grade It button when done.

When the student clicks the Grade It button for evaluation, the course delivers student feedback (correct, incorrect, or unknown response) in the bottom frame, as shown in Figure 11-3.

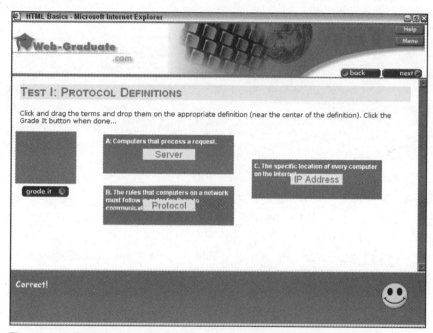

Figure 11-3: Student feedback from the drag-and-drop question in the HTML Basics course

The course author's perspective

Now let's look at the same drag-and-drop interaction from the course author's perspective. Figure 11-4 shows interaction open in Dreamweaver MX.

The interaction is a Drag_ManyToMany template, as identified in the Properties panel. This particular interaction contains a matching drag element for every target element. CourseBuilder offers many variations on the drag-and-drop interaction, as you'll see later in the chapter.

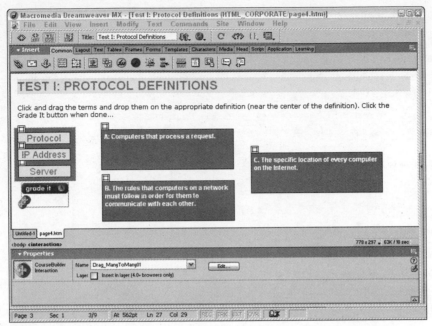

Figure 11-4: The example drag-and-drop question open in Dreamweaver MX

To create this drag-and-drop interaction, follow these steps (assuming you've opened the file within the frameset):

1. Click the Insert CourseBuilder Interaction button on the Learning tab. The CourseBuilder Interaction dialog box displays, with the CourseBuilder Gallery active.

2. Choose the Drag and Drop category to display the seven drag-and-drop templates (see Figure 11-5). Each template is different in terms of the number of drag and target elements, the elements that can be moved, and the sequence of each drag-and-drop.

For this example, we want to

- Allow only the drag elements (terms) to move, meaning that the target elements remain stationary.

- Have multiple drag elements (three terms) and multiple target elements (three definitions), with each drag element having only one correct match, giving us a total of three correct pairs (match-ups).

- Students to click the Grade It button when they are ready for evaluation. This affords students the opportunity to change their minds (and their responses) until they click the Grade It button.

3. Select the `Drag_ManyToMany` template, which best meets our requirements. CourseBuilder inserts a working copy of the template into your Dreamweaver MX page, and activates the additional tabs for that template (General, Elements, Pairs, Action Mgr) in the dialog box, as shown in Figure 11-5.

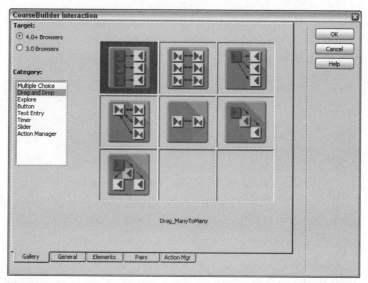

Figure 11-5: The CourseBuilder Gallery with the Drag_ManyToMany template selected

4. Click the General tab (shown in Figure 11-6) to define the general properties for the interaction.

5. Select Judge Interaction on a specific event (set using the Judge Interaction) to require students to click the Grade It button for evaluation.

   The Correct When field specifies All Correct and None Incorrect by default. Maintain this setting because we *only* want to declare an answer as correct when the student correctly matches *all three* pairings.

6. Uncheck the Create a Reset button option because the design of this interaction does not call for one. CourseBuilder removes the Reset button from the interaction in the Dreamweaver MX page.

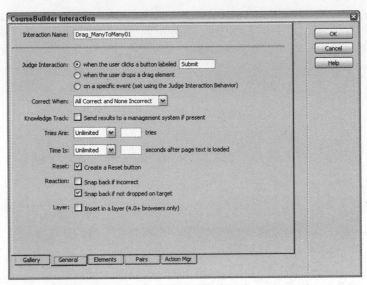

Figure 11–6: General tab for the Drag_ManyToMany interaction

7. Select your snap back options in the Reaction field, which is unique to drag-and-drop interactions. It has two snap back settings:

- **Snap back if incorrect.** If checked, this setting specifies that drag elements dropped anywhere except on the correct target are automatically returned to their original position. Use this setting if you do not want to allow incorrect answers (for example, when creating activities). By default, this is not checked, so we don't need to change the setting for this interaction.

- **Snap back if not dropped on target.** If checked, this setting specifies that drag elements dropped anywhere except on a target (correct or incorrect) are automatically returned to their original position. Use this setting if you do not want to allow drag elements to be dropped into non-target areas. It is selected by default, so uncheck it for this interaction.

8. Click on the Elements tab (shown in Figure 11-7) to define each element in the interaction.

With the other interactions, you typically define both the options (choices in Multiple Choice, responses in Text Entry, ranges in Sliders, hot areas in Explore) and the judgment of correct and incorrect on a single tab (Choices tab for Multiple Choice, Responses tab for Text Entry, Ranges tab for Sliders, Hot Areas tab with Explore). With drag-and-drop interactions, however, you need to define more information about the options, so the definitions are spread across *two* tabs: Elements and Pairs.

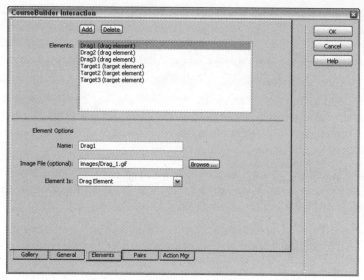

Figure 11-7: The Elements tab for a drag-and-drop interaction.

The Elements tab defines each element used in the drag-and-drop interaction, and identifies each element as a drag element, a target element, or both. Since our interaction has three drag elements and three target elements, which is the default, we don't need to add or subtract elements. (To add an element, simply click the Add button, and then define the new element's characteristics in the Element Options section of the tab. To delete an element, highlight it and click the Delete button.)

Note that various templates provide different numbers and definitions of elements on this tab. The Drag_2wayManyToMany template, for example, includes a total of six elements, each set to be Both Drag and Target on the Element Is field (because the template allows any element to be dragged to any other element, so all elements in effect are drag elements *and* target elements).

By default, each drag element is named Drag (Drag1, Drag2, Drag3) and each target element is named Target (Target1, Target2, Target3). Since the name is used only for internal processing, we do not need to change them.

If you add more elements (for example, an additional drag and target element), they will be named unnamed1 and unnnamed2. You can then manually change their names to be Drag4 and Target4. Adding more elements just continues this numbering sequence of unnamed3, unnamed4, and so forth.

The Image File field identifies an image to be contained within an element. If you are using images for drag or target elements, you can browse to each image file to specify the image for that element. By default, CourseBuilder uses placeholder images that you replace in Dreamweaver MX with images, text, or other objects.

The Element Is drop-down menu identifies whether an element is a drag element, a target element, or both. If an element is identified as either a drag element or both a drag and target element, it can be moved and dropped. Target elements remain stationary.

The terms in our example are defined as drag elements and the definitions are defined as target elements, so students can move the terms to the definitions, but they cannot move the definitions.

9. Click the Pairs tab (see Figure 11-8) to define each correct *and* incorrect pairing (match-up) of drag element to target element.

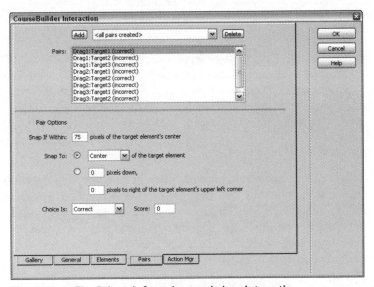

Figure 11-8: The Pairs tab for a drag-and-drop interaction

The Pairs tab enables you to identify the correct (and incorrect) match-ups based on the elements you defined in the Elements tab. By default, CourseBuilder defines each matching drag and target number as correct, and all other matches as incorrect. So, for example, Drag1 to Target1, Drag2 to Target2, and Drag3 to Target3 are, by default, correct, and Drag2 to Target1, Drag3 to Target1, and so forth are incorrect.

If you add more elements to the mix, CourseBuilder does not define those elements by default. You must manually add them from the Pairs drop-down menu (see in Figure 11-9). The addition of just two drag and two target elements dramatically increases the number of possible combinations, as the figure shows.

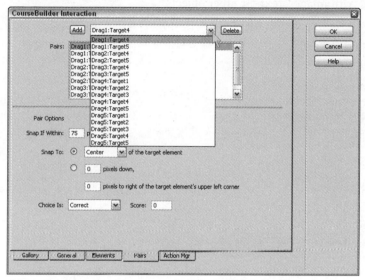

Figure 11-9: The Pairs tab showing additional pairs (match-up combinations) when other elements were added on the Elements tab

TIP

If you have many possible pairings of drag and target elements, a quicker approach is to define only correct pairs t. Then, when you create the processing logic in the Action Manager, you can set two conditions: `if Correct` and `else`. If the student answers correctly, the `if Correct` logic is processed; all other answers are processed by the `else` condition.

The Pairs tab is discussed more fully later in this chapter, in the section titled, "Defining the Elements and Pairs Tab Properties."

10. Click the Action Manager (Action Mgr) tab. CourseBuilder displays the default rules for processing this interaction, defining CourseBuilder actions for correct, incorrect, and unknown student responses.

11. Delete each Popup Message in the Action Manager and insert a Set Text of Frame action instead. By default, the Action Manager displays a popup message saying "Correct" for the `if Correct` condition, and a popup message saying "Incorrect" for the `else if Incorrect` condition. Highlight each Popup Message action in the Action Manager tab and click the Cut button to delete it.

12. Click the `if Correct` condition in the Action Manager, as shown in Figure 11-10.

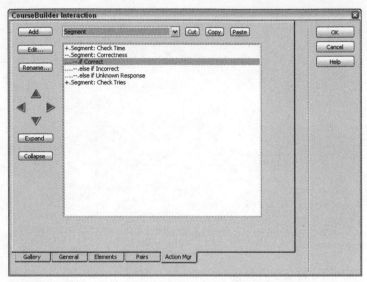

Figure 11-10: The Action Manager after the Popup Message actions have been deleted and before the Set Text of Frame actions are added

Now that the `if Correct` condition is active (highlighted), any actions we add are added to it.

13. Select the Set Text of Frame action from the Action Manager drop-down menu, and click the Add button.

CourseBuilder displays the Set Text of Frame dialog box.

14. Select the `blackboard` frame from the Frame drop-down menu.

15. Enter the text for the message that you want displayed in the `blackboard` frame when students answer correctly. You can enter simple text, or you can format that text with HTML tags, depending on the effect you want.

You can enter simple text, or you can format that text with HTML tags, depending on the effect you want.

16. Repeat Steps 12–15 for the `if Incorrect` and `if Unknown Response` conditions as well. Figure 11-11 shows the HTML tags for the incorrect state of this interaction in the *HTML Basics* course.

17. Click OK when you've completed defining the rules in the Action Manager. CourseBuilder writes the processing rules into the HTML file, and displays the drag-and-drop interaction in Dreamweaver MX, similar to Figure 11-12.

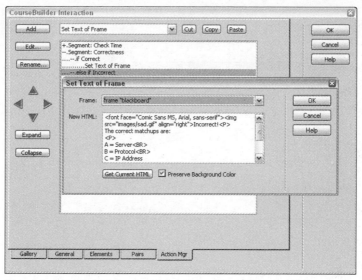

Figure 11-11: This feedback text is written to the frame named blackboard when the student answers incorrectly.

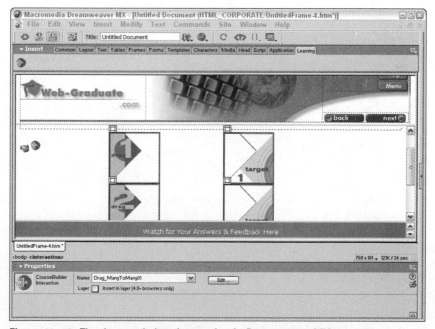

Figure 11-12: The drag-and-drop interaction in Dreamweaver MX

Figure 11-13 shows a flowchart of the decisions and actions taken by the Action Manager when processing this drag-and-drop interaction.

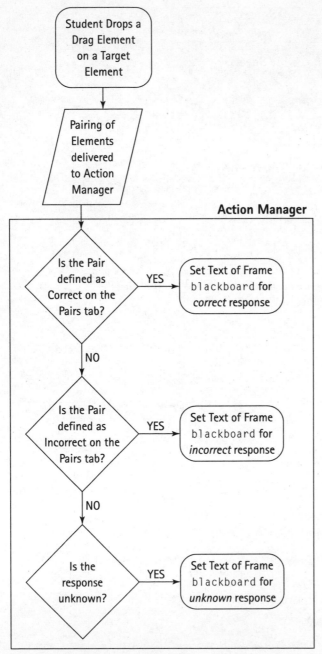

Figure 11–13: Processing of the drag–and–drop interaction in the Action Manager

Once the interaction is written into Dreamweaver MX, you can rearrange the layout. In the *HTML Basics* course, for example, the images in the drag elements and target elements were replaced with text, and the layers containing the text were stylized using Cascading Style Sheets.

Choosing Your Drag-and-Drop Template

The CourseBuilder Gallery contains seven drag-and-drop templates, as shown in Figure 11-14.

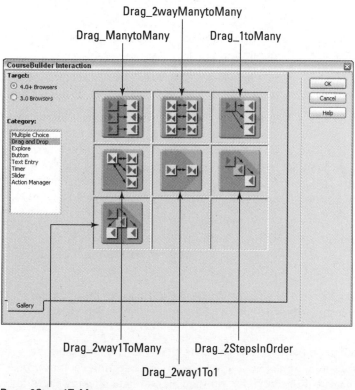

Figure 11-14: Drag-and-drop templates available in the CourseBuilder Gallery

The significant differences between the seven templates are the number of elements, the number of moveable and stationary elements, and whether or not sequence matters.

Choosing multiple drag and target elements (Drag_ManyToMany)

Use the `Drag_ManyToMany` template when you want an interaction that has multiple drag and multiple target elements, with the target elements remaining stationary. By default, this interaction

- ◆ Judges the interaction when students click a Submit button. Other options are for automatic judgment (when the student drops a drag element) and for initiating judging by a specific event, such as a button or slider interaction (General tab).

- ◆ Judges an answer correct if *all* are correct and *none* incorrect (General tab).

- ◆ Inserts a Reset button to allow students to return elements to their original position and start over (General tab).

- ◆ Snaps elements back to their original position if they are dropped anywhere but on a target (General tab).

- ◆ Provides six elements: three drag elements named `Drag1` through `Drag3`, and three target elements named `Target1` through `Target3` (Elements tab).

- ◆ Names any additional drag and target elements that you add as unnamed (`unnamed1`, `unnamed2`, `unnamed3`, and so forth) regardless of whether the added element is a drag or target. You can rename them in the Name field (If you highlight a drag element and click the Add button, CourseBuilder adds an additional drag element. If you highlight a target element and click the Add button, CourseBuilder adds an additional target element.) (Elements tab).

- ◆ Defines all nine possible pairings, with three pairs (`Drag1:Target1`, `Drag2:Target2`, and `Drag3:Target3`) set to correct: All other possible combinations are set to incorrect (Pairs tab).

- ◆ Sets each drag element to snap to the center of a target if the student drops that element within 75 pixels of a target's center. See the section, "Pairs tab," later in this chapter for more details (Pairs tab).

- ◆ Does not include in the Pairs list any new elements you added on the Elements tab. You add the new ones manually be selecting each new possible pair from the drop-down list on the Pairs tab and clicking the Add button (Pairs tab).

You can modify these defaults on the General, Elements, and Pairs tabs. Figure 11-15 shows the default layout for the `Drag_ManyToMany` interaction after it is inserted into Dreamweaver MX.

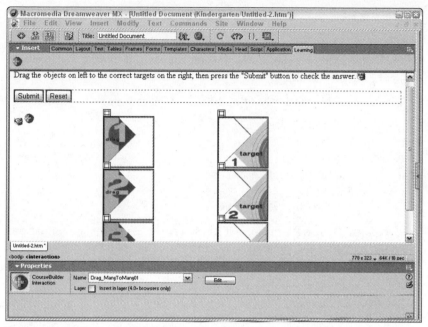

Figure 11-15: The Drag_ManyToMany interaction, inserted into Dreamweaver MX

Choosing multiple elements, all dragable to each other (Drag_2wayManyToMany)

Use the Drag_2wayManyToMany template when you want an interaction that uses multiple elements, each serving as both drag *and* target elements (you can drag any element to any other element). By default, this interaction

◆ Judges the interaction when students click a Submit button. You can select automatic judgment (when the student drops any element); or you can have the interaction judged by a specific event, such as a button or slider interaction (General tab).

◆ Judges an answer correct if *all* are correct and *none* incorrect (General tab).

◆ Inserts a Reset button to allow students to return elements to their original positions and start over (General tab).

◆ Provides six elements, each serving the dual role of drag element *and* target element, allowing all six elements to move: DragTarget1 through DragTarget6. If this template were used in the *HTML Basics* drag-and-drop interaction for protocol definitions, for example, students would have the option of dragging terms to the definitions *or* definitions to the terms (Elements tab).

◆ Names any additional drag and target elements that you add as unnamed (unnamed1, unnamed2, unnamed3, and so forth). You can rename them in the Name field (If you highlight any element and click the Add button, CourseBuilder adds an additional element that is both a drag and target element.) (Elements tab).

◆ Defines 18 possible pairings out of 30, with 6 pairs set to correct:

```
DragTarget1:DragTarget4 (correct)
DragTarget4:DragTarget1 (correct)
DragTarget2:DragTarget5 (correct)
DragTarget5:DragTarget2 (correct)
DragTarget3:DragTarget6 (correct)
DragTarget6:DragTarget3 (correct)
```

Twelve pairings are set to incorrect (these are the additional combinations available by pairing DragTarget elements in the left-hand grouping with DragTarget elements in the right-hand grouping):

```
DragTarget1:DragTarget5 (incorrect)
DragTarget1:DragTarget6 (incorrect)
DragTarget5:DragTarget1 (incorrect)
DragTarget6:DragTarget1 (incorrect)
DragTarget2:DragTarget4 (incorrect)
DragTarget2:DragTarget6 (incorrect)
DragTarget4:DragTarget2 (incorrect)
DragTarget6:DragTarget2 (incorrect)
DragTarget3:DragTarget4 (incorrect)
DragTarget3:DragTarget5 (incorrect)
DragTarget4:DragTarget3 (incorrect)
DragTarget5:DragTarget3 (incorrect)
```

There are 12 additional possible combinations that you can add but are not initially defined in the Pairs list. These additional combinations are pairings within a grouping (DragTarget1:DragTarget3, DragTarget4:DragTarget5, and so forth) (Pairs tab).

◆ Sets each element to snap to the center of another element if the student drops it within 75 pixels of any other element's center. See the section, "Pairs tab," later in this chapter for more details (Pairs tab).

◆ Does not include in the Pairs list any new elements you added on the Elements tab. You can add them manually by selecting each new possible pair from the drop-down list on the Pairs tab and clicking the Add button (Pairs tab).

You can modify these defaults on the General, Elements, and Pairs tabs. Figure 11-16 shows the default layout for the Drag_2wayManyToMany interaction after it is inserted into Dreamweaver MX.

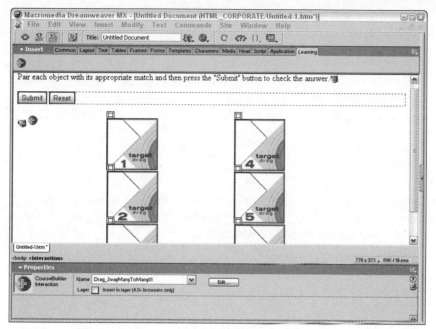

Figure 11-16: The Drag_2wayManyToMany interaction, inserted into Dreamweaver MX

Choosing one drag element with multiple targets (Drag_1ToMany)

Use the Drag_1ToMany template when you want an interaction that has a single drag element that can be dragged to one correct target element among multiple target distractors, with the target elements remaining stationary. By default, this interaction

- ◆ Judges the interaction automatically when a student drops the drag element onto any target element. You can choose the option to have the interaction judged when the student clicks a Submit button, or by a specific event, such as a button or slider interaction (General tab).

- ◆ Judges an answer correct if *any* are correct and *none* incorrect (General tab).

- ◆ Inserts a Reset button to allow students to return elements to their original position and start over (General tab).

- ◆ Snaps elements back to their original position if they are dropped anywhere but onto a target (General tab).

- ◆ Provides four elements: one drag element named Drag1, and three target elements named Target1 through Target3 (Elements tab).

◆ Names additional drag and target elements that you add as unnamed (unnamed1, unnamed2, unnamed3, and so forth). You can rename them in the Name field (If you highlight a drag element and click the Add button, CourseBuilder adds an additional drag element. If you highlight a target element and click the Add button, CourseBuilder adds an additional target element.) (Elements tab).

◆ Defines all three possible pairings, with the first pair set to correct (Pairs tab):

```
Drag1:Target1 (correct)
Drag1:Target2 (incorrect)
Drag1:Target3 (incorrect)
```

◆ Sets a drag element to snap to the center of a target if the student drops it within 75 pixels of a target's center. See the section, "Pairs tab," later in this chapter for more details (Pairs tab).

◆ Does not include on the Pairs list any new elements you added on the Elements tab. You can add them manually by selecting each new possible pair from the drop-down list on the Pairs tab and clicking the Add button (Pairs tab).

You can modify these defaults on the General, Elements, and Pairs tabs. Figure 11-17 shows the default layout for the Drag_1ToMany interaction after it is inserted into Dreamweaver MX.

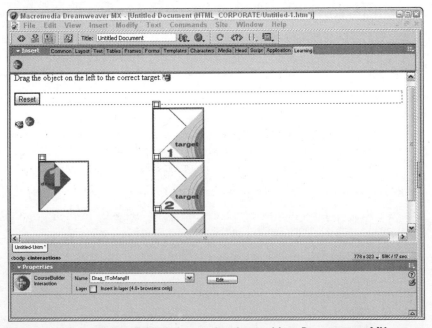

Figure 11-17: The Drag_1ToMany interaction, inserted into Dreamweaver MX

Choosing one drag element with multiple targets, all dragable to each other (Drag_2way1ToMany)

Use the `Drag_2way1ToMany` template when you want an interaction that only uses elements that are both drag and target elements, so that all elements can be moved. By default, this interaction

- ◆ Judges the interaction automatically when a student drops the drag element onto any target element. You can choose to have the interaction judged when the student clicks a Submit button, or by a specific event, such as a button or slider interaction (General tab).

- ◆ Judges an answer correct if *any* are correct and *none* incorrect (General tab).

- ◆ Inserts a Reset button to allow students to return elements to their original positions and start over (General tab).

- ◆ Provides four elements (`DragTarget1` through `DragTarget4`), each serving the dual role of drag element *and* target element, and allows all four elements to move. Students can drag any element to any other element (Elements tab).

- ◆ Names additional drag and target elements that you add as unnamed (`unnamed1`, `unnamed2`, `unnamed3`, and so forth). You can rename them in the Name field (If you highlight any element and click the Add button, CourseBuilder adds an additional element that is both a drag and target element.) (Elements tab).

- ◆ Defines six possible pairings out of 12, with two pairs set to correct:

  ```
  DragTarget1:DragTarget2 (correct)
  DragTarget2:DragTarget1 (correct)
  ```

  The other four defined pairings — the additional combinations available by pairing `DragTarget1` with the remaining elements — are set to incorrect:

  ```
  DragTarget1:DragTarget3 (incorrect)
  DragTarget1:DragTarget4 (incorrect)
  DragTarget3:DragTarget1 (incorrect)
  DragTarget4:DragTarget1 (incorrect)
  ```

  There are six additional possible combinations that you can add but which are not initially defined in the Pairs list. These additional combinations are pairings within the grouping of multiple elements (`DragTarget2:DragTarget3`, `DragTarget4:DragTarget3`, and so forth) (Pairs tab).

◆ Sets each element to snap to the center of another element if the student drops it within 75 pixels of any other element's center. See the section, "Pairs tab," later in this chapter for more details (Pairs tab).

◆ Does not include in the Pairs list any new elements you added on the Elements tab. You can add them manually by selecting each new possible pair from the drop-down list on the Pairs tab and clicking the Add button (Pairs tab).

You can modify these defaults on the General, Elements, and Pairs tabs. Figure 11-18 shows the default layout for the Drag_2way1ToMany interaction after it is inserted into Dreamweaver MX.

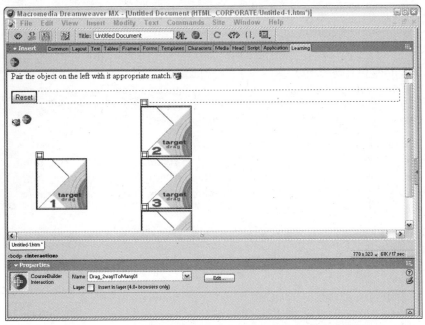

Figure 11-18: The Drag_2way1ToMany interaction, inserted into Dreamweaver MX

Choosing two elements, both dragable (Drag_2way1To1)

Use the Drag_2way1To1template when you want a drag-and-drop interaction that has two elements, both of which are target and drag elements. This template is typically used for demonstration purposes. By default, this interaction

- Judges the interaction automatically when students drop the drag element onto any target element. You can choose to have the interaction judged when the student clicks a Submit button or by a specific event, such as a button or slider interaction (General tab).

- Judges an answer correct if *any* are correct and *none* incorrect (General tab).

- Inserts a Reset button to allow students to return elements to their original positions and start over (General tab).

- Provides two elements (DragTarget1 and DragTarget2), each serving the dual role of drag element and target element, and allows both elements to move. Students can drag any element to any other element (Elements tab).

- Names additional drag and target elements that you add as unnamed (unnamed1, unnamed2, unnamed3, and so forth). You can rename them in the Name field (If you highlight any element and click the Add button, CourseBuilder adds an additional element that is both a drag and target element.) (Elements tab).

- Defines both possible pairings as not judged:

```
DragTarget1:DragTarget2 (not judged)
DragTarget2:DragTarget1 (not judged)
```

- Sets each element to snap to the center of another element if the student drops it within 75 pixels of any other element's center. See the section, "Pairs tab," later in this chapter for more details (Pairs tab).

- Does not include in the Pairs list any add new elements you added on the Elements tab. You can add them manually by selecting each new possible pair from the drop-down list on the Pairs tab and clicking the Add button (Pairs tab).

You can modify these defaults on the General, Elements, and Pairs tabs. Figure 11-19 shows the default layout for the Drag_2way1To1interaction after it is inserted into Dreamweaver MX.

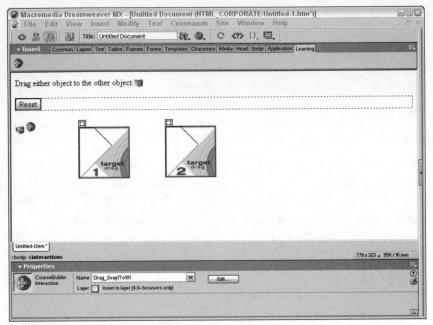

Figure 11-19: The Drag_2way1To1 interaction, inserted into Dreamweaver MX

Choosing a multi-step sequence (Drag_2StepsInOrder)

Use the Drag_2StepsInOrder template when you want an interaction that has a single drag element that is dropped on multiple target elements in a specific sequence, with the target elements remaining stationary. By default, this interaction

- ◆ Judges the interaction automatically when students drop the drag element onto any target element. You can choose to have the interaction judged when the student clicks a Submit button; or by a specific event, such as a button or slider interaction (General tab).

- ◆ Judges an answer correct if *any* are correct and *none* incorrect (General tab).

- ◆ Inserts a Reset button to allow students to return elements to their original position and start over (General tab).

- ◆ Snaps elements back to their original position if they are dropped anywhere but onto a target (General tab).

◆ Provides three elements: one drag element (Drag1) and two target elements (Target1 and Target2), where students must drop the Drag1 element on Target1 before they drop it on Target2 (Elements tab).

◆ Names additional drag and target elements that you add as unnamed (unnamed1, unnamed2, unnamed3, and so forth). You can rename them in the Name field. If you highlight a target element and click the Add button, CourseBuilder adds an additional target element. If you decide to add more target elements, note that you will need to add the processing rules to test the sequence for those new elements in the Action Manager (Elements tab).

◆ Defines both possible pairings as not judged:

```
Drag1:Target1 (not judged)
Drag1:Target2 (not judged)
```

All pairings are set as not judged because the decision about correct or incorrect depends on the sequence the student chooses and is handled through conditions in the Action Manager.

◆ Sets a drag element to snap to the center of a target if the student drops it within 75 pixels of a target's center. See the section, "Pairs tab," later in this chapter for more details (Pairs tab).

◆ Does not include in the Pairs list any new elements you added on the Elements tab. You can add them manually by selecting each new possible pair from the drop-down list on the Pairs tab and clicking the Add button (Pairs tab).

You can modify these defaults on the General, Elements, and Pairs tabs. Figure 11-20 shows the default layout for the Drag_2StepsInOrder interaction after it is inserted into Dreamweaver MX.

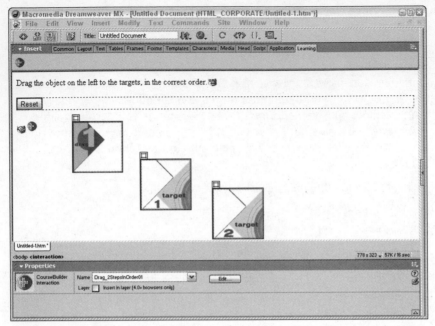

Figure 11-20: The Drag_2StepsInOrder interaction, inserted into Dreamweaver MX

Choosing a multi-step sequence with a distractor (Drag_2Steps1ToMany)

Use the Drag_2Steps1ToMany template when you want an interaction that has a single drag element that is dropped on multiple target elements in a specific sequence, with target distractors added, and with the target elements remaining stationary. By default, this interaction

- ◆ Judges the interaction automatically when students drop the drag element onto any target element. You can choose to have the interaction judged when the student clicks a Submit button; or by a specific event, such as a button or slider interaction (General tab).

- ◆ Judges an answer correct if *any* are correct and *none* incorrect (General tab).

- ◆ Inserts a Reset button to allow students to return elements to their original positions and start over (General tab).

- Snaps elements back to their original position if they are dropped anywhere but onto a target (General tab).

- Provides four elements: one drag element (Drag1) and 3 target elements (Target1 through Target3) (Elements tab).

- Initially names additional drag and target elements sequentially as unnamed (unnamed1, unnamed2, unnamed3, and so forth) regardless of whether the added element is a drag element or target element. If you highlight a target element and click the Add button, CourseBuilder adds an additional target element. If you decide to add more target elements, note that you will need to add the processing rules to test the sequence for those new elements in the Action Manager (Elements tab).

- Defines three possible pairings as not judged:

```
Drag1:Target1 (not judged)
Drag1:Target2 (not judged)
Drag1:Target3 (not judged)
```

All pairings are set as not judged because the decision about correct or incorrect depends on the sequence the student chooses and is handled through conditions in the Action Manager.

- Sets a drag element to snap to the center of a target if the student drops it within 75 pixels of a target's center. See the section, "Pairs tab," later in this chapter for more details (Pairs tab).

- Does not include in the Pairs list any new elements you added on the Elements tab. You can add them manually by selecting each newly possible pair from the drop-down list on the Pairs tab and clicking the Add button (Pairs tab).

You can modify these defaults on the General, Elements, and Pairs tabs. Figure 11-21 shows the default layout for the Drag_2Steps1ToMany interaction after it is inserted into Dreamweaver MX.

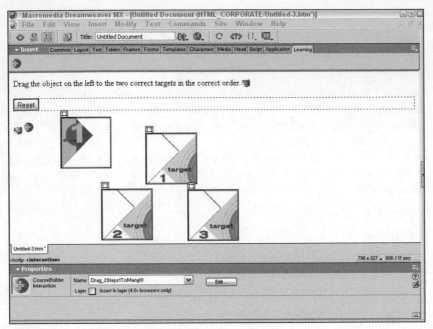

Figure 11-21: The Drag_2Steps1ToMany interaction, inserted into Dreamweaver MX

Defining the Elements and Pairs Tab Properties

Drag-and-drop interactions are the only interactions that require two unique tabs to define the interaction properties:

- ◆ The Elements tab defines each element used in the interaction – that is, each layer that becomes a drag element or target element (or both).

- ◆ The Pairs tab defines match-ups between elements and identifies each match-up as correct, incorrect, or not judged.

Elements tab

A drag-and-drop interaction involves dragging and dropping content contained within layers. Although the content is important, what really matters to CourseBuilder is not the content, but that layers containing the content.

The Elements tab, shown in Figure 11-22, defines each layer used in the drag-and-drop interaction, regardless of the element's function.

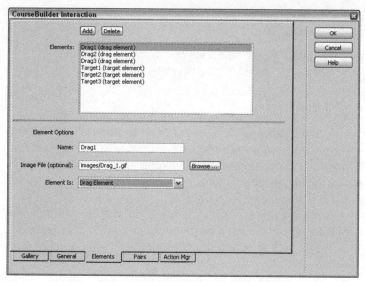

Figure 11-22: The Elements tab for the Drag_ManyToMany interaction

On the Elements tab, you:

◆ Create each element (layer) used in the interaction. By default, each inter-action provides different numbers of drag and target elements, depending on what makes sense for that interaction.

◆ Add or delete elements. Add new elements by clicking the Add button, or delete existing elements by highlighting an existing element and clicking the Delete button. If you highlight a drag element and click the Add but-ton, CourseBuilder adds an additional drag element; if you highlight a tar-get element and click the Add button, CourseBuilder adds an additional target element; and if you highlight a drag and target element and click the Add button, CourseBuilder adds an additional drag and target element.

◆ Specify a name for the element, which is an internal name used for processing.

◆ Insert an image file (optional) as the content for the element within the layer. Select this option if your interaction uses images as drag or target elements.

◆ Choose each element's function. The Element Is field identifies the func-tion of an element as a

■ Drag Element, meaning the layer can be dragged and dropped.

■ **Target Element**, meaning the layer is stationary, waiting for a drag element to be dropped on it.

■ **Both Drag and Target**, meaning the layer can both be dragged and dropped and can have other elements dropped on it.

Pairs tab

Individual elements have little meaning in a drag-and-drop interaction. The true purpose of the interaction is to enable students to demonstrate knowledge of relationships between elements. If, for example, you have term elements and definition elements, the importance of the interaction is the correct pairing of terms with definitions.

The Pairs tab, shown in Figure 11-23, defines the rules for possible pairings. This list of combinations can become quite large as the number of elements increases, especially if elements serve as both drag and target elements.

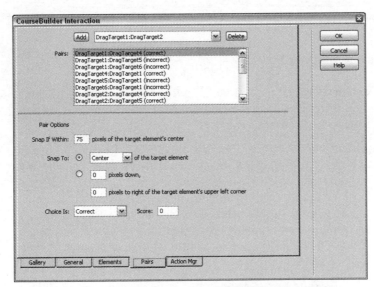

Figure 11-23: The Pairs tab for the Drag_ManyToMany interaction.

On the Pairs tab, you:

◆ Specify each possible pairing for which you want to issue a response. Templates that define separate drag and target elements define all possible pairs in the Pairs list. Templates that define dual-role elements (where a single element is *both* a drag and target element) define only those pairs that generally make sense for that interaction – pairing `DragTarget` elements in the "left" group with `DragTarget` elements in the "right" group. Although all other pairings can be defined in the Pairs list, they aren't listed there by default. The bottom line is that if you want to respond to a possible pairing that the student might attempt, you need to define that possible pairing in the Pairs list.

◆ Define the Snap If Within option. This defines when to snap a dropped drag element to a target element. For example, the Snap If Within option shown in Figure 11-23 is set to 75 pixels, so that if a student drops a drag element within 75 pixels of the target, that element snaps to the target and becomes a pairing.

Figure 11-24 shows that the snap is determined by how close the student drops a drag element to a target element – basically defining the student's intent on declaring a match.

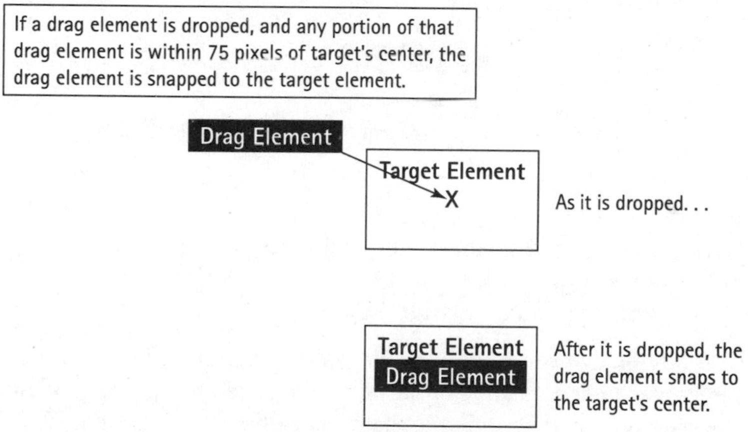

Figure 11-24: Defining when to snap a dropped drag element to a target element

◆ Define the Snap To options. After you define when to snap a drag element to a target element (how close the elements must be to cause a snap), you define *where* to snap the drag element in relation to the target. Figure 11-25 shows examples of the first option, in which you can snap the drag element to the center, left, right, top, or bottom of the target element, and the second option, in which you specify the number of pixels down and to the right of a target's top-left corner to snap the top-left corner of the drag element.

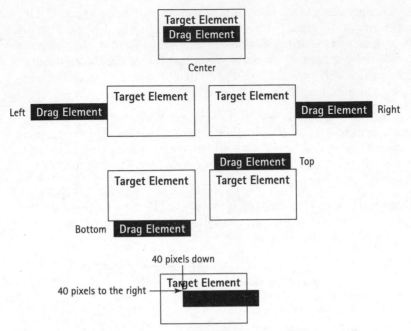

Figure 11-25: Defining where to snap a dropped drag element in relation to a
target element

◆ Specify whether each pair should be judged as Correct, Incorrect, or Not
   Judged by selecting a judgment from the Choice Is drop-down menu. This
   field determines the evaluation for a pair.

   You obviously need to define all correct pairs. You may, however, find it
   beneficial to define some or all incorrect pairs as well. For example, you
   may include specific incorrect pairs that give you the opportunity to
   explain to the student exactly why the pairing is incorrect. Or you may
   define incorrect pairs so that you can define a snap back for incorrect
   matches.

◆ Define the score for each pairing. Scoring and tracking is covered in detail
   in Part IV of this book. Briefly, the score is the numeric value you put on
   each pair. You'd usually set positive values for correct pairs, and a zero
   value for incorrect pairs.

Application Examples

Drag-and-drop interactions can be a lot of fun, particularly when working with
animations and movies. Let's look at two examples that show how drag-and-drop
interactions "bring things to life."

Example: The Beginnings of Animation

The Beginnings of Animation example provides a match-up of animation timeframes (on theater tickets) with images from actual animation samples (Figure 11-26).

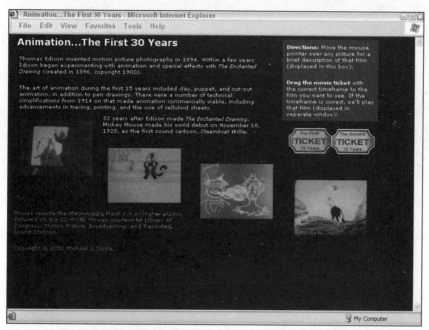

Figure 11–26: In The Beginnings of Animation page students must know a film's animation timeframe to see the movie.

If the student drops a ticket with the correct timeframe on an animation image, the student is rewarded with a trip to the movies—well, not exactly; the original animation movie plays in Macromedia Flash, as shown in Figure 11-27.

This interaction was created using the Drag_ManyToMany template (default of three drag elements and three target elements), with some modifications. To create this interaction we:

- ◆ Defined the interaction to be

    - Judged when the user drops a drag element (a ticket).

    - Correct when *any* are correct and *none* are incorrect, because there are four different correct answers.

    - Snap back drag element (ticket) to the starting position if the ticket is not dropped on a correct target.

Figure 11-28 shows the definitions on the General tab for this interaction.

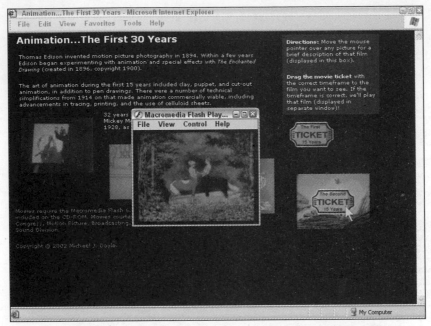

Figure 11-27: When a correct match is made, the movie automatically plays.

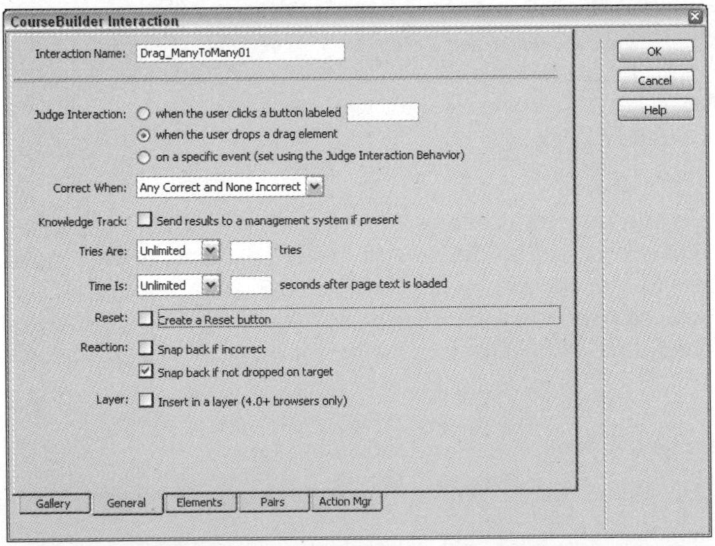

Figure 11-28: The General tab of the Drag_ManyToMany interaction in
The Beginnings of Animation

◆ Deleted a drag element and added a target element to the template, for a total of two drag elements (two tickets), and four target elements (the still pictures representing each movie), as the Elements tab in Figure 11-29 shows.

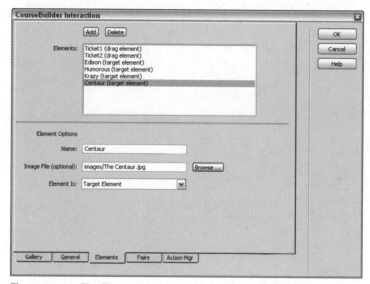

Figure 11-29: The Elements tab of the Drag_ManyToMany interaction in The Beginnings of Animation

Notice that in this example the name of each element was changed to reflect the content for the element, and that the images were included using the Image File field.

◆ Defined only the correct pairs on the Pairs tab, as shown in Figure 11-30.

◆ Removed the standard conditions (if Correct, else if Incorrect, and else if Unknown Response) in the Action Manager. Why? Because they don't allow different actions based on different pairings in the interaction. For example, how could you distinguish between the correct pairing of Ticket1:Edison (playing the Edison animation) and the correct pairing Ticket1:Humorous (playing the Humorous animation)?

To distinguish between each pairing, we used JavaScript, as shown in Figure 11-31. The JavaScript allows us to define a different action (play a different movie) for each correct answer by testing conditions. The example shows a test to see if Ticket1 is dropped on Edison (a correct pair); if it is, the Action Manager plays the movie Edison.swf in a new browser window.

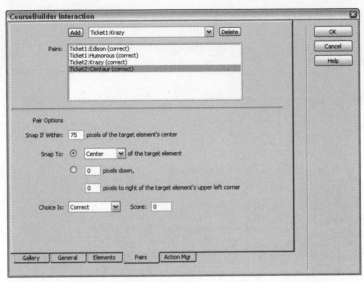

Figure 11-30: The Pairs tab of the Drag_ManyToMany interaction in
The Beginnings of Animation

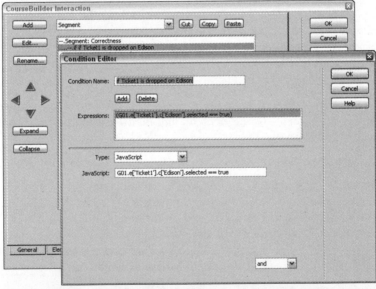

Figure 11-31: The condition that tests for each correct pairing is created
using the Condition Editor within the Action Manager. Each correct pairing
launches a different action (plays a different movie).

The JavaScript is written by CourseBuilder; you just need to tweak values
for it. Using JavaScript to test conditions is discussed in Chapter 17.

Example: My House

My House is a drag-and-drop interaction in which beginning reading students drag basic words to representative images, as shown in Figure 11-32.

Figure 11-32: My House is a simple matching exercise that enables students to match words to images.

When students correctly match a word to an image, the image becomes animated (the bird flies, the car runs, the girl bounces a soccer ball, and so forth). This example of the Drag_ManyToMany interaction shows how you can attach numerous actions in the Action Manager to each different pairing and bring things to life!

Figure 11-33 shows the Action Manager processing for this interaction. As with *The Beginnings of Animation,* this interaction uses JavaScript to define different actions for each pairing. When a student drops a correct word on an image, the image "comes to life" because the Action Manager swaps the still image with an animated image.

Once the image begins animation, the layer containing the word is also hidden through a Show-Hide Layers action set for each term. (Using JavaScript to define distinct actions is discussed in Chapter 17.)

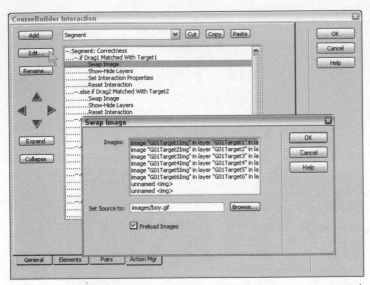

Figure 11-33: Images in My House come to life because a correct match calls for a Swap Image action in the Action Manager, swapping the still image with an animated image.

Summary

In this chapter you learned

- ◆ About the various drag-and-drop templates, differentiated mainly by the number of elements, type of elements (drag, target, or both), and sequence of dropping.

- ◆ How drag-and-drop interactions work from both the student and course author's perspectives.

- ◆ To define each element on the Elements tab, which is unique to drag-and-drop interactions.

- ◆ To define matches (correct, incorrect, and no response) on the Pairs tab, which is also unique to drag-and-drop interactions.

- ◆ About the concept of snapping elements.

- ◆ That drag-and-drop interactions can provide different actions in the Action Manager for different pairings.

The next chapter describes how to create Explore (hot-area) interactions.

Chapter 12

Explore (Image Hot Area) Interactions

IN THIS CHAPTER

♦ Examining explore interactions from student and course author perspectives

♦ Working with layers and the Z-Index

♦ Choosing different explore templates for different applications

♦ Understanding teaching about and testing on software user interfaces

EXPLORE INTERACTIONS are variations on traditional "hot area" graphics such as HTML image maps, where students click different areas of a graphic and receive distinct responses from each hot area. The concept of an explore interaction is to superimpose "hot areas" over an image, and to have those hot areas, when clicked, launch different actions in the Action Manager. Figure 12-1 shows the concept of hot areas superimposed over a graphic (the hot areas are represented by the dashed rectangles).

Explore interactions offer many possibilities for implementation. For example, you could use the interaction to

♦ Teach students about a software program by superimposing hot areas over a screen capture, and displaying descriptive text when students click different hot areas. We'll discuss an example of this idea (the GUI example on the CD-ROM) at the end of this chapter.

♦ Test students on parts of an engine by setting each hot area to display a test question.

♦ Study human anatomy by defining hot areas on an image of a body that, when clicked, launch a Flash movie about that part of the anatomy.

The key limitation of the interaction is that hot areas must be square or rectangular because, unlike other hot-area technologies such as image maps in HTML, the explore interaction uses layers to define hot areas, and layers are limited to rectangles and squares (see Chapter 3 for a discussion of layers).

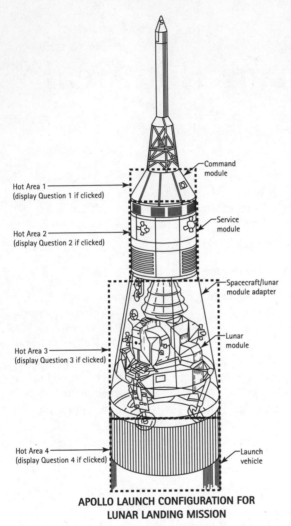

Hot Area 1
(display Question 1 if clicked)

Command
module

Hot Area 2
(display Question 2 if clicked)

Service
module

Spacecraft/lunar
module adapter

Lunar
module

Hot Area 3
(display Question 3 if clicked)

Hot Area 4
(display Question 4 if clicked)

Launch
vehicle

**APOLLO LAUNCH CONFIGURATION FOR
LUNAR LANDING MISSION**

Figure 12–1: In an explore interaction, rectangular hot areas
are superimposed over an image.

Understanding How Explore Interactions Work

To grasp the concepts behind explore interactions, it is important that you understand the process for an interaction from both the student's perspective (how it works) and a course author's perspective (how you create it). Let's take a look at one interaction from the student perspective first.

The student's perspective

The *HTML Basics* course uses an explore interaction to teach students about uniform resource locators (URLs). Figure 12-2 shows the page from the course segment on Internet protocol definitions.

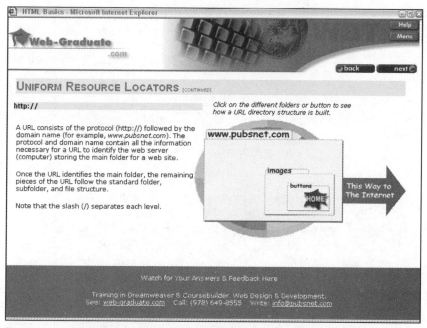

Figure 12-2: An explore interaction from the HTML Basics course

Although you can't really see it in the figure, the background image is a spinning disk. The three folder images are three overlapping hot areas; each folder changes color as the mouse moves over it. When a student clicks a folder, the directory path for that folder is displayed at the upper left of the page, as shown in Figure 12-3.

The course author's perspective

Now let's look at the same explore interaction from the course author's perspective. Figure 12-4 shows the interaction open in Dreamweaver MX.

The interaction is identified in the Properties panel as an Explore_Random interaction. It contains a different folder within each hot area, and the hot areas are layered on top of each other (see the sidebar "Understanding the Z-Index" for information about overlapping layers).

Notice that the URL changes as you click on different folders.

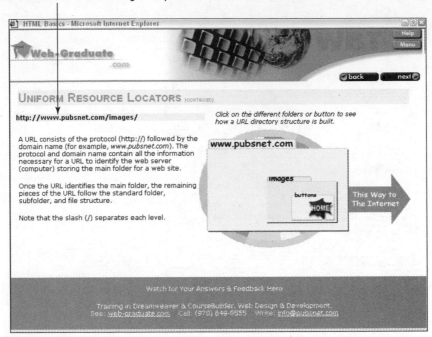

Figure 12-3: A student has clicked the images folder, and the URL at the top left of the page reflects the path to the selected folder.

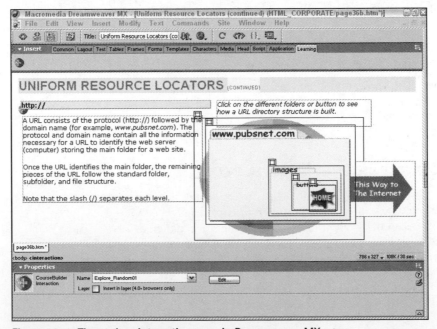

Figure 12-4: The explore interaction open in Dreamweaver MX

Understanding the Z-Index

Many CourseBuilder interactions (including drag and drop and explore) rely on the use of layers, which are rectangular containers used to position content exactly where you want it in the browser window. Layers are unique from other types of HTML content in several ways; for example, layers can be:

◆ Moved to any position on a Web page by students (made dragable).

◆ Animated by using timelines in Dreamweaver MX.

◆ Positioned to overlap each other.

The capability of layers to overlap each other is the hallmark of layers (and the reason for their name). Of course, this all begs the question: if layers overlap, what determines which layer stays in the foreground, and which layer moves to the background? The answer is that the order of that overlap is determined by the Z-Index.

The Z-Index is simply a whole number entered into the Z-Index field on the Properties panel when a layer is selected. If layers overlap, the layer with a higher numbered Z-Index moves to the foreground, and the layer with a lower numbered Z-Index moves to the background wherever the layers overlap.

As you draw successive layers on your Web page, Dreamweaver assigns each new layer a Z-Index setting that increments the previously highest setting by one. For example, if your page contains a single layer with a Z-Index setting of 5, the next layer you draw is assigned the Z-Index of 6, and so forth. You can always change the Z-Index for a layer in the Properties panel.

Figure 12-5 shows the results of three separate, overlapping layers. LayerC, which has a Z-Index setting of 3, remains in the foreground, overlapping LayerB and LayerA. LayerB remains in the foreground where it overlaps LayerA, but is in the background where it overlaps LayerC.

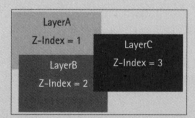

Figure 12-5: The order of precedence for overlapping layers is determined by the layers' Z-Index values.

This interaction example requires us to create a layer for feedback (the layer that displays different path names when hot areas containing folders are clicked). We need to create the feedback layer *before* we insert the CourseBuilder interaction, so that we can use the Set Text of Layer action in the Action Manager.

We'll assume the starting point for this example to be as shown in Figure 12-6, with some initial text already in the file. (The file already has the style sheet html.css from the styles folder attached.)

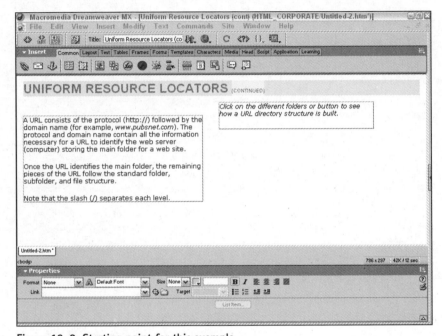

Figure 12–6: Starting point for this example

To create the interaction, follow these steps (since this example does not refer to other frames, you do *not* need to edit it inside the frameset):

1. Click the Draw Layer icon on the Insert panel's Common tab to draw a layer for feedback. Draw the layer whatever size you want, because we will define the correct dimensions in the Properties panel.

2. Select the new layer (named Layer3 in this example) and change the settings for that layer on the Properties panel as follows (see Figure 12-7):

    Layer ID: url

    L (pixels from left): 13

    T (pixels from top): 51

    W (width): 360

H (height): 15

Z-Index: 3

Bg Color: #F0F0F0 (using zeroes, not the letter O)

Vis: visible

Overflow: visible

3. Type the initial text inside the feedback layer (and bold it), as follows:

   http://

4. Click the Insert CourseBuilder Interaction button on the Learning tab. The CourseBuilder Interaction dialog box displays, with the CourseBuilder Gallery active.

5. Choose the Explore category to display the three explore templates.

   We want students to click on a series of folders or the Home button (home.gif), and to view the path names (URLs) for different folders and files within a Web site, so we need to use several hot areas that each contain an image. The interaction that fits our requirements is the Explore_Random template. (We discuss the details of each explore template later in the chapter.)

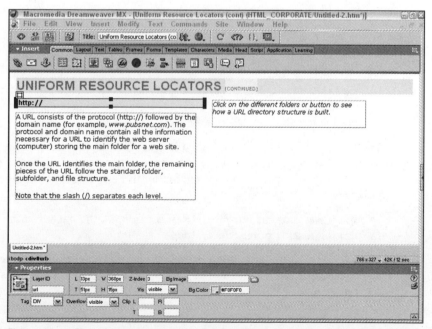

Figure 12-7: Changing the properties of the feedback layer on the Properties panel

6. Click the `Explore_Random` template. CourseBuilder inserts a working copy of the template into your Dreamweaver MX page, and activates additional tabs for that template (General, Hot Areas, Action Mgr), as shown in Figure 12-8.

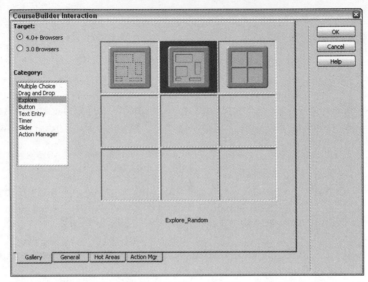

Figure 12-8: The CourseBuilder Gallery with the explore template `Explore_Random` **selected**

7. Click the General tab (shown in Figure 12-9) to define the general properties for the interaction.

In using this interaction, the student only needs to click a hot area to initiate judgment automatically. This is the default setting, so you do not need to change it.

The Backdrop Image (optional) field lets you specify the image that serves as the background image for the hot areas. For instance, the backdrop image specified for the explore interaction in Figure 12-1 is the Apollo 11 spacecraft.

In some cases, such as our *HTML Basics* example, the backdrop image (a spinning disk) is purely decorative.

The `ExploreRandom` template's default backdrop image, which is used as the backdrop image if you don't specify one, is stored in the images folder as `ExploreRandom_Bkgnd.GIF` (it is copied there when you copy the CourseBuilder support files).

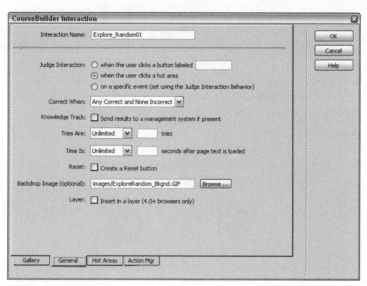

Figure 12-9: General tab for the Explore_Random interaction

8. Click the Browse button to select the Backdrop Image file. Select the disk.gif file from the images folder in the *HTML Basics* root folder.

   CourseBuilder updates the Explore_Random template in Dreamweaver MX with the backdrop image of the spinning disk, as shown in Figure 12-10.

   Once you define the backdrop image, the next step is to define the content for each hot area.

9. Click the Hot Areas tab (shown in Figure 12-11) to define each element in the interaction.

   By default, the Explore_Random interaction includes five hot areas, each initially set up with a default image (named ExploreRandom_1.GIF through ExploreRandom_5.GIF).

   Our *HTML Basics* interaction needs only four hot areas (one each for the three folders and the Home button).

10. Highlight the hot area we don't need, HotArea5, and click the Delete button. CourseBuilder deletes HotArea5, leaving us with four hot areas.

    By default, hot areas are set to Not Judged. *If* you were using the explore interaction as a test, you could judge hot areas as answers to test questions. For example, you might ask, "Which part of the car cools the engine?" and students would answer by clicking on the radiator within a picture of an engine. For the *HTML Basics* interaction, though, leave the default setting Not Judged.

    Now we need to identify the image that each hot area will contain.

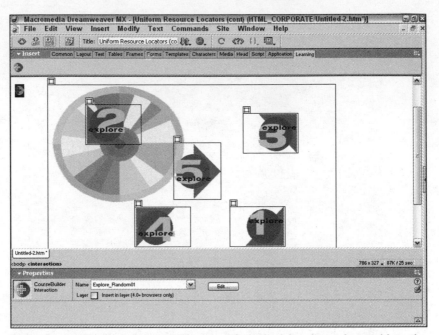

Figure 12-10: The Dreamweaver MX page with the backdrop image inserted into the background layer

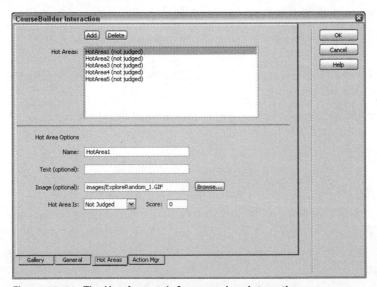

Figure 12-11: The Hot Areas tab for an explore interaction

11. Highlight `HotArea1` in the Hot Areas list and click the Browse button to replace the placeholder image `ExploreRandom_1.GIF`. Select the `folder-large.gif` file from the `images` folder in the *HTML Basics* root folder.

    Specify the images for the remaining hot areas as follows:

    HotArea2: `images/folder-medium.gif`

    HotArea3: `images/folder-small.gif`

    HotArea4: `images/home.gif`

12. Click the Action Mgr tab to display the Action Manager (see Figure 12-12). The initial settings for this interaction include more processing than you've seen with other interactions.

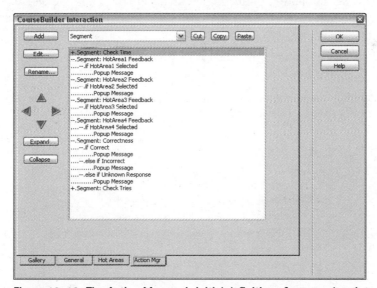

Figure 12-12: The Action Manager's initial definitions for an explore interaction

CourseBuilder displays the default rules for processing this interaction, defining CourseBuilder actions for correct, incorrect, and unknown student responses. However, those definitions are irrelevant to this interaction, because we aren't evaluating student responses for correctness.

What *is* relevant are the conditions inserted automatically for each hot area (`if Hot Area1 selected`, and so forth). Each of these conditions tests to see if a hot area has been selected (clicked on). The Action Manager then determines which hot area was clicked, and processes the actions for that area.

By default, a click in a hot area launches a Popup Message action that identifies the area. Instead, we want the clicks to change the text in the feedback layer named `url`.

13. Highlight each Popup Message action in the Action Manager tab and click the Cut button to delete it (this must be done for each message; there is no way to cut multiple actions at once).

14. Click the first condition, if HotArea1 Selected, to highlight it. This condition tests to see if the student clicked the hot area named HotArea1. If the student clicked the large folder (represented by HotArea1), the Action Manager processes the actions for that condition.

    With the if HotArea1Selected condition active (highlighted), we can add actions to that specific highlighted condition.

15. Select the Set Text of Layer action from the Action Manager drop-down menu.

16. Click the Add button on the Action Manager tab to add the Set Text of Layer action to the if HotArea1 Selected condition. CourseBuilder displays the Set Text of Layer dialog box.

17. Select the layer "url" from the Layer drop-down menu on the Set Text of Layer dialog box.

18. Type the text you want to display in the layer named url if the student clicks HotArea1 (the large folder), as shown in Figure 12-13.

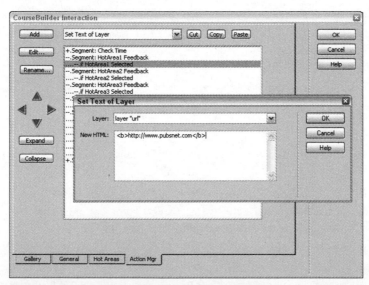

Figure 12-13: Inserting a Set Text of Layer action for the if HotArea1 Selected condition

In this example, the text entered for the Set Text of Layer action for HotArea1 (the large folder) is http://www.pubsnet.com.

19. Repeat Steps 16-18 for the `if HotArea2`, `ifHotArea3`, and `if HotArea4` conditions, using the following text for each Set Text of Layer action:

    HotArea2: `<b>http://www.pubsnet.com/images/</b>`

    HotArea3: `<b>http://www.pubsnet.com/images/buttons/</b>`

    HotArea4: `<b>http://www.pubsnet.com/images/buttons/ home.gif</b>`

20. Click OK when you've completed defining the rules in the Action Manager. CourseBuilder writes the processing rules into the HTML file. If the page looks like a mess, everything was probably done correctly, as you can see in Figure 12-14.

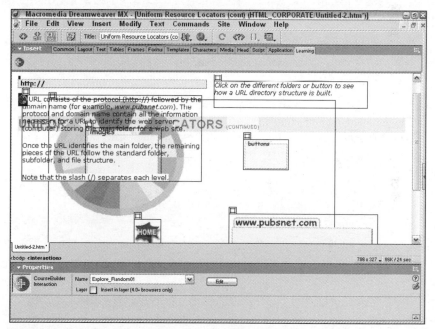

Figure 12-14: The explore interaction inserted into Dreamweaver MX

When the explore interaction is inserted into your Dreamweaver MX page, the hot area names (`HotArea1` through `HotArea4`) all contain the prefix G01 on the Properties panel. This prefix is to distinguish hot areas if you insert multiple interactions on a single page. The remainder of this chapter continues to refer to hot area names without the prefix, for the sake of simplicity.

There are only two tasks remaining to complete the interaction: arranging all of the elements into their final positions, and setting the Z-Index for HotArea1 through HotArea4 to ensure proper layering of each image.

When CourseBuilder inserts the explore interaction into your Dreamweaver MX page, the backdrop layer is initially assigned a Z-Index value of 1, and the hot areas are assigned a Z-Index value of 2. We need to make sure the hot area layers are differentiated from each other, because we are going to layer the four hot areas.

HotArea1 (the large folder) already has a Z-Index of 2 (one higher than the backdrop image), so we only need to change HotArea2 through HotArea4. Here's how:

1. Select the layer named HotArea2 (containing the medium folder).

2. Change the Z-Index to 3 in the Properties panel.

3. Repeat steps 1 and 2 for HotArea3 and HotArea4, so that the final Z-Index values for the hot areas are

    HotArea1 (the large folder):   2

    HotArea2 (the medium folder): 3

    HotArea3 (the small folder):   4

    HotArea4 (the Home button):   5

Finally, arrange all of the layers by dragging them into their proper positions, as shown in Figure 12-15.

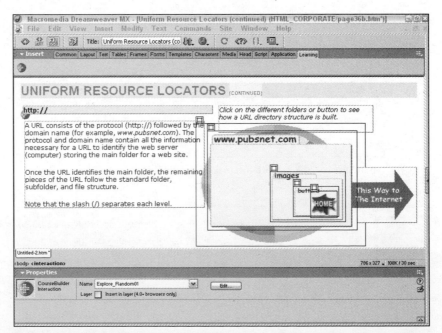

Figure 12–15: The final position of layers in the explore interaction from the HTML Basics course

Figure 12-16 shows a flowchart that diagrams the decisions and actions taken by the Action Manager when processing this explore interaction.

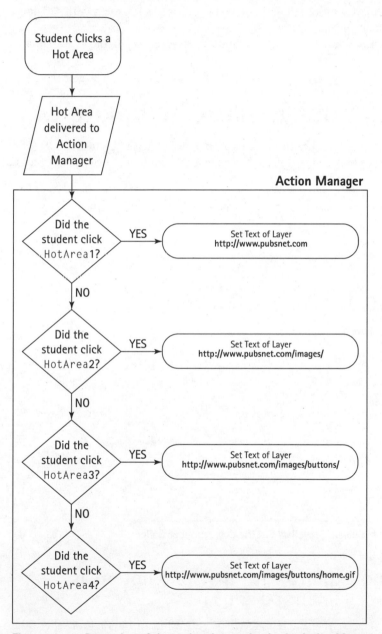

Figure 12–16: Processing of the explore interaction in the Action Manager

Each folder uses a mouseover effect that changes the folder with a darkened version of itself when the student moves the mouse pointer over that folder. This effect was added by adding a Swap Image behavior in Dreamweaver MX, swapping each image with an "on" version of itself (`folder-large.gif` is swapped with `folder-largeon.gif`, and so forth).

Chapter 3 describes how to create a mouseover effect with the Swap Image behavior.

Choosing Your Explore Template

The CourseBuilder Gallery contains three explore templates (see Figure 12-17). The significant difference between them is in the appearance and layout of the hot areas.

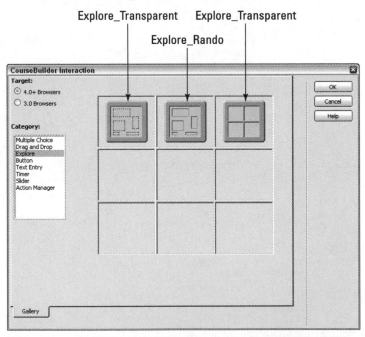

Figure 12-17: Explore templates available in the CourseBuilder Gallery

Choosing explore with invisible hot areas (Explore_Transparent)

Use the `Explore_Transparent` template when you want an interaction where the backdrop image becomes the center of attention, so to speak, for the test or activity. (Both GUI examples described in the section named "Application Examples" at the end of this chapter use the `Explore_Transparent` template to superimpose hot areas over a software screen capture). Because CourseBuilder creates transparent hot areas for this interaction, only the backdrop image is visible to students.

Although there are transparent hot areas superimposed in layers, it appears to students as if they are clicking different areas of a single image (the backdrop), and getting different reactions depending on where they click. By default, this interaction

◆ Judges the interaction automatically when a student clicks a hot area. You have the option to have the interaction judged when the student clicks a Submit button; or you can have the interaction judged by a specific event, such as a button or slider interaction (General tab).

◆ Judges an answer correct if *any* are correct and *none* incorrect (General tab).

◆ Sets the Backdrop Image (optional) to `Explore_random.gif`, stored in the `images` folder (General tab).

 It is a little confusing, but the default backdrop image for the `Explore_Transparent` template really is named Explore_random.gif.

◆ Provides five hot area layers: `HotArea1` through `HotArea5` (Hot Areas tab).

◆ Names any additional hot areas that you add as unnamed (`unnamed1`, `unnamed2`, `unnamed3`, and so forth). You can rename them in the Name field (Hot Areas tab).

◆ Provides a Text (optional) field where you can add text to the hot area. If you include an image, the text is placed to the right or below the image in the layer, depending on space available in the layer (Hot Areas tab).

◆ Provides an Image (optional) field where you can add an image to the hot area. By default, each hot area contains the image file `transparentSquare.gif`, a transparent 100x100 pixel graphic file stored in the `images` folder (Hot Areas tab).

◆ Sets all hot areas to Not Judged (Hot Areas tab).

Obviously, adding text or images to a hot area defeats the purpose of transparent hot areas. You can modify these defaults on the General and Hot Areas tabs. Figure 12-18 shows the default layout for the `Explore_Transparent` interaction after it is inserted into Dreamweaver MX.

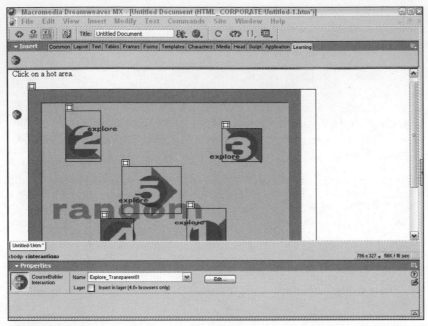

Figure 12–18: The `Explore_Transparent` interaction, inserted into Dreamweaver MX. The numbers and graphics are part of the backdrop image, and not contained within the layers.

Choosing explore with visible hot areas (`Explore_Random`)

Use the `Explore_Random` template when you want an explore interaction where the backdrop image remains in the background and hot areas contain an image or text that is visible to students. The example explore interaction we discussed earlier in the chapter used this template by filling the hot areas with images of folders. By default, this interaction

- ◆ Judges the interaction automatically when a student clicks a hot area. You have the option to have the interaction judged when the student clicks a Submit button; or you can have the interaction judged by a specific event, such as a button or slider interaction (General tab).

- ◆ Judges an answer correct if *any* are correct and *none* incorrect (General tab).

- ◆ Sets the Backdrop Image (optional) to `ExploreRandom_Bkgnd.GIF`, stored in the `images` folder (General tab).

- ◆ Provides five hot areas layers: `HotArea1` through `HotArea5` (Hot Areas tab).

◆ Names any additional hot areas that you add as unnamed (unnamed1, unnamed2, unnamed3, and so forth). You can rename them in the Name field (Hot Areas tab).

◆ Provides a Text (optional) field where you can add text to the hot area. If you include an image, the text is placed to the right or below the image in the layer, depending on space available in the layer (Hot Areas tab).

◆ Provides an Image (optional) field where you can add an image to the hot area. By default, each hot area contains a different graphics file stored in the images folder and named ExploreRandom_1.GIF through ExploreRandom_5.

◆ Sets all hot areas to Not Judged (Hot Areas tab).

You can modify these defaults on the General and Hot Areas tabs. Figure 12-19 shows the default layout for the Explore_Random interaction after it is inserted into Dreamweaver MX.

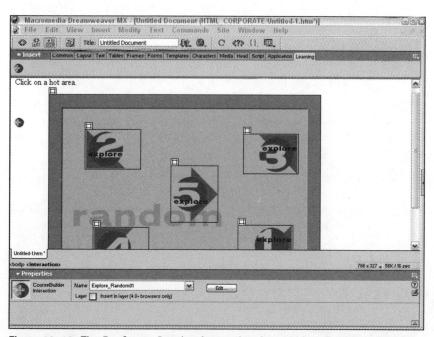

Figure 12-19: The Explore_Random interaction, inserted into Dreamweaver MX. The numbers and graphics are contained within each layer, and not part of the backdrop image.

▦ Choosing explore without a backdrop image (`Explore_Areas`)

Use the `Explore_Areas` template when you want to set up image hot areas without a backdrop image. By default, this interaction

- ◆ Judges the interaction automatically when a student clicks a hot area. You have the option to have the interaction judged when the student clicks a Submit button; or you can have the interaction judged by a specific event, such as a button or slider interaction (General tab).

- ◆ Judges an answer correct if *any* are correct and *none* incorrect (General tab).

- ◆ Does not include a backdrop image. This is the key differentiator between the `Explore_Areas` template and other explore templates (General tab).

- ◆ Provides four hot area layers: `HotArea1` through `HotArea4` (Hot Areas tab).

- ◆ Names any additional hot areas that you add as unnamed (`unnamed1`, `unnamed2`, `unnamed3`, and so forth. You can rename them in the Name field (Hot Areas tab).

- ◆ Provides a Text (optional) field where you can add text to the hot area. If you include an image, the text is placed to the right or below the image in the layer, depending on space available in the layer (Hot Areas tab).

- ◆ Provides an Image (optional) field where you can add an image to the hot area. By default, each hot area contains a different graphics file stored in the `images` folder and named `Explore1.GIF` through `Explore4.GIF` (Hot Areas tab).

- ◆ Sets all hot areas to Not Judged (Hot Areas tab).

You can modify these defaults on the General and Hot Areas tabs. Figure 12-20 shows the default layout for the `Explore_Areas` interaction after it is inserted into Dreamweaver MX.

Application Examples

Explore interactions are highly visual, and can be one of the most engaging and effective types of interactions, particularly when tests and activities are high in visual content. Let's look at two examples that demonstrate how to use the explore interaction to teach and test about software. Both examples are on the CD-ROM (in the GUI folder) that shipped with this book.

Example: teaching about a graphical user interface

The Explore_Transparent interaction enables you to superimpose transparent hot areas over any backdrop image so that as students click different areas of the image they are actually clicking on "invisible" hot areas, launching specific, different actions from each one.

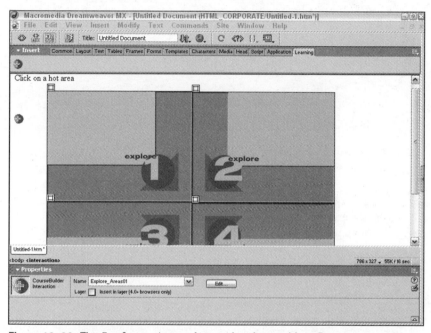

Figure 12-20: The Explore_Areas interaction, inserted into Dreamweaver MX

Figure 12-21 shows an Explore_Transparent interaction that uses a screen capture from the CourseBuilder Interaction dialog box as an example of describing different areas of a GUI (graphical user interface).

From the student's perspective, there is a single image that they click on to launch different actions (in this case, change the text to information specific to the area of the screen clicked). For example, when the student clicks on the area discussing targets, it displays a write-up about targets and browser versions.

This particular example has five separate hot areas defined, which you can see when the file is open in Dreamweaver MX (see in Figure 12-22).

To the right of the screen capture, layered on top of each other, are five layers, all of similar size, each describing a portion of the screen defined by a hot area. When a student clicks on a hot area of the screen, the Action Manager shows (makes visible) the layer containing the description related to the hot area clicked, and hides all other descriptive layers.

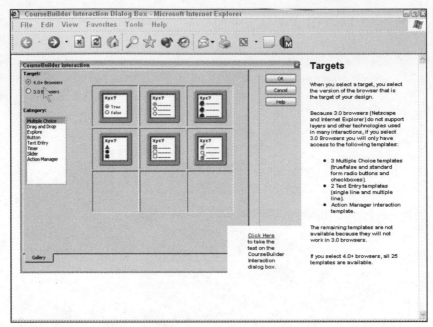

Figure 12-21: Using the explore interaction to enable students to learn and explore different areas of a GUI screen capture

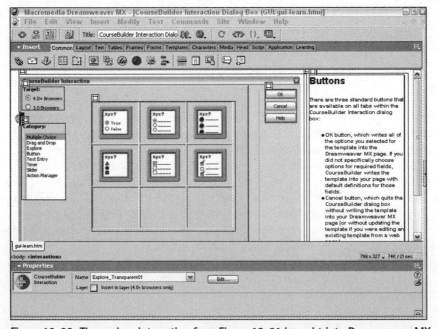

Figure 12-22: The explore interaction from Figure 12-21 brought into Dreamweaver MX

Figure 12-23 shows the Action Manager logic for processing the Show-Hide Layers action for each hot area. You can see, for example, when students click on HotArea1, the Action Manager shows the layer named target, and hides (makes invisible) the other four layers containing descriptions of the other hot areas.

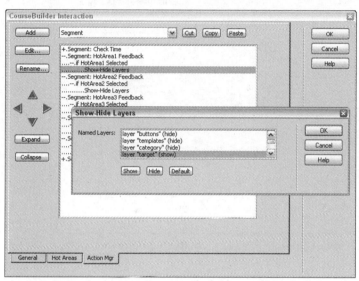

Figure 12-23: The Action Manager uses the Show–Hide Layers action to make different layers visible and invisible depending on the hot area clicked by students.

Example: testing on a graphical user interface

The Explore_Random interaction enables you to superimpose images or text in hot areas over a backdrop image. Figure 12-24 shows this interaction being used to test students on GUI from the preceding example. For the test, the GUI elements are removed from the background image and replaced with five visible hot areas, each containing a different question.

From the student's perspective, there are five different areas on the screen, labeled by text as Question 1 through Question 5. When students click on a question (hot area), CourseBuilder opens a separate browser window containing a question related to the hot area. So, for example, when the student clicks Question 1, CourseBuilder launches a question on target browsers.

Each question is a separate hot area, as is shown in Figure 12-25.

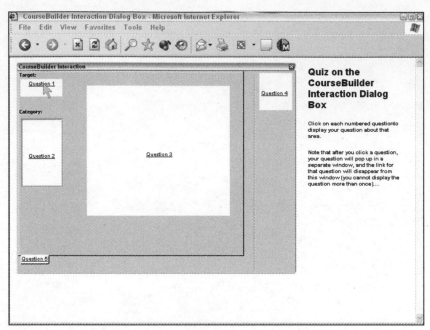

Figure 12-24: Using an explore interaction to test students on different areas of a GUI screen capture

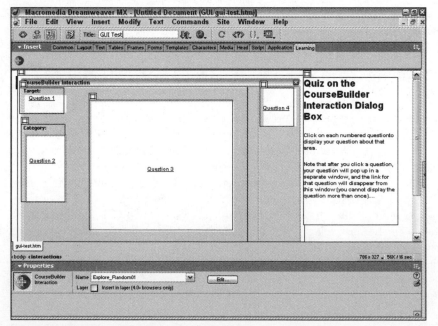

Figure 12-25: The explore interaction from Figure 12-24 brought into Dreamweaver MX

Figure 12-26 shows the Action Manager logic for processing the interaction. Each hot area has *two* separate actions associated with it:

◆ Show-Hide Layers, which hides the layer containing the clickable question number (Question 1, Question 2, and so forth) that was clicked.

◆ Open Browser Window, which opens a different browser window that displays the pertinent question.

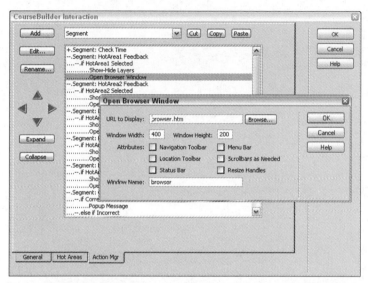

Figure 12-26: The Action Manager launches two separate actions when the student clicks a hot area: a Show–Hide Layers action and the Open Browser Window action.

When students click on a hot area, that hot area opens an HTML file containing the multiple-choice question (interaction), as shown in Figure 12-27.

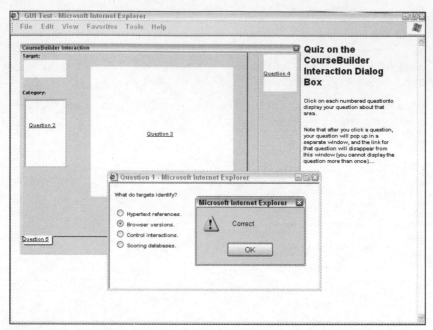

Figure 12-27: Each hot area launches a multiple-choice question related to that hot area.

Summary

This chapter described

- The different applications for the explore interaction, which is probably the toughest interaction to grasp conceptually.

- The example of the explore interaction from the *HTML Basics* course.

- The differences between the three explore interaction templates.

- Examples of both `Explore_Random` and `Explore_Transparent` used on a software screen capture.

The next chapter describes how to use sliders as test and activity interactions.

Chapter 13

Slider Interactions

IN THIS CHAPTER

- ◆ Examining the parts of a slider
- ◆ Using sliders for multiple-choice tests, and as control interactions for navigating and selecting options
- ◆ Exploring ranges, and mapping numeric range definitions in CourseBuilder
- ◆ Selecting the appropriate template for tests and for control
- ◆ Creating custom sliders from any images (.GIF or .JPG formats)

SLIDER INTERACTIONS are used both as a form of multiple-choice interactions and as control interactions. Sliders are a particularly well-suited interaction when you want to provide students with a wide range of answers, such as numbers on a scale; the students can select answers within ranges that you specify.

A slider consists of two images (see Figure 13-1): a track, which is stationary, that represents the scale being used, and a thumb, which students click and slide (drag) to a point on the track (scale) that they choose.

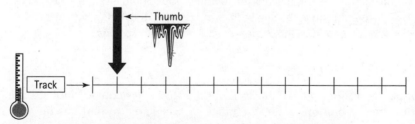

Figure 13-1: Every slider consists of two images: a track and a thumb.

Sliders allow students to select a *specific range location* from a range of numbers. When you create your slider interaction, you specify the total range of numbers on the General tab as well as the graphical image that represents the thumb and track. CourseBuilder automatically calculates each range location based on the size of the graphical image representing the slider track. For example, if you have a

311

track that is five inches wide and specify a range of 1 to 10, CourseBuilder spaces each range location a half-inch apart.

Slider interactions offer many possibilities for implementation because you can select whatever images you want to represent the track and thumb. For example, you could

◆ Use a historical figure or object as a thumb, and a timeline for the track.

◆ Use a railroad car as a thumb, and a railroad track as a track with different stations along the way.

◆ Use a baseball player as a thumb, and the chalk line between two bases as a track.

The fun part of working with sliders is that it is extraordinarily easy to develop custom sliders (tracks and thumbs), so you can select images that represent your subject matter.

The sliders that ship with CourseBuilder are shown in Chapter 6.

Understanding How Slider Interactions Work

To understand the concepts behind slider interactions, you should examine the process for an interaction from the student's perspective (how it works) and the course author's perspective (how you create it). This section describes both perspectives.

The student's perspective

Let's take a look at a slider interaction from the *HTML Basics* course. Students are asked to select any resolution within the range of acceptable resolutions for Web graphics. Using an overall range from 0 to 300, the correct range is anywhere between 72 and 96, as you can see in Figure 13-2.

The track in this example is an ordinary graphic of a bar, and the thumb is an animated graphic of an information highway traveling into a computer monitor (reinforcing the "download" concept that drives the question). The specific location on the range location is indicated numerically in a separate text area that shows the exact location of the thumb on the track.

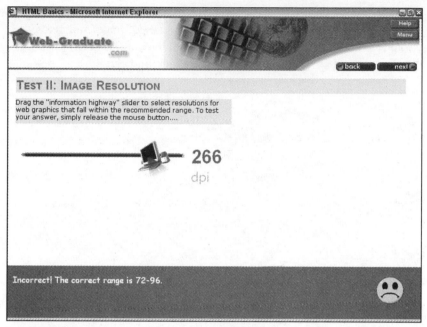

Figure 13-2: A slider interaction from the HTML Basics course after a student selects the location 266 in the range

The course author's perspective

Now let's look at the same slider interaction from the course author's perspective. To create this drag-and-drop interaction, follow these steps (assuming you've opened the file within the frameset):

1. Click the Insert CourseBuilder Interaction button on the Learning tab. The CourseBuilder Interaction dialog box displays, with the CourseBuilder Gallery active.

2. Choose the Slider category to display the two slider templates. Reviewing the profile of what we want to have happen, we want students to

   Have a range of numbers (0 to 300) from which to choose.

   Identify ranges 0–71 and 97–300 as incorrect, and range 72–96 as correct.

   Click and slide the animated computer monitor to select their choice, and have their responses automatically judged as soon as they release the mouse button.

   The slider template that fits these requirements is Slider_CorrectRange.

3. Click the `Slider_CorrectRange` template. CourseBuilder inserts a working copy of the template into your Dreamweaver MX page, and activates the additional tabs for that template (General, Ranges, Action Mgr), as shown in Figure 13-3.

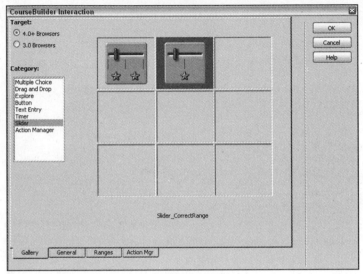

Figure 13-3: The CourseBuilder Gallery with the `Slider_CorrectRange` template selected

4. Click the General tab (Figure 13-4) to define the general properties for the interaction.

This example assumes we previously created a custom slider named `monitor` (creating custom sliders is described later in this chapter). You select custom sliders in the same fashion as you select pre-designed sliders that ship with CourseBuilder. For the purposes of this exercise, we assume the custom slider is already created.

5. Select the slider from the Appearance drop-down menu. For this example, we're selecting the custom slider `monitor` (see Figure 13-5).

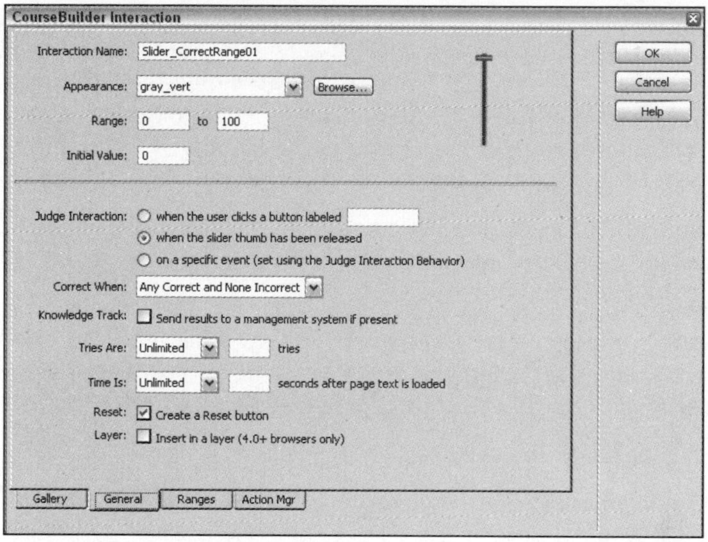

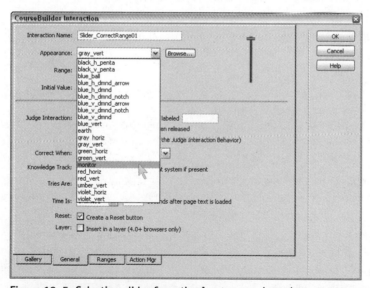

Figure 13-4: General tab for the Slider_CorrectRange interaction

Figure 13-5: Selecting slider from the Appearance drop-down menu

6. Choose the numbers for the beginning and end of the overall range of your track. The numbers you select should correlate to the numbers on the actual scale you are using. If you were representing the Celsius scale, for instance, you would use 0 to 100 to show the range from freezing to boiling points; or if you were representing the months of the year, you would use 1 to 12 to show the range of months from January through December.

    For our example, we are using an arbitrary range of numbers (0 to 300) representing potential resolution levels for images. Enter **0** and **300** in the Range fields.

7. Enter the location on the track where you want the thumb initially positioned. The Initial Value field identifies the initial position of the thumb on the scale. Typically, the initial positions for a thumb is

    Start of range (in our example, 0)

    Middle point of range (in our example, 150)

    End of range (in our example, 300)

    The slider in our example is initially placed in the center of the track, so enter **150** in the Initial Value field.

8. Select Judge Interaction when the slider thumb has been released. (Sliders are controls, making it cumbersome to use buttons or other events to launch judgment of the interaction.)

    The Correct When field specifies Any Correct and None Incorrect by default. This setting is irrelevant to our example because we have only one correct range. There might be circumstances, however, where multiple ranges of numbers could be correct, and in those cases *any* versus *all* correct would make a difference.

9. Uncheck the Create a Reset button option to remove the Reset button. The Reset button is checked (included) by default. If you judge an interaction automatically, reset does not make sense.

10. Click on the Ranges tab. Here you define each range (subdivision) of the overall range defined on the General tab. By identifying each range in the overall range, you can define different judgments and actions for each range. By default, `Slider_CorrectRange` defines three ranges:

    `Range1`: **0 to 48**, incorrect

    `Range2`: **49 to 51**, correct

    `Range3`: **52 to 100**, incorrect

If defining correct and incorrect ranges in the Action Manager, any gaps in range definitions are judged by the Action Manager as an Unknown Response. For example, if you define an overall range of 0 to 300 on the General tab, and define two ranges on the Ranges tab (Range1 as 0 to 100, and Range2 as 101 to 200), any numbers falling in the undefined portion of the range (201 to 300) are judged as an Unknown Response.

Because the default provides the number of ranges we need, we don't need to add or subtract any (if we did, we would simply click Add to add one, or highlight a range and click Delete to delete one).

In our example, the overall range on the General tab is defined as 0 to 300, and the correct answer to the question on resolutions for images includes any answer from 72 and 96 (dpi). We need to define the three ranges on the Ranges tab to evaluate students:

> 0 to 71 (set to Incorrect)
>
> 72 to 96 (set to Correct)
>
> 97 to 300 (set to Incorrect)

11. Highlight the first range (Range1) if it is not already highlighted, and enter a range of **0** to **71** (see Figure 13-6). Be sure that Range1 is set to incorrect.

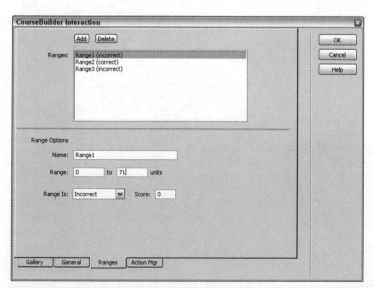

Figure 13-6: The Ranges tab for a slider interaction

12. Repeat Step 11 for the other two ranges, so that their final range definitions match the following:

   Range2: **72** to **96** (set to Correct)

   Range3: **97** to **300** (set to Incorrect)

13. Click the Action Mgr (Action Manager) tab. CourseBuilder displays the rules for processing this interaction, defining CourseBuilder actions for correct, incorrect, and unknown student responses.

   By default, the Action Manager (see Figure 13-7) tests a condition if Range1 Selected to see if the slider was released in Range1; if it was, the Action Manager pops up a message that says, "Too Low." The Action Manager also tests a condition if Range3 Selected to see if the slider was released in Range3, and if it was, the Action Manager pops up a message that says, "Too High." Range2 is set to correct, launching the actions under the if Correct condition.

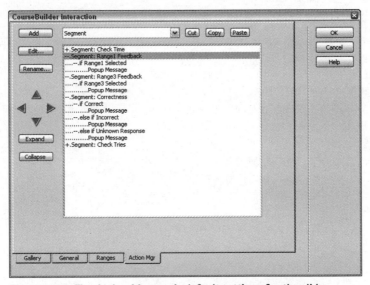

Figure 13-7: The Action Manager's default settings for the slider interaction

If you want to test for specific conditions such as ranges, Chapter 17 describes these capabilities fully.

14. Highlight and delete (by clicking the Cut button) the `Segment: Range 1 Selected` and the `Segment: Range 3 Selected` segments since the design of the *HTML Basics* course sends student feedback to the bottom frame (`blackboard`) for correct and incorrect responses.

15. Highlight each `Popup Message` action in the `if Correct` and `else if Incorrect` conditions and click the Cut button to delete them (this must be done for each message; there is no way to cut multiple actions at once).

16. Highlight the `else if Unknown Response` and click the Cut button to delete the unknown response condition.

17. Highlight the `if Correct` condition, select the Set Text of Frame action from the Action Manager drop-down menu, and click the Add button.

    CourseBuilder displays the Set Text of Frame dialog box.

18. Select the frame named `blackboard` from the Frame drop-down menu.

    When you add your feedback text, you can enter simple text or you can format that text with HTML tags, depending on the effect you want.

19. Enter the code for a correct answer, as follows:

    ```
    <font face="Comic Sans MS, Arial, sans-serif"><img
    src="images/smiley.gif" align="right">Correct!</font>
    ```

20. Highlight the `else if Incorrect` condition and click the Add button on the Action Manager tab to add the Set Text of Frame action to the `else if Incorrect` condition, as shown in Figure 13-8 (be sure to select the frame named `blackboard`).

21. Click OK when you've completed defining the rules in the Action Manager. CourseBuilder writes the processing rules into the HTML file, and displays the slider interaction in Dreamweaver MX, similar to Figure 13-9.

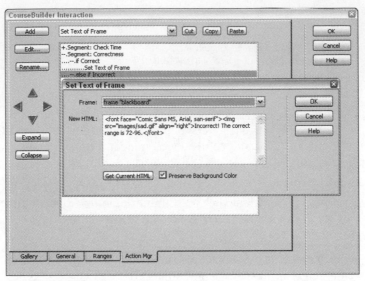

Figure 13-8: Entering the text for student feedback when they select a number in the incorrect ranges

Text box (inserted by default) that displays the current numeric location of the thumb on the track as students slide the thumb

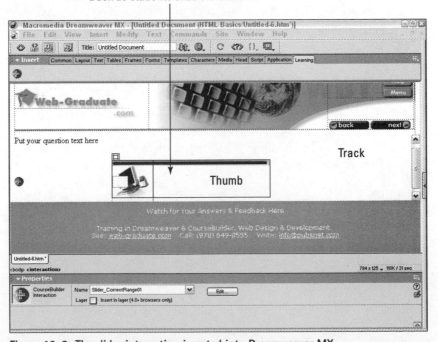

Figure 13-9: The slider interaction inserted into Dreamweaver MX

After you insert the interaction, you can rearrange the layers and text box to the final format. For instance, the text box in the *HTML Basics* example (see Figure 13-10) is dragged into a separate layer to display the numeric location of the thumb on the track. It has style characteristics attached from an external Cascading Style Sheet that changes the numbers to blue and enlarges the font.

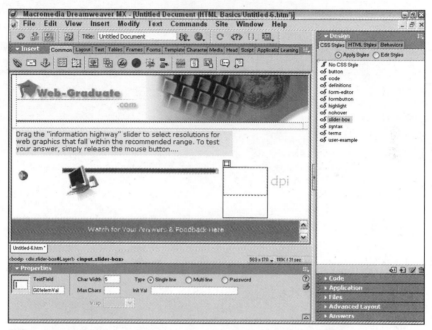

Figure 13-10: Rearrange the interaction's layers in Dreamweaver MX.

Figure 13-11 shows a flowchart that diagrams the decisions and actions taken by the Action Manager when processing this slider interaction.

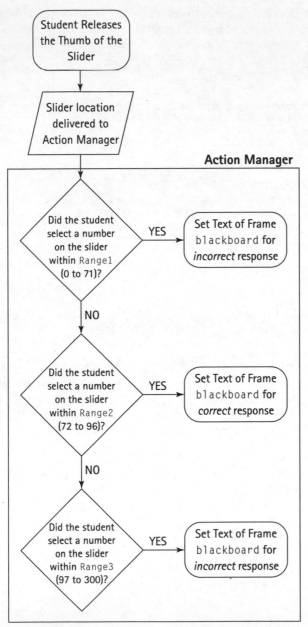

Figure 13–11: Processing of the slider interaction in the Action Manager

Creating Custom Sliders

Creating custom sliders is a relatively straightforward task. Every custom slider consists of three components, all stored in the sliders folder within the images folder:

- ◆ The image for the track (.gif or .jpg file).
- ◆ The image for the thumb (.gif or .jpg file).
- ◆ The thumbnail (100x100-pixel representation of the slider) displayed on the General tab in the CourseBuilder Interaction dialog box when you select the custom slider (.gif or .jpg file).

CourseBuilder sliders fall into two categories:

- ◆ Horizontal sliders, where the track has a horizontal orientation and the thumb moves from left to right (the far left is a value of 0, and the far right is the high end of the range).
- ◆ Vertical sliders, where the track has a vertical orientation and the thumb moves from bottom to top (the bottom is a value of 0, and the top is the high end of the range).

You implicitly specify the orientation for a slider by the naming convention you follow when you deposit your thumb, track, and thumbnail images into the sliders folder (subfolder within the images folder). Table 13-1 lists these conventions, which are added to the end of the image name. For example, a GIF image named pencil that you want to use as a thumb on a horizontal slider would be named pencil_hor_thm.gif.

TABLE 13-1 SLIDER IMAGE NAMING CONVENTIONS

Slider Orientation	GIF Image	JPG Image
Horizontal	_hor_thm.gif (thumb)	_hor_thm.jpg (thumb)
	_hor_tnail.gif (thumbnail)	_hor_tnail.jpg (thumbnail)
	_hor_trk.gif (track)	_hor_trk.jpg (track)
Vertical	_ver_thm.gif (thumb)	_ver_thm.jpg (thumb)
	_ver_trk.gif (track)	_ver_trk.jpg (track)
	_ver_tnail.gif (thumbnail)	_ver_tnail.jpg (thumbnail)

In the *HTML Basics* slider example, the custom slider `monitor` can be found in the Appearance drop-down menu on the General tab. CourseBuilder automatically abstracts that name because it found the following files in the `sliders` folder: `monitor_hor_thm.gif`, `monitor_hor_track.gif`, and `monitor_tnail.gif`.

You cannot mix and match graphics types (.GIF and .JPG) for a single slider; also, CourseBuilder will not display the slider as an option in the General tab unless all three necessary images (thumb, track, and thumbnail) are present in the `sliders` folder.

Although the track and thumb can be whatever size you want, the thumbnail graphic should be sized to 100 by 100 pixels. Since the only purpose of the thumbnail is to represent the slider in the dialog box, it does not really matter if the image is somewhat distorted by resizing.

Of course, the real challenge in creating tracks is making sure each location on the track accurately represents the sub-ranges. See "Example: *The Mesozoic Era* (as a multiple-choice test)" at the end of this chapter for directions on how to proportionally match a graphical track to the ranges defined in the slider interaction.

Choosing Your Slider Template

The CourseBuilder Gallery contains two slider templates, as shown in Figure 13-12. The significant difference between the two templates is that one slider is designed as a multiple-choice test, and the other slider is designed as a control interaction.

Choosing a slider as a control interaction (`Slider_2Ranges`)

Use the `Slider_2Ranges` template when you want to use a slider interaction for control, *without* judging choices. By default, this interaction

◆ Displays all of the sliders in the `sliders` folder for that site. CourseBuilder lists any slider that provides the three necessary files for each slider, discussed earlier in this chapter (General tab).

◆ Sets the overall range at 0 to 100 (General tab).

◆ Sets the initial value to 0, which means that the thumb is initially positioned to the far left on horizontal sliders or at the bottom of vertical sliders. You can select any number within the overall range as the starting point for the thumb (General tab).

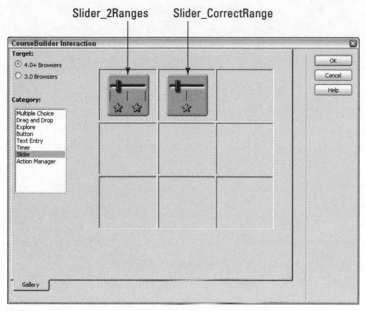

Figure 13-12: Slider templates available in the CourseBuilder Gallery

◆ Judges the interaction automatically when the student releases the slider thumb (General tab).

◆ Judges an answer correct if *any* are correct and *none* incorrect, although this setting is irrelevant because the ranges on the Ranges tab are not judged (General tab).

◆ Inserts a Reset button to allow students to return elements to their starting position and start over (General tab).

◆ Provides two sub-ranges: Range1, which is initially set at 0 to 49; and Range2, which is initially set at 50 to 100 (Ranges tab).

◆ Sets all ranges to Not Judged (Ranges tab).

◆ Inserts segments that include conditions for every range defined on the Ranges tab: if Range1 Selected, if Range2 Selected, and so forth (Action Mgr).

You can modify these defaults on the General and Ranges tabs. Figure 13-13 shows the default layout for the Slider_2Ranges interaction after it is inserted into Dreamweaver MX.

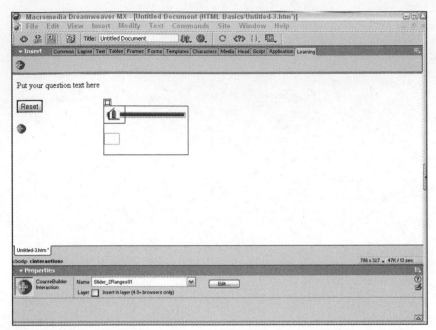

Figure 13-13: The `Slider_2Ranges` interaction, inserted into Dreamweaver MX.
In addition to the slider, CourseBuilder automatically inserts a text box that displays
the numeric location of the thumb on the slider at any given point.

Choosing a slider for multiple choice (`Slider_CorrectRange`)

Use the `Slider_CorrectRange` template when you want to use a slider interaction
for multiple choices, where each range is judged as correct or incorrect. By default,
this interaction

- Displays all of the sliders in the `sliders` folder for that site. CourseBuilder
  lists any slider that provides the three necessary files for each slider, discussed earlier in this chapter (General tab).

- Sets the overall range at 0 to 100 (General tab).

- Sets the initial value to 0, which means that the thumb is initially positioned to the far left on horizontal sliders or at the bottom of vertical sliders. You can select any number within the overall range as the starting
  point for the thumb (General tab).

- Judges the interaction automatically when the student releases the slider
  thumb (General tab).

- Judges an answer correct if *any* are correct and *none* incorrect (General tab).

- Inserts a Reset button to allow students to return elements to their original position and start over (General tab).

- Provides three sub-ranges: Range1, which is initially set at 0 to 48; Range2, which is initially set at 49 to 51; and Range3, which is initially set to 52 to 100 (Ranges tab).

- Sets Range1 and Range3 to Incorrect, and Range2 to correct (Ranges tab).

- Inserts segments that include conditions for both incorrect ranges defined on the Ranges tab: if Range1 Selected, and if Range3 Selected (Action Mgr).

- Includes the standard conditions under the Correctness segment (if Correct, else if Incorrect, and else if Unknown Response), each containing a Popup Message as the action (Action Mgr).

You can modify these defaults on the General and Ranges tabs. Figure 13-14 shows the default layout for the Slider_CorrectRange interaction after it is inserted into Dreamweaver MX.

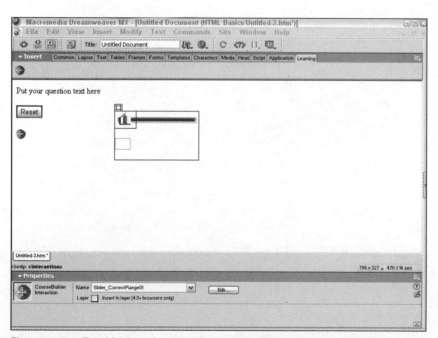

Figure 13-14: The Slider_CorrectRange interaction, inserted into Dreamweaver MXCourseBuilder automatically inserts a text box that displays the numeric location of the thumb on the slider at any given point.

Application Examples

Slider interactions provide students with a strong feeling of interactivity with a course. The examples described in this section both use the same slider: one as a means for control, the other for answering a multiple-choice question.

Example: The Mesozoic Era (as a multiple-choice test)

The Slider_CorrectRange template enables you to create a slider that judges each range on the track. Students answer each question by sliding the thumb to the correct location on the track and then releasing the thumb. *The Mesozoic Era* uses a slider consisting of a Triceratops thumb that moves along a timeline track to answer questions.

The slider is set to provide three options for student answers (as shown in Figure 13-15): Triassic, Jurassic, or Cretaceous.

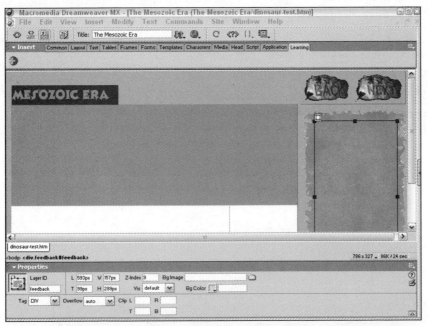

Figure 13-15: The Mesozoic Era as a multiple-choice test, where students use the slider to answer questions that are subsequently judged

Before inserting the interaction, the page was generally laid out, as shown in Figure 13-16. Of particular importance is the creation of the layer named feedback, which is used by the Action Manager as the location for conveying feedback to students.

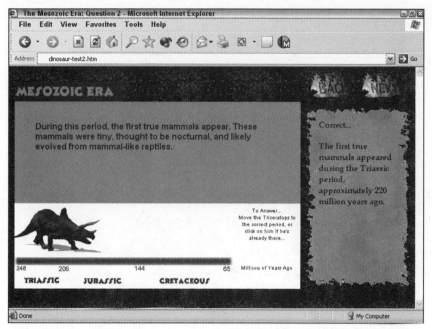

Figure 13-16: The Mesozoic Era web page before the slider interaction is inserted into the page

To create this example, select a `Slider_CorrectRange` template, because that template judges student answers. To begin defining your slider, select the Appearance for the slider – in this case, a custom slider named `dino`. This custom slider is automatically listed (by the unique part of the filename, `dino`) in the slider interaction General tab because these three files were deposited into the `sliders` folder:`dino_hor_thm.gif` (thumb), `dino_hor_trk.gif` (track), and `dino_hor_tnail.gif` (thumbnail).

As shown in Figure 13-17, you can define the ranges in "reverse order", so to speak, to match the orientation of the range of years on the track. Enter the overall range as 248 to 65. Since these numbers are only used for determining position on the track, you do not need to add the extra zeroes to make the numbers "millions".

If you wanted to represent the full number of years, such as 248,000,000 to 65,000,000, you could do so. However, you cannot enter separators such as commas or decimal points in the Range fields, so you'd use 248000000 to 65000000.

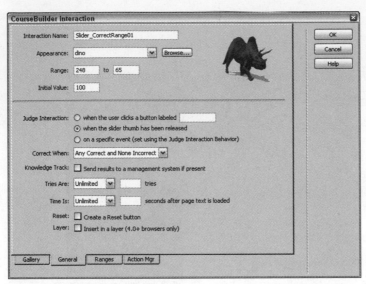

Figure 13-17: The Mesozoic Era covers the years from 248 million years ago until 65 million years ago. You can enter the range in reverse order on the General tab.

The Reset button is omitted for this interaction.

The next step in the process is to define the sub-ranges on the Ranges tab. These sub-ranges equate to each main period in *The Mesozoic Era,* as follows:

◆ Triassic, from 248 to 206 millions of years ago

◆ Jurassic, from 206 to 144 millions of years ago

◆ Cretaceous, from 144 to 65 millions of years ago

Notice that the range numbers overlap. For example, Triassic ends in 206 and Jurassic begins in 206; so when students pick 206, what period are they choosing? If ranges overlap, CourseBuilder associates the overlapped portion with the earliest defined range, so if 206 is selected, CourseBuilder associates it to the Triassic range.

Figure 13-18 shows the definitions of each range on the Ranges tab, with Triassic set as correct and Jurassic and Cretaceous set to incorrect. We've given each range the name of the Mesozoic period so that it is easier to follow the logic once we go to the Action Manager.

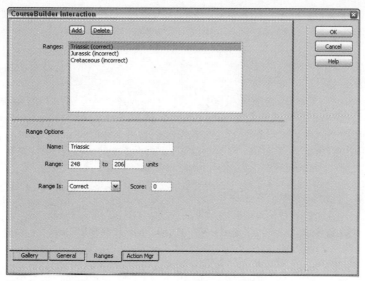

Figure 13-18: Defining each range on the Ranges tab

The trick with ranges is to proportionally match the sub-ranges with locations on the graphical representation of the range (the track image). To do so we need to gather the following information:

◆ The width of the graphic that represents the track (represented by the graphics file `dino_hor_trk.gif`). You can obtain the width by opening the file in a graphics program and looking at the width settings of the file. This file is 420 pixels wide.

◆ The percentage of the overall range that each sub-range represents. To determine the percentage of a specific range, divide a sub-range by the overall range. For example, if the overall range is 183 (248 minus 65), the sub-ranges are

Triassic: 42 (248 minus 206)

Jurassic: 62 (206 minus 144)

Cretaceous: 79 (144 minus 65)

Now that you know the overall range and each sub-range, you can figure out the percentages that each sub-range covers (numbers are rounded):

Triassic: 23% (42 divided by 183)

Jurassic: 34% (62 divided by 183)

Cretaceous: 43% (79 divided by 183)

In our example, the horizontal track is 420 pixels wide. With the percentages information and the width of the track, we can determine where each range should begin and end on the graphic:

Triassic begins at location 0 and ends at location 97 (23% from the left of the track).

Jurassic begins at location 97 and ends at location 240 (add the Jurassic 34% to the Triassic 23%).

Cretaceous begins at location 240 and ends at location 420 (the end of the scale).

You can place the beginning and ending markers for sub-ranges as exactly as you need in a graphics program such as Macromedia Fireworks MX, as long as the program provides rulers, as shown in Figure 13-19.

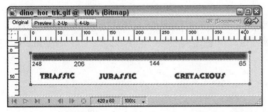

Figure 13-19: The track for The Mesozoic Era brought into Macromedia Fireworks MX. Using rulers allows you to precisely map locations on a graphical track to ranges used in slider interactions.

Once the ranges are defined on the Ranges tab, you are ready to define the processing rules in the Action Manager. By default, CourseBuilder creates a feedback segments for each range, as well as the standard Correctness segments.

CourseBuilder only creates feedback segments for every other feedback segment when you use the `Slider_CorrectRange` template (a known bug in CourseBuilder at the time of the writing of this book). If you want all feedback segments created, you can create your slider interaction using the `Slider_2Ranges` template and change the "Not Judged" ranges to either correct or incorrect, as appropriate.

Since the design of our course has us judging for the correctness of answers to questions, we can delete the feedback segments and just use the Correctness segment. As shown in Figure 13-20, we remove the feedback segments and the Popup Message conditions in the Correctness segment, and replace them with Set Text of Layer actions that write feedback into the layer named `feedback`.

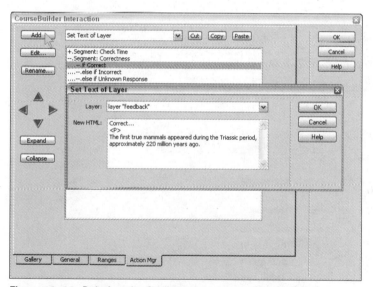

Figure 13-20: Deleting the feedback segments and replacing the Popup Message actions with Set Text of Layer actions in the Correctness segment

Once you complete your processing rules in the Action Manager and click OK, CourseBuilder inserts the thumb (Triceratops) and track (Mesozoic timeline) into layers, which you can drag and rearrange into their proper position. CourseBuilder also inserts a text box to display the numeric values for the range as students move the slider (as in the *HTML Basics* example). That text box was deleted for this example.

Example: The Mesozoic Era (as a control)

This example also uses the custom slider dino. However, instead of using the slider to answer questions (as with the Slider_CorrectRange template), it uses the dino slider for navigating to different pages.

When students slide the Triceratops to different periods on the Mesozoic timeline, CourseBuilder loads different pages depending on where the thumb is released on the slider. For example, when students slide the Triceratops to the Jurassic period and release it, CourseBuilder loads the page named dinosaur-jurassic.htm into the browser window (see Figure 13-21). The only function of the slider in the Slider_2Ranges template is to control selection of options without judgment.

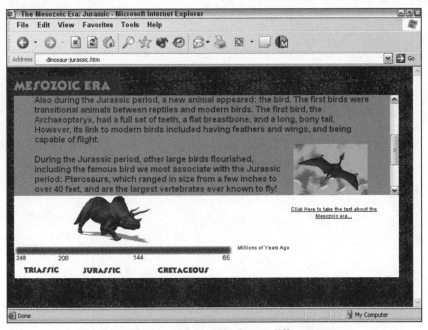

Figure 13-21: The slider dino used for navigating to different pages

You create this interaction with the Slider_2Ranges template. There are two key differences between this interaction and the interaction in the preceding example (Slider_CorrectRange). First, because we are using the dino slider for navigation, we need to add a third range for the Cretaceous period, and set all ranges to Not Judged, as shown in Figure 13-22.

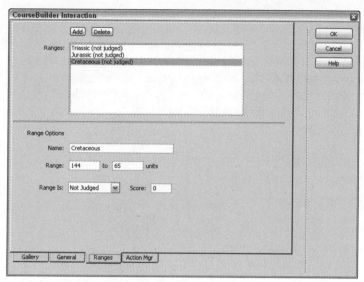

Figure 13-22: The Ranges tab when the `dino` slider is used for navigation.
None of the ranges are judged.

Second, when we look at the Action Manager tab, as shown in Figure 13-23, we see that it only contains feedback segments, and does not contain the standard Correctness segment.

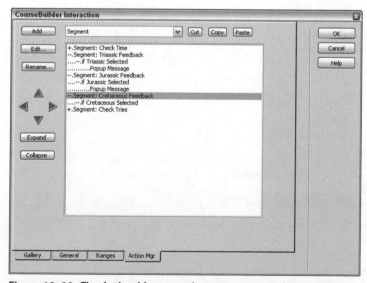

Figure 13-23: The Action Manager when you create an interaction using the `Slider_2Ranges` interaction for navigation and control

Remember, when a student drags the Triceratops to the Jurassic period, we want CourseBuilder to replace the current file with `dinosaur-jurassic.htm`. To direct CourseBuilder to load a new file into the browser, you need to replace the Popup Message actions under each segment with a Go To URL action for each segment, and specify the appropriate HTML file for each segment, as shown in Figure 13-24. (Note that the third segment, Cretaceous Feedback, does not contain a Popup Message because that segment was added on the Ranges tab).

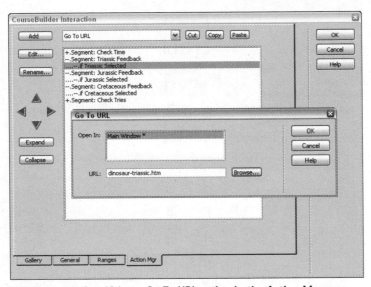

Figure 13-24: Specifying a Go To URL action in the Action Manager

Summary

This chapter described how to

- ◆ Use sliders for either multiple-choice tests or as controls.

- ◆ Create custom sliders from any images, including information on accurately scaling graphical representations of ranges.

- ◆ Select the appropriate slider templates.

- ◆ Apply sliders through several examples (*HTML Basics* and *The Mesozoic Era,* both on your CD-ROM).

The next chapter describes the control and processing of interactions.

Part III

Controlling and Processing Interactions

Chapter 14

Understanding Control and Processing Interactions

IN THIS CHAPTER

- ◆ Understanding the basics of control interactions (buttons, sliders, timers)
- ◆ Understanding how control and processing interactions work together

COURSEBUILDER has three controls that enable you to manage interactivity between students and course content:

- ◆ Buttons, which students click to indicate their selection.
- ◆ Sliders, which students slide and release to indicate their selection.
- ◆ Timers, with which you can set time limits for tests and activities, and trigger the testing of conditions or performance of actions at any interval along the way.

CourseBuilder processing rules enable you to manage the logic for judging and processing student tests and activities with the Action Manager, which is accessible in two ways:

- ◆ The Action Mgr tab on every interaction (you've seen this view of the Action Mgr in all of the previous chapters discussing interactions).
- ◆ The Action Manager interaction in the CourseBuilder Gallery, a separate interaction that you can include in your page to process multiple interactions in one place.

Enabling Student Interactivity with Buttons and Sliders

As you learned in earlier chapters, you can set up interactions so that they automatically process (judge interaction) when students

- Click a choice in a multiple-choice interaction

- Drop a drag element in a drag-and-drop interaction

- Exit a text field in a text-entry interaction

- Click a hot area in an explore interaction

- Release the thumb of a slider in a slider interaction

Sometimes, however, other events can be set up to initiate judgment. And that's where football comes in. . . ,

In football, for example, before the kickoff, the kicker places the ball on a tee. Until the kicker kicks the ball, that ball just sits on that tee. . . *waiting*. Once the ball is kicked, it's in play, and the fun begins!

You can construct CourseBuilder interactions to use buttons and sliders in roughly the same way. That is, you can set test and activity interactions to *wait* for buttons and sliders to kick them into play. Here's the general process:

1. Insert a test or activity interaction such as a multiple-choice question or a drag-and-drop activity.

2. Set the interaction to *wait* for the button or slider.

3. Insert the button or slider.

4. Instruct the button or slider to "kick" the test or activity interaction into play.

You set interactions to wait by specifying that the interaction be judged on a specific event. And just as the football waits, not knowing who or what will kick it into play, the test and activity interactions don't know what will kick them into play – they just sit there and wait for it (I realize this analogy is a bit anthropomorphic!). You set an interaction to wait by choosing the Judge Interaction on a specific event (set using the Judge Interaction Behavior) option. Figure 14-1 shows a multiple-choice interaction being set to wait.

Now you need to get the kicker on the field, show him the ball, and let him kick. And that's where the button or slider comes in. You instruct the button or slider to judge the interaction by selecting the Judge Interaction action on the button or slider's Action Mgr tab. Figure 14-2 shows a button being set up to judge the multiple-choice interaction shown in Figure 14-1.

Specify that a test or activity interaction wait for a button,
slider, or some other event to kick the interaction into play.

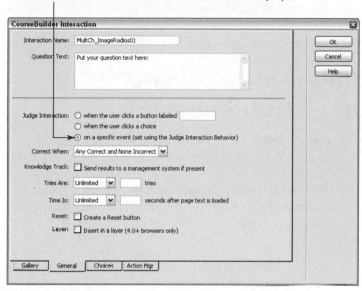

Figure 14-1: Setting an interaction to wait for a button or slider to
initiate judgment

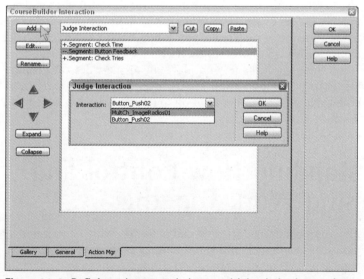

Figure 14-2: Defining a button to judge a multiple-choice interaction
when the student clicks the button

Once the student clicks the button, the Action Manager for that button begins processing and finds a single instruction: start processing the rules for the multiple-choice interaction, as defined by the Judge Interaction action inserted into the Action Manager.

Managing Complex Processing with the Action Manager

Continuing the football analogy, where's the coach? The coach on a football team drives everything. From calling plays to making decisions during the game, the coach manages all of the team's activities.

In CourseBuilder, the coach is the Action Manager. It is the Action Manager that determines how to process and respond to student actions. By combining rules for interactions in the Action Manager, you can create complex tests and activities without being a programmer!

Typically the Action Manager on an interaction's Action Mgr tab is used to define processing rules for that single interaction. For example, a button might have a single action defined on its Action Mgr tab, which is to initiate judgment of another interaction using the Judge Interaction action. Or, a drag-and-drop exercise might evaluate each pair and, if correct, display a popup message that is specific to each pairing.

The Action Manager interaction, on the other hand, is frequently used to process the rules and actions for multiple interactions, rather than defining those rules on each interactions Action Mgr tab. For example, you might have a test that has 10 multiple choice questions (similar to the *HTML Basics* final examination), leave the Action Mgr tab for each interaction blank, and place all of the rules on a single Action Manager interaction that evaluates the 10 responses and calculates a grade.

The procedures for developing processing rules on the Action Mgr tab and in the Action Manager interaction are identical.

Understanding How Control and Processing Work Together

CourseBuilder lets you control the time for tests and activities with Timer interactions. Timers are separate interactions that begin timing as soon as the page loads, and provide different graphical representations to students to enable them to "watch the clock," so to speak.

Timers allow you to define triggers that fire at specific intervals up to and including the time when the timer expires. Because timers are interactions, they include an Action Manager that lets you test conditions or perform actions at the intervals you specify.

The power of control and processing interactions is really in the assemblage of complex tests and activities that provide substantial interactivity for students as well as the ability to provide students with context-specific feedback and events.

Figure 14-3 shows the control and processing pieces pulled together into an interactive student experience.

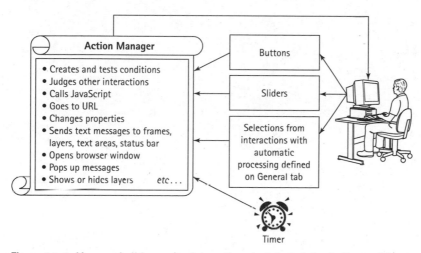

Figure 14-3: You can build complex interactions by intertwining buttons, sliders, behaviors, timers, and the Action Manager.

The chapters in Part III will help you use CourseBuilder control interactions and the Action Manager to build highly interactive e-Learning content.

Summary

This chapter described the concepts of the CourseBuilder interactions that manage control and processing of interactions.

The next chapter describes button interactions.

Chapter 15

Button Interactions

BUTTONS ARE USED for many reasons in Web-based training. For example, the *HTML Basics* course uses buttons to

◆ Navigate the course (Back and Next)

◆ Launch the student blackboard for each blackboard exercise

◆ Display sample HTML code you write by launching the code into a browser

◆ Initiate evaluation of a test or activity interaction

You can easily insert a button into any Web page within Dreamweaver MX by inserting a rollover image and attaching behaviors to it. So why use a button *interaction?* Because each button interaction lets you define processing rules in the Action Manager for that button, just as you define processing rules for any other interaction.

Probably the most common use of button interactions is to initiate the judgment of other CourseBuilder interactions. In the *HTML Basics* course, for example, a Grade It button is inserted as a button interaction, which initiates the judgment of many of the test and activity interactions in the course.

You can use any graphical images for button interactions, including buttons that ship with CourseBuilder (see Chapter 6) or custom buttons, described later in this chapter. This remainder of this chapter describes how to use button interactions.

Understanding How Button Interactions Work

To help you understand the concepts behind button interactions, let's examine the process for a button interaction from both the student's perspective (how it works) and the course author's perspective (how you create it).

The student's perspective

Let's first look at a button interaction from the *HTML Basics* course from the student's perspective. Figure 15-1 shows a sample button interaction from one of the tests.

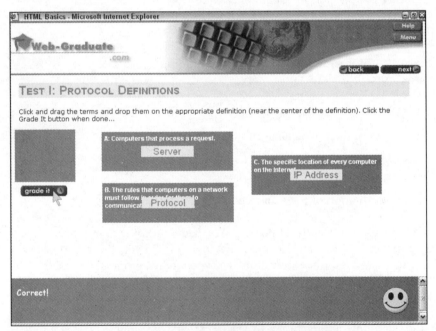

Figure 15-1: A button interaction in the HTML Basics course that initiates judgment of a drag-and-drop interaction

The student is instructed to click and drag the appropriate terms to each definition. When students drag and drop a term on a definition, they do not receive immediate feedback — in fact, they can continue rearranging dropped terms even after they've dropped them all onto definitions. To initiate judgment and receive feedback, students must explicitly click the Grade It button, which initiates processing of the button interaction's Action Manager. Of course, from the student's perspective, they cannot tell the difference between a button and a button interaction.

The course author's perspective

From the course author's perspective, there are *two separate* interactions required:

◆ A drag-and-drop interaction that enables students to click and drag terms to definitions. Students can move the drag elements as often as they'd like, because the interaction "waits" (so to speak) for the student to click the Grade It button before judging the interaction.

◆ A button interaction that, when clicked, includes an action in the button's Action Manager to initiate the processing of rules in the drag-and-drop Action Manager.

You can use a button interaction to launch judgment (processing) of any test or activity interaction, including multiple choice, drag and drop, explore, and text entry. (Although you could initiate judgment of a slider with a button, such design would be silly since sliders are also control interactions.)

Setting up a button interaction to launch a test or activity interaction is a two-step process. First, you must set the Judge Interaction option for that test or activity interaction to initiate processing *on a specific event,* as shown in Figure 15-2. In effect, this setting tells the interaction (a drag-and-drop in this example) to "wait" for some outside event to initiate judgment; it doesn't specify what the outside event is.

Second, you initiate processing of the test or activity interaction by adding a Judge Interaction action to the *button* interaction's Action Manager.

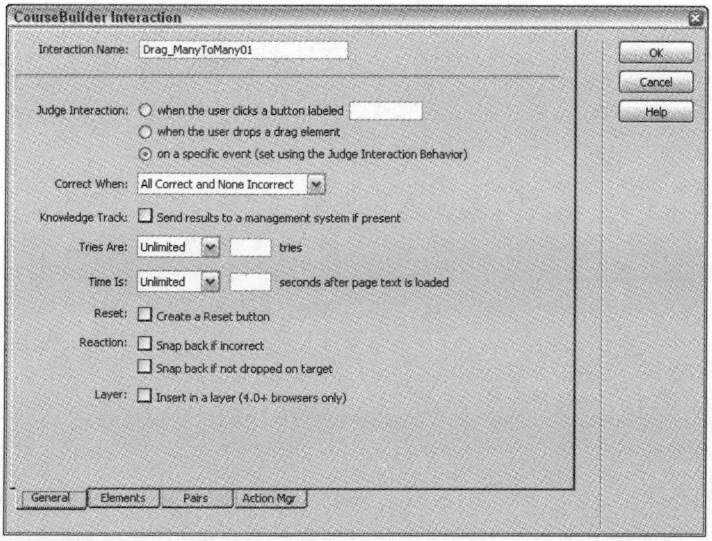

Figure 15-2: Specify that a drag-and-drop interaction should wait for some other event to initiate judgment.

To insert a button interaction that initiates judgment of the drag-and-drop interaction (assuming the drag-and-drop interaction is already inserted into the Web page), follow these steps:

1. Click the mouse pointer at the location in the Web page where you want that button to be located. In our example, we've included the button just below the drag-and-drop interaction.

2. Click the Insert CourseBuilder Interaction button on the Learning tab. The CourseBuilder Interaction dialog box displays, with the CourseBuilder Gallery active.

3. Select the Button category to display the two button templates (see Figure 15-5).

4. Click the Button_Push template. CourseBuilder inserts a working copy of the template into your Dreamweaver MX page, and activates the additional tabs for that template (General and Action Mgr), as shown in Figure 15-3.

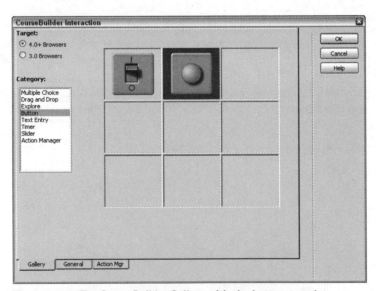

Figure 15-3: The CourseBuilder Gallery with the button template Button_Push selected

5. Click the General tab (see Figure 15-4) to define the general properties for the interaction.

6. Select the custom button grade from the Appearance drop-down menu, as shown in Figure 15-5.

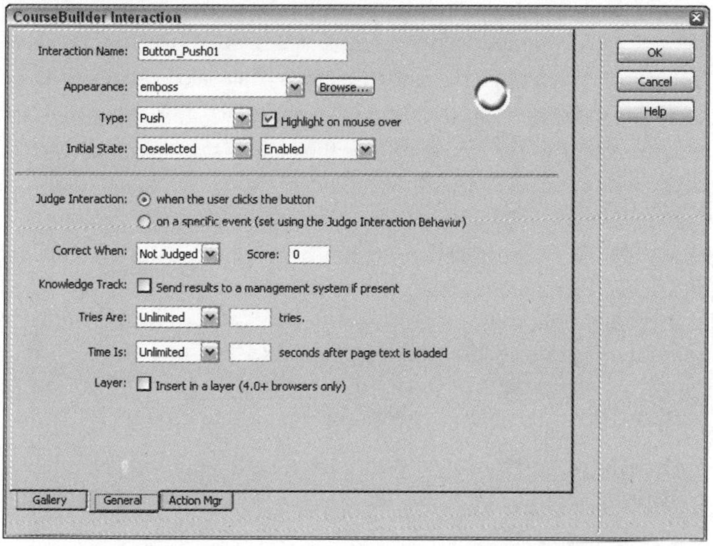

Figure 15-4: General tab for the Button_Push interaction

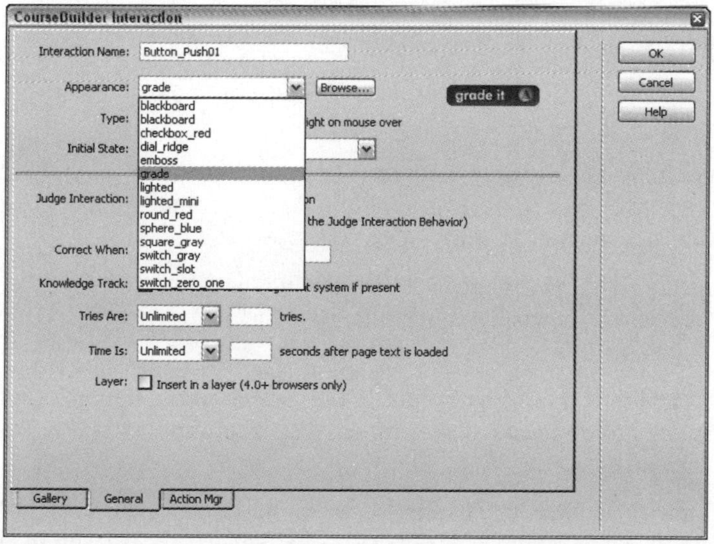

Figure 15-5: Selecting the custom button from the Appearance
drop-down menu

grade is a custom button we created, as described later in this chapter. You select custom buttons the same way that you select pre-designed buttons that ship with CourseBuilder: from the Appearance drop-down menu. For the purposes of this exercise, we assume the custom button is already created.

7. Leave the Type of button set to Push. The Type drop-down field indicates either a Toggle or Push button. If you selected the Button_Toggle template, this field defaults to a Toggle button; if you selected the Button_Push template, this field defaults to Push button. (Toggle and push buttons are explained more fully in the "Understanding Button Interaction Types and States" section later in this chapter.)

8. Leave the Highlight on Mouse Over checked. If you uncheck this, CourseBuilder will not swap an alternate image when the student moves the mouse pointer over the button.

9. Leave the Initial State set to Deselected (the Selected state is the mouse over state). Button states are explained more fully in the "Understanding Button Interaction Types and States" section later in this chapter.

    Leave the button Enabled. When the button is enabled, it is operational; when the button is disabled, it is not operational until some action makes it operational.

11. Leave the Judge Interaction set to When the User Clicks the Button. Rarely does it make sense to have another interaction initiate judgment of a button, so leave this setting just as it is.

12. Leave the Correct When field set to Not Judged (almost always the case) by default. To associate judgment (correct or incorrect) with the button itself, you set this to Up or Down options.

13. Click the Insert in a Layer option at the bottom of the General tab to insert the button inside a layer for easy repositioning within Dreamweaver MX.

14. Click the Action Mgr tab. CourseBuilder displays the default rules for processing this interaction, which consists of a segment named Button Feedback that includes a Popup Message (that says "Button Pushed") by default.

15. Highlight Popup Message and click Cut.

16. Highlight the Button Feedback segment, select the Judge Interaction action from the Action Manager drop-down menu, and click the Add button. CourseBuilder displays the Judge Interaction dialog box.

The Judge Interaction action enables you select the interaction to be processed when students click the button.

17. Select the `Drag_ManyToMany01` interaction in the Judge Interaction dialog box, as shown in Figure 15-6, and Click OK.

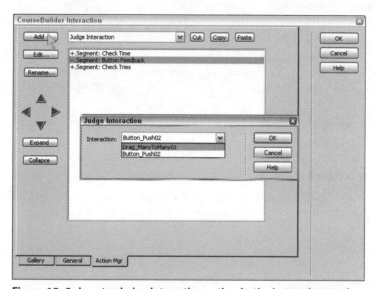

Figure 15-6: Insert a Judge Interaction action in the button interaction to identify the interaction that should be judged when students click the button.

18. Click OK when you've completed defining the rules in the Action Manager. CourseBuilder writes the processing rules into the HTML file, and displays the button interaction in Dreamweaver MX, similar to Figure 15-7.

Figure 15-8 shows a flowchart that diagrams the decisions and actions taken by the Action Manager when processing this button interaction.

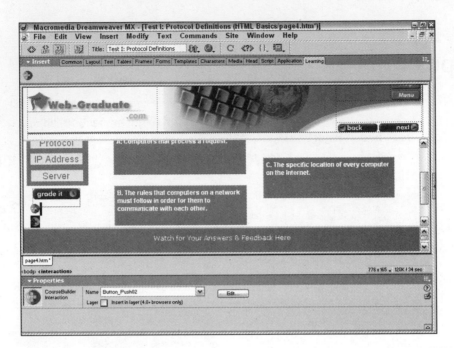

Figure 15-7: The button interaction inserted into the Dreamweaver MX Web page. It initiates judgment of the drag-and-drop interaction when students click it.

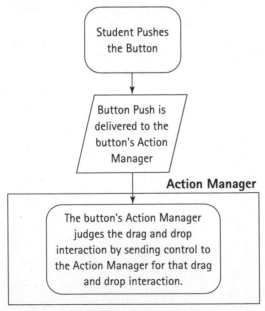

Figure 15-8: Processing of the button interaction in the Action Manager

Understanding Button Interaction Types and States

A sample file called button-states.htm on the CD-ROM demonstrates the different default states for a button when students mouseover and click. The concepts described in this section will be much easier to understand if you read them.

To allow you to build highly interactive buttons, CourseBuilder provides multiple *states* for each button. Each button has six possible states, depending on student actions and properties you might set for a button. For example, when the student moves the mouse pointer over a button graphic, that button is in the highlighted state; and when the student clicks the mouse pointer on that button graphic, that button is in the selected and highlighted state.

Each button state has an associated (and typically different) graphic button that CourseBuilder displays when the button changes state. For example, a button in the highlighted state might use a version of the button with shadowed letters, and a button in the selected state might use an embossed version of the button.

All button interactions use the same states for a button. However, there are two *types* of button interactions *(toggle and push)* that differ in *how* they use button states and how they define default actions in the Action Manager.

A sample file called button-states.htm on the CD-ROM demonstrates the different states for a toggle and push button when students mouse-over and click it. The concepts described in this section will be much easier to understand if you view the sample file while reading about them here.

Toggle buttons work similar to light switches by toggling between on and off. When a student clicks a toggle button, that button remains in the selected state until the toggle button is clicked again, at which point it returns to the normal state (just as a light switch stays in the off position until moved to the on position, and vice versa).

Toggle buttons have two unique characteristics. First, the graphic representing the normal (deselected) state remains until the button is clicked, at which point it is replaced by the graphic representing the selected state. Second, the Action Manager for toggle buttons tests for two conditions: if Selected and else if Deselected, providing the opportunity to define *different* actions for each state.

A good example of a toggle button is shown in the *Movie Controller* example on the CD-ROM. When you initially load the page, the page includes a Play button that, when clicked, plays a movie; as soon as you click the Play button, the movie plays *and* that Play button becomes (toggles to) a Stop button. When you click the Stop button, the movie stops playing *and* the Stop button toggles back to a Play button. Students can toggle between Play and Stop as much as they want.

Table 15-1 shows the different button states that are automatically applied for toggle buttons.

TABLE **15-1 DEFAULT STATES FOR TOGGLE BUTTON GRAPHICS**

State	Displays When	Graphic File Naming Convention
Normal	Normal (how it looks when a page first opens).	`*.gif`
Highlighted	Mouse pointer is over the button graphic.	`*_hlt.gif`
Selected *and* Highlighted	Mouse pointer is over the button graphic and is clicked (selected), and remains over button graphic.	`*_sel_hlt.gif`
Selected	Mouse pointer moves off previously clicked (selected) button.	`_sel.gif`

Whereas toggle buttons work similar to light switches, push buttons work similar to doorbells. When students click a push button, that button remains selected *only* as long as the mouse button remains clicked; once the mouse button is released, the push button automatically pops back to the normal state. Furthermore, unlike the toggle button, push buttons do *not* test for conditions in the Action Manager; rather, they automatically run any actions you specify in a segment named `Button Segment`.

A good example of a push button is also shown in the *Movie Controller* example on the CD-ROM. The page includes a Rewind button that only rewinds the movie.

Table 15-2 shows the different states that are automatically applied for push buttons.

When you use button interactions, there may be cases where you disable a button by selecting Disabled on the button interaction's General tab, or by using the Set Interaction Properties action in the Action Manager. You might, for example, disable a button when a student reaches the time limit for a test or activity. Or you might initially disable a button until the student performs a specific action.

TABLE 15-2 DEFAULT STATES FOR PUSH BUTTON GRAPHICS

State	Displays When	Graphic File Naming Convention
Normal	Normal (how it looks when the Web page opens).	*.gif
Highlighted	Mouse pointer is over button graphic.	*_hlt.gif
Selected *and* Highlighted	Mouse pointer is over button graphic and is clicked and held.	*_sel_hlt.gif then automatically displays *hlt.gif when mouse button is released

If a button is disabled, CourseBuilder uses different graphic states to show that the button is disabled. Table 15-3 shows the two possible disabled states (and their associated graphics) for buttons.

TABLE 15-3 THE TWO DISABLED STATES FOR BUTTON GRAPHICS

State	Displays When	Graphic File Naming Convention
Disabled	Button is disabled (can't be clicked).	*_dis.gif
Selected and Disabled	Button was previously clicked but is now disabled.	*_sel_dis.gif

Creating Custom Buttons

To create a custom button, you need to create a graphic file for each of the six button states *plus* a thumbnail graphic used to represent the button on the General tab. Although you create buttons for the different states, CourseBuilder knows which button to use for each state by the graphics file naming conventions.

Although you need to create the different graphic files for each button, you can reuse the same graphic (with the appropriate names) if you decide to reuse the same graphical look in different states. For example, if you decide you want the "selected and highlighted" state of a button to be the same as "selected", simply use the same graphic file twice (once with the _sel_hlt.gif suffix, and once with the _sel.gif suffix).

Table 15-4 shows the seven graphics you can create for a button.

TABLE 15-4   REQUIRED GRAPHIC FILES FOR CUSTOM BUTTONS

State	Graphic File Naming Convention	Example
{default}	*.gif	
Highlighted (Mouse is over button.)	*_hlt.gif	
Selected & Highlighted (Button is clicked; mouse remains over it.)	*_sel_hlt.gif	
Selected (Button is clicked; mouse moves off button.)	_sel.gif	
Disabled (Button disabled by course author in Action Manager.)	_dis.gif	
Selected & Disabled (Button was clicked by student; now disabled by course author in Action Manager.)	_sel_dis.gif	
Thumbnail (100x100-pixel representation of button; used only on the General tab.)	_tnail.gif	

Assume you had a button named Score represented by a graphics file named score.gif. To create the images for this button, create the following seven graphics files:

```
score.gif

score_hlt.gif

score_sel_hlt.gif

score_sel.gif

score_dis.gif

score_sel_dis.gif

score_tnail.gif
```

To make a button available to your site, simply deposit the seven graphic files into the `buttons` folder (within the `images` folder of your Dreamweaver MX site). CourseBuilder then automatically includes the button in the Appearances field on the General tab when you select the button interaction.

Choosing Your Button Template

The CourseBuilder Gallery contains two button templates, as shown in Figure 15-9. The significant difference between them is in how they use the different button states, and the default conditions and segments they insert into the Action Manager.

Button_Toggle   Button_Push

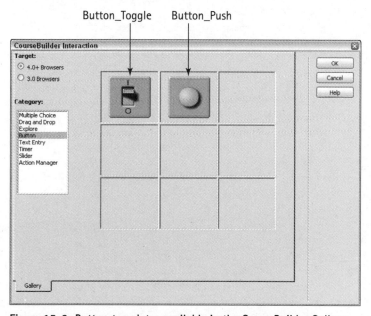

Figure 15-9: Button templates available in the CourseBuilder Gallery

Choosing a toggle button (`Button_Toggle`)

Use the `Button_Toggle` template when you want to use a button interaction that works like a light switch. When students click a toggle button, it remains in the clicked (selected) position until they click it again. By default, this interaction

◆ Displays all of the buttons in the `buttons` folder for that site. CourseBuilder automatically lists all graphics in the `buttons` folder as buttons in the Appearance drop-down menu (General tab).

◆ Sets the Type to Toggle (General tab).

♦ Sets the Initial State to Deselected (displays the `*.gif` graphic) — a value of Selected displays the `*_sel.gif` graphic — and Enabled, meaning the button is operational. A value of Disabled turns the button to non-operational, and it remains in that state unless you specifically change it back to Enabled in the Action Manager (General tab).

♦ Judges the interaction automatically when the student clicks the button (General tab).

♦ Provides `if Selected` and `else if Deselected` conditions in the Action Manager, as shown in Figure 15-10. By providing separate conditions for these two button states, CourseBuilder enables you to easily define different actions for each time the student clicks the button (each button click toggles between each state) (Action Mgr tab).

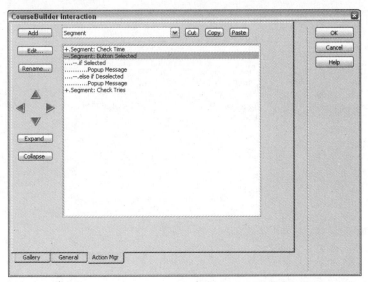

Figure 15-10: The `Button_Toggle` interaction default settings in the Action Manager

You can modify these defaults on the General and Action Mgr tabs.

Choosing a push button (`Button_Push`)

Use the `Button_Push` template when you want to use a button interaction that works like a doorbell. When students click a push button, it automatically pops back to its original state (original image) when released. By default, this interaction

♦ Displays all of the buttons in the `buttons` folder for that site. CourseBuilder automatically lists all graphics in the `buttons` folder as buttons in the Appearance drop-down menu (General tab).

- Sets the Type to Push (General tab).

- Sets the Initial State to Deselected (displays the file name `*.gif`) — a value of Selected displays the file named `*_sel.gif` — and Enabled, meaning the button is operational. A value of Disabled turns the button to non-operational, and it remains in that state unless you specifically change it back to Enabled in the Action Manager (General tab).

- Judges the interaction automatically when the student clicks the button (General tab).

- Provides a Button Feedback segment, as shown in Figure 15-11, but does not provide `if Selected` or the `else if Deselected` conditions because push buttons don't remain in the selected state (Action Mgr tab).

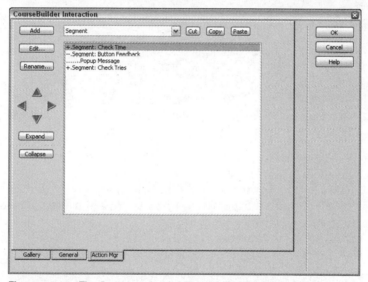

Figure 15-11: The `Button_Push` interaction defaults in the Action Manager

You can modify these defaults on the General and Action Mgr tabs.

Application Example

Although button interactions are most often used to launch the judgment of other interactions (see the *HTML Basics* example described earlier in this chapter), they can easily be used to control any of the actions available within the Action Manager. Let's look at an example in which buttons control the playing of a Flash movie (see Figure 15-12).

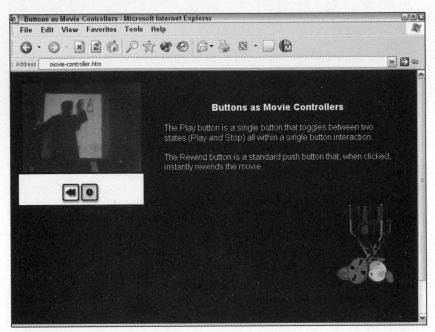

Figure 15-12: This example uses both push (Rewind) and toggle (Play/Stop) buttons.

To see how this works, take a look at the *Movie Controller* example on the CD-ROM (as shown in Figure 15-12).

When students click the Rewind button, the Flash movie returns to the very first frame in the movie. Because of the nature of the Rewind function (a single click and the movie instantly moves to the first frame of the movie), it makes sense to use a push button. I created two states of the button (plus a thumbnail):

```
rewind.gif

rewind_hlt.gif
```

The Play and Stop functions are a little more complex because they are combined into a single button interaction, enabling students to toggle between play and stop. To create this interaction, I created four states of the button:

```
play.gif

play_hlt.gif

play_sel.gif (an image of the stop button)

play_sel_hlt.gif (an image of the stop button highlighted)
```

When the student clicks the Play button, the movie plays and the button turns into the Stop button so that the student can click it to stop playing the movie. If the student clicks the Stop button, the movie pauses and the button turns into a Play button. The student can toggle between Play and Stop as often as they want.

Let's follow the processing logic for the toggle button interaction (see Figure 15-13):

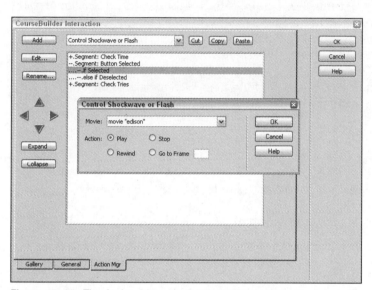

Figure 15-13: The Action Manager for the Button_Toggle interaction lets you easily define actions for both the Selected or Deselected states of the button.

1. The student clicks the Play button (play.gif), meaning that the Play button is selected. The Action Manager sees that the button is selected and performs the action directed by the if Selected condition, which in this case is a Control Shockwave or Flash action defined to play the Flash movie.

   The movie plays and CourseBuilder swaps the button image to play_sel.gif (the Stop button), which is the selected version of the button (if the student's mouse pointer is over the button, CourseBuilder displays the selected and highlighted version of the image, which is the Stop button highlighted).

2. The student clicks the Stop button, meaning that the button toggles back to the original image, the Play button (`play.gif`). The Action Manager sees that the button is deselected and performs the `else if Deselected` condition, which in this case is a Control Shockwave or Flash action defined to stop the Flash movie.

   The movie stops and CourseBuilder swaps the button image to the original image `play.gif` (the Play button), which is the deselected version of the button (if the student's mouse pointer is over the button, CourseBuilder displays the deselected and highlighted version of the image, which is the Play button highlighted).

It's the second click that toggles the button interaction back to the original state. If the student again clicks the button, the process repeats with Step 1.

Summary

This chapter discussed the types and states of buttons, as well as how to

- ◆ Use buttons to initiate judgment of other interactions.
- ◆ Use buttons to launch other actions within the Action Manager.
- ◆ Create custom buttons.

The next chapter describes how to use timers to control the amount of time students have to complete a test or activity.

Chapter 16

Timer Interactions

IN THIS CHAPTER

◆ Understanding the purpose of timer interactions

◆ Using timer interactions to control time for tests and activities

◆ Creating custom timers

TIMER INTERACTIONS can be used for any function, although their key utilization within CourseBuilder is to provide a countdown clock for test questions and activities. Timers enable you to create a countdown clock that can

◆ Count for as long as you would like.

◆ Trigger warnings and other actions after specific time has elapsed.

◆ Launch any actions you want through the Action Manager when time runs out.

To see how timers and triggers work, take a look at Figure 16-1. Timers are defined in numbers of seconds, regardless of the length of the timing. In this example, the timer is set for 6 minutes total (360 seconds).

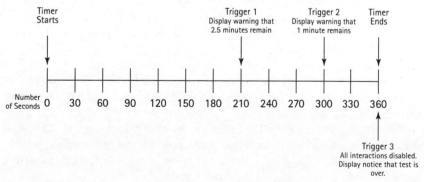

Figure 16-1: How timers and triggers work in CourseBuilder

Triggers are used along the way to display warnings about time remaining (triggers are set to fire after so many seconds into the timer). Like other CourseBuilder interactions, triggers can launch any actions in the Action Manager. The example shown in Figure 16-1 uses three triggers:

◆ Trigger 1 fires at 210 seconds (3.5 minutes) into the timer, and displays a warning to the student that 2.5 minutes remain.

◆ Trigger 2 fires at 300 seconds (5 minutes) into the timer, and displays a warning to the student that 1 minute remains.

◆ Trigger 3 fires when the timer expires, using the Action Manager to disable all of the interactions on the page. This function is similar to "Time's up; put your pencils away!"

Understanding How Timer Interactions Work

To understand the concepts behind timer interactions, you should be familiar with the interaction from the student's perspective (how it works) and from the course author's perspective (how you create it). This section describes both perspectives.

The student's perspective

To see how timer interactions work from a student's perspective, take a look at a timer interaction from the *HTML Basics* course. Figure 16-2 shows a sample timer interaction from the final examination section.

The counter shows the time remaining for the test. When the student has 2 minutes remaining (240 seconds into the test), the timer triggers a warning in the bottom frame telling the user there are 2 minutes remaining, as shown in Figure 16-3. The notice remains in the frame for 15 seconds and then disappears, and the student continues working on the test.

Figure 16-4 shows an example of the test in which the student answered the first 9 questions, but did not finish Question 10 when time expired. If the student has not completed the exam before time elapses, the timer immediately disables the test and provides a score for work completed.

In this example, the student got all questions right except for Question 10, which is marked incorrect because it is incomplete. After scoring, the test displays a message next to each question showing whether each question was correct, incorrect by choice, or incorrect because of a lack of response.

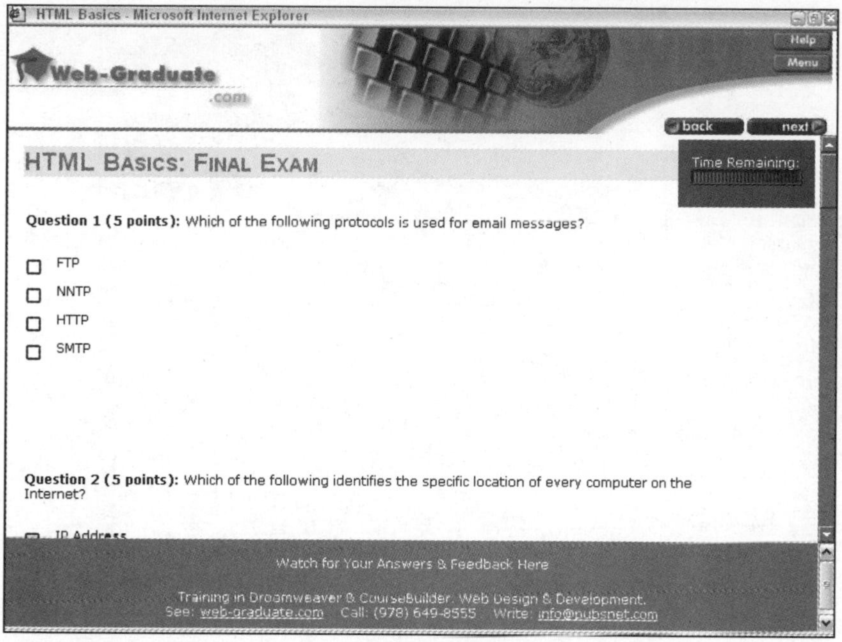

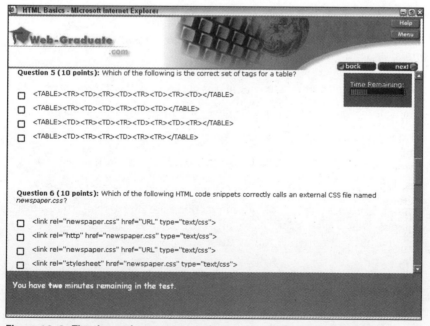

Figure 16-2: A timer interaction in the HTML Basics course that allots 6 minutes for completion of the final examination

Figure 16-3: The timer triggers two warnings to the student: when there are 2 minutes and 1 minute remaining in the exam.

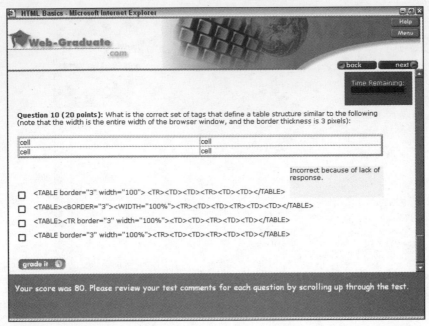

Figure 16-4: When time expires, the timer disables unanswered questions and then scores the exam.

The course author's perspective

From the course author's perspective, this test involves the assemblage of the following interactions:

◆ 10 multiple-choice interactions, one for each question.

◆ 1 button interaction that students click when they've completed the test.

◆ 1 timer interaction set for 360 seconds (6 minutes).

◆ 1 Action Manager interaction that judges each of the 10 multiple-choice interactions, and processes the scoring at the end of the exam.

This example assumes that all of the interactions are already inserted into the file. To understand how the Action Manager works, refer to Chapter 17.

To insert the timer into the file, follow these steps:

1. Ensure that the file is at the proper starting point (10 multiple-choice, button, and action manager interactions are already inserted).

2. Click the Insert CourseBuilder Interaction button on the Learning tab. The CourseBuilder Interaction dialog box displays, with the CourseBuilder Gallery active.

3. Choose the Timer category to display the two timer templates (see Figure 16-5).

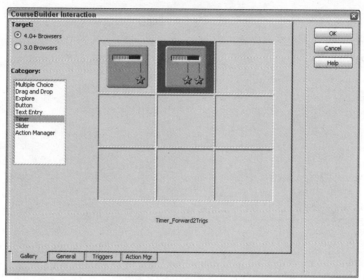

Figure 16-5: The CourseBuilder Gallery with the timer template Timer_Forward2Trigs selected

4. Click the Timer_Forward2Trigs template (we'll have five triggers to define). CourseBuilder inserts a working copy of the template into your Dreamweaver MX page, and activates the additional tabs (General, Triggers, and Action Mgr) for that template, as shown in Figure 16-5.

5. Click the General tab (see Figure 16-6) to define the general properties for the interaction.

Select custom button Small_Gradient from the Appearance drop-down menu.

Enter **360** in the Duration: field. This defines the total duration of the timer in seconds. We're allotting six minutes for the test, and that's 360 seconds.

Select the Reverse image order option. The timer will start with a filled image and "empty" as time passes. Normally (with the option unchecked), timers begin with a blank image and "fill up" as time passes.

Since we want the timer to begin when the page loads, leave the default setting for Judge Interaction, which automatically starts the timer when the page finishes loading (only select the On a Specific Event option if you want some outside action to start the timer).

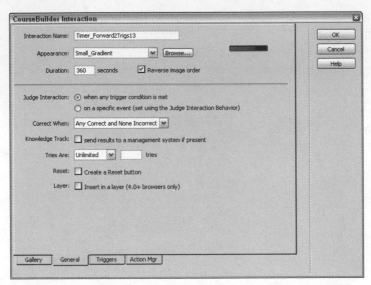

Figure 16-6: General tab for the `Timer_Forward2Trigs` **interaction**

The Correct When field is also irrelevant, because we aren't judging the timer for correctness. Again, leave the default selected.

The knowledge track is irrelevant for control interactions (knowledge tracking uses different properties to track time for interactions). Do not select this option.

The Tries Are field and the number of tries field are immaterial because the concept does not make sense in terms of a timer interaction. Just leave these as they are.

The Reset button would defeat the purpose of the timer (why have a timer if the student can continually request additional time?). There may be circumstances where the Reset button would be handy — in cases where you want "beat the clock" type timing for an activity — but not for the timing of a test. Uncheck the Create a Reset button field.

6. Click the Triggers tab to define the triggers for the interaction. CourseBuilder displays the Triggers tab.

   We need to define a total of five triggers for our interaction, so highlight `Trigger2` and click the Add button three times. CourseBuilder adds three triggers (`unnamed1`, `unnamed2`, and `unnamed3`), bringing the total number of triggers to five.

For consistency, rename the triggers we just added. Highlight unnamed1 and type **Trigger3** in the name field; highlight unnamed2 and type **Trigger4** in the name field; and then highlight unnamed3 and name it **Trigger5.**

Define the times for each trigger to fire. To do so, highlight each trigger and, in the Trigger Once After field, enter the number of seconds at which it will fire. Here are the firing times:

Trigger1: 240 seconds

Trigger2: 255 seconds

Trigger3: 300 seconds

Trigger4: 315 seconds

Trigger5: 360 seconds

Figure 16-7 shows the Triggers tab after as the time for Trigger5 is set.

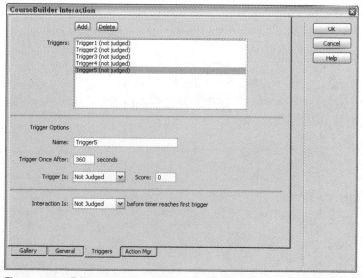

Figure 16-7: Triggers tab for the Timer_Forward2Trigs **interaction**

With the timing set, we're ready to specify the *actions* for the triggers.

7. Click the Action Mgr tab to display the Action Manager. CourseBuilder displays the default rules for processing this interaction, as shown in Figure 16-8.

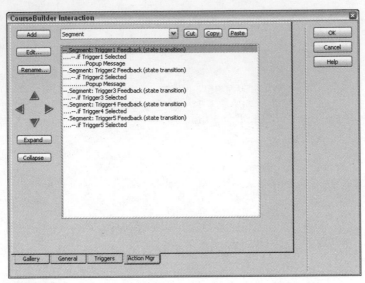

Figure 16–8: Action Mgr tab for the `Timer_Forward2Trigs` interaction, with initial settings for the five triggers set on the Triggers tab

Begin by removing the two Popup Messages (CourseBuilder adds Popup Message actions for the two original triggers, but not for additional triggers that you added on the Triggers tab). To do so, highlight each Popup Message and press the Cut button.

We now need to add the appropriate actions to each trigger, as follows:

Highlight the Trigger1 condition `if Trigger1 Selected`, select the action Set Text of Frame from the action drop-down menu, and click the Add button. CourseBuilder displays the Set Text of Frame dialog box (see Figure 16-9). Select the frame in which the message will display (the bottom frame, named `blackboard`). In the New HTML field, type the following message, and then click OK to close the Set Text of Frame dialog box:

```
<font face="Comic Sans MS, Arial, sans-serif">You have
<b>two</b> minutes remaining in the test.</font>
```

Highlight the Trigger2 condition `if Trigger1 Selected`, select the action Set Text of Frame from the action drop-down menu, and click the Add button. Select the frame `blackboard` and leave the New HTML field blank so that this trigger action writes nothing to the frame, effectively "erasing" the Trigger1 message. The result is that the two-minute warning (Trigger1) displays for 15 seconds and then disappears (Trigger2) from the student's screen. Click OK.

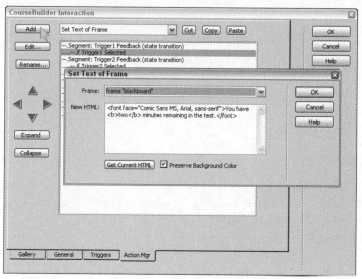

Figure 16-9: Adding a Set Text of Frame action to the
`if Trigger1 Selected` condition in the Action Manager. We add
the message we want displayed into the New HTML text box.

Highlight the Trigger3 condition `if Trigger1 Selected`, select the
action Set Text of Frame from the action drop-down menu, and click
the Add button. Select the frame `blackboard`, type the following message, and then click OK:

```
<font face="Comic Sans MS, Arial, sans-serif">You have
<b>one minute remaining in the test.</font></b>
```

Highlight the Trigger4 condition `if Trigger1 Selected`, select the
action Set Text of Frame from the action drop-down menu, and click
the Add button. Select the frame `blackboard` and leave the New HTML
field blank to "erase" the Trigger3 message. Click OK.

Trigger5 fires *only* if the timer expires before the student presses the
Grade It button. If Trigger5 fires, we need to disable the Grade It button
so that students can't continue to enter answers; and we need to send
control to the Action Manager to process all of the multiple-choice
interactions and provide a total score.

Highlight the Trigger5 condition (`if Trigger5 Selected`). Select the
action Set Interaction Properties from the action drop-down menu and
click the Add button. CourseBuilder displays the Set Interaction
Properties dialog box. Set the property of the button interaction
(named `Button_Push12`) to disabled, following the settings in Figure
16-10, and click OK.

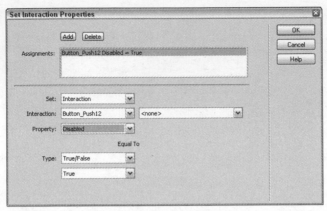

Figure 16-10: Disabling the button interaction `Button_Push12` in the Set Interaction Properties dialog box

Highlight the Set Interaction Properties action that was inserted into the Action Manager. Select the action Judge Interaction from the action drop-down menu and click the Add button. CourseBuilder displays the Judge Interaction dialog box. Select the ActionMgr11 interaction from the Judge Interaction dialog box, as shown in Figure 16-11, and click OK.

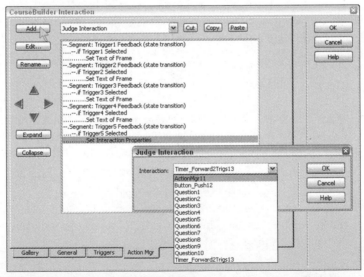

Figure 16-11: Calling the Action Manager interaction from the timer, using the Judge Interaction action

The timer is now inserted into the final exam page. As Figure 16-12 shows, if the student clicks the Grade It button before time expires on the timer, the Grade It button interaction launches the Action Manager interaction; if time expires before the student clicks the Grade It button, the timer launches the Action Manager interaction.

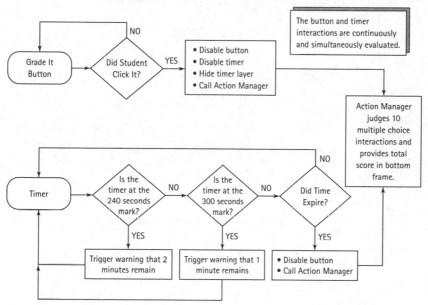

Figure 16-12: Both the button and timer interactions are continuously and simultaneously tested until either a student pushes the button or time expires.

TIP Notice that the layer containing the timer remains displayed in the upper right corner of the frame `mainFrame`? That is because the layer uses persistent layers, a capability available through a free extension to Dreamweaver MX available on the Macromedia Exchange for Dreamweaver (`http://exchange.macromedia.com`). Search for the name of the extension, Persistent Layers, created by Marja Ribbers-de Vroed.

Creating Custom Timers

Like animated graphics for the Web, CourseBuilder timers are simply a series of images that display sequentially to give the illusion of animation. However, unlike animated graphics, CourseBuilder timers do not stack the images into a single animated GIF file.

To build custom timers, you need to understand how CourseBuilder uses the graphics representing the timer. Let's look at an existing timer, the Small_Gradient timer used in the *HTML Basics* course. The Small_Gradient timer consists of 30 different files (see in Figure 16-13).

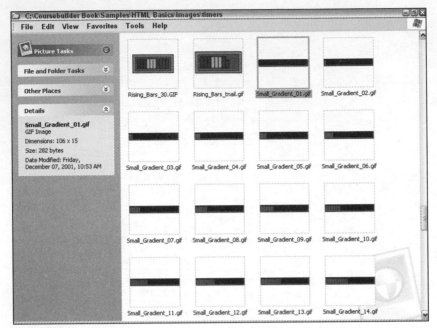

Figure 16-13: Some of the 30 graphics files that make up the timer `Small_Gradient`

Visually, the starting point for a timer depends on the order you select. If Reverse Image Order is *not checked* on the General tab, the first graphic used by the Small_Gradient timer is `Small_Gradient_01.gif` (empty). The second graphic used by the Small_Gradient timer is named `Small_Gradient_02.gif` (one bar); the third is `Small_Gradient_03.gif` (two bars), and so forth. If Reverse Image Order *is checked,* the first graphic used is `Small_Gradient_30.gif` (full), the second is `Small_Gradient_29.gif` (full minus one bar), and so forth.

You can have as few or as many images as you'd like for your timer, as long as their filenames end sequentially (`_01.gif`, `_02.gif`, `_03.gif` and so forth). For example, if you created a timer named Ball_Drop, you would name the files `Ball_Drop_01.gif`, `Ball_Drop_02.gif`, `Ball_Drop_03.gif`, and so forth.

So, the next logical question is, "how do the images relate to time?" That part is also pretty straightforward. CourseBuilder reviews the `timers` folder to determine the number of images associated with a particular timer. The Small_Gradient timer, for example, consists of 30 images progressing from the "empty" to the "full" state of the image (CourseBuilder is able to determine this because the files are named `Small_Gradient_01.gif` through `Small_Gradient_30.gif`).

To determine the replacement timing for each image, CourseBuilder divides the value you enter for Duration by the total number of images for the specified timer. In the *HTML Basics* course, for example, we defined the total duration of the timer to be 360 seconds. Because we selected the Small_Gradient timer, which consists of 30 images in the timer, we know that each image is replaced every 12 seconds.

If we use the same Small_Gradient timer for a timer with a total duration of 60 seconds, each image is replaced every 2 seconds.

Choosing Your Timer Template

The CourseBuilder Gallery contains two timer templates, as shown in Figure 16-14.

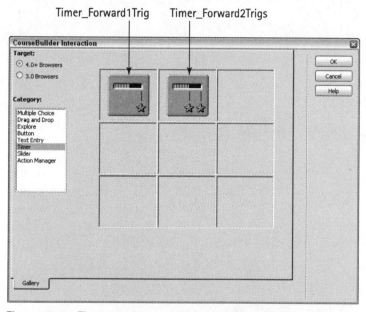

Figure 16–14: Timer templates available in the CourseBuilder Gallery

The significant difference between the two templates is in the number of triggers each template initially contains.

Choosing a timer with a single trigger (Timer_Forward1Trig)

Use the Timer_Forward1Trig template when you want to use a timer interaction with a single trigger. By default, this interaction

- Displays all of the timers in the timers folder for that site. CourseBuilder automatically lists all graphics ending in _01.gif in the timers folder as timers in the Appearance drop-down menu (General tab).

- Selects the Hourglass timer on the Appearance drop-down menu (General tab).

◆ Sets the Duration to 30 seconds (General tab).

◆ Displays images in normal order because Reverse image order is *not* selected (General Tab).

◆ Creates a Reset button (General tab).

◆ Includes a single trigger named Trigger1 that fires at 30 seconds, which is the end of the timer (Triggers tab).

◆ Displays a Popup Message in the Action Manager when Trigger1 fires (Action Mgr tab).

Figure 16-15 shows the default Action Manager processing for this single-trigger interaction.

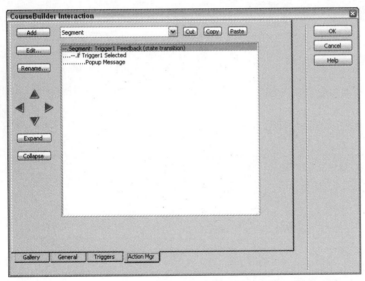

Figure 16-15: The Timer_ Forward1Trig interaction displays a "Time Expired" popup message when the timer ends.

You can modify these defaults on the General, Triggers, and Action Mgr tabs.

Choosing a timer with two triggers (Timer_Forward2Trigs)

Use the Timer_Forward2Trigs template when you want to use a timer interaction with two triggers. By default, this interaction

◆ Displays all of the timers in the timers folder for that site. CourseBuilder automatically lists all graphics ending in _01.gif in the timers folder as timers in the Appearance drop-down menu (General tab).

- ◆ Selects the Gradient timer on the Appearance drop-down menu (General tab).

- ◆ Sets the Duration to 30 seconds (General tab).

- ◆ Displays images in normal order because Reverse image order is *not* selected (General Tab).

- ◆ Creates a Reset button (General tab).

- ◆ Includes two triggers: `Trigger1` fires at 15 seconds, and `Trigger2` fires at 30 seconds (Triggers tab).

    `Trigger1` displays a Popup Message ("Trigger 1 hit") in the Action Manager when `Trigger1` fires (Action Mgr tab).

    `Trigger2` displays a Popup Message ("Trigger 2 hit") in the Action Manager when `Trigger2` fires (Action Mgr tab).

Figure 16-16 shows the default Action Manager processing for this two-trigger interaction. You can modify these defaults on the General, Triggers, and Action Mgr tabs.

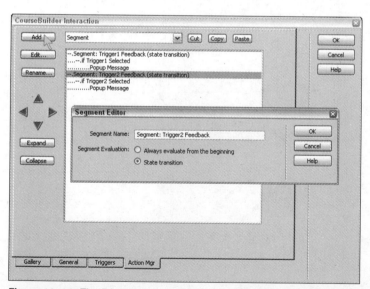

Figure 16-16: The `Timer_Forward2Trigs` interaction displays a popup message when each trigger fires.

Each segment includes a state transition phrase after the segment (segments are discussed fully in Chapter 17). When you create segments in CourseBuilder, you can specify a Segment Evaluation of State transition, which simply tells the Action Manager that if the conditions in the segment have been met, it should skip past them—when the `Trigger1` condition is met, the Action Manager only checks for `Trigger2`. This saves some processing time.

Application Example

Timer interactions are most often used to limit the amount of time for a test or activity. Let's look at an example that uses a custom timer to limit the time for a test.

In the *Speed Limits* example test, the student is given 75 seconds to understand the test and answer four questions. When the student opens *Speed Limits,* the timer begins by displaying a speed limit of 5. Every five seconds, the timer changes the posted speed limit sign, enabling the student to gauge his progress (see in Figure 16-17).

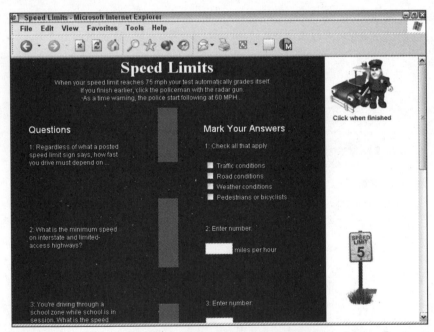

Figure 16–17: When Speed Limits loads into the browser, the timer begins. Every five seconds, the speed limit sign increments by 5.

When the posted speed limit reaches 60, the course displays a graphic of a speeder pulled over, as shown in Figure 16-18.

Trigger fires at 60 seconds, displaying animated graphic in previously hidden layer

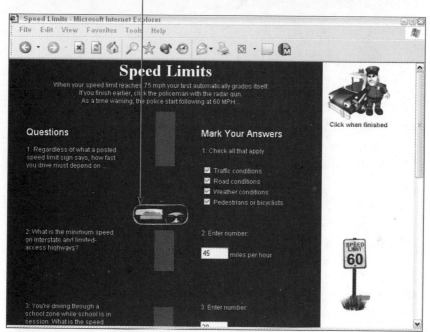

Figure 16-18: When Speed Limits reaches the 60 mph mark, a graphic of a speeder being pulled over appears on the divider lines.

The test ends in one of two ways (similar to the *HTML Basics* final examination described earlier in this chapter):

◆ The student clicks the police button when he has finished answering the four questions.

◆ Time expires at 75 seconds and the timer automatically disables the test interactions and grades whatever work was completed.

The first step in creating this timer interaction is to generate the graphics for the speed limit sign. If we have a 75-second timer and want to update that timer every 5 seconds, then we need 16 different graphics, as shown in Figure 16-19.

Although the creation of so many graphics may look like a daunting task, it isn't that bad! The quickest way to create images for custom timers is to open the starting image in a graphics program and just tweak and save each file (following the file naming conventions for timers, and saving the images to the `timers` folder for that site). Remember, you can use as few or as many images as you want; however, a greater number of images provides for a more animated timer.

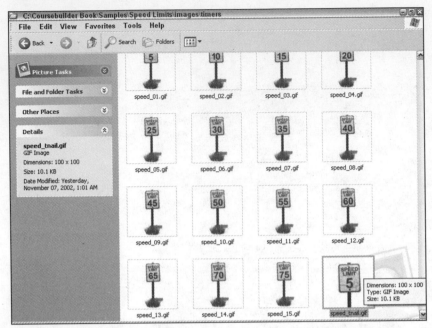

Figure 16-19: The speed limit timer uses 15 different graphics files to display the timer.

In addition to the timer graphics, the timer also requires a thumbnail graphic used on the General tab of the CourseBuilder Interaction dialog box, as shown in Figure 16-19.

After the timer images are created and stored in the timers folder, you can insert that timer in any Web page. To insert it in the *Speed Limits* test, click the Insert CourseBuilder Interaction icon on the Learning tab. From the CourseBuilder gallery, select the Timer interaction, and then select the Timer_ Forward2Trigs.

Click on the General tab and select the speed timer from the Appearance drop-down menu. Notice that CourseBuilder displays the thumbnail graphic (speed_tnail.gif) when you select the speed timer, as shown in Figure 16-20.

Set Duration to 75, and uncheck the Create a Reset button field.

On the Triggers tab, define Trigger1 to fire at 60 seconds and Trigger2 to fire at 75 seconds.

Then on the Action Mgr tab, we define the actions that the two triggers initiate (see Figure 16-21).

Trigger1, which fires at 60 seconds, initiates a Show-Hide Layers action that shows the layer containing the animated graphic of the pulled-over speeder. Trigger2, which fires at 75 seconds, initiates a Judge Interaction that judges the 4 questions and displays feedback for each question using an Action Manager interaction (Action Manager interactions are fully discussed in Chapter 17).

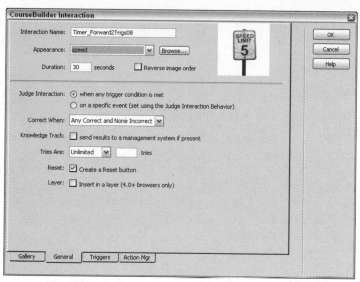

Figure 16-20: When the speed timer is selected, CourseBuilder displays the thumbnail graphic on the General tab.

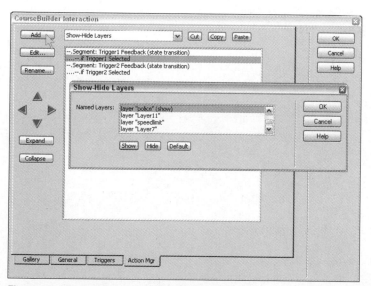

Figure 16-21: Setting the actions for the triggers

Summary

This chapter described how to:

- ◆ Use of timers to control the allotted times for tests and activities.
- ◆ Add multiple triggers to control actions at timed intervals.
- ◆ Create custom timers.

The next chapter describes how to make full use of the Action Manager to process interactions.

Chapter 17

Processing Interactions with the Action Manager

IN THIS CHAPTER

- ◆ Examining how the Action Manager drives all processing for CourseBuilder interactions

- ◆ Comparing the Action Mgr tab and the Action Manager interaction

- ◆ Using the Action Manager interface to enter and modify processing rules

- ◆ Working with segments, conditions, and actions

- ◆ Testing the condition of interaction and interaction element properties

- ◆ Scoring single-page and multiple-page examinations

A point of frequent misunderstanding with the Action Manager is that course authors can define the rules for the Action Manager in two places:

- ◆ The Action Mgr tab

- ◆ The Action Manager interaction

It may help you avoid confusion to think of the Action Manager as one room (with two doors: Action Mgr tab and Action Manager interaction. That is, you can define the same rules on the Action Mgr tab that you define on the Action Manager interaction. While they both enable you to perform the same task, you typically use the Action Mgr tab to define the rules for processing when you have one or two interactions on a single page. You normally use the Action Manager interaction to define the rules for processing when you have several or many interactions on a single page. The key benefit of the Action Manager interaction is that it allows you to modify all of the processing rules for a page (regardless of how many interactions you have) in a single location.

References throughout this book to the "Action Manager" refer to both the Action Manager available to individual interactions through the Action Mgr tab, and the Action Manager as an interaction.

Regardless of which path to the Action Manager you choose, you always end up in the same "room," shown in Figure 17-1.

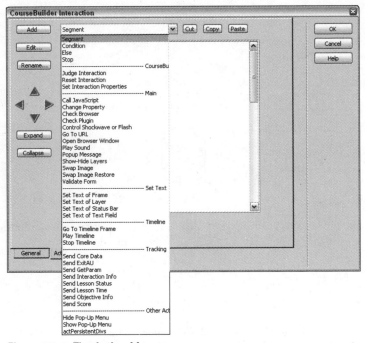

Figure 17-1: The Action Manager

The Action Manager drop-down menu shows all of the actions available. The bottom of the list includes other behaviors you have installed through the use of the Extension Manager in Dreamweaver MX. (The composite graphic in Figure 17-1 shows a complete list.)

The Action Manager as an interaction

We've seen plenty of examples throughout this book of the Action Mgr tab. Let's pick door number 2 and build a more complex set of rules using the Action Manager as an interaction. We won't be seeing this project from the student's perspective, because students see no difference at all whether you've defined rules using the Action Mgr tab or the Action Manager interaction.

In Chapter 16 we discussed an example in which timers were used to manage the time allotted for the final exam in the *HTML Basics* course. (If you haven't already tried the exam, I recommend you take it now. The experience will make it much easier for you to follow the concepts presented in this chapter.)

To build that final exam required

◆ 10 multiple-choice interactions, one for each question

◆ 1 button interaction that students press when they've completed the test

◆ 1 timer interaction set for 360 seconds (6 minutes)

◆ 1 Action Manager interaction that judges each of the 10 multiple-choice interactions, and processes the scoring at the end of the exam

Figure 17-2 shows a portion of the final exam for the *HTML Basics* course. When students take the exam, they have six minutes to answer 10 questions.

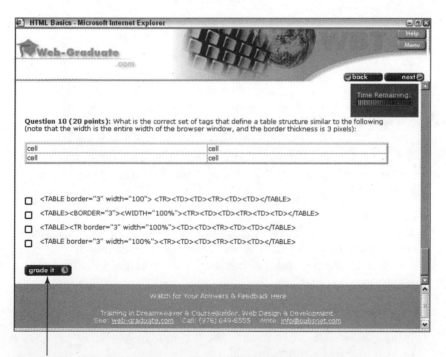

The 10 multiple choice interactions are not evaluated until student presses the Grade It button. Then all 10 interactions are evaluated once, and feedback is written to the bottom frame.

Figure 17-2: Students don't receive evaluation or feedback on the HTML Basics final examination until it is judged.

When students finish the exam and click the Grade It button at the end of the exam @or when time expires – they receive their grade in the bottom frame (blackboard) of the frameset, as shown in Figure 17-3. Students also receive feedback on each question, which is displayed in hidden feedback layers positioned next to each question.

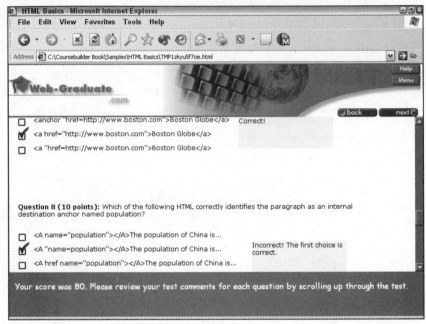

Figure 17-3: Students receive their grade in the bottom frame, as well as specific feedback on each answer.

To centralize the processing of the rules for the 10 multiple-choice questions, we left the Action Mgr tab for all 10 multiple-choice interactions empty.

We want to create an Action Manager interaction that is initiated by the Grade It button, and which then

1. Processes the rules for each of the 10 multiple-choice questions:

    If the student answered correctly, the Action Manager writes the word Correct in the hidden feedback layer.

    If the student answered incorrectly, the Action Manager writes the word Incorrect and identifies the correct answer in the hidden feedback layer.

    If the student didn't answer, the Action Manager writes the phrase "Incorrect because of lack of response" in the hidden feedback layer.

2. Calculates and displays the total score in the bottom frame.

3. Shows (makes visible) all hidden feedback layers so the student can see the feedback for each question.

The following example describes how to insert the hidden feedback layers; insert the Action Manager; and insert the button that "kicks it into play" (initiates processing). We assume that the 10 multiple-choice questions are already included in the file, and that the Action Mgr tab for each of those interactions is blank.

1. Move to the top of the final exam page, if not already there.

2. Insert the 10 student feedback layers, which will be hidden from view until the exam is evaluated. To do so, click the Draw Layer icon on the Insert panel's Common tab. Dreamweaver changes the cursor into cross-hairs.

3. Position the cursor near Question 1 and draw a small rectangular layer (don't worry about the size now; we'll change it to exact dimensions later).

4. Click on the newly-drawn layer to view its properties in the Properties panel. Change its properties as follows (see Figure 17-4):

   Layer ID to Q1feedback. When you create feedback layers in a Dreamweaver page, it is better to use a specific name related to the function of that layer. That way, it is easier to identify specific layers when, for example, you need to refer to them in defining rules in the Action Manager.

   W (width) to 180 and **H** (height) to 60. By setting the layer size numerically, you can ensure that all feedback layers are exactly the same size.

   Z-Index is 30 (as discussed earlier in this book, higher numbered Z-Index layers will display in front of lower numbered Z-Index layers should they overlap).

   Vis (visible) to hidden. We don't want the student to see these layers until after the examination, so we want the initial state of them to be hidden.

   Bg Color to #FFFFCC (to give it contrast to the background).

   Overflow to auto, meaning that if the text exceeds the defined size of the layer, the layer automatically adds scrollbars.

5. Repeat steps 2–4 for questions 2–10. The only differences between layers are the Layer ID name (use names Q2feedback through Q10feedback) and the placement of each feedback layer next to the corresponding question.

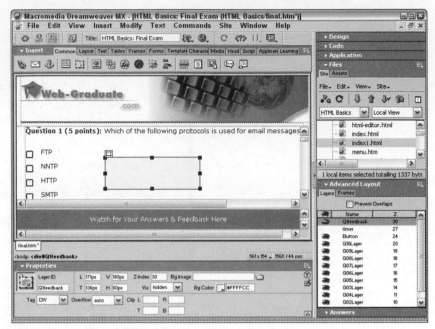

Figure 17-4: Changing the properties of the hidden feedback layer

6. Click anywhere within the file to insert the Action Manager interaction. Although the location of the Action Manager doesn't matter for processing purposes, I generally find it easier to locate the Action Manager if I put it either at the beginning or end of the file, rather than intermingled among test and activity interactions.

7. Click the Insert CourseBuilder Interaction button on the Learning tab. The CourseBuilder Interaction dialog box displays, with the CourseBuilder Gallery active.

8. Choose the Action Manager category to display the Action Manager template (see Figure 17-5).

9. Click the ActionMgr template. CourseBuilder inserts an additional CourseBuilder interaction invisible element (placeholder) into the Web page, and displays the General and Action Mgr tabs. It does not insert anything that would be visible to the student.

10. Click the General tab (see Figure 17-6) to define the general properties for the Action Manager. There aren't as many definitions on this General tab as there are for other interactions.

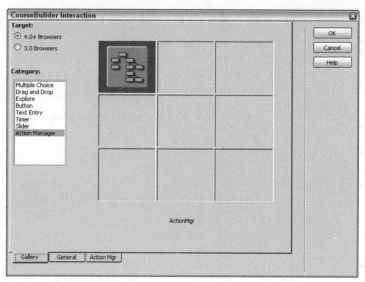

Figure 17-5: Selecting the Action Manager category from the CourseBuilder Gallery

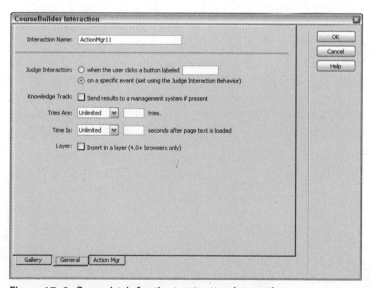

Figure 17-6: General tab for the `ActionMgr` interaction

11. Keep the default settings on the General tab.

The most important field to us at this point is Judge Interaction, defining what initiates judgment of this Action Manager interaction. By the design of our test, either the Grade It button or the timer can initiate processing of the rules defined in the Action Manager, so we need to specify that this Action Manager wait for another event to kick it into action. Because the default setting is to Judge Interaction on a specific event, we do not need to change anything.

12. Click the Action Mgr tab. By default, the tab is empty, since there is no context for the interaction. We need to insert processing rules for each of the 10 multiple-choice questions that follow the logic shown in Figure 17-7.

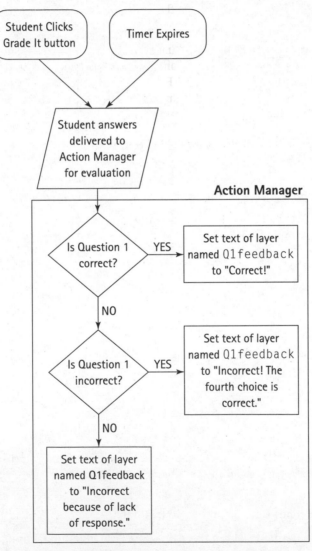

Figure 17-7: The processing logic for evaluating each of the
10 multiple-choice questions

The Action Manager displays the Segment option on the drop-down menu. Because you must always precede rules with a segment identifier, our first step is to create a segment. (Although you must have at least one segment in the Action Manager, its role is similar to comments in a computer program or HTML – they simply serve to identify a section, and do not affect processing in any way.)

13. Click the Add button to add a segment. CourseBuilder displays the Segment Editor dialog box.

    Because our first segment judges the first question out of 10, we'll call the segment Judge Question 1.

14. Type **Judge Question 1** in the Segment Editor dialog box, as shown in Figure 17-8. There are two additional options in the dialog box, which we'll discuss later in this chapter. For this exercise, accept the default: Always evaluate from the beginning. Click OK in the Segment Editor dialog box.

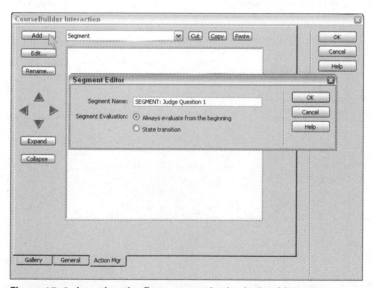

Figure 17-8: Inserting the first segment in the Action Manager

With the first segment identified, we can enter the conditions and actions for it.

15. Select Condition from the Action Manager drop-down menu and click the Add button. CourseBuilder launches the Condition Editor, which is the tool you use to define conditions in the Action Manager.

    The first condition we must test for (as the flowchart in Figure 17-8 shows) is whether the student's answer to Question 1 is correct.

16. Type **Question 1 Correct** in the Condition Name field. The text you type here is displayed as an `if` statement (`if Question 1 Correct`) in the Action Manager.

17. Keep the default Interaction for the first Type field, since we are testing a condition for an interaction (the Question 1 multiple-choice interaction).

    Because we are defining rules for an interaction, we must tell the Condition Editor exactly what interaction to test. The Interaction drop-down menu (shown in Figure 17-9) displays all of the interactions available on the page (displayed by the name you specified in the Interaction Name field for each interaction on the General tab).

18. Select `Question1` from the Interaction drop-down menu.

    The drop-down menu to the right of the Interaction field (which currently displays "<none>"), lets you select a specific element for testing. Do not change this option, since we are only testing for the overall correctness of the interaction. (You can read more about testing conditions for individual elements in the section named "Conditions" later in this chapter.)

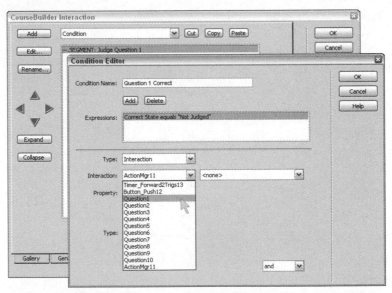

Figure 17-9: Selecting the specific interaction about which you are testing conditions

The property we want to test for is the correctness of the student's answer. By default, the Property field tests for Correct State, so we don't need to change this option.

There are three possible Correct States: Correct, Incorrect, or Not Judged. We want to test that the Correct State for Question1 is Correct. (We'll test for Incorrect in another condition.)

19. Select Correct from the second drop-down menu under the second Type field (below Select), as shown in Figure 17-10.

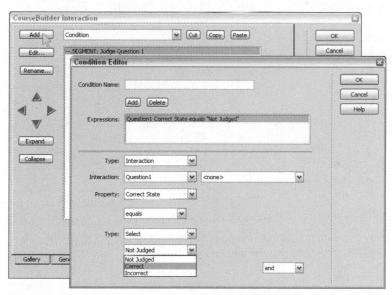

Figure 17-10: Selecting the specific Correct State for testing

20. Click the OK button in the Condition Editor dialog box. CourseBuilder inserts the name of your condition into the Action Manager, preceded by the if condition (if Question1 Correct). Any actions (one or many) that you insert under the condition are automatically executed if the condition is met; if the condition is not met, the actions are passed by until the conditions *are* met.

We next have to define the action we want performed if the condition is met, which is to set the layer named Q1feedback to display "Correct!"

21. Select the Set Text of Layer action from the Action Manager and click the Add button. The Set Text of Layer dialog box displays.

22. Type **Correct!** in the New HTML field, as shown in Figure 17-11, and click the OK button in the Set Text of Layer dialog box.

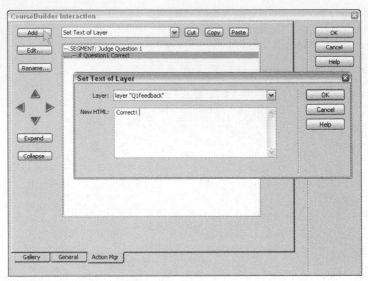

Figure 17-11: Adding the Set Text of Layer action

You now have a completed condition that launches a specific action. We need to repeat the process to test for Correct State equals Incorrect, and to display the appropriate message if the student's answer is incorrect. To add additional conditions to the same segment, you must highlight the previous condition before clicking the Add button (the hierarchy of the Action Manager is discussed in detail later in this chapter).

When you insert additional conditions to an if condition, the Action Manager automatically inserts them as else if statements, as follows:

    if condition1
        perform condition1 actions

    else if condition2
        perform condition2 actions

    else if condition3
        perform condition3 actions

The Action Manager tests for condition1; if condition1 is true, the Action Manager processes the condition1 actions and does *not* test the remaining conditions in the group. If condition1 is false, the Action Manager tests condition2. If condition2 is true, the Action Manager processes the condition2 actions and again does *not* test the remaining conditions in the group.

If you want to insert actions for the Action Manager to perform *only when* a group of if and else if tests are all false, insert an Else statement from the Action Manager drop-down menu at the end of the group of tests.

23. Highlight the `if Question1 Correct` condition.

24. Select Condition from the Action Manager drop-down menu and click the Add button. CourseBuilder again launches the Condition Editor.

25. Modify the Condition Editor to follow the settings shown in Figure 17-12:

Condition Name:	Question1 Incorrect
Type:	Interaction
Interaction	Question1
Property:	Correct State
Type:	Select
	Incorrect

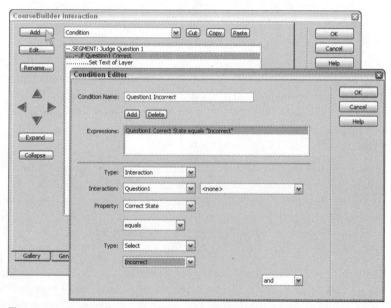

Figure 17-12: Inserting a condition to test for an incorrect student answer

The two differences between the previously defined `if Question1 Correct` condition and this `if Question1 Incorrect` condition are the Condition Name fields and the last field that tests for Incorrect from the second drop-down menu under the second Type field (below Select). Click OK in the Conditions Editor dialog box.

26. Select the Set Text of Layer action from the Action Manager and click the Add button. The Set Text of Layer dialog box opens.

27. Type **Incorrect! The fourth choice is correct.** in the New HTML field, as shown in Figure 17-13, and click the OK button in the Set Text of Layer dialog box.

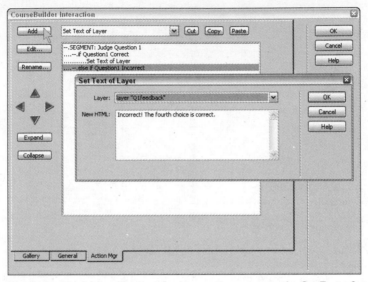

Figure 17-13: Adding the text for incorrect answers to the Set Text of Layer field

Finally, students may skip over a question entirely, leaving it unanswered. We want to mark it incorrect, but the Action Manager will not see the question as either correct or incorrect, because there is no response to judge. We can, however, add an Else statement in the Action Manager, which indicates the action to run if all of the other conditions (Is it correct? Is it incorrect?) are not true.

28. Select the Else statement (just below Condition) from the Action Manager drop-down menu and click the Add button. CourseBuilder inserts the Else statement in the Action Manager.

29. Select the Set Text of Layer action from the Action Manager and click the Add button. The Set Text of Layer dialog box opens.

30. Type **Incorrect because of lack of response.** in the New HTML field, as shown in Figure 17-14, and click the OK button in the Set Text of Layer dialog box.

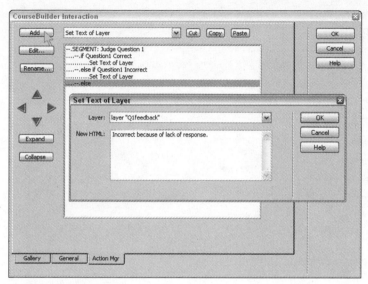

Figure 17–14: Adding the text for unanswered questions to the
Set Text of Layer field

Now that you've completed the entire segment for Question1, you need to repeat it for the remaining questions. Seems like a daunting task. However, given that each segment is so similar, we can take a shortcut that will save us significant time: copy and paste the first segment nine times and tweak the settings.

1. Highlight the segment named SEGMENT: Judge Question 1 and click the Copy button (to the right of the drop-down menu). CourseBuilder stores the entire segment, including all conditions and actions, into the paste buffer.

2. Click the Paste button nine times. CourseBuilder inserts nine clones of the segment (see Figure 17-15).

3. Edit the remaining segments, conditions, and actions by highlighting each, clicking the Edit button, and making the following edits:

   Edit each segment name to increment the question number.

   Edit each if Question Correct Condition Name and Interaction to increment the question number in the Condition Editor.

   Edit each else if Question Incorrect Condition Name and Interaction to increment the question number in the Condition Editor.

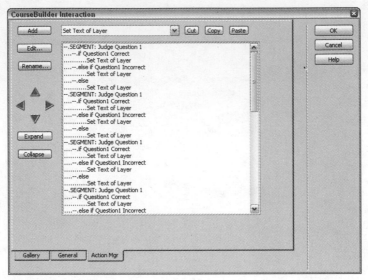

Figure 17-15: Copying and pasting segments can save substantial time
if the segments are structured similarly.

On the Set Text of Layer action under the `else if Question
Incorrect` condition, select the appropriate layer for each question
number, and modify the New HTML field to indicate the correct choice
for each question (for Question 2 type **Incorrect! The first choice is
correct.** ; for Question 3 type **Incorrect! The first choice is correct.** ;
and so forth...).

When you have updated all of these settings, you should have 10 segments, as shown in Figure 17-16.

Our final task is to include a segment that displays the student's score in the bottom frame, and then shows (makes visible) all of the student feedback layers. Here's
what to do:

1. Highlight the last segment, `SEGMENT: Judge Question 10`.

2. Select Segment from the Action Manager drop-down menu and click the
   Add button.

3. Name the additional segment `SEGMENT: Show Score` in the Segment
   Editor and click OK.

   Regardless of how many questions students answer, and whether the
   exam ends by the student clicking the Grade It button or time expiring,
   students are entitled to evaluation. That means that this segment should
   always run, regardless of conditions. If we simply add actions rather than
   conditions, those actions will always run.

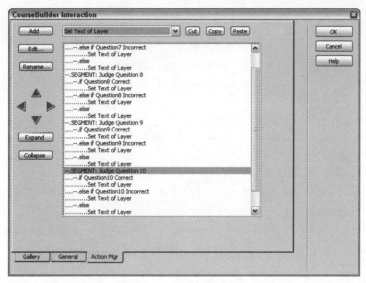

Figure 17-16: The multiple-choice questions after you edit each segment

4. Select the Set Text of Frame action from the Action Manager drop-down menu and click the Add button to add it to the Show Score segment. The Set Text of Frame dialog box opens. Add the following the text and code (see Figure 17-17) to calculate and display the final exam score, and then click OK in the dialog box:

```
<font face="Comic Sans MS, Arial, sans-serif">Your score
was{G01.score+G02.score+G03.score+G04.score+G05.score+G06.
score+G07.score+G08.score+G09.score+G10.score}. Please
review your test comments for each question by scrolling up
through the test.</font>
```

The calculation of student scores is discussed later in this chapter; however, everything you need to do to calculate the score is shown in Figure 17-18 — CourseBuilder automatically assigns all of the values to variables.

5. Select the Show-Hide Layers action from the Action Manager drop-down menu and click the Add button. The Show-Hide Layers dialog box opens.

6. Highlight feedback layer Q1feedback and click the Show button, and repeat the process for the rest of the feedback layers (Q2feedback through Q10feedback) (see Figure 17-18). Click OK in the Show-Hide Layers dialog box.

Click OK in the CourseBuilder Interaction dialog box to the page in Dreamweaver MX. Notice that there's no visible evidence of all that work! The Action Manager is specifically meant for behind-the-scenes processing.

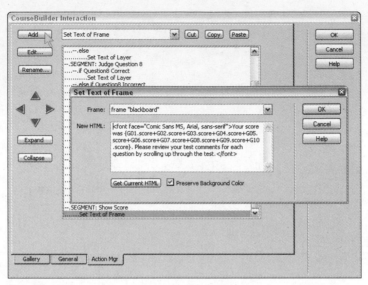

Figure 17-17: Inserting the text and code to calculate and display the student's score in the bottom frame named `blackboard`

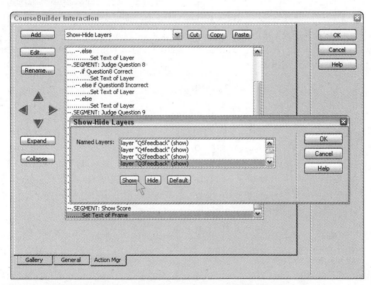

Figure 17-18: Setting the feedback layers to Show (making them visible to students)

Using the Action Manager

The Action Manager is a hierarchical structure that consists of rules for processing interactions. Understanding that hierarchy is important to proficient use of the Action Manager. Figure 17-19 shows an example of an Action Manager hierarchy that we can use for discussion.

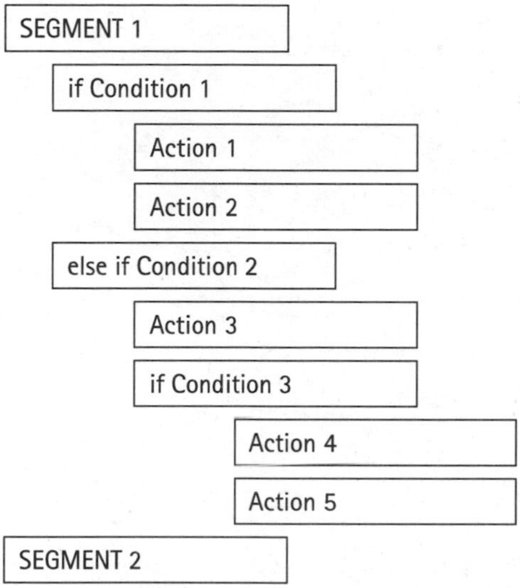

```
SEGMENT 1
    if Condition 1
            Action 1
            Action 2
    else if Condition 2
            Action 3
            if Condition 3
                    Action 4
                    Action 5
SEGMENT 2
```

Figure 17–19: Example of the Action Manager hierarchy

All of the buttons in the Action Manager assume their context from the active rule, which is the segment, condition, or action highlighted (clicked on) in the Action Manager. If you are modifying an existing rule with Edit, Rename, Promote/Demote (arrows), Expand, Collapse, Cut, or Copy, for example, you are modifying the highlighted rule. If you are inserting a new rule with Add or Paste, the highlighted rule becomes the location reference for the new rule.

The concept of modifying is straightforward because the context never changes. For example, if you highlight SEGMENT 1 and click Edit, you edit SEGMENT 1 in the Segment Editor; if you highlight Action 3 and click Edit, you edit Action 3.

The concept of inserting new rules is not so straightforward because the placement of the added or pasted rules depends on what is highlighted and what you are adding. For example, if you highlight SEGMENT 1 and add a new segment, CourseBuilder inserts the new segment after SEGMENT 1; if you highlight the else if Condition 2 condition and add a new condition, CourseBuilder adds the new condition after Condition 2 and just above SEGMENT 2.

As you add groups of conditions to segments, the number of conditions in the Action Manager can get rather lengthy. For easier viewing, you can expand or collapse segments and groups of rules by highlighting a segment or if statement and clicking the Expand or Collapse buttons. Figure 17-20 shows the Action Manager for the *HTML Basics* final examination, where all segments have been collapsed except for the first segment.

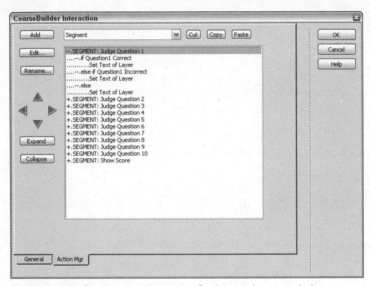

Figure 17-20: Segments and groups of rules can be expanded or collapsed in the Action Manager.

Table 17-1 describes each of the buttons on the Action Manager.

TABLE 17-1 ACTION MANAGER BUTTONS

Button	Description
Add	Adds the segment, condition, or action selected in the drop-down menu.
Edit...	Edits the rules for the highlighted segment, condition, or action in the appropriate editor. For example, conditions are edited in the Condition Editor.
Rename...	Renames the text displayed in the Action Manager window for a highlighted segment, condition, or action. Does not allow you to edit the rules.

Button	Description
▲ ◄ ► ▼	Up and down arrows move the highlighted condition or action up or down the set of rules to allow reordering of rules.

Left and right arrows promote or demote conditions and actions, which may change their priority in the hierarchy.

For example, if you highlight the if Condition 3 condition in Figure 17-20 and press the left arrow, CourseBuilder changes the condition to an if else condition at an equal hierarchical level as the two conditions above it. |
| Expand | Segments and conditions that have a minus sign to the left are expanded, meaning that all rules are visible. In Figure 7-21, the first segment is expanded.

If a segment or condition displays a plus sign (meaning there are rules not visible), you can expand the segment or condition by highlighting it and clicking the Expand button. |
| Collapse | Segments and conditions that have a plus sign to the left are collapsed, meaning that some conditions and actions are not visible. In Figure 17-21, all segments except the first segment are collapsed.

If a segment or condition displays a minus sign, you can collapse the segment or condition by highlighting it and clicking the Collapse button. |
| Cut | Cuts the highlighted segment, condition, or action, including all dependent conditions and actions.

In Figure 17-21, for example, if you highlighted SEGMENT: Judge Question 1 and pressed the Cut button, CourseBuilder would delete the entire segment, including the three conditions and three actions that are dependents of that segment.

On the other hand, if you highlighted the else if Question1 Incorrect condition and pressed the Cut button, CourseBuilder would delete that condition plus the Set Text of Layer action beneath it. |
| Copy | Copies the highlighted segment, condition, or action and moves it (plus any dependent conditions or actions) into the paste buffer. |
| Paste | Pastes the segment, condition, or action previously copied or cut (plus any dependent conditions or actions) below the highlighted segment, condition, or action in the Action Manager. CourseBuilder inserts the pasted rules into an appropriate position in the hierarchy. |

Segments

Segments are similar to comments in programming languages or markup languages: they categorize the content below. However, segments are different from comments in one key aspect: *every* condition or action must be a dependent of a segment.

When you insert a segment, CourseBuilder displays the Segment Editor, as shown in Figure 17-21.

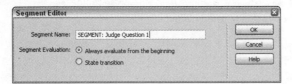

Figure 17-21: The Segment Editor in the Action Manager

The Segment Evaluation field provides two options that affect processing of interactions:

◆ **Always evaluate from the beginning.** This setting says that every time the segment is evaluated (on the same page load), it must be evaluated beginning at the first line.

◆ **State transition.** This setting says that if a segment was previously evaluated with some conditions met (and others not), that the conditions that were met must not be reevaluated.

Conditions

Conditions are the heart and soul of highly interactive CourseBuilder courses, because conditions enable you to define different responses to different student actions. Throughout this book you've seen some of the power of using conditions such as `if Correct` and `if Incorrect`, but those conditions are literally the tip of the iceberg.

When you add a condition into the Action Manager, CourseBuilder displays the Condition Editor, shown in Figure 17-22.

The core function of the Condition Editor is to build expressions (logical tests, so to speak) that test properties of interactions and elements. Each expression consists of two parts: Part A is the hypotheses and Part B is the actual state. The Condition Editor basically compares the two components in this question: Does Part A (hypothesis) [meet the specified condition of] Part B (actual state)?

Part A is the condition you are testing for

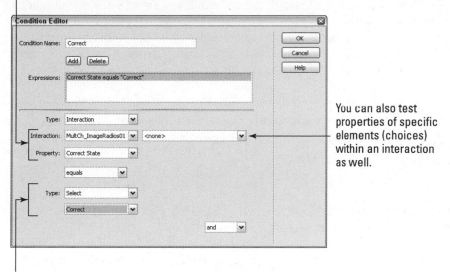

You can also test properties of specific elements (choices) within an interaction as well.

Part B is the actual state of the condition

Figure 17-22: The Condition Editor in the Action Manager

Expressions can be defined to highly granular levels, such as the following:

If student selects choice 3 (*hypothesis*) is true (*actual state*)

If total score for interaction (*hypothesis*) equals 5 (*actual state*)

If time for interaction (*hypothesis*) equal or greater than 10 (*actual state*)

You can also define multiple expressions within a single condition, where both expressions must be true for the condition to be true. For example,

If student selects choice 3 (*hypothesis*) is true (*actual state*) **and**

If total score for interaction (*hypothesis*) equals 5 (*actual state*)

To add more than one expression to a condition, simply click the Add button to define additional expressions. In the bottom right of the Condition Editor you can choose:

- and, which means both expressions must be true for the condition to be true

- or, which means the condition is true as long as at least one expression is true.

Once you create a condition in the Condition Editor, CourseBuilder displays that condition within the Action Manager by the name you specified in the Condition Name field, preceded by either an `if` or `else if` clause, depending on where you insert the condition. So the example shown in Figure 17-22 would be inserted as either `if Correct` or `else if Correct`. You can then insert actions underneath the condition, and those actions will only be performed if the condition is true.

 Although there are four types of conditions (Interaction, Action Manager, Document Tag, JavaScript) that you can test, this book mainly focuses on testing conditions for interactions.

USING CONDITION PLANNERS FOR TESTING PROPERTIES

You can define conditions that test properties of

- Interactions as a whole. You test properties on an interaction as long as the drop-down elements menu to the right does not select a specific element.

- Specific elements within an interaction. You test properties on a specific element (such as a specific choice for multiple choice or hot area for explore) if you select that element from the elements menu.

Properties always relate to either an interaction *or* element, but not both. For example, the Score property is the score for each choice, whereas the Total Score property is the sum of the scores of the choices for a specific interaction.

To facilitate the planning of conditions, the toolkit includes two planners that help you relate conditions to actions on a single sheet:

- Condition Planner for Interaction Properties
- Condition Planner for Interaction *Element* Properties

Suppose, for example, that you want to create a condition that tests a multiple-choice interaction named `MultCh_ImageRadios01` to see if the student answered correctly and, if the student did answer correctly, you want to define an action that initiates judgment of the second multiple-choice question, `MultCh_ImageRadios02`. The Condition Planner for Interaction Properties, shown in Figure 17-23, helps you identify the appropriate condition in the Condition Editor as well as the action in the Action Manager.

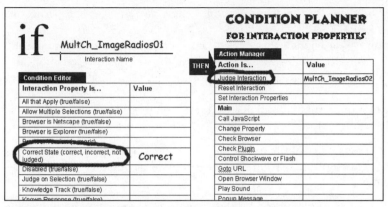

Figure 17-23: Use the Condition Planner for Interaction Properties to identify appropriate conditions and actions.

The Condition Planner for Interaction Element Properties is similar in design, only it lists property *elements*.

A BUG FOR ELEMENTS

As you know, the Condition Editor lets you select specific elements within an interaction. However, there is a bug in some versions of CourseBuilder that only enables you to select every other element.

Figure 17-24, for example, shows the Condition Editor for a multiple-choice interaction that has four elements (buttons).

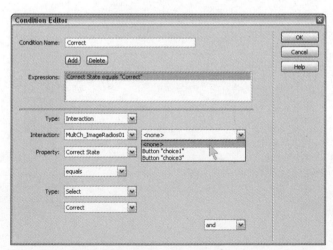

Figure 17-24: A bug that allows the Condition Editor to recognize only every other element

With choices only for Button 1 and Button 3, how can you test properties on Button 2 and Button 4?

The workaround is to change the view to JavaScript and manually make the changes. Assume we are working with the same multiple-choice interaction and want to define a condition if the student selects Button 2. We would

1. Select any button that is available (it doesn't matter which one, so let's just select Button 3).

2. Define the remainder of the expression the way you want to test the desired button, Button 2. Your expression should be complete before moving to Step 3.

3. Select the JavaScript option from the Type drop-down menu, as shown in Figure 17-25.

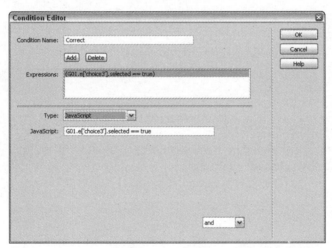

Figure 17-25: The JavaScript view of Button 3, which we want
to change to Button 2

4. Change the JavaScript to reflect the element you actually want the condition to test. Because this is a multiple-choice interaction, Button 3 is represented by the JavaScript `choice3`; change it to `choice2` and click OK to return to the Action Manager.

Although the JavaScript changes for different interactions, it should always be obvious what change you need to make to reference a different element. For example, you might want to test a pairing in a drag-and-drop interaction that shows Drag1:Target1 and Drag1:Target3. To test the pairing Drag1: Target2, select any paired elements (for example, Drag1: Target3):

```
G01.e['Drag1'].c['Target3'].selected == true
```

Change the pair elements to match the desired elements (Drag1:Target2) as follows:

```
G01.e['Drag1'].c['Target2'].selected == true
```

Be sure to click OK *without* reselecting the Interaction type; otherwise, the Condition Editor changes the element back to the originally selected element.

Thanks to author Betsy Bruce for suggesting this workaround!

Properties

This section describes the properties of interactions that you can test by creating expressions in the Condition Editor, or set values for by using the Set Interaction Properties from the drop-down menu in the Action Manager.

Each property consists of data that is stored in a specific data type, including

◆ **True/false.** When a property is a true/false data type, it has three possible values: true, false, and null (empty). For example, the Time Limit property for an interaction can be true (time limit has been reached) or false (time limit has not been reached).

◆ **Numeric.** When a property has a numeric data type, it is stored as a number. Numeric values can be tested with typical numeric operators: equal to, not equal to, greater than, less than, equal or greater than, equal of less than. For example, the Possible Correct property for an interaction is the number of choices that were defined as correct when the interaction was created.

◆ **Select.** When a property is a select list, it can only contain properties from that list. For example, the Correct State property for an interaction uses a select list with three options: correct, incorrect, or not judged.

◆ **Text.** When a property is a text data type, it can be any text string. For example, the Tracking Interaction ID is the text entered for an interaction on the Tracking tab when the interaction was created.

PROPERTIES OF INTERACTIONS

Interaction properties are always associated with a single interaction, and are referenced by the object identifier.

Table 17-2 describes the interaction properties that are available for all interactions.

TABLE 17-2 PROPERTIES OF INTERACTIONS

Property	Data Type	Description
All that Apply	True/False	Does the student need to select all of the correct answers to be correct? True means yes; false means no.
Allow Multiple Selections	True/False	Can the student select more than one choice? True means yes; false means no.
Browser is Explorer	True/False	Is the browser Internet Explorer? True means yes; false means no.
Browser is Netscape	True/False	Is the browser Netscape? True means yes; false means no.
Browser Version	Numeric	Is the browser {equal to, not equal to, greater than, less than, equal or greater than, equal of less than} the version number you specify?
Correct State	Select	Is the interaction correct, incorrect, or not judged?
Disabled	True/False	Is the interaction disabled? True means disabled; false means enabled.
Judge on Selection	True/False	Is the interaction automatically judged when students make selection? True means it is set to automatically judge; false means judgment is launched by some other event.
Knowledge Track	True/False	Is the interaction set up for knowledge tracking? True means yes; false means no.

Property	Data Type	Description
Known Response	True/False	Is there a known response (either correct *or* incorrect) to the interaction? True means yes; false means no.
OS Is Macintosh	True/False	Is the student using a Macintosh system? True means yes; false means no.
OS Is Windows	True/False	Is the student using a Windows system? True means yes; false means no.
Possible Correct	Numeric	Possible correct refers to the total number of answers in the interaction that are marked as correct. Is the number of possibly correct answers {equal to, not equal to, greater than, less than, equal or greater than, equal of less than} the number you specify?
Possible Incorrect	Numeric	Possible incorrect refers to the total number of answers in the interaction that are marked as incorrect. Is the number of possibly incorrect answers {equal to, not equal to, greater than, less than, equal or greater than, equal of less than} the number you specify?
Time	Numeric	Is the amount of time spent on the page {equal to, not equal to, greater than, less than, equal or greater than, equal of less than} the number you specify.
Time At Limit	True/False	If the interaction has a time limit set, has time expired? True is yes; false is no.
Time Left	Numeric	If the page has a time limit set, is the amount of time left on the timer {equal to, not equal to, greater than, less than, equal or greater than, equal of less than} the number you specify?

Continued

TABLE 17-2 PROPERTIES OF INTERACTIONS *(Continued)*

Property	Data Type	Description
\Time Limit	Numeric	If the page has a time limit set, is the total amount of time in the time limit {equal to, not equal to, greater than, less than, equal or greater than, equal of less than} the number you specify?
Total Correct	Numeric	Is the total number of correct answers selected by the student {equal to, not equal to, greater than, less than, equal or greater than, equal of less than} the number you specify?
Total Elements	Numeric	Is the total number of elements in an interaction {equal to, not equal to, greater than, less than, equal or greater than, equal of less than} the number you specify?
Total Incorrect	Numeric	Is the total number of incorrect answers selected by the student {equal to, not equal to, greater than, less than, equal or greater than, equal of less than} the number you specify?
Total Score	Numeric	Is the total score for the specified interaction {equal to, not equal to, greater than, less than, equal or greater than, equal of less than} the number you specify?
Tracking Interaction ID	Text	Is the text for the Interaction ID entered on the Tracking tab when the interaction was created the same as the text you specify?
Tracking Objective ID	Text	Is the text for the Objective ID entered on the Tracking tab when the interaction was created the same as the text you specify?
Tracking Question Type	Text	Is the text for the Tracking Question Type defined when the interaction was created the same as the text you specify?

Property	Data Type	Description
Tracking Weight	Numeric	Is the weight for the interaction entered on the Tracking tab when the interaction was created {equal to, not equal to, greater than, less than, equal or greater than, equal of less than} the number you specify?
Tries	Numeric	Is the number of tries the student has made to answer the interaction {equal to, not equal to, greater than, less than, equal or greater than, equal of less than} the number you specify?
Tries At Limit	True/False	Is the number of tries the student has made to answer the interaction at the limit defined by the tries limit property? True is yes; false is no.
Tries Limit	Numeric	Is the number of tries the student is allowed {equal to, not equal to, greater than, less than, equal or greater than, equal of less than} the number you specify?
Unknown Correctness	Select	If the student does not respond, is the interaction correct, incorrect, or not judged?

TESTING PROPERTIES OF ELEMENTS

Interaction *element* properties are always associated with elements within an interaction, such as a specific choice in a multiple-choice interaction or a specific hot area on an explore interaction.

Table 17-3 describes the interaction properties that are available for interaction elements. Many of the elements are available only to specific interactions. For example, the Is Toggle property is specific to button interactions.

TABLE 17-3 PROPERTIES OF ELEMENTS WITHIN INTERACTIONS

Property	Data Type	Description
Alignment	Select	Is a drag element snapped to the {center, left, right, top, bottom, or top left} in relation to a target? For drag-and-drop interactions.
Correctness	Select	Is a specific student choice set to correct, incorrect, or not judged? For all interactions.
Disabled	True/False	Is the interaction disabled? True means yes; false means no. For all interactions.
Expected Value	Select, True/False, Text, Numeric	Is the expected value for the element the value you specify? Expected values vary depending on the type of interaction. For example, an expected value for a text entry might be the word "President"; expected values for buttons would be true or false, and so forth. For all interactions.
Initial Value	Select, True/False, Text, Numeric	Is the initial value (value before student makes a choice) for the element the value you specify? Values vary depending on type of interaction. For example, values for text entry would be text; values for buttons would be true or false, and so forth. For all interactions.
Is Toggle	True/False	Is the button set to work like a toggle switch? True is yes; false is no. For button interactions.

Property	Data Type	Description
Match Case	True/False	Is the text that students enter required to match the case of the correct answer to be correct?
		True is yes; false is no.
		For text-entry interactions.
Match Entire Word	True/False	Is the text that students enter required to match the entire word or phrase of the correct answer to be correct?
		True is yes; false is no.
		For text-entry interactions.
Maximum Value	Numeric	Is the maximum value on the slider {equal to, not equal to, greater than, less than, equal or greater than, equal of less than} the number you specify?
		For slider interactions.
Minimum Value	Numeric	Is the minimum value on the slider {equal to, not equal to, greater than, less than, equal or greater than, equal of less than} the number you specify?
		For slider interactions.
Original X Position	Numeric	Is the original X-axis position (using browser coordinates) of a specific drag element the number you specify?
		For drag-and-drop interactions.
Original Y Position	Numeric	Is the original Y-axis position (using browser coordinates) of a specific drag element the number you specify?
		For drag-and-drop interactions.
Score	Numeric	Is the designated score for an interaction {equal to, not equal to, greater than, less than, equal or greater than, equal of less than} the number you specify?
		For all interactions.

Continued

TABLE 17-3 PROPERTIES OF ELEMENTS WITHIN INTERACTIONS *(Continued)*

Property	Data Type	Description
Selected	True/False	Is the element selected?
		For all interactions.
Snap Back on Incorrect	True/False	Is drag element set to snap back if student drops it on incorrect target?
		True means yes; false means no.
		For drag-and-drop interactions.
Snap Back on Miss	True/False	Is drag element set to snap back if student misses targets?
		True means yes; false means no.
		For drag-and-drop interactions.
Snaps To	True/False	Is the drag element set to snap to target element?
		True is yes; false is no.
		For drag-and-drop interactions.
Tolerance	Numeric	Is the number of pixels that causes a snap to target around a target element the number you specify?
		For drag-and-drop interactions.
Value	Select, True/False, Text, Numeric	Is the value for the element the value you specify?
		Values vary depending on type of interaction. For example, values for text entry would be text; values for buttons would be true or false, and so forth.
		For all interactions.
X Offset	Numeric	Is the number of pixels added to or subtracted from the drag-and-drop snap-to location on the X-axis the number you specify?
		For drag-and-drop interactions.

Property	Data Type	Description
Y Offset	Numeric	Is the number of pixels added to or subtracted from the drag-and-drop snap-to location on the Y-axis the number you specify?
		For drag-and-drop interactions.

Actions

The definition of actions within the Action Manager has been discussed extensively throughout this book, particularly in Chapter 3, which discusses Dreamweaver MX actions, and Chapter 6, which discusses actions available in Dreamweaver MX.

Tracking actions are discussed in Chapter 19, which discusses sending results to a Learning Management System.

However, one area of actions that needs further discussion is how to convey feedback to students through Action Manager actions.

An important aspect of any Web-Based Training course is giving students the feeling that they are interacting with the course – that is, the feeling that they are involved in two-way communications. Such interactivity not only requires the student to "click and type and do" to interact with the course, it also requires the course to provide plenty of feedback in response to the student's actions ("That is correct", "That is incorrect because...," "Your first two answers are correct, but the third answer...") and so forth.

Substantial feedback is important to students (and therefore to the success of your WBT). And although decisions about "how and where" to deliver feedback is not officially part of the Learning Site definition, it is an important factor in finalizing your decisions about layout style.

You can easily deliver context-sensitive text feedback by selecting any of the following actions in the Action Manager:

◆ Set Text of Frame to send text feedback to a specific frame. For example, the tests in the *HTML Basics* course (on the CD-ROM) send feedback to the bottom frame.

The main advantage of using a frame is that it is a consistent location for feedback; the main disadvantage of using a frame is that you lose that portion of the browser window for the duration of a course.

◆ Set Text of Layer to send text feedback to a specific layer. For example, the Cloze Tests (on the CD-ROM) send feedback to layers that are initially hidden near the content, and then made visible when feedback is written to them.

The main advantages of layers is that they don't take up screen real estate until they are necessary, and they are displayed right next to the question; the main disadvantage of layers is that you must create them for every single interaction.

- ◆ Set Text of Status Bar to send feedback to the status bar (at the bottom of the browser window). I do not recommend ever using this capability, because the text is not very visible to students.

- ◆ Set Text of Text Field to send feedback to a text area box in a form. For example, the Presidential Files example (on the CD-ROM) sends feedback to a text area within the file.

  The main advantage of a text area is that it works even with older browsers; the main disadvantage of a text area is that it requires constant real estate.

- ◆ Popup Message to send feedback to a popup message, similar to an error message box. For example, the Presidential Files example also uses popup messages to indicate wrong choices. Popup messages are fine, but because popups are most often used on operating systems for "wrong" events (errors, for example), they suffer guilt by association.

  The main advantage of using popup messages is that they are often the default feedback for interactions; the main disadvantages of popup messages is that they require students to click them (to close the popup) each time they are displayed, and they are associated with "wrong" events.

Scoring Exams

Can you imagine what our education system would be like without scoring? ("Dad, I brought home my report card. It's blank again!")

CourseBuilder offers many capabilities for scoring, whether or not you write those scores to a database. This section discusses scoring and tracking without writing to a database. See Chapters 18 and 19 for information about tracking with a database.

When you create an interaction, you can create a score for every single correct answer in the exam. For example, you can create a multiple-choice, "check-all-that-apply" interaction that has two correct answers, assigning a value of 5 points to each answer.

You specify the score for an element on the tab that defines the element:

- ◆ Choices tab for multiple-choice interactions.

- ◆ Pairs tab for drag-and-drop interactions.

◆ Hot Areas tab for explore interactions.

◆ Responses tab for text-entry interactions.

◆ Ranges tab for slider interactions.

Figure 17-26 shows the score field for a multiple-choice interaction. In this particular example, each correct choice is assigned a score of 5 points, meaning that students have three possible scores for this interaction:

◆ 0 points if they do not select any correct choice.

◆ 5 points if they select one correct choice.

◆ 10 points if they select both correct choices.

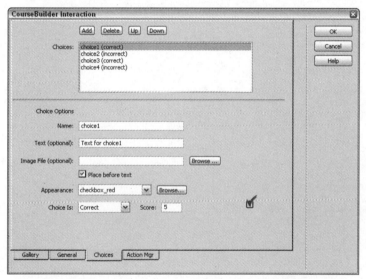

Figure 17-26: Defining the score for each choice in a multiple-choice interaction

Scoring for a single page

When you insert an interaction in a page, CourseBuilder provides that interaction with an object identifier. For example, look at the HTML code for the first multiple-choice interaction inserted into the *HTML Basics* final examination:

```
<interaction name="Question1" object="G01" template="010_Multiple
Choice/030_MultCh_ImageRadios_04.agt"
includesrc="interactionClass.js,elemIbtnClass.js">
```

This object identifier (object=*) is automatically created by CourseBuilder when you insert the interaction, and is included regardless of the type of interaction. Take a look at the following example from the same final examination – the button interaction that sends the examination to the Action Manager for processing:

```
<interaction name="Button_Push12" object="G12"
template="040_Button/020_Button_Push_04.agt"
includesrc="interactionClass.js,elemIbtnClass.js">
```

If you read through the entire HTML page for the final examination, you'd find the following object identifiers:

Question 1 (G01)

Question 2 (G02)

Question 3 (G03)

Question 4 (G04)

Question 5 (G05)

Question 6 (G06)

Question 7 (G07)

Question 8 (G08)

Question 9 (G09)

Question 10 (G10)

Action Manager (G11)

Button (G12)

Timer (G13)

There are certain scoring properties that are automatically maintained by CourseBuilder, as shown in Table 17-4. These properties can be changed numerous times while a page is loaded into the browser. But when the page changes, these properties are erased.

There is an example on scoring properties on the CD-ROM that may help you understand how these scoring properties work. The example is Understanding Scoring Properties.htm stored in the samples folder named Scoring.

TABLE 17-4 SCORING PROPERTIES OF INTERACTIONS ON A SINGLE PAGE

Property Name	Description
score	A numeric property that indicates the student's score for an interaction, with an initial value of 0. This property represents the student's grade for the interaction, based on his answers.
totalCorrect	A numeric property that indicates the total number of correct answers that the student selected in an interaction, with an initial value of 0.
totalIncorrect	A numeric property that indicates the total number of incorrect answers that the student selected in an interaction, with an initial value of 0.
possCorrect	A numeric property that indicates the total number of answers identified as correct in an interaction. Does not vary based on student answers.
possIncorrect	A numeric property that indicates the total number of answers identified as incorrect in an interaction. Does not vary based on student answers.
correct	A true/false property that indicates whether the student's answer is correct, based on the answers that the student selected and the definition of "correct" defined on the General tab for that interaction.

You can use these properties in many ways on a single page, and specify the exact interaction property by preceding the scoring property with the object identifier. For example, to refer to the total correct property for an interaction with the object identifier G03, you would refer to the property G03.totalCorrect.

For example, the final examination for the HTML Basics course creates a Set Text of Frame action at the end of the test that contains the following text:

```
Your score was {G01.score+G02.score+G03.score+G04.score+G05.
score+G06.score+G07.score+G08.score+G09.score+G10.score}. Please
review your test comments for each question by scrolling up through
the test.
```

When the text is written to the frame, it replaces the equation between the curly braces with the numeric answer for that equation. For example, if the answer to the equation was 70, it writes: Your score was 70. Please review your test comments....

CourseBuilder restarts the numbering of object identifiers with each page. That means the first object identifier on each and every page is G01, making it impossible to carry values across pages.

Scoring and tracking across multiple pages without using a database

The challenge of tracking in a browser without using a database is finding a way to get information from one page to another. If the student scores 5 points for Question 1 and moves to another page containing Question 2, how do you get the score from the previous page containing Question 1 to the current page containing Question 2? The answer is *frames*.

We've already looked at frames extensively because Learning Site uses frames to separate navigation (navFrame) from content (mainframe). We've also seen additional frames easily added to an already framed site — for example, we added the frame blackboard to the bottom of the *HTML Basics* course to display student feedback.

So why frames for tracking in a browser? Because frames can store variables that can be passed to other frames in a frameset. And as long as the tracking frame storing the variables is never refreshed or loaded with other content, and remains loaded in the browser window, the variables are available.

CourseBuilder lets you easily add a tracking frame to an existing framed or non-framed course. The tracking frame is nearly invisible to the student, but remains constantly loaded into a frameset (see Figure 17-27) as a container for variables that can be accessed or modified by every file that passes through the *other* frames in the frameset.

When you create a tracking frame, CourseBuilder

- ◆ Creates a frameset if you add tracking to a Web page, or adds an embedded frameset if you add tracking to an existing frameset (such as a Learning Site site).

- ◆ Creates a tracking frame named cmiresults.

- ◆ Creates a file named results.htm, which remains resident in the cmiresults frame, storing variables in the browser's memory.

The next section, "Application Example: Creating Multipage Tests that Track Scores," demonstrates how to create a tracking frame.

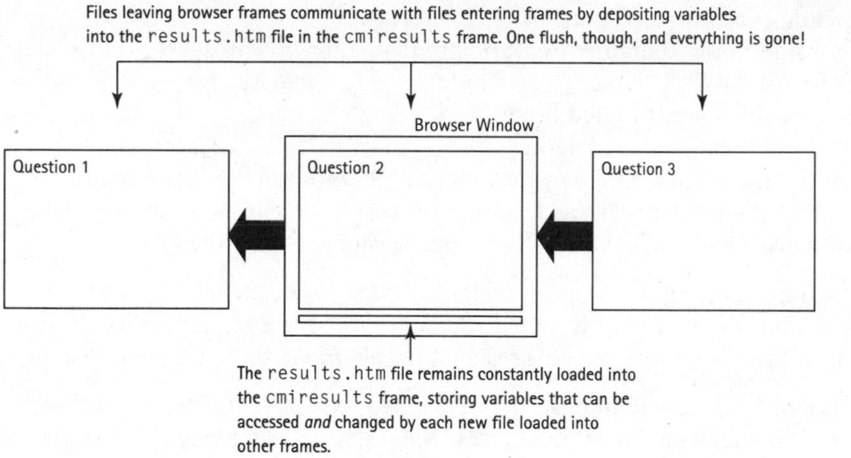

Files leaving browser frames communicate with files entering frames by depositing variables into the `results.htm` file in the `cmiresults` frame. One flush, though, and everything is gone!

Browser Window

| Question 1 | Question 2 | Question 3 |

The `results.htm` file remains constantly loaded into the `cmiresults` frame, storing variables that can be accessed *and* changed by each new file loaded into other frames.

Figure 17-27: The `results.htm` file remains resident in the tracking frame named `cmiresults`.

 If you use this approach to passing variables between frames, the student could "flush" all stored values by refreshing or reloading the browser window. To minimize the chances of this, I recommend launching the test in a separate browser window without navigation buttons, inserting only the necessary navigation buttons, as demonstrated in the application example in the next section.

Application Example: Creating Multipage Tests that Track Scores

The original final exam for the *HTML Basics* course consisted of 10 multiple-choice questions as well as the directions for that final exam all contained on a single page. This example shows the *HTML Basics* final exam restructured into a separate series of pages (one question per page plus a separate page for directions) loaded into a newly-created frameset.

By creating a frameset (named `exam-directions-frameset.htm`), we can reserve a frame as the container for variables that store student scores across multiple pages. Although it looks like a single page loading (see Figure 17-28), the frameset actually consists of two frames:

- A frame named `content`, which receives 99% of the browser window. The initial file loaded into this frame is `exam-directions.htm`. Each question is subsequently loaded into this frame as students take the exam.

- A frame named `cmiresults`, which receives 1% of the browser window, making it practically invisible to students. The file `results.htm` is loaded into this frame, and remains resident in this frame throughout the exam.

  The directions were moved to a file named `exam-directions.htm`, which also included an image of an arrow linking to a page named `Question1.htm`.

- The questions were moved to files named Question1.htm through Question10.htm (one question per page), each page including an image of an arrow linking to the next question (the arrow in Question1.htm linked to Question2.htm, and so forth).

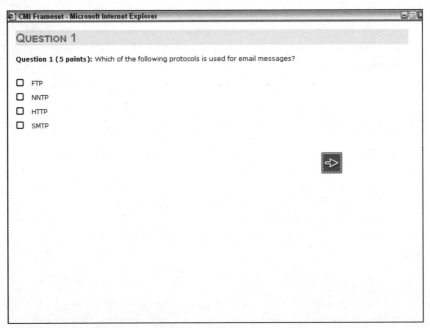

Figure 17-28: The tracking frameset named `exam-directions-frameset.htm` loaded into a new browser window

This example is on the CD-ROM as an example of scoring and tracking across multiple pages, in the folder `Muliple Pages Scoring`. Try it out!

To create the tracking frameset at this point:

1. Open the directions page named `exam-directions.htm`, which is the first page of the final exam.

2. Choose Modify → CourseBuilder → Create Tracking Frameset from the Dreamweaver MX menu.

   CourseBuilder displays the Create Tracking Frameset dialog box, as shown in Figure 17-29.

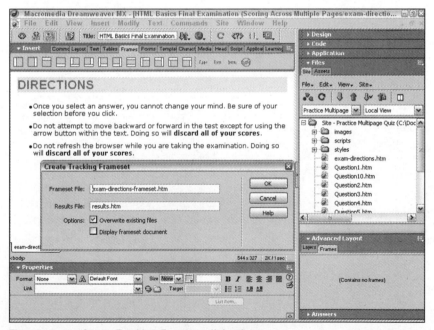

Figure 17-29: Create Tracking Frameset dialog box

By default, CourseBuilder names the tracking frameset using the filename that was open in Dreamweaver MX when you chose the option from the menu. Since we had `exam-directions.htm` opened, CourseBuilder defaults to naming the frameset `exam-directions-frameset.htm`. You can name this file whatever you want, but keep in mind that this frameset will become the initial file for the final exam.

CourseBuilder defaults to naming the Results File `results.htm`. There is absolutely no reason to rename this file, since it is basically hidden and must not be modified while the exam is in the browser window (otherwise you will flush all variables from the browser).

3. Accept the defaults for the Create Tracking Frameset dialog box by clicking the OK button. CourseBuilder adds the frameset file named `exam-directions-frameset.htm` and the results file `results.htm` to your site.

   If you dig into the HTML code, you will see that CourseBuilder added a frame named `cmiresults`, and set the source of that frame to `results.htm`.

4. Open the `results.htm` file in Dreamweaver MX. We need to define the following variables in that `results.htm` file:

   - `total` (the cumulative score for the exam, which starts at 0 and increments by the score value for each correct question).

   - `numQuestions` (a counter that tallies the number of questions in the exam, incremented by 1 for each question asked).

   - `numCorrect` (a counter that tallies the number of correct answers, incremented by 1 for each correct answer).

 JavaScript variables are *case sensitive*. Enter them exactly as shown.

We add these variables (as well as initial values) to the `results.htm` page by using a Call JavaScript behavior that loads the variables with initial values as soon as the `results.htm` file is loaded into the `cmiresults` frame.

5. Click the `<BODY>` tag in the tag selector.

6. Click the Add Behavior button on the Behaviors panel, as shown in Figure 17-30.

7. Select the Call JavaScript behavior from the popup menu. Dreamweaver MX displays the Call JavaScript dialog box.

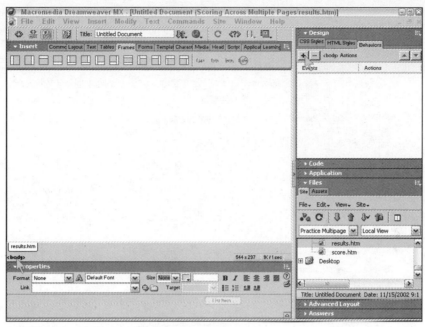

Figure 17-30: Adding a behavior to the `<BODY>` tag

8. Enter the following code into the Call JavaScript dialog box (see Figure 17-31), exactly as shown (remember, the variables are case sensitive). Basically, the JavaScript code is identifying new variables and setting their initial values to 0.

```
total=0, numQuestions=0, numCorrect=0;
```

Click OK to add the newly-defined behavior to the Behaviors panel. Be sure that the behavior has `onLoad` under the Events column (if not, you can click on the arrow to display the events drop-down menu and select `onLoad`).

TIP

Although this approach is designed specifically for carrying scoring variables between pages, you can easily use the same structure to carry any variables between content pages within a frame site. For example, you can gather the student's name and continually refer to the student by name. Just remember to initialize the variable in the `results.htm` file, just as you initialized the scoring and tracking variables.

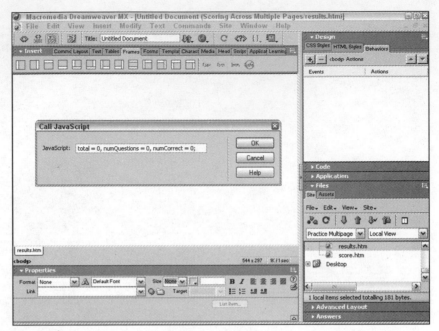

Figure 17-31: Defining and initializing the variables in the `results.htm` file

9. Save and close the file. Now that the variables are initialized and defined, you can call or change them from any file loaded into the frameset.

Our next task is to modify the variables within each question based on student answers for each question.

10. Open the frameset file `exam-directions-frameset.htm`. You will need to edit all question files within the frameset because of the variable definitions.

11. Click in the frame named `content` (the main content window) and choose File → Open in Frame from the Dreamweaver MX menu.

12. Open the `Question1.htm` file.

13. Highlight the invisible element for the `MultCh_ImageRadios01` interaction and click the Edit button on the Properties panel. CourseBuilder opens the interaction in the CourseBuilder Interaction dialog box.

Be sure the following settings are in effect:

- Judge Interaction when the user clicks a choice (General tab)
- Correct When All Correct and None Incorrect (General tab)
- Create a Reset button is unchecked (General tab)
- Incorrect choices have a Score of 0 (Choices tab)
- The Correct choice has a Score of 5 (Choices tab)

We're ready to edit our rules in the Action Manager, but let's take a little time out here to review what we want to accomplish:

◆ Increment the variable `total` by the score value entered on the Choices tab for correct answers if the student answers correctly.

◆ Increment the variable `numQuestions` by 1 for each question.

◆ Increment the variable `numCorrect` by 1 for each correct answer.

Although there are many ways to design this interaction, I wanted to separate the question counter and score updating (which always update) from the number of correct (which only updates based on the student's performance).

Also, because we judge the interaction automatically when the student clicks a choice, we need to disable the interaction immediately after the student selects a choice. Otherwise, the student could continually select and unselect the correct choice, continuously incrementing the variables during the process.

Considering these circumstances, I made the following design decisions:

◆ Update the `numCorrect` variable within an `if Correct` condition on the Action Manager for the multiple-choice interaction, because this variable should update *only* if the student answers correctly.

◆ Disable the multiple-choice interaction as soon as the student makes a selection.

◆ Update the `total` and `numQuestions` automatically on the Action Manager for the arrow button, because these variables should always be updated and don't need conditions related to the student's performance on the multiple-choice interaction.

Now let's continue with our tracking frameset.

14. Click on the Action Manager tab for the `MultCh_ImageRadios01` interaction in the CourseBuilder Interaction dialog box.

15. Cut all segments, actions, and conditions from the Action Manager except for the `Segment:Correctness` segment and the `if Correct` condition.

16. Highlight the `Segment:Correctness` segment. We are going to add an action that disables the multiple-choice question as soon as the student selects an answer.

17. Select the Set Interaction Properties action from the Action Manager drop-down menu and click the Add button. CourseBuilder displays the Set Interaction Properties dialog box (see Figure 17-32), which by default contains the settings to disable the multiple-choice `MultCh_ImageRadios01` interaction (the default for this action is to disable an interaction; the multiple-choice question is the default because it is the only interaction on the page).

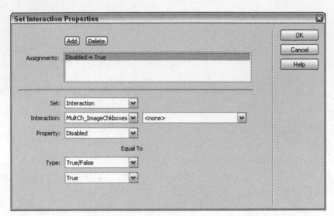

Figure 17-32: Inserting a Set Interaction Properties action that disables the multiple-choice question as soon as the student answers

18. Click OK to insert the Set Interaction Properties that disables the multiple-choice interaction.

19. Highlight the `if Correct` condition.

20. Select the Call JavaScript action from the Action Manager drop-down menu and click the Add button. CourseBuilder displays the Call JavaScript dialog box.

21. Enter the following code into the Call JavaScript dialog box (see Figure 17-33), exactly as shown (remember, the variables are case sensitive).

```
top.cmiresults.numCorrect ++
```

The code indicates the

- Location of the variable (`top.cmiresults`, where `top` indicates the top level in the browser window, and `cmiresults` is the name of the frame at the top level containing the variable).

- Variable name (`numCorrect`) and the level of incrementation (++ indicates that the variable is a counter and should be incremented by 1).

22. Click OK to insert the Call JavaScript into the Action Manager.

Each Call JavaScript action was renamed to show its function within the Action Manager. If you want to rename the Call JavaScript action, highlight the action in the Action Manager and click the Rename button.

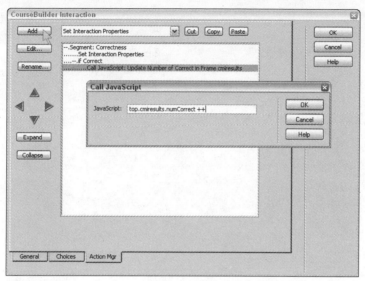

Figure 17-33: Entering the JavaScript code that updates the number of correct (numCorrect) counter maintained in the cmiresults frame

23. Click OK again to update the multiple-choice interaction with the new rules and close the CourseBuilder Interaction dialog box.

Our final task is to insert the arrow button that updates the score (total) and number of questions (numQuestions).

24. Click the cursor at the location on the page where you want to insert the arrow button, and then click Insert CourseBuilder Interaction button on the Learning tab. CourseBuilder displays the CourseBuilder Interaction dialog box, with the CourseBuilder Gallery active.

25. Choose the Button category to display the two button templates.

26. Click the Button_Push template. CourseBuilder displays the General and Action Mgr tabs.

27. Click the General tab and select the custom Next button from the Appearance drop-down menu. Accept the remaining defaults, as shown in Figure 17-34.

28. Click the Action Manager tab and remove (cut) everything except for the Segment: Button Feedback segment. We need to add three actions:

- Call JavaScript that updates the numQuestions variable by 1.

- Call JavaScript that updates the total variable by the score the student received on the question.

- Go To URL action that loads the next question into the content frame.

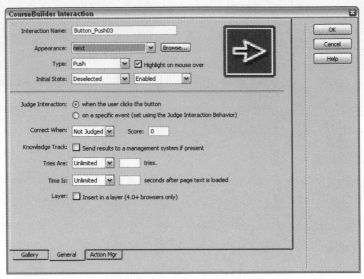

Figure 17-34: The General tab for the button interaction that will insert the arrow button into `Question1.htm`

29. Select the Call JavaScript action from the Action Manager drop-down menu and click the Add button. CourseBuilder displays the Call JavaScript dialog box.

30. Enter the following code into the Call JavaScript dialog box (see Figure 17-35), exactly as shown (remember, the variables are case sensitive) and then click OK:

```
top.cmiresults.numQuestions ++
```

The code increments the number of questions (`numQuestions`) counter by 1.

31. Select the Call JavaScript action from the Action Manager drop-down menu and click the Add button. CourseBuilder displays the Call JavaScript dialog box.

32. Enter the following code into the dialog box (see Figure 17-36), exactly as shown (remember, the variables are case sensitive), and then click OK:

```
top.cmiresults.total += G01.score
```

The code increments the score (`total`) by the value assigned to the correct answer. Notice that whereas the other variables were incremented by 1 (++), this variable is incremented by the assigned value for the score (+=G01.score).

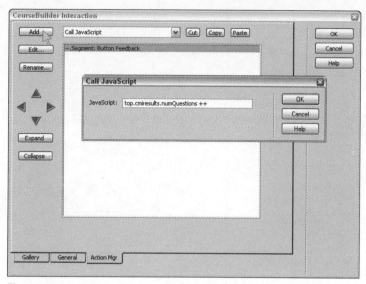

Figure 17-35: Entering the JavaScript code that updates the number of questions (numQuestions) counter maintained in the cmiresults frame

33. Select the Go To URL action from the Action Manager drop-down menu and click the Add button. CourseBuilder displays the Go To URL dialog box.

34. Highlight the frame named content, because we want to load the next question into the same frame.

35. Browse to the file Question2.htm and click OK. Figure 17-37 shows the completed Go To URL action.

36. Click OK to insert the new button interaction into the Question1.htm file.

37. Repeat Steps 11–36 for each question file (Question2.htm through Question10.htm), making the appropriate changes in the Go To URL action. (All variables stay the same.)

    Because the actions remain the same for the button, you can simply cut and paste the button (including the interaction code) into each subsequent question file to save time.

At the end of the exam (or anywhere along the way, for that matter) you can write the variables stored in the cmiresults frame into any page in the content frame. In our example, we created a link for the arrow in Question10.htm that loads a file named score.htm into the frame named content. The score.htm file contains a Set Text of Layer that writes the feedback for the test to a layer, as shown in Figure 17-38.

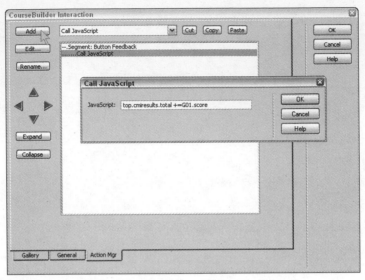

Figure 17-36: Entering the JavaScript code that updates the score (total) variable maintained in the cmiresults frame

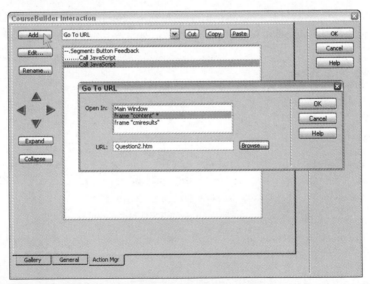

Figure 17-37: Inserting the Go To URL action that loads the next question into the current frame, named content

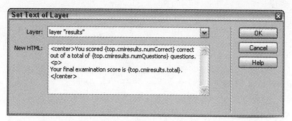

Figure 17-38: Variables in the feedback to students are replaced with the actual values.

When the text is written on the screen, the student sees (with his specific values filled in, of course):

You scored 7 correct out of a total of 10 questions.

Your final examination score is 75.

Regardless of the design of your interactions, you must ensure that variables only change once during judgment, otherwise students could easily skew the scoring. For example, if you have multiple-choice questions judged automatically, you should disable the interaction as soon as the student makes a choice; otherwise, each call to the Action Manager could increment scores, correct choices, and number of questions.

Summary

This chapter described how to

◆ Use either the Action Mgr tab on an interaction or the Action Manager interaction to define the processing rules for a single CourseBuilder interaction or multiple CourseBuilder interactions.

◆ Use the Action Manager interface proficiently.

◆ Work with segments, conditions, and actions.

◆ Test properties of interactions and interaction elements.

◆ Score single-page and multiple-page examinations.

The next chapter describes how to make full use of the Learning Site Microsoft Access Database as a Learning Management System.

Part IV

Tracking Results

Chapter 18

Using the Learning Site Microsoft Access Database

IN THIS CHAPTER

- ◆ Installing a testing Web server on your computer

- ◆ Defining tracking information within Learning Site

- ◆ Creating a database to store information about students and activities

- ◆ Enabling CourseBuilder interactions to track student performance

- ◆ Using the Record Administrator to manage students and activities in Learning Site

- ◆ Testing and uploading your site

- ◆ Exploring the Microsoft Access database that Learning Site creates

LEARNING SITE ships with Learning Management System (LMS) functionality contained within Learning Site, driven by a number of scripts and a pre-built Microsoft Access database all contained within Learning Site.

This chapter walks you through the basic steps of setting up your Learning Site to include database and tracking (the sections are in the sequence you must follow):

1. Create and define a Web server for testing.

2. Create your Learning Site LMS.

3. Copy the Learning Site administration files into your site.

4. Define tracking for each CourseBuilder interaction in your course.

5. Upload your site to the Web server for testing.

6. Use the Record Administrator to set up and test your course.

7. Publish your course to make it "live."

To test your Learning Site LMS, you need to use a Web server, which runs the ASP scripts that drive processing for the Learning Site LMS.

You can choose to use a remote Web server or, if you are running a Microsoft Windows system, you can set your system to work like a remote server using Internet Information Server (IIS) for Microsoft Windows NT, 2000, or XP Professional systems.

 Learning Site does not support Windows 98 or Windows ME as of the printing of this book.

If you are using a Macintosh system, you need to set up a remote server.

Throughout the remainder of this chapter, the phrase *Web server* refers to the location you chose for your remote server, whether it is truly remote or on your Windows system working like a remote server.

Creating and Defining Your Web Server

If you are working on a Microsoft Windows system, the easiest approach to testing your Learning Site LMS is to set up a Web server on your own system. This server operates like a Web server on the Internet, processing scripts, working with databases, and so forth.

To use a Web server on your Windows system, you need to

1. Create and install a Web server on your Microsoft Windows system using Internet Information Server (IIS).

2. Create a folder on the Web server to store your site, including the tracking database and processing scripts that Learning Site LMS creates.

3. Define the Remote Info and Testing Server categories in your Dreamweaver MX site to point to the Web server.

Creating and installing a Web server

To install IIS on your Windows NT, 2000, or XP Professional systems:

1. Insert your Windows NT, 2000, or XP Professional CD in the CD-ROM drive.

2. Choose Start → Control Panel. Windows displays the Control Panel window.

3. Click the Add or Remove Programs icon. Windows displays the Add or Remove programs window.

4. Click the Add/Remove Windows components button. Windows displays the Windows Components Wizard.

5. Select the Internet Information Services (IIS) component checkbox as shown in Figure 18-1, and click the Next button.

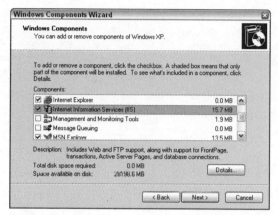

Figure 18-1: The Windows Components Wizard shows the IIS component on a Microsoft Windows XP system.

6. Follow the dialog procedure for installing IIS.

IIS creates a directory on your C:\ drive that serves as the Web server root directory, similar in function to the root directory on any Web server on the Internet. The path to that directory is `C:\inetpub\wwwroot\`.

Once you install your Web server, it starts automatically each time you start your system. You can, however, explore and manage your Web server, should the need arise: IIS is accessible through Start → Control Panel, and then select the Administrative Tools icon.

Creating a Web site folder on your Web server

With your Web server installed, you need to create a folder (subdirectory) with proper permissions on the server to which you can upload your Dreamweaver MX site for testing.

To show this process, let's create a folder named `Learning-Remote`:

1. Create a new folder within the `C:\inetpub\wwwroot\` folder by using File → New → Folder from Windows Explorer or My Computer. Name it `Learning Remote`. This is the folder that will store your site on the Web server.

2. Right-click the new `Learning-Remote` folder and select Properties at the bottom of the popup list. Windows displays the Properties dialog box for the folder.

3. Click on the Web Sharing tab of the Properties dialog box.

4. Select the Share this folder option. By default, the folder is shared using an alias (used by the Web server) that is the same name as the folder (in this case, `Learning-Remote`).

5. Click on Edit Properties button to edit the properties of that folder. Be sure that Read access permissions and Scripts application permissions are checked (they should be by default). Figure 18-2 shows these settings on a Windows XP system.

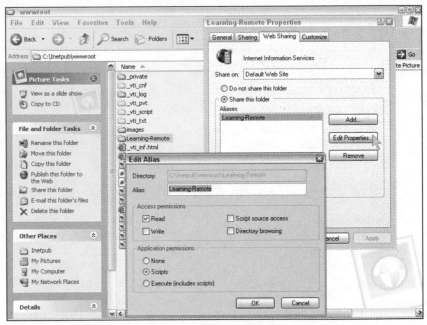

Figure 18-2: Changing the properties of the `Learning-Remote` folder on your Web server

6. Click OK to save the permissions, and OK again to save the properties.

Your computer is now set up as a Web server, which you can access through the browser by specifying *localhost* in the URL. For example, if the `Learning-Remote` folder had a file named `index.html` in it, you could type **http://localhost/**

Learning-Remote/index.html in your browser, and the browser would retrieve that file (located at C:\inetpub\wwwroot\Learning-Remote\index.html) like it would any other URL.

If you want to create additional folders for other Web sites, follow this same process for each site, giving them unique folders within the C:\inetpub\wwwroot\ directory.

Specifying Web server settings within your Dreamweaver MX site

Although you have created a Web server with a folder named Learning-Remote, that folder is empty. The next step is to create a site within Dreamweaver MX that uses C:\inetpub\wwwroot\Learning-Remote as the remote Web server for that site. To do so, follow these steps (if you have an existing site, select Site → Edit Sites and begin with Step 3):

1. Choose Site → New Site from the Dreamweaver MX menu to display the Edit Sites dialog box. Select the Advanced tab.

2. Enter the Site Name and Local Root Folder. For this example, the Site Name is Learning Site LMS, and the Local Root Folder is Learning-Local.

3. Click the Remote Info category to set up your connection to the Web server.

4. Select Local/Network from the Access drop-down menu.

5. Browse to the Learning-Remote folder in C:\inetpub\wwwroot\Learning-Remote to select the Remote Folder (see Figure 18-3). Click Select.

6. Now that the Remote Folder is identified, you need to specify the Testing Server settings. Click the Testing Server category.

7. Select the Server Model ASP VBScript, which is the scripting language used to develop the Learning Site LMS scripts.

8. Select Local/Network from the Access drop-down menu. By default, Dreamweaver MX defines the Testing Server folder to be the same folder as the Remote Folder, which is what we want.

9. Click OK to exit the Site Definition dialog box and save your settings. Figure 18-4 shows the settings for Testing Server being entered on the Site Definition dialog box within Dreamweaver MX.

Note that you will now have *two* copies of the site. One will be the local copy, wherever you happen to store it, the other will be the "remote" copy (in the wwwroot folder) that you can upload files to through Dreamweaver MX.

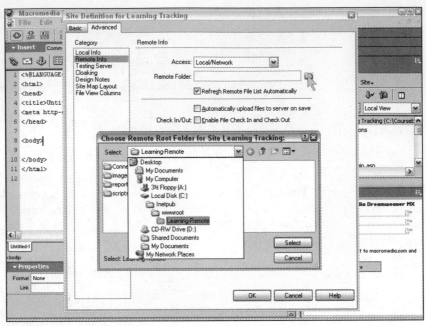

Figure 18-3: Setting up the `C:\inetpub\wwwroot\Learning-Remote` **folder as the Remote Folder within Dreamweaver MX**

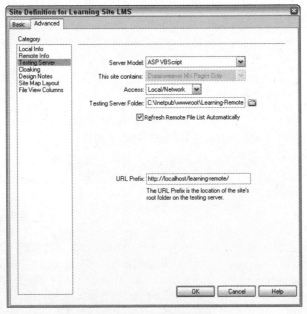

Figure 18-4: Setting up the Testing Server

Creating Your Learning Site LMS

You've created a local Web server and are ready to turn your Learning Site into a Learning Management System. To do so, you need to create a Learning Site (or modify an existing Learning Site) to include tracking information. Specifically, you need to

1. Define tracking information.

2. Create a Microsoft Access database to store student, administrator, and activity (course) data.

3. Define the Data Source Name (DSN) to allow the Web server to communicate with the database.

4. Define the student login and results pages.

 Although these tasks are documented in separate sections, you would normally define them all at once in Learning Site. The steps in each section assume you remain in Learning Site until you finish defining the student login and results pages, so the step numbers "carry through" each section.

After you create your Learning Site LMS, the main page of your course is automatically changed by Learning Site to redirect access attempts to an authorization form, so that only authorized students can access the course.

Defining Tracking Information

Once you have your Web server and Dreamweaver MX set up properly, you are ready to create a Learning Site that includes tracking information:

1. Be sure that the Dreamweaver MX site that will contain your Learning Site LMS is open.

2. Choose Site → Learning Site → Create Learning Site. The Learning Site dialog box displays.

3. Check the Data Tracking checkbox. Learning Site displays three additional tracking tabs (Tracking, Login, and Results), as shown in Figure 18-5.

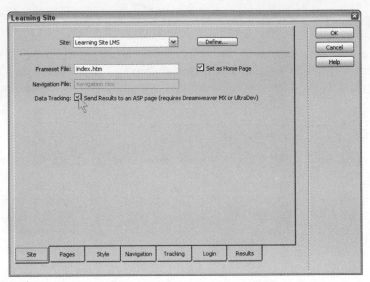

Figure 18-5: Learning Site with data tracking enabled

 At this point you can insert sample pages and select a different style, or enter them later. If you want to test tracking, however, you will need to include at least one CourseBuilder interaction in your Learning Site.

4. Click the Tracking tab. At the Learning Site level, an activity is a single course, typically defined by a single Dreamweaver MX site. The top of the Tracking tab contains two default definitions for the activity:

Activity ID, which is by default set to 100. The Activity ID can be up to 50 alphanumeric characters, and is used in reports that refer to the activity. Normally, the Activity ID would reflect the course content, such as HTML Basics for the *HTML Basics* course.

Activity Name, which is by default set to the name of your Dreamweaver MX site.

Our example maintains the default values.

Creating a Microsoft Access database

You have to create a Microsoft Access database that will store all of the student, activity, and tracking information:

5. Click the Create Microsoft Access (.mdb) file button in the Learning Site dialog box. Learning Site displays the Save Tracking Database As dialog box.

6. Use the drop-down menu to select the `Learning-Remote` folder in `C:\inetpub\wwwroot\`.

7. Enter the name of the file for your database as shown in Figure 18-6, and click Save. (In our example, we use `corporate-training.mdb` as the name of the database, because we may want to add more courses later.)

Learning Site creates the Microsoft Access database `C:\inetpub\www-root\Learning-Remote\corporate-training.mdb`.

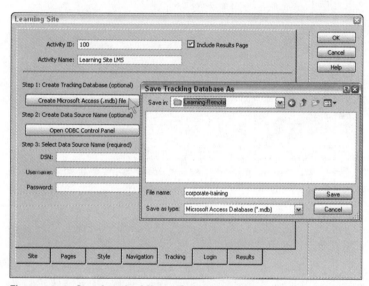

Figure 18-6: Creating the Microsoft Access database in the Learning-Remote folder on the Web server

Defining the System Data Source Name (DSN)

You must define the System Data Source Name (DSN) to allow the ASP tracking page to find the Microsoft Access database on the Web server:

8. Click the Open ODBC Control Panel. Windows displays the ODBC Data Source Administrator.

9. Click the System DSN tab to define a system DSN. Windows displays a Create New Data Source menu (see Figure 18-7).

10. Select the Microsoft Access Driver (.mdb) and click the Finish button.

Of course, we're not really finished! Windows displays the ODBC Microsoft Access Setup dialog box.

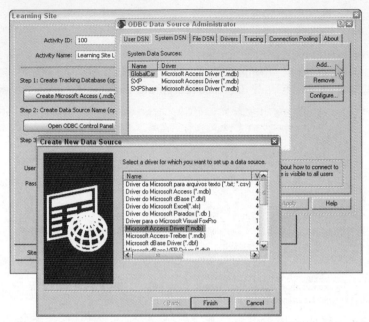

Figure 18-7: Selecting the Microsoft Access Driver as the data source
for defining the new system DSN

11. Enter a Data Source Name (used internally only). Our example uses
    `Corporate Training Database`.

12. Click the Select button to specify the name of the Microsoft Access data-
    base we just created. Windows displays the Select Database dialog box.
    Browse to the database on the Web server, as shown in Figure 18-8.

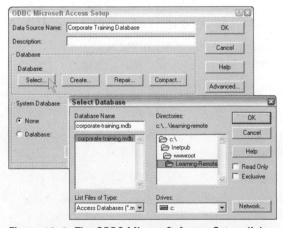

Figure 18-8: The ODBC Microsoft Access Setup dialog
box and the Select Database dialog box

13. Select the database, click OK, and OK again to save the ODBC settings and return to the Tracking tab in Learning Site.

14. Click the Select ODBC button (the icon of the globe) to the right of the DSN field. Windows displays the Select ODBC DSN menu, as shown in Figure 18-9. Select your database (Corporate Training Database, in this example) and click OK.

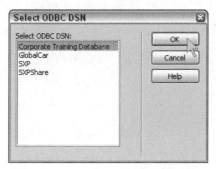

Figure 18-9: Selecting the newly-defined Corporate Training Database as the DSN pointer to the Microsoft Access database

Defining the student login and results pages

The final phase in this mini-journey is to define the student login and results pages:

15. Click the Login tab. The student login page is the ASP script that authorizes students to access the course. Learning Site modifies the site so that students accessing the course are redirected to the student login (studentLogin.asp) page to ensure authorization to take the course.

    Learning Site displays the Login tab settings.

16. Accept the default Login File Name studentLogin.asp, or enter a new ASP file name.

17. Accept the default Login Title (displayed in the browser title bar), or enter a new title.

18. Choose the graphic displayed on the login page by selecting a graphic (logo) that matches the style for your course, or by selecting a custom graphic, as shown in Figure 18-10.

    Select the login logo that is most appropriate for the style of your course, or select a custom graphic by selecting the Custom option.

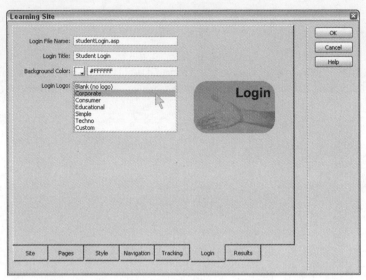

Figure 18-10: Selecting a graphic for your login page that matches the design of your course

19. Click the Results tab. The results page displays the results of the student's performance on the tracked test. (You specify the circumstances for displaying the results page (results.asp) on the Navigation tab for the Learning Site. (See Chapter 7 for a description of the first four tabs in the Learning Site dialog box.)

    Learning Site displays the Results tab settings, as shown in Figure 18-11.

20. Accept the default Results File Name results.asp, or enter a new ASP file name.

21. Accept the default Results Title (displayed in the browser title bar) or enter a new title.

22. Choose the graphic displayed on the results page by selecting a graphic (logo) that matches the style for your course, or by selecting a custom graphic, as shown in Figure 18-11 (click Open when you select a custom graphic).

23. Click OK on the Learning Site dialog box to return to Dreamweaver MX. Learning Site writes the new definitions and files to your Dreamweaver MX site. In addition, if you inserted CourseBuilder interactions on the Pages tab, Learning Site prompts you to insert the CourseBuilder support files as well. (See Chapter 7 for a discussion of the Pages tab.)

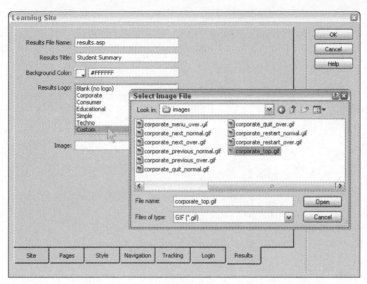

Figure 18-11: Selecting a graphic for your results page that matches the design of your course. This examples shows a custom graphic being chosen.

Understanding the additional files added to your Dreamweaver MX site

When you finish entering your definitions for tracking, Learning Site writes the standard Learning Site files (such as navigation.htm, menu.htm, and so forth) to your Dreamweaver MX site. Learning Site also writes the following additional files in your Learning-Local site folder:

◆ Connections, which contains a single file named LearningSite.asp that enables the scripts to find the Microsoft Access database on the Web server.

◆ global.asa, which is used by the Web server to maintain information about users, machine names, and so forth.

◆ tracking.asp, which processes tracking information.

◆ studentLogin.asp, which is used by students to log into the course.

◆ results.asp, which is used to display the results of tests to student.

Copying the Administration Files

Before you can use the Records Administrator (to create student accounts, run reports, and so forth), you need to copy the administration files into your site. To do so, choose Site → Learning Site → Copy Admin Files. Learning Site displays the Copy Learning Site Admin Files dialog box.

The only field you are required to enter in the dialog box is the DSN you identified earlier when creating the Learning Site. The DSN Corporate Training Database (or whatever you named the site's DSN) should display by default. To confirm, click OK.

If the DSN does not display automatically, you can click the Select ODBC button (the icon of the globe) to the right of the DSN field. Windows displays the Select ODBC DSN menu, as shown in Figure 18-12.

Figure 18-12: Selecting the DSN before copying the administration files into your site

Select your DSN, click the OK button, and OK again to copy the administration files. Learning site copies three files and a folder into the root folder for your site:

- ◆ adminLogin.asp, which enables you to log into the Records Administrator (by default, the username and password are both admin).

- ◆ adminmenu.asp, which displays the Record Administrator menu of options.

- ◆ global.asa, a system definitions file.

- ◆ reports folder, which contains nine additional .asp files which drive the administration interface for the Record Administrator.

Defining Tracking for Each CourseBuilder Interaction

To define tracking information in CourseBuilder, you must first understand scores, weights, and the grading scale. Then you can use the Question Developer planning document on the toolkit to design a test that gives the desired value to each question.

Understanding scores, weights, and the grading scale

The total score for a test using Learning Site LMS is based three different factors: score, weight, and grading scale.

SCORE

The score is defined for each correct answer on the

- ◆ Choices tab for multiple-choice interactions

- ◆ Responses tab for text-entry interactions

- ◆ Pairs tab for drag-and-drop interactions

- ◆ Ranges tab for slider interactions

- ◆ Hot areas tab for explore interactions

Each correct answer should have a score defined for it, reflecting its point value. It is possible for a single interaction to have more than one correct answer, each of which should be assigned a specific score.

WEIGHT

The weight is defined for each interaction on the Tracking tab for that interaction. There is only one weight value for each interaction, and it is used to give more or less importance to a specific interaction in relation to other interactions in the test.

For example, assume Question 1 and Question 2 each have one correct answer worth 2 points. However, if Question 1 has a weight of 1 and Question 2 has a weight of 3, the weighted score for a correct choice in Question 1 would be 2 points, and for Question 2 it would be 6 points (score × weight).

You certainly do not need to use weighted scores. To let the question scores stand on their own; you can enter a weight value of 1 for every question. Figure 18-13 shows the relationship between weights and scores.

GRADING SCALE

Finally, for the Learning Site LMS, a grading scale of 100 is used for all tests. That means the scores and weights you define ultimately are translated into proportional pieces of a 100-point scale.

For example, assume a test consists of 5 questions (Q1 through Q5), each with a score of 5 points. Furthermore, assume Q1 through Q3 are weighted at 2, and Q4 through Q5 are weighted at 1. If a student answered all but Q3 correctly, the total weighted score would be 30 ((5 × 2) + (5 × 2) + (0 × 2)) + ((5 × 1)+ (5 × 1)).

To compute the total score on a grading scale of 100, Learning Site would divide the total weighted score by the total possible weighted score of 40 (the weighted score if the student answered *all* correctly), and multiply the result by 100. In this example, the total score would be 75 ((30/40) × 100).

Question 1 (weight = 2)

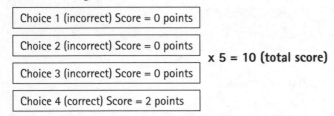

| Choice 1 (correct) Score = 2 points |
| Choice 2 (incorrect) Score = 0 points |
| Choice 3 (incorrect) Score = 0 points |
| Choice 4 (incorrect) Score = 0 points |

x 2 = 4 (total score)

Question 2 (weight = 5)

| Choice 1 (incorrect) Score = 0 points |
| Choice 2 (incorrect) Score = 0 points |
| Choice 3 (incorrect) Score = 0 points |
| Choice 4 (correct) Score = 2 points |

x 5 = 10 (total score)

Figure 18-13: Understanding the relationship between scores
and weights

To help you better understand the relationship of score, weight, and grading
scale, Table 18-1 shows example tests consisting of two or three questions with
various scores and weights. (Note the Learning Site LMS rounds off total scores.)

TABLE 18-1 SCORING EXAMPLES

	Score	Weight	Student Answer is...	Test Score on a 100-Point Scale
Test 1				
Question 1	4	1	Correct	15
Question 2	22	1	Incorrect	
Test 2				
Question 1	2	14	Incorrect	91
Question 2	55	5	Correct	

	Score	Weight	Student Answer is...	Test Score on a 100-Point Scale
Test 3				
Question 1	13	1	Correct	4
Question 2	300	1	Incorrect	
Test 4				
Question 1	14	2	Correct	21
Question 2	55	5	Incorrect	
Question 3	15	3	Correct	

When Learning Site scores a course, it does not have a setting that shows the total number of questions in the course, so the final test score is always based on the number of questions that the student actually answers.

For example, if a course has 10 questions, students normally would need to answer the 10 questions correctly to receive a grade of 100. However, if a student answers a single question correctly and exits the course, that student's grade will be recorded as 100, but the scoring reports will show that the student only answered a single question.

Defining tracking for each interaction

Once you create a Learning Site LMS, you must be sure of two things:

◆ Interactions that you want tracked have the Knowledge Track option on the General tab selected.

◆ Interactions that you *don't* want tracked *do not* have the Knowledge Track option on the General tab selected.

These might seem like obvious points, but remember that buttons, sliders, and timers are also interactions, and you probably don't want to track them.

When you check the Knowledge Track option on the General tab, CourseBuilder displays an additional tab named Tracking. To complete the Tracking definitions on that tab:

1. Enter the name of an Interaction ID. The ID will be used in the database (and in reports) to show student performance for that specific interaction. Normally, I use an ID that reflects the number of the question — Question1, Question2, and so forth. You cannot use spaces in the ID (text beyond a space is discarded from the database). Figure 18-14 shows the Tracking tab's fields.

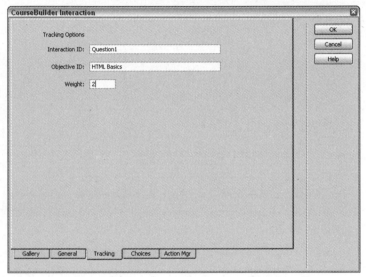

Figure 18-14: Enter tracking information on the Tracking tab for each interaction.

2. Enter a single word (no spaces) Objective ID that identifies related interactions. For example, if you have a series of questions on HTML tables, you could enter tables for the Objective ID to show that the questions are related.

When you enter an Objective ID with spaces, Learning Site inserts other fields such as weight and latency in the wrong fields. Do *not* insert spaces into the Objective ID.

3. Enter the weight for that specific interaction. Be sure you understand the consequences of the weight value (read the previous section on scores, weights, and the grading scale).

4. Click OK to insert the interaction into your Dreamweaver MX page.

Be sure to attach tracking information to every interaction that you want tracked. Also note that you may only have one tracked interaction per page, and that interaction must be the G01 interaction (see Chapter 17 for a discussion of the G01 interaction).

Because it takes a couple of seconds for Learning Site to write data to the database, students "flying" through an exam may have their answers lost. I highly recommend inserting a 3-second timer that initiates *after* the interaction is judged and then displays a message such as "OK, proceed to next question." Or at a minimum include a message to the student describing the need to proceed slowly.

Uploading Your Site to the Web Server

To test your Learning Site LMS, you need to upload it to your Web server. Because you defined the Remote Info earlier in this chapter, you can simply click the Put button (the up arrow) to upload the entire site to the Web server, as shown in Figure 18-15.

Figure 18-15: Uploading your site to your Web server for testing

Dreamweaver MX moves your entire site up to the Web server, and you're ready to create student accounts and test your course!

 Using the Records Administrator to Set Up and Test Your Course

The Records Administrator is a tool. You use it to administer your database. The Records Administrator enables you to

- Add, modify, and delete students and other administrators in the database
- View student and activity reports
- Search the student or activity database

To access the Records Administrator, type **http://localhost/Learning-Remote/adminlogin.asp** in your browser's address bar and press the Enter key:

You must type the address in your Web browser. Using File → Open from your browser will not work, because that bypasses the Web server.

Also, if you receive an error message referring to the file named global.asa (an optional system definitions file), delete that file and click the Refresh button. The loss of the file will have no impact on your testing.

Your browser now displays the Records Administration login screen (see Figure 18-16). Enter the default User ID (**admin**) and Password (**admin**).

After your User ID and Password are authorized, the Records Administrator displays the Admin Menu, as shown in Figure 18-17.

You have to add a student user before you can test your course. We'll do that in the next section.

Managing students and administrators

There are two types of users in a Learning Site LMS:

- Students, who gain access to the course.
- Administrators, who gain access to the Admin Menu.

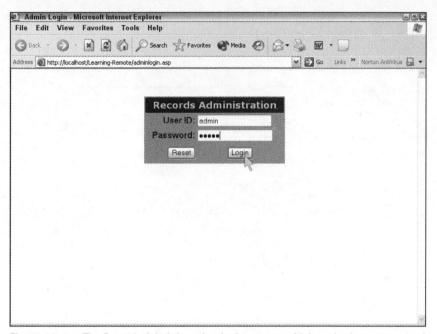

Figure 18-16: The Records Administration login screen, which authorizes access to the administration account for the Learning Site LMS

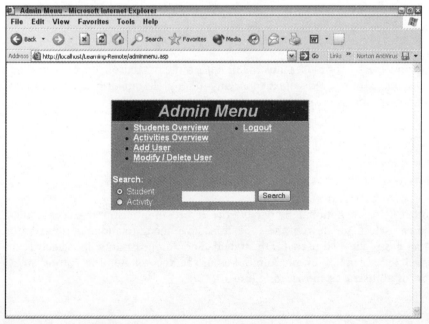

Figure 18-17: The Admin Menu

To add students and administrators to the Records Administrator, select the Add User option on the Admin Menu. The Records Administrator displays the Add New User form, as shown in Figure 18-18.

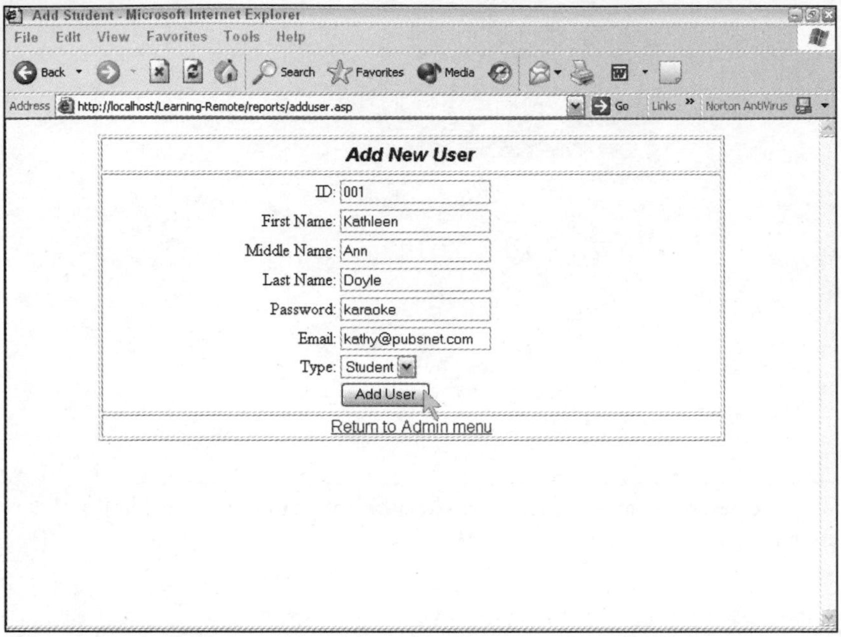

Figure 18–18: Adding a new student or administrator to the database

The ID you specify for a user must be unique in the database. You can choose to use a last name, a numbered sequence, or any other alphanumeric characters.

The remaining fields are self-explanatory. You *must* specify

◆ ID

◆ Last Name

◆ Password

The other fields are optional. By default, the Records Administrator adds a Student user; you can select Admin from the Type drop-down menu to add an administrator.

You can easily view all users (both students and administrators) by selecting the Modify/Delete User option on the Admin Menu. The Records Administrator displays the report of all users, as shown in Figure 18-19.

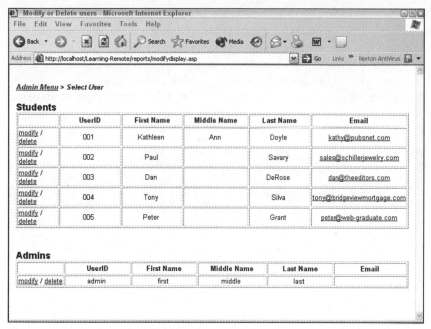

Figure 18-19: You can view, modify, and delete students and administrators when you select the Modify/Delete User option.

With the Modify/Delete User results displayed, you can modify or delete any user by selecting modify or delete from the left-hand column in the same row that contains that user's information. The only field that you *cannot* change for students or administrators is UserID.

Viewing reports

The Records Administrator provides access to reports on students and activities (courses). Let's take a look at all of the reports you can retrieve.

The reports are all driven by ASP pages (scripts) stored in a folder named `reports` within your site. This folder was created when you selected a Microsoft Access database in the Learning Site dialog box.

STUDENT REPORTS

The Record Administrator provides three reports about students, each with greater detail: Students Overview, Student Summary, and Student Detail.

Author, please provide The Students Overview report lists all students in the database. Access this report by selecting the Students Overview option from the Admin Menu. The Records Administrator provides a listing of students, as shown in Figure 18-20.

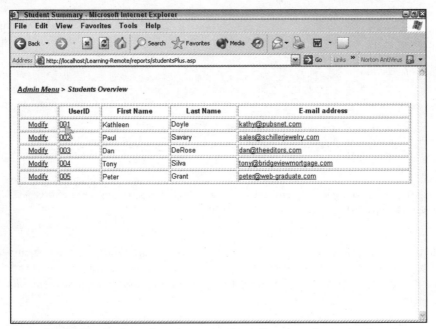

Figure 18-20: The Students Overview report lists all students in the database.

The Student Summary report, which provides details about a student's course activities, is accessed by clicking on the student's ID in the Students Overview report. (Typically, each course is a separate activity, as defined on the Tracking tab for the Learning Site dialog box.)

The Student Detail report lists the results of each interaction for an activity. Access the detail report by clicking on an Activity Name in the Student Summary report. The Records Administrator displays the Student Detail report, as shown in Figure 18-22.

The Student Detail report contains two fields that are confusing because of the labels:

◆ **User Response** lists the answer selected by the student (choice selected, text typed, and so forth).

◆ **Result** lists the judgment of the User Response.

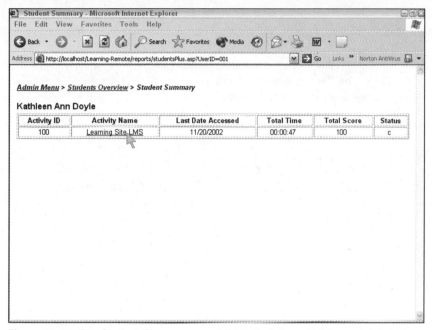

Figure 18-21: The Student Summary report lists all of the activities completed by the student selected from the Students Overview report.

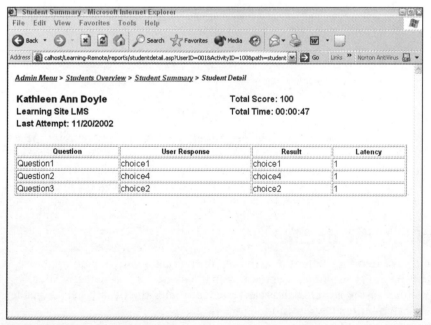

Figure 18-22: The Student Detail report, which lists the student's performance for each interaction in the activity (course)

ACTIVITY REPORTS

The Record Administrator provides two reports about activities: Activities Overview and Activity Summary.

The Activities Overview report (see Figure 18-23) lists all activities in the Learning Site LMS. The Record Administrator displays this report when you select the Activities Overview option from the Admin Menu.

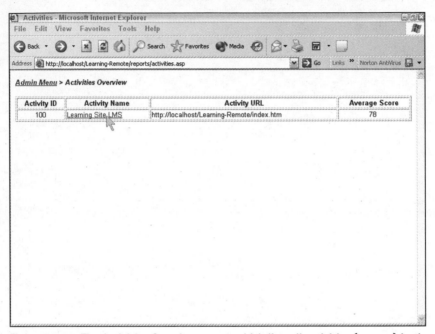

Figure 18-23: The Activities Overview report, which lists all activities (courses) in the database

The Activity Summary report provides further detail about any activity. Access this report by clicking on the Activity Name in the Activities Overview report. When we click on the Learning Site LMS activity, for example, the Records Administrator displays a report listing all students who have taken the activity, and the results of their testing, as shown in Figure 18-24.

Searching the database

You can also search for students *or* activities by entering a search word or phrase in the Search field. For example, if you know that a student's last name is Silva, you can type Silva in the search field, select Student under the Search category, then click the Search button, as shown in Figure 18-25.

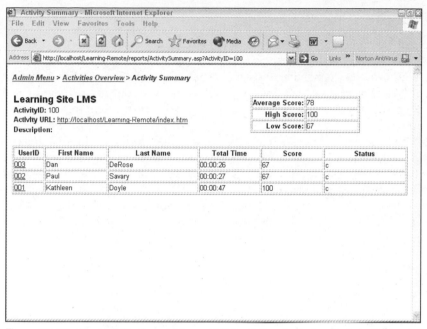

Figure 18-24: The Activity Summary report lists all the students who have taken the activity, and shows the results of their testing.

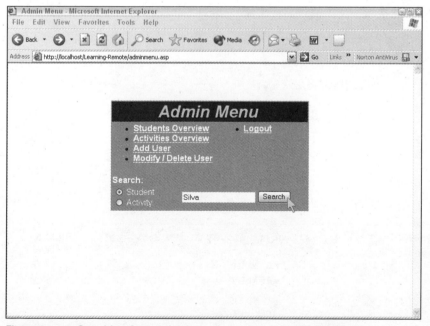

Figure 18-25: Searching for numbers, words, or phrases in the Student or Activity records

Testing the course

You can test the course as a student as soon as you add a student to the Records Administrator. To access the course as a student, type the name of the frameset file in your Web browser. Remember to type the name of the frameset file *stored on your local Web server* (index.htm by default, but whatever you specified on the Site tab of the Learning Site dialog box): **http://localhost/Learning-Remote/index.htm**.

Anyone trying to access the course is automatically redirected to the student login page, which asks for the student's User ID and Password (use the ID and password of a student added using the Records Administrator). When the User ID and Password are authorized, the Learning Site LMS displays the index.htm file (or whatever you selected as the frameset file).

You can then test the course by taking it as a student. When you finish, the final page in the course (selected from the Results tab of the Learning Site dialog box) will be the summary of the student's performance (yours, in this test) on the tests, as shown in Figure 18-26.

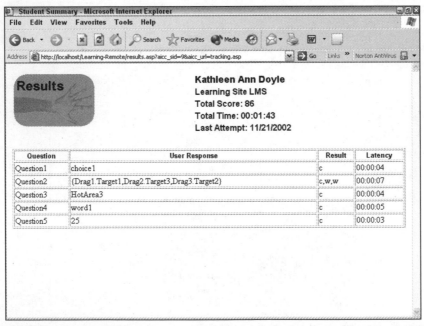

Figure 18–26: The results.asp page in the course displays the student's performance results for each interaction in the course.

In this example, the test consists of five questions:

◆ Question 1 is a multiple-choice question with one correct choice (correct score is 20, weight is 1)

◆ Question 2 is a drag-and-drop question, with 3 correct pairings (correct score is 7 per correct pairing, weight is 1)

◆ Question 3 is an explore question, with 1 correct hot area (correct score is 20, weight is 1)

◆ Question 4 is a text-entry question, with 1 correct answer (correct score is 20, weight is 1)

◆ Question 5 is a slider question, with 1 correct range of 0-49 (correct score is 20, weight is 1)

This example's results show that Kathleen answered questions 1, 3, 4, and 5 correctly. However, on the drag-and-drop exercise, she correctly matched Drag1:Target1, but incorrectly matched the other pairs, scoring only 33% of the 20 points, giving a final rounded score of 86 for the examination.

The Results page's User Response column includes braces around answers that are partially correct, and the Result column indicates which specific answers were correct (c) or incorrect (w).

Redesigning ASP pages

The ASP files that Learning Site inserts into your Dreamweaver MX site are. . . hmmmm. . . how to say this. . . ugly! The good news is that ASP files can be redesigned in Dreamweaver MX just like any other page. You can, for example, use Cascading Style Sheets to change the styles used by the page.

When you edit an ASP page, be sure to change only the content, and not the server behaviors or other database and script definitions. Dreamweaver MX uses curly braces, highlighting, and other visual aids to help you distinguish definitions from "regular" content, as seen in Figure 18-27.

You can safely change text content. For example, in the Student Summary there are two headings that I consider to be rather cryptic: User Response and Result. You could change these headings, which would more properly be named Student's Answer and Judged As.

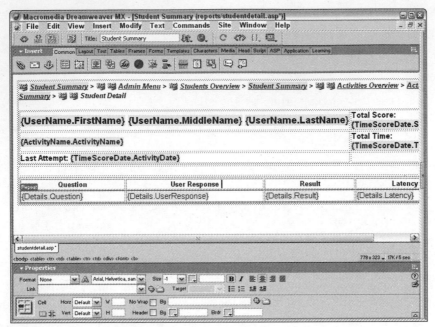

Figure 18-27: The Student Summary being editing in Dreamweaver MX

Table 18-2 lists the ASP pages created by Learning Site. You can make content style changes to any of them except the ones clearly marked "Do not modify this file."

TABLE 18-2 ASP PAGES CREATED BY LEARNING SITE

ASP Page	Folder Location	Description
LearningSite.asp	connections	The DSN definition. **Do not modify this file.**
activities.asp	reports	The Activities Overview report that you select from the Admin Menu.
Activitysummary.asp	reports	The Activity Summary report accessed when you click on an activity name in the Activities Overview report.

ASP Page	Folder Location	Description
adduser.asp	reports	The Add New User form that displays when you select Add User from the Admin Menu.
deleteuser.asp	reports	The confirmation page that displays when you delete a user through the Modify/Delete user report.
modify.asp	reports	A user record that displays when you select the modify option from either the Student Overview report or the Modify/Delete User report.
modifydisplay.asp	reports	The Modify/Delete user report that displays when you select Modify/Delete User from the Admin Menu.
SearchResults.asp	reports	The search results that displays when you search for student or activity data from the Admin Menu.
studentdetail.asp	reports	The Student Detail report that displays when you select a User ID from the Activity Summary report.
studentsPlus.asp	reports	Either the Student Overview report (displays when Student Overview is selected from the Admin Menu) or and the Student Summary report (displays when you select a User ID from the Student Overview).
adminLogin.asp	Root directory	The login screen for administrators.
adminmenu.asp	Root directory	The Admin Menu.
results.asp	Root directory	The results page that displays when the student completes the course.
studenLogin.asp	Root directory	The login screen for students.
tracking.asp	Root directory	Connection information. **Do not modify this file.**

Going Live

When you have tested your course and are satisfied with the data being captured in the database, you are ready to publish it on your "live" Web server (assuming you have been using a testing Web server to this point). There are two main tasks you must perform first:

1. Update the Remote Info fields in the Dreamweaver MX site (Site → Edit Sites from the Dreamweaver MX menu). You need to collect the connection information for the "live" location and insert it into the Remote Info dialog box.

2. Create a Data Source Name (DSN) on the "live" system that matches the DSN created on your testing system; ask your Webmaster, system administrator, ISP, or whomever else is responsible for the administration of that system to create a DSN for your Microsoft Access database.

   If the task falls on your shoulders, refer to the instructions earlier in this chapter regarding the creation of a DSN.

Windows NT/2000 systems have built in support for ASP, but Unix/Linux systems do not. If you are using a Unix/Linux web host, make sure that they are running ChiliSoft for ASP support. Otherwise, the site will not function properly.

Understanding the Microsoft Access Database

You can certainly use and manage your Learning Site LMS without working in Microsoft Access. However, if you run into database problems, or decide you want to make modifications to the database, this section provides a description of the tables and fields within that database.

Microsoft Access is a relational database, and relational databases store data in a series of interrelated tables that are similar in structure to a spreadsheet. The power of a relational database is the key fields that link one table to another, allowing for complex storage, reporting, and computation of data.

For example, Figure 18-28 shows two of the tables within the Microsoft Access database created by Learning Site. The Student_Data table (top table) is linked to the Activity_Detail table (bottom table) through the key field User ID.

This Microsoft Access database was created in Microsoft Access 97, and works on any version of Microsoft Access through the current version. You do not have to convert the database to use it, even if you are running a more recent version.

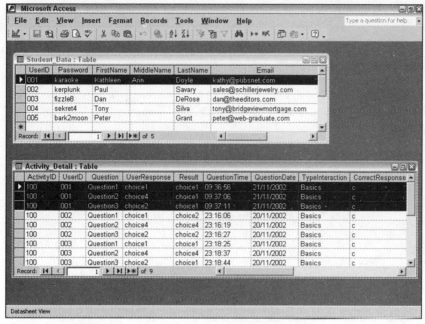

Figure 18-28: The Microsoft Access database created by Learning Site stores information in various tables within the database.

Understanding the tables created by Learning Site

Learning Site creates six tables within the Microsoft Access Learning Site database:

- Activities
- Activity_Detail
- Activity_Status
- Admin_Data
- Session_IDs
- Student_Data

Each of the following sections describes a table and the fields contained within it. Note that some tables contain fields that are not currently used, such as the ActivityDescription field in the Activities table.

Key fields are identified by the image of a key in the Field column.

ACTIVITIES TABLE

The Activities table contains a listing of each activity (course) in the database. The information is written to the database the first time a student accesses that activity.

Figure 18-29 shows an example of the Activities table, and Table 18-3 defines its fields.

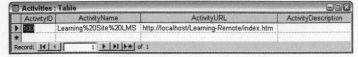

Figure 18-29: The Activities table

TABLE 18-3 FIELDS IN THE ACTIVITIES TABLE

Field	Data Type	Required?	Size	Description
ActivityID 🔑	Text	Yes	50	Unique identifier for activities that you entered on the Tracking tab of the Learning Site dialog box.
ActivityName	Text	No	50	Activity Name field that you entered on the Tracking tab of the Learning Site dialog box.
ActivityURL	Text	No	50	Automatically added by Learning Site when you create the database on the Tracking tab within Learning Site.
ActivityDescription	Memo	No	N/A	Not currently used.

ACTIVITY_DETAIL TABLE

The Activity_Detail table contains details about a specific activity (course) in the database. Figure 18-30 shows an example of the Activity_Detail table, and Table 18-4 defines its fields.

ActivityID	UserID	Question	UserResponse	Result	QuestionTime	QuestionDate
100	001	Question1	choice1	choice1	09:36:56	21/11/2002
100	001	Question2	choice4	choice1	09:37:06	21/11/2002
100	001	Question3	choice2	choice1	09:37:11	21/11/2002
100	002	Question1	choice1	choice2	23:16:06	20/11/2002
100	002	Question2	choice4	choice4	23:16:19	20/11/2002
100	002	Question3	choice2	choice2	23:16:27	20/11/2002
100	003	Question1	choice1	choice1	23:18:25	20/11/2002
100	003	Question2	choice4	choice4	23:18:37	20/11/2002
100	003	Question3	choice2	choice1	23:18:44	20/11/2002

Figure 18-30: The Activity_Detail table (Not all of the fields can be seen in this figure.)

TABLE 18-4 FIELDS IN THE ACTIVITY_DETAIL TABLE

Field	Data Type	Required?	Size	Description
ActivityID	Text	No	255	Unique identifier for activities that you entered on the Tracking tab of the Learning Site dialog box.
UserID	Text	No	255	Unique identifier for students and administrators. Specified by the administrator when a new user is added.
Question	Text	No	255	The text that identifies a specific interaction, entered in the Interaction ID field on the Tracking tab for an interaction.
UserResponse	Text	No	255	The choice selected by the student. Automatically recorded when the interaction is judged.
Result	Text	No	255	The judgement of the User Response. Automatically recorded when the interaction is judged.
QuestionTime	Text	No	255	The time when the interaction was judged.
QuestionDate	Text	No	255	The date when the interaction was judged.
TypeInteraction	Text	No	255	Stores codes representing the interaction: f for Text Entry; m for Drag and Drop; c for everything else.
CorrectResponse	Text	No	255	The correct answer for the interaction.
ResponseValue	Text	No	255	Not used.
Weight	Text	No	255	The weight that you specify on the Tracking tab when you create the interaction.

Continued

TABLE 18–4 FIELDS IN THE ACTIVITY_DETAIL TABLE *(Continued)*

Field	Data Type	Required?	Size	Description
Latency	Text	No	255	The amount of time that the page is loaded before the student answers. Automatically recorded when the interaction is judged.
ObjectiveID	Text	No	255	The Objective ID entered on the Tracking tab when the interaction was created. (See Caution about this field under the section "Defining tracking for each interaction" earlier in this chapter.)

ACTIVITY_STATUS TABLE

The Activity_Status table contains information about each student's status for each course in the database (such as his final score for a course). Figure 18-31 shows an example of the Activity_Status table, and Table 18-5 defines its fields.

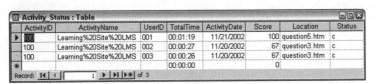

Figure 18-31: The Activitiy_Status table

ADMIN_DATA TABLE

The Admin_Data table contains the login information for each administrator in the database. Figure 18-32 shows an example of the Admin_Data table, and Table 18-6 defines its fields.

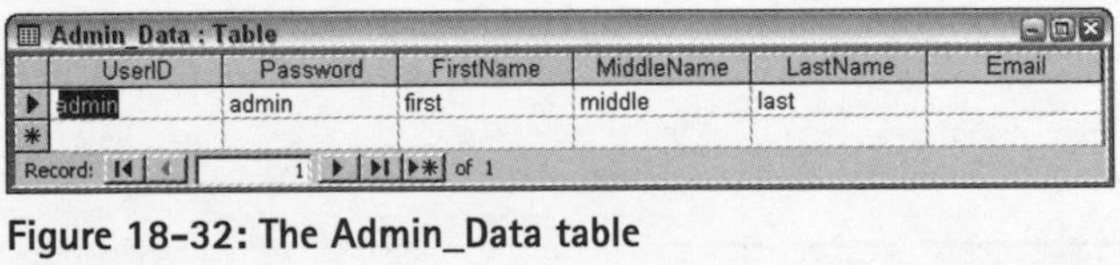

Figure 18-32: The Admin_Data table

TABLE 18-5 FIELDS IN THE ACTIVITY_STATUS TABLE

Field	Data Type	Required?	Size	Description
ActivityID 🔑	Text	No	50	Unique identifier for activities that you entered on the Tracking tab of the Learning Site dialog box.
ActivityName	Text	No	255	Activity Name field that you entered on the Tracking tab of the Learning Site dialog box.
UserID 🔑	Text	No	255	Unique identifier for students and administrators. Specified by the administrator when a new user is added.
TotalTime	Text	No	50	Total time for a session, starting with the first judged interaction.
ActivityDate	Date/Time	No	N/A	Date for the session.
Score	Number	No	Double	Total score, calculated as described in the section on scoring earlier in this chapter. Remember, if students don't answer all the questions, their score is calculated based their partial answers as if they were the complete test.
Location	Text	No	255	Last page (with a judged interaction) that the student accessed for the activity.
Status	Text	No	255	Indicates if the activity is complete (C) or incomplete (I). Students receive an incomplete if they quit the course before the results.asp page is processed.

TABLE 18-6 FIELDS IN THE ADMIN_DATA TABLE

Field	Data Type	Required?	Size	Description
UserID 🔑	Text	Yes	50	Unique identifier for students and administrators. Specified by the administrator when a new user is added.
Password	Text	Yes	255	Specified by administrator when adding or modifying user.
FirstName	Text	Yes	255	Specified by administrator when adding or modifying user.
MiddleName	Text	No	255	Specified by administrator when adding or modifying user.
LastName	Text	Yes	255	Specified by administrator when adding or modifying user.
Email	Text	No	50	Specified by administrator when adding or modifying user.

SESSION_IDS TABLE

The Session_IDs table contains information about each student's latest session. Each time a student logs in to the course, Learning Site creates a new SessionID in the database. Figure 18-33 shows an example of the Session_IDs table, and Table 18-7 defines its fields.

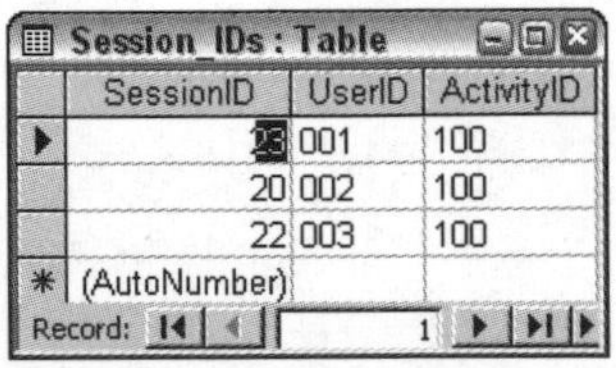

Figure 18-33: The Session_IDs table

TABLE 18-7 FIELDS IN THE SESSION_IDS TABLE

Field	Data Type	Required?	Size	Description
SessionID	AutoNumber	N/A	Long Integer	Unique identifier automatically created by Learning Site each time a student logs into the course.
UserID	Text	No	50	Unique identifier for students and administrators. Specified by the administrator when a new user is added.
ActivityID	Text	No	50	Unique identifier for activities that you entered on the Tracking tab of the Learning Site dialog box.

STUDENT_DATA TABLE

The Student_Data table contains information about each student in the database. Figure 18-34 shows an example of the Student_Data table, and Table 18-8 defines its fields.

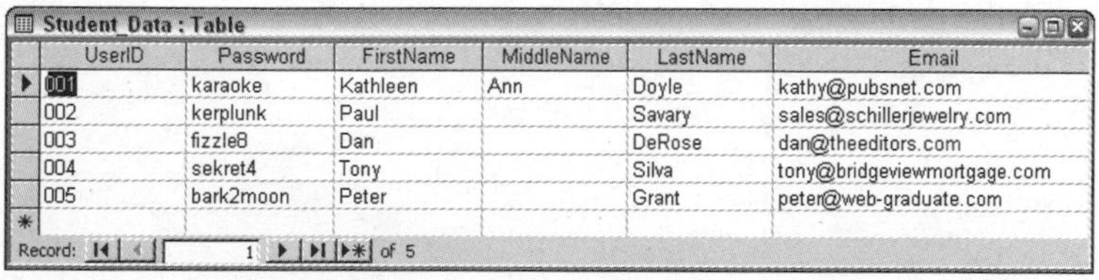

UserID	Password	FirstName	MiddleName	LastName	Email
001	karaoke	Kathleen	Ann	Doyle	kathy@pubsnet.com
002	kerplunk	Paul		Savary	sales@schillerjewelry.com
003	fizzle8	Dan		DeRose	dan@theeditors.com
004	sekret4	Tony		Silva	tony@bridgeviewmortgage.com
005	bark2moon	Peter		Grant	peter@web-graduate.com

Record: |◄| ◄ | 1 | ► | ►| | ►* | of 5

Figure 18-34: The Student_Data table

TABLE 18-8: FIELDS IN THE STUDENT_DATA TABLE

Field	Data Type	Required?	Size	Description
UserID 🔑	Text	Yes	50	Student's user ID for logging in, specified by the administrator when adding a new user.
Password	Text	Yes	255	Student's password, specified by administrator when adding or modifying user.
FirstName	Text	No	255	Student's first name, specified by administrator when adding or modifying user.
MiddleName	Text	No	255	Student's middle name, specified by administrator when adding or modifying user.
LastName	Text	Yes	255	Student's last name, specified by administrator when adding or modifying user.
Email	Text	No	50	Student's email, specified by administrator when adding or modifying user.

Using one database for multiple courses

You can easily use a single database for multiple activities (courses), which enables you to use central data management for your e-Learning courses. When you create additional courses, simply point to the same database.

◆ Each activity (course) must have a unique Activity ID specified on the Tracking tab for the Learning Site dialog box when you create the course.

◆ Each activity must point to the same DSN, because the DSN identifies the data source.

Summary

This chapter described how to

◆ Install and set up the Learning Management System that ships with Learning Site.

◆ Add tracking capabilities to CourseBuilder interactions.

◆ Track results for students and activities (courses).

◆ Publish your course to a live system, including all tracking and reporting capabilities.

Chapter 19

Sending Results to a Learning Management System

LEARNING MANAGEMENT Systems (LMS) are software programs that facilitate the delivery and administration of online training by authorizing students, tracking student performance, providing management reports, and so forth.

Brandon Hall, one of the best-known consultants in the e-Learning industry, publishes an annual review of LMS that, for the 2002 report, covered more than 70 different LMS systems. There are some emerging standards (discussed later in), but those standards are still in their infancy.

CourseBuilder is able to communicate with any LMS system that is AICC-compliant (defined later in this chapter); however, CourseBuilder is limited to sending information *to* an LMS, and cannot receive information *from* an LMS.

This chapter describes the tasks you need to perform on the CourseBuilder side to enable communications with a Learning Management System. Given that there are 70+ possibilities on the "other side of the house", you will need to consult your LMS documentation for that side of the conversation.

Communicating with an LMS

Enabling communications between a CourseBuilder course and an LMS requires work at both the CourseBuilder and LMS levels.

Here are the steps to enable a CourseBuilder course to communicate to the LMS:

1. Create a tracking frameset.

2. Select Knowledge Track on the General tab for each interaction.

3. Accept the default communications or select specific tracking actions in the Action Manager.

Refer to your LMS documentation to understand how it will communicate with CourseBuilder.

Create a tracking frameset

A CourseBuilder course uses a hidden tracking frameset to communicate with the LMS. You can create this hidden frameset regardless of whether your course currently uses a frameset (if your site does use a frameset, CourseBuilder adds that frameset into the tracking frameset).

For example, if we want to include a tracking frameset for *The Presidential Files* course (which does not currently use frames), here's what we'd do:

1. Open the initial page for the course, `presidents1.htm`.

2. Choose Modify → CourseBuilder → Create Tracking Frameset from the Dreamweaver MX menu. CourseBuilder displays the Create Tracking Frameset dialog box, as shown in Figure 19-1.

3. By default, CourseBuilder names the tracking frameset by adding a suffix of `-frameset` to the original filename, creating a new frameset file named `presidents1-frameset.htm`.

   CourseBuilder also creates a file named `results.htm`, which remains resident in the hidden frame, named `cmiresults`.

   Accept the defaults by clicking the OK button. CourseBuilder adds the frameset file and the results file (`results.htm`) to your site.

The hidden frame has minimal impact on what the student sees (see Figure 19-2).

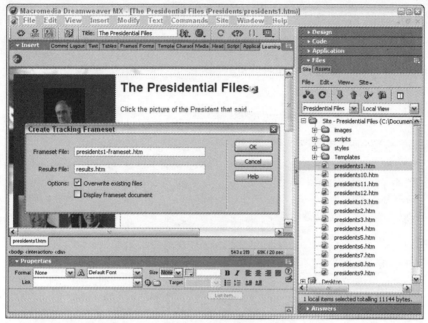

Figure 19-1: Create Tracking Frameset dialog box.

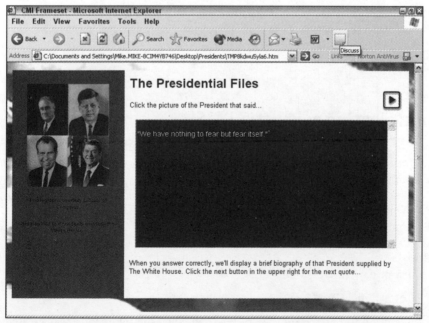

Figure 19-2: The hidden frame cmiresults is virtually invisible to students.

Enabling interactions for tracking

Communications between your course and an LMS is at the interaction level. You specify those communications by selecting the Knowledge Track option (see Figure 19-3) on *every* interaction that you want to communicate with the LMS.

Select Knowledge Track to track interaction results

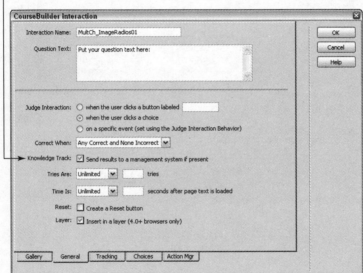

Figure 19-3: Enable tracking for each interaction that will communicate with the LMS.

Communicating with the LMS

When a CourseBuilder interaction is judged, that interaction automatically passes certain information to an LMS if tracking is enabled. You can, however, initiate specific communications through the Action Manager of any interaction.

INFORMATION AUTOMATICALLY COMMUNICATED

CourseBuilder automatically communicates the following information if Knowledge Tracking is enabled:

- ◆ Current date (DD/MM/YYYY)
- ◆ Current time (HH:MM:SS)
- ◆ Interaction ID entered on the Tracking tab when the interaction was created
- ◆ Objective ID entered on the Tracking tab when the interaction was created
- ◆ Type of interaction

- ◆ Correct answer
- ◆ Student's answer
- ◆ Response judged correct or incorrect?
- ◆ Weight
- ◆ Time it took for student to answer (latency)

The Activities Detail table in Chapter 18 provides descriptions of these fields.

INFORMATION YOU CAN SEND FROM THE ACTION MANAGER

CourseBuilder provides eight actions that you can select to initiate specific communications with an LMS (although CourseBuilder cannot receive communications *from* an LMS). Those actions can be initiated like any other action within the Action Manager.

By using actions in the Action Manager, you can pass different interaction values to an LMS. To pass those values, you must understand how they are stored as JavaScript variables.

JavaScript variables for tracking use the format G01.*variable*, where G01 is the CourseBuilder variable identifying the specific interaction, and *variable* is the tracking variable for score. For example, the score for the second interaction on a page (G02) is stored in the JavaScript variable G02.score.

These variables are automatically tracked for every interaction, so you simply need to reference the variable. Table 19-1 lists the tracking variables available for each interaction.

TABLE 19-1 COURSEBUILDER JAVASCRIPT VARIABLES FOR TRACKING

Variable	Description
score	Numeric score for the interaction.
totalCorrect	Number of correct responses the student selected.
totalIncorrect	Total number of incorrect responses the student selected.
possCorrect	Total number of correct choices of elements defined for the interaction.
possIncorrect	Total number of incorrect choices or elements defined for the interaction.
correct	True if student answer is judged as correct, false if student answer is judged as incorrect.
tries	Number of attempts the student made in answering.

Continued

TABLE **19-1** COURSEBUILDER JAVASCRIPT VARIABLES FOR TRACKING *(Continued)*

Variable	Description
triesLimit	Number of attempts the student is allowed to make.
time	Amount of time (HH:MM:SS format) elapsed for an interaction.
timeLimit	Amount of time (HH:MM:SS format) the student is allowed to enter an answer.
trackIntId	The Interaction ID as entered on the Tracking tab for the interaction.
trackObjectiveID	The Objective ID as entered on the Tracking tab for the interaction.
trackQType	String identifying the type of interaction.
trackWeight	Weight as entered on the Tracking tab for the interaction.

Table 19-2 lists the different tracking actions that are available from within the Action Manager drop-down menu.

TABLE **19-2** ACTION MANAGER TRACKING ACTIONS

Send Action	Description
Core Data	
Status	Select from: Passed, Completed, Failed, Incomplete, Browsed, Not Attempted.
Location	URL (address) of the LMS.
Score	As a JavaScript expression for the score, using CourseBuilder variables, such as {G01.score+G02.score}.
Time	As a JavaScript expression, such as {G01.time}.
ExitAU	
ExitAU	Sends a notice to the LMS to exit the Assignable Unit. CourseBuilder cannot process any returned data.

Send Action	Description
GetParam	
GetParam	Not operational.
Interaction Info	
Interaction ID	As defined on the Tracking tab for the interaction, such as {G01. trackIntId}.
Objective ID	As defined on the Tracking tab for the interaction, such as {G01. trackObjectiveID}.
Interaction Type	Select from: True/False, Multiple Choice, Fill-in-the-blank, Matching, Simple Performance, Sequencing, Linkert, Unanticipated.
List Correct Response(s)	However the correct responses are defined on the appropriate interaction's tab (Choices, Responses, Pairs, Hot Areas, Ranges).
List Student Response(s)	However the student responses are defined for the answers they selected, which are also defined on the appropriate interaction's tab (Choices, Responses, Pairs, Hot Areas, Ranges).
List Result(s)	How the interaction was judged (c=correct, w=incorrect, n=not answered).
Weight	The weight as defined on the Tracking tab for the interaction, such as {G01. TrackWeight}.
Latency	Entered in the format 00:00:00 (hours:minutes:seconds).
Lesson Status	
Lesson Status	Select from: Passed, Completed, Failed, Incomplete, Browsed, Not Attempted.
Lesson Time	
Lesson Time	Either choose a specific interaction from a drop-down menu, or choose <custom> from the drop-down menu and define the time for an interaction explicitly or using the JavaScript variables, such as {G01.time}.

Continued

TABLE **19-2** ACTION MANAGER TRACKING ACTIONS *(Continued)*

Send Action bjective Info	Description
Interaction	Either choose from a specific interaction from a drop-down menu, or choose <custom> from the drop-down menu. If you choose <custom>, two additional fields are displayed: Objective ID and Score.
Status	Select from: Passed, Completed, Failed, Incomplete, Browsed, Not Attempted.
Objective ID	As defined on the Tracking tab for the interaction, such as {G01. trackObjectiveID}.
Score	As a JavaScript expression for the score, using CourseBuilder variables, such as {G01.score+G02.score}.
Score	
Score	As a JavaScript expression for the score, using CourseBuilder variables, such as {G01.score+G02.score}.

Reviewing Standards

e-Learning technology is still in its infancy. Because of this, the state of standards is also in its infancy. There are two standards, however, that have received considerable attention in the e-Learning world:

◆ A guideline published by the AICC (Aviation Industry CBT Committee), which specifies guidelines for communications between courseware and Learning Management Systems. This is often referred to as the Computer Managed Instruction (CMI) standard.

AICC-compliancy requires two-way communications between the LMS and courseware. CourseBuilder can communicate with an LMS that is AICC-compliant, it cannot receive communications and is thus itself *not* AICC-compliant.

◆ The Sharable Content Object Reference Model (SCORM), standards developed by the Advanced Distributed Learning initiative, which enables interoperability, accessibility and reusability of Web-based learning content.

Again, CourseBuilder is not SCORM-compliant. However, Tom King has created two extensions to help (both available at www.macromedia.com/exchange/):

Manifest Maker for ADL SCORM Extension, which creates a default content packaging manifest for compliance with the ADL SCORM Version 1.2 specification.

SCORM Runtime Wrapper, which inserts the required JavaScript code and HTML attributes for compliance with the ADL SCORM Version 1.2 specification.

There are a number of organizations working toward standards for learning technology. Table 19-3 provides an overview of the most notable organizations and the focus of their efforts.

TABLE 19-3 DEVELOPING STANDARDS FOR LEARNING TECHNOLOGY

Organization	Description
ADL (Advanced Distributed Learning)	**Focus:** The Sharable Content Object Reference Model (SCORM), standards that enable interoperability, accessibility and reusability of Web-based learning content.
	Web site: www.adlnet.org
ALIC (Advanced Learning Infrastructure Consortium)	**Focus:** (Asian focus) Creates learning environments that enable anyone to learn anytime and anywhere, according to the goals, pace, interests, understanding of individuals and groups.
	Web site: www.alic.gr.jp/
ARIADNE Foundation	**Focus:** (European focus) Creates tools and methodologies for producing, managing and reusing computer-based training elements.
	Web site: www.ariadne-eu.org/

Continued

TABLE 19-3 DEVELOPING STANDARDS FOR LEARNING TECHNOLOGY *(Continued)*

Organization	Description
AICC (Aviation Industry CBT Consortium)	**Focus:** Originally focused on the aviation industry, its Computer Managed Instruction (CMI) guidelines have become an industry standard for development, delivery, and evaluation of computer-based training technologies. **Web site:** www.aicc.org
IEEE Learning Technology Standards Committee (Institute of Electrical and Electronic Engineers)	**Focus:** Chartered by the parent IEEE organization to develop accredited technical standards, practices and guidelines for learning technology. **Web site:** http://grouper.ieee.org/LTSC/
IMS Global Management Systems (Instructional Management Systems)	**Focus:** Develops and promotes open specifications for facilitating online distributed learning activities such as locating and using educational content, tracking learner progress, reporting learner performance, and exchanging student records between administrative systems. **Web site:** www.imsglobal.org

Summary

This chapter described how to

- Set up CourseBuilder to communicate student performance information to an LMS.
- Use JavaScript variables that CourseBuilder automatically creates and maintains to collect student performance data.

It also discussed the various organizations and standards that are defining the emerging e-Learning industry.

Part V

Appendixes

Appendix A

What's on the CD-ROM

THIS APPENDIX PROVIDES you with information on the contents of the CD that accompanies this book. (For the latest and greatest information, please refer to the ReadMe file located at the root of the CD.) Here is what you will find:

- ◆ System Requirements
- ◆ Using the CD with Windows and Macintosh
- ◆ What's on the CD
- ◆ Troubleshooting

System Requirements

Make sure that your computer meets the minimum system requirements listed in this section. If your computer doesn't match up to most of these requirements, you may have a problem using the contents of the CD.

For Windows:

- ◆ Intel Pentium II processor or equivalent 300+ MHz
- ◆ Windows 98, 2000, NT, ME or XP
- ◆ 96MB of available RAM (128MB recommended)
- ◆ Internet Explorer or Netscape Navigator 4.0 or greater
- ◆ 275MB available disk space
- ◆ 256-color monitor capable of 800x600 resolution (1024x768, millions of colors recommended)
- ◆ A CD-ROM drive

For Macintosh:

◆ Power Mac G3 or better

◆ Mac OS 9.1 or higher, or Mac OS X 10.1 or higher

◆ Internet Explorer or Netscape Navigator 4.0 or later

◆ 96MB of RAM (128MB recommended)

◆ 275MB available disk space

◆ 256-color monitor capable of 800x600 resolution (1024x768, millions of colors recommended. Thousands of colors required for OS X.)

Using the CD with Windows

To install the items from the CD to your hard drive, follow these steps:

1. Insert the CD into your computer's CD-ROM drive.

   The CD displays a menu with the following options: Install, Browse, eBook, Links, and Exit.

2. Choose one of the following options from the CD menu:

   Install: Gives you the option to install the supplied software and/or the author-created samples on the CD-ROM.

   Browse: Allows you to view the contents of the CD-ROM in its directory structure.

   eBook: Allows you to view an electronic version of the book.

   Links: Opens a hyperlinked page of Web sites.

   Exit: Closes the CD menu.

If the CD menu does not display, follow the steps below to access the CD.

1. Click Start → Run.

2. Type **d:\setup.exe** in the Run dialog box, where *d* is the letter of your CD-ROM drive. The CD displays the CD menu.

3. Choose the Install, Browse, eBook, Links, or Exit option from the CD menu. (See Step 2 in the preceding list for a description of these options.)

Using the CD with the Mac OS

To install the items from the CD to your hard drive, follow these steps:

1. Insert the CD into your CD-ROM drive.

2. Double-click the icon for the CD after it appears on the desktop.

3. Open the program's folder on the CD and double-click the Install or Installer icon. Note: To install some programs, just drag the program's folder from the CD window and drop it on your hard drive icon.

What's on the CD

The following sections provide a summary of the software and other materials you'll find on the CD.

Author-created materials

All author-created material from the book, including code listings and samples, is on the CD in the folder named "Author".

The following folders are contained in the Author folder on the CD:

Planning Documents. Includes the various planners that assist you in organizing, designing, and implementing your Web-Based Training course with CourseBuilder and Learning Site. Also includes a storyboard (.TIF file) for each Learning Site Template.

Samples. Includes 12 fully functioning samples showing various capabilities of CourseBuilder and Learning Site. Of particular note is the *HTML Basics* sample, which is a complete three-hour course demonstrating all of the capabilities of CourseBuilder and Learning Site using an actual course.

Learning Site Templates. Includes 12 specially designed templates only available to users of this book. These templates, along with their associated Cascading Style Sheets, provide you with tremendous flexibility in the visual design of your courses.

Applications

The following applications are on the CD:

Acrobat 5.0 Reader, from Adobe Systems, Inc.

Freeware for Windows and Macintosh. Lets you view and print PDF documents. For more information, check out www.adobe.com.

CourseBuilder for Dreamweaver MX Extension, from Macromedia, Inc.

Freeware for Windows and Macintosh. Quickly create compelling Web-based instructional content that works across multiple platforms and browsers with this powerful extension. For more information, go to www.macromedia.com/exchange/.

Dreamweaver MX, from Macromedia, Inc.

30-day Trial Version for Windows and Macintosh. The most popular Web editing tool in the world lets you work in a single environment to quickly create, build, and manage Web sites and Internet applications. Dreamweaver MX combines strong visual layout tools with rapid Web application development into one complete, integrated solution. For more information, check out www.macromedia.com.

Fireworks MX, from Macromedia, Inc.

30-day Trial Version for Windows and Macintosh. A powerful tool for creating Web graphics that seamlessly integrate with Dreamweaver MX. Macromedia Fireworks MX is the easiest way to create, optimize, and export Web-optimized graphics. For more information, check out www.macromedia.com.

Flash MX, from Macromedia, Inc.

30-day Trial Version for Windows and Macintosh. A powerful tool that lets you create browser-independent movies integrating videoand other media into highly interactive and engaging productions. For more information, go to www.macromedia.com/exchange/.

Flash 6 Player, from Macromedia, Inc.

Freeware for Windows and Macintosh. With almost a half *billion* users on the planet, Flash is the most extensively used plug-in on the Web. Lets you play Flash movies integrated into *or* separately from your Web browser. For more information, go to www.macromedia.com.

Learning Site for Dreamweaver MX Extension, from Macromedia, Inc.

Freeware for Windows and Macintosh. Assemble a training course that combines pages from multiple sources, including Dreamweaver MX Web pages and CourseBuilder interactions. Lets you easily assemble all the pieces of a course, and automatically builds a navigation and menu system. For more information, go to `www.macromedia.com/exchange/`.

 Learning Site does not support Windows 98 or Windows ME as of the printing of this book.

Macromedia Extension Manager 1.5, from Macromedia, Inc.

Freeware for Windows and Macintosh. Use Macromedia Extension Manager to install extensions (such as CourseBuilder and Learning site) into Macromedia products. There are literally hundreds of free extensions that extend the capabilities of Macromedia products by integrating additional options into the products. For more information, check out `www.macromedia.com/exchange/`.

Shareware programs are fully functional, trial versions of copyrighted programs. If you like particular programs, register with their authors for a nominal fee and receive licenses, enhanced versions, and technical support. *Freeware programs* are copyrighted games, applications, and utilities that are free for personal use. Unlike shareware, these programs do not require a fee or provide technical support. *GNU software* is governed by its own license, which is included inside the folder of the GNU product. See the GNU license for more details.

Trial, demo, or evaluation versions are usually limited either by time or functionality (such as being unable to save projects). Some trial versions are very sensitive to system date changes. If you alter your computer's date, the programs will "time out" and will no longer be functional.

eBook version of the Macromedia Dreamweaver MX e-Learning Toolkit

The complete text of this book is on the CD in Adobe's Portable Document Format (PDF). You can read and search through the file with the Adobe Acrobat Reader (also included on the CD).

Bonus content

The CD also includes *Using Macromedia Flash MX Learning Interactions*, from Barbara Nelson and Macromedia. A PDF file that describes how to use Flash MX to create e-Learning content.

Troubleshooting

If you have difficulty installing or using any of the materials on the companion CD, try the following solutions:

- ◆ **Turn off any anti-virus software that you may have running.** Installers sometimes mimic virus activity and can make your computer incorrectly believe that it is being infected by a virus. (Be sure to turn the anti-virus software back on later.)

- ◆ **Close all running programs.** The more programs you're running, the less memory is available to other programs. Installers also typically update files and programs; if you keep other programs running, installation may not work properly.

- ◆ **Reference the ReadMe:** Please refer to the ReadMe file located at the root of the CD-ROM for the latest product information at the time of publication.

If you still have trouble with the CD, please call the Wiley Customer Care phone number: (800) 762-2974. Outside the United States, call 1 (317) 572-3994. You can also contact Customer Service by e-mail at techsupdum@wiley.com. Wiley Publishing, Inc. will provide technical support only for installation and other general quality control items; for technical support on the applications themselves, consult the program's vendor or author.

Appendix B

Installing, Using, and Customizing the Learning Site Templates

A LEARNING SITE STYLE CONSISTS of all the graphics, buttons, and HTML used to create the top frame (`navigation.htm`) of a Learning Site. A Learning Site template consists of all the elements for a single Learning Site style. You select a Learning Site style on the Style tab of the Learning Site dialog box.

This appendix explains how to install the additional templates from this book's CD-ROM. If you are content with the templates, that's all you need to do!

However, there may be situations where you want to create a completely customized template and install your custom template into Learning Site – this appendix also explains the procedure for creating and installing your custom templates so they are available from within the Learning Site Styles tab.

Understanding the Folders and Files

Whether you install the additional templates from the CD-ROM or create your own custom templates, you need to understand the folders and files used by Learning Site to recognize the templates on the Style tab. There are three key folders:

◆ `Navigation`, which contains the following for *each* template: a text file containing HTML markup as well as a folder containing all associated images. For example, the Business1 template consists of a text file named `business1.txt` and a folder named `Business1` that contains the images used by that template.

  In addition, the `Navigation` folder contains a folder named `Thumbnails`, which includes a thumbnail .GIF file for each template.

◆ `Commands`, which contains (among other things) a file named `Learning Site.htm`. It's this file that processes the menu of templates on the Learning Site Style tab.

◆ `Images`, which contains the images used for the login and results pages *if* you enable tracking for your Learning Site.

Folder locations

The location of the `Navigation`, `Commands`, and `Images` folders varies, depending on operating system, as shown in the following list. Wherever you see `username` in the path name, that is your name as recognized by the system (it should be obvious when browsing because the folder usually contains the same username that you use to log into the system).

Windows NT systems

The `Navigation` folder is located at

```
C:\WinNT\profiles\username\Application
Data\Macromedia\Dreamweaver
MX\Configuration\Shared\Learning\Navigation
```

The `Commands` folder is located at

```
C:\WinNT\profiles\username\Application
Data\Macromedia\Dreamweaver MX\Configuration\Commands
```

The `Images` folder is located at

```
C:\WinNT\profiles\username\Application
Data\Macromedia\Dreamweaver
MX\Configuration\Shared\Learning\Tracking\Images
```

Windows 2000 and Windows XP systems

The `Navigation` folder is located at

```
C:\Documents and Settings\username\Application
Data\Macromedia\Dreamweaver
MX\Configuration\Shared\Learning\Navigation
```

The `Commands` folder is located at

```
C:\Documents and Settings\username\Application
Data\Macromedia\Dreamweaver MX\Configuration\Commands
```

The `Images` folder is located at

```
C:\Documents and Settings\username\Application
Data\Macromedia\Dreamweaver MX\Configuration\
Shared\Learning\Tracking\Images
```

On Windows XP systems these folders may be contained in hidden folders. From My Computer select Tools → Folder Options. On the View tab, under the Hidden files and folders category, click the Show hidden files and folders category to show all folders.

Mac OS X systems

The `Navigation` folder is located at

```
Hard disk/Users/username/Library/Application
Support/Macromedia/Dreamweaver
MX/Configuration/Shared/Learning/Navigation
```

The `Commands` folder is located at

```
Hard disk/Users/username/Library/Application
Support/Macromedia/Dreamweaver MX/Configuration/Commands
```

The `Images` folder is located at

```
Hard disk/Users/username/Library/Application
Support/Macromedia/Dreamweaver
MX/Configuration/Shared/Learning/Tracking/Images
```

 Hereafter in this Appendix we will refer to the `Navigation`, `Commands`, `Images`, **and** `Thumbnails` **folders knowing that the path to them is system-specific.**

Existing files

Assuming that you haven't created or installed additional templates, your `Navigation` folder contains the folders and files shown in Figure B-1. These are the files for the six templates installed by Learning Site.

Consumer		File Folder
Corporate		File Folder
Custom		File Folder
Educational		File Folder
Scripts		File Folder
Simple		File Folder
Techno		File Folder
Thumbnails		File Folder
consumer.txt	4 KB	Text Document
corporate.txt	5 KB	Text Document
custom.txt	3 KB	Text Document
educational.txt	4 KB	Text Document
menu.htm	1 KB	HTML Document
simple.txt	4 KB	Text Document
techno.txt	4 KB	Text Document

Figure B-1: The original folders and files contained within the Navigation folder

Your `Commands` folder contains many different HTML and JavaScript files, which are used by CourseBuilder and Learning Site to process specialized functions. To modify the list of templates available on the Styles tab within the Learning Site dialog box, we are only concerned with a single file in this folder: `Learning Site.htm`, as shown in Figure B-2.

CourseBuilder Template Fix.js	3 KB	JScript Script File
Create Learning Site.htm	1 KB	HTML Document
Create Pathware Frameset.htm	3 KB	HTML Document
Create Pathware Frameset.js	4 KB	JScript Script File
Create Tracking Frameset.htm	3 KB	HTML Document
Cut Interaction.htm	2 KB	HTML Document
Cut Interaction.js	2 KB	JScript Script File
Learning Site.htm	79 KB	HTML Document
Learning Site.js	37 KB	JScript Script File
Modify Learning Site.htm	1 KB	HTML Document
Name Editor.htm	2 KB	HTML Document
Name Editor.js	2 KB	JScript Script File
Paste Interaction.htm	3 KB	HTML Document
Paste Interaction.js	2 KB	JScript Script File
Segment Editor.htm	2 KB	HTML Document
Segment Editor.js	2 KB	JScript Script File

Figure B-2: The `Learning Site.htm` file in the Commands folder contains the menu of templates displayed by the Style tab in the Learning Site dialog box.

Your `Images` folder (within the `Tracking` folder) contains two images for each of Learning Site's five templates. Learning Site uses these images, shown in Figure B-3, when you enable tracking, which creates a login page and results page for each course.

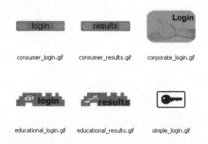

consumer_login.gif   consumer_results.gif   corporate_login.gif

educational_login.gif   educational_results.gif   simple_login.gif

Figure B-3: Images used by Learning Site on the login and results pages when tracking is enabled

Installing the Templates on the CD-ROM

The word "installation" might be a little bit of a misnomer for this task, because all you need to do is copy files from the CD-ROM to the folders and *voila,* they're installed! Because Learning Site reads the Learning Site.htm file to determine the menu for the Style tab, we are going to copy a new version of that file, one that includes the 12 additional templates in the Style tab menu.

Follow these steps to replace your existing Navigation folder and Learning Site.htm file with the new versions on the CD-ROM:

1. Rename the existing Navigation folder on your system. (Choose a name such as Navigation-Archive.) That way, if you encounter problems you can easily return to your original state.

2. Copy the entire Navigation folder from the CD-ROM and place it in the same folder (Learning) as the original.

3. Rename the existing Learning Site.htm file in the Commands folder on your system to something like Learning Site Archive.htm, again to maintain the original in case you encounter problems.

4. Copy the Learning Site.htm file from the CD-ROM and place it in the same Commands folder as the original.

5. Rename the existing Images folder in the Tracking folder on your system to a different name, such as Images Archive. (Because Images is such a common name for folders, be sure you are renaming the Images folder contained within the Tracking folder.)

6. Copy the Images folder from the CD-ROM and place it in the same folder (Tracking) as the original.

You can check the installation of the new templates by creating a new or modifying an existing Learning Site. The Style tab should now show all of the new templates as well as Learning Site's original templates, as shown in Figure B-4.

If you already have Dreamweaver MX open, you may need to close it and then reopen it to see the new templates.

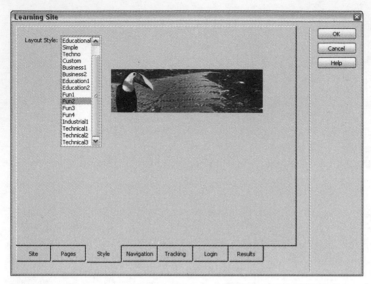

Figure B-4: The new templates are merged with the original Learning Site templates, ready to be used.

Using the Associated Cascading Style Sheets

Each template on the CD-ROM includes a Cascading Style Sheet (CSS) that enables you – in a single step – to attach style characteristics to every page in your course (of course, using the CSS is entirely optional on your part – you can still use the templates without using the associated CSS files).

Although the CSS files are not strictly part of a Learning Site template, you can use them to change many of the style characteristics of the content for a course to match the design of the navigation frame (navFrame), giving your course a unified design.

Each of the 12 additional templates has a unique CSS that follows the naming convention of the template. So, for example, the template education1 has a CSS named education1.css.

In addition to defining fonts and colors for many elements of content (paragraphs, lists, table, headers, and so forth), each CSS also includes a set of seven "highlight markers" that you can use to highlight important points, much like a student highlighting important text in a textbook. (To highlight text in a file that has a CSS attached, simply select the text and choose Text → CSS Styles from the Dreamweaver MX menu, and you'll see the 7 highlight markers listed: blue, cream, gray, green, pink, purple, and yellow.)

When you want to use a particular CSS, copy it from the CD-ROM and paste it into the `styles` folder within your Dreamweaver MX site (or wherever you store your CSS files), and attach the CSS to each file, as described in Chapter 3.

Creating Custom Learning Site Styles

The biggest trick to creating a custom Learning Site style is understanding the files and folders that are involved. If you are going to create a custom Learning Site style, I highly recommend that you install the additional templates from the CD-ROM (even if you don't plan on using them) just to get a feel for the files, folders, and process for adding new templates.

When you create a custom Learning Site style, you give yourself complete control over the visual design of your course. You can include your company logo, use background graphics, insert special effects — you're in complete control!

Here's the general process for creating a custom template (we'll take a look at the details in the following sections):

1. Select a name for your template.

2. Design the layout of the navigation in a Dreamweaver MX page.

3. Attach the appropriate behaviors to each button.

4. Save the page as a text file, with portions of the HTML removed.

5. Copy the files into the `Navigation` folder.

6. Save a thumbnail image of the design in the `Thumbnail` folder within the `Navigation` folder.

7. Save a login and results image of the design in the `Images` folder within the `Tracking` folder (optional; do this only necessary if you use tracking).

8. Update the `Learning Site.htm` menu to list your new template on the Styles tab.

Selecting a name

Select a *single word* as the name for your template. Choose one that is different from the existing template names, which are shown in Table B-1.

TABLE B-1 LEARNING SITE TEMPLATES

Existing Templates	Additional Templates from CD	
Corporate	Business1	Fun3
Consumer	Business2	Fun4
Educational	Education1	Industrial1
Simple	Education2	Technical1
Techno	Fun1	Technical2
Custom	Fun2	Technical3

Designing the layout and attaching button behaviors

When you design your template, keep in mind that there are six buttons in Learning Site that can be programmed to perform navigation functions: Next, Previous, Quit, Menu, Restart, and Finish.

The easiest way to design the layout in Dreamweaver MX is to create a Dreamweaver MX site that contains a folder named images. Then, open the file named navigation-javascript.htm on the CD-ROM (in the Learning Site Templates folder), as shown in Figure B-5.

This file is set up with a properly sized table (100% width by 100 pixels high) and, more importantly, includes a text button that includes all the necessary JavaScript behaviors for processing the navigation for that button. All you need to do is replace the text buttons with your image buttons:

1. Highlight the text for a button. For example, highlight the text for Next.

2. Insert the image for the Next button by clicking the Image icon on the Common tab of the Insert Panel, or by choosing Insert → Image from the Dreamweaver MX main menu. (Be sure to store *all* images for the template in the images folder of your Dreamweaver MX site.)

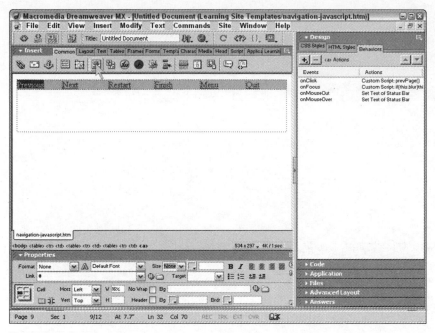

Figure B-5: Opening the `navigation-javascript.htm` file, which lets you easily create a custom template that includes the JavaScript navigation already attached to each text button

Figure B-6 shows the file after the image for the Next button is inserted. Notice that the image file for the Previous button is selected (as shown in the Properties panel), and that the image file also has the behaviors attached, as shown on the Behaviors panel.

Once you replace each text button with an image button, you can rearrange the image buttons, attach behaviors to buttons, add other images for decoration, add a background tile, and so forth.

If you try to replace the text button using a rollover image, Dreamweaver MX will *not* insert the necessary JavaScript behaviors that allow the button to be used for Learning Site navigation. If you want a rollover image, replace the text button with an image, and then attach a Swap Image behavior to that image.

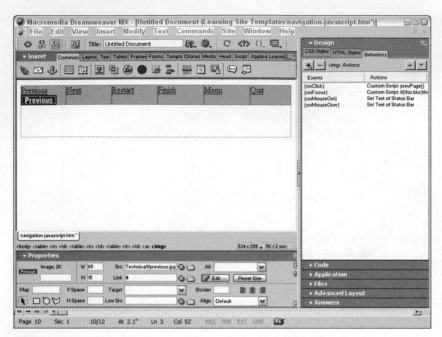

Figure B-6: Inserting graphics and buttons into the navigation table

Saving the page as a text file

HTML files used for a Learning Site template must contain *only* the code between the `<BODY>` and `</BODY>` tags, and be saved as a text file. (Check any of the text files in the `Navigation` folder.)

To save your HTML file as a Learning Site template text file, first save your file as an HTML file. Although Learning Site won't be able to use this version, you'll have it in case you want to make changes in your template later.

Next, change to code view and remove any HTML above the `<BODY>` tag and below the `</BODY>` tag. Then save the remaining code as a text file by choosing File → Save As and choosing a Save as Type Text Files (*.txt), as shown in Figure B-7. Use the name you selected for your template as the file name for the text file; for example, when I created the Fun2 template, I saved the text file for that template as `fun2.txt`.

Copying the files into the `Navigation` folder

The next step in the process is to copy *both* the text file and the `images` folder from your Dreamweaver MX site to the `Navigation` folder used by Learning Site (you do not need to copy the HTML source).

After you copy them into the `Navigation` folder, you need to need to rename the `images` folder using your template name (for example, when I created the Fun2 template I renamed the `images` folder `Fun2`).

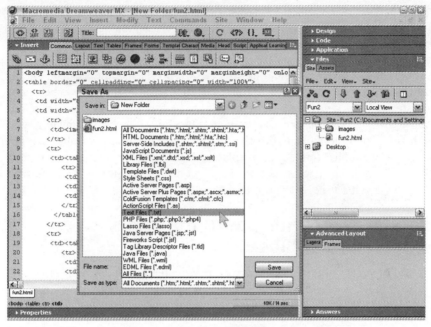

Figure B-7: Saving the HTML as a text file named after your template

 You might be asking why you can't just name your `images` folder to the template name *before* moving it, instead of dealing with this renaming business. **You cannot!** When you copy the text file and images folder to the Navigation folder, they become a Learning Site template. However, if you look at the image references in the text files in the `Navigation` folder, you will see they point to a folder named images. Whenever you *apply* a Learning Site template, Learning Site copies the images from the Navigation folder into the Dreamweaver MX site that applied the template, and stores them in a folder named `images`.

When you're finished, you should have a text file and the newly named folder within the `Navigation` folder. When I created the `Fun2` template, those files were named `fun2.txt` and the `Fun2` folder (capitalization of the name doesn't matter).

Creating the thumbnail, results, and login images (optional)

There are three additional graphics that Learning Site uses for each template: the thumbnail, results, and login graphics. (The creation of these graphics is optional; the template will work without them.)

The thumbnail graphic is a .GIF preview graphic that Learning Site displays on the Style tab of the Learning Site dialog box when you select a template. Use the name of the template, and be sure to save it as a .GIF file in the Thumbnails folder within the Navigation folder. The Fun2 template's thumbnail graphic, for example, is named Fun2.gif. Thumbnail graphics should be sized at 290 pixels wide by 82 pixels high.

The results and login graphics are used in the results and login pages when your Learning Site uses tracking (see Chapters 18 and 19 for more information about results and login pages). You can size your graphics to whatever dimensions you want. Each file should be named with the template name plus the results or login suffix. So, for example, the Fun2 template's login graphic would be named Fun2_login.gif and the results graphic Fun2_results.gif. Store them both in the Images folder within the Tracking folder.

Adding your new template to the Styles, Login, and Results tabs

Now that you've created the files necessary for your template, the final step is to get the new template name displayed in the following locations in your Learning Site dialog box:

- ◆ List of templates on the Style tab
- ◆ List of login logos on the Login tab
- ◆ List of results logos on the Results tab

To insert the new template, open the Learning Site.htm file (located in the Commands folder) in Dreamweaver MX, and edit it from Code view. You will need to add an option for your new template in three different options lists (one for Style, one for Login, and one for Results) within the LearningSite.htm file (Figure B-8 shows a sample option list for Style).

 I highly recommend making a backup copy of LearningSite.htm before you edit it; that way, you have a backup copy to fall back on should you run into problems when editing the file.

You need to insert the same code at the end of the option list for each tab (replacing your new template name where you see the example template Fun2, just above the end tag </SELECT>):

```
<OPTION>Fun2</OPTION>
```

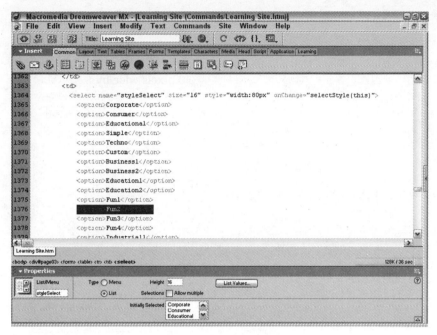

Figure B-8: Updating the `Learning Site.htm` file

To easily find these lists in the file, you can search for the opening of each list, as follows:

◆ **Style options list:** `<select name="styleSelect"`

◆ **Login options list:** `<select name="loginLogoSelect"`

◆ **Results options list:** `<select name="resultsLogoSelect"`

It is important that the name you use between the `<OPTION></OPTION>` tags matches the name of the text file and the folder containing the images for the new template — that is how Learning Site makes the connection between the option name and the template files. You can arrange additional template names however you want, as long as they fall below the Custom template option.

Appendix C

Creating Custom CourseBuilder Interactions

IF YOU FIND YOURSELF modifying a CourseBuilder interaction often in approximately the same way, consider creating a custom CourseBuilder interaction, which is a fairly simple process.

For example, assume you create a multiple-choice question that uses custom graphics for the buttons, or that has specific rules defined in the Action Manager to send feedback to a frame. Each time you insert that multiple-choice interaction, you must modify the settings for it. A custom interaction enables you to make the changes once, store a copy of the interaction in the CourseBuilder Gallery, and then insert the modified interaction wherever you need it!

When you create the custom interaction, CourseBuilder maintains your settings from *all* tabs for that interaction. You could change the settings on the General tab, Choices tab, and Action Manager tab, and all those settings would be saved. You can create a custom interaction for any of the eight categories of interaction or create a custom category as well.

In addition, CourseBuilder saves any style characteristics and reformatting of the interaction that you do before saving it as a custom interaction. As a general rule, whatever Dreamweaver MX highlights as part of the interaction when you select the interaction will be saved as part of the custom interaction.

Creating your Custom Interaction

To copy a modified interaction into the CourseBuilder Gallery (thus creating a custom interaction), you:

1. Select an inserted interaction in Dreamweaver MX by clicking on the invisible element representing the interaction, or by clicking on the <INTERACTION> tag in the tag selector.

2. Choose Modify → CourseBuilder → Add Interaction to Gallery from the Dreamweaver MX. CourseBuilder displays the Add Interaction to Gallery dialog box.

3. Choose to include the custom interaction in an existing category or click New to type in the name of a new category. (A new category name is limited to 20 characters.)

4. Determine whether your interaction should be available to all browsers (3.0), or just 4.0 and later (4.0+) browsers. (Unless there are unusual circumstances, you would normally select 4.0+ browsers.) Remember, all interactions are available for 4.0 browsers, and only a select few are available for 3.0 browsers.

5. Name your custom interaction (template) using up to 20 characters. The Existing drop-down menu shows the existing interactions for the category you chose. Figure C-1 shows a custom interaction being named `doyle_custom`.

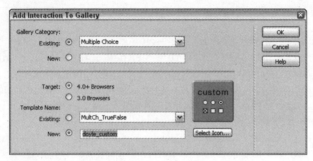

Figure C-1: Adding a modified interaction to the CourseBuilder Gallery

 Although you can select an existing template name for your custom interaction, doing so will delete the existing template. I highly recommend against selecting an existing template.

6. You can create a custom icon to represent your new CourseBuilder interaction, or you can keep the default custom icon. If you decide to create a new icon, the graphic must by an 80x80-pixel .GIF file that is stored in the appropriate category folder within the `Gallery` folder described in the next section, "Deleting Custom Interactions and Replacing the Gallery Icon."

7. Click OK to create your custom CourseBuilder interaction.

After you create a custom interaction, that interaction is available to any site you edit. You select and insert a custom interaction from the CourseBuilder Gallery in the same way that you insert any other CourseBuilder interaction, as shown in Figure C-2.

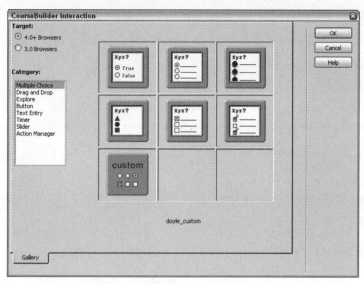

Figure C-2: Inserting a custom CourseBuilder interaction from the CourseBuilder Interaction dialog box

Deleting Custom Interactions and Replacing the Gallery Icon

CourseBuilder Gallery interactions are stored in `C:\Program Files\Macromedia\ Dreamweaver MX\CourseBuilder\Gallery`.

Within the `Gallery` folder are eight folders, one for each category of CourseBuilder interaction. CourseBuilder creates an additional folder for each new category if you choose to create a new category in the Add Interaction to Gallery dialog box.

Our `doyle_custom` template (remember, interactions in the CourseBuilder Gallery are called templates), for example, appears in the `Multiple Choice` folder (see Figure C-3). CourseBuilder has added the new icon .GIF file (`100_doyle_ custom_04.gif`) and an .AGT file (`100_doyle_custom_04.agt`), which contains the actual definitions for the interaction.

If you choose to create a different icon in the future, simply replace the icon .GIF file with a new .GIF file.

If you want to delete a custom interaction entirely, simply delete the appropriate .GIF and .AGT files.

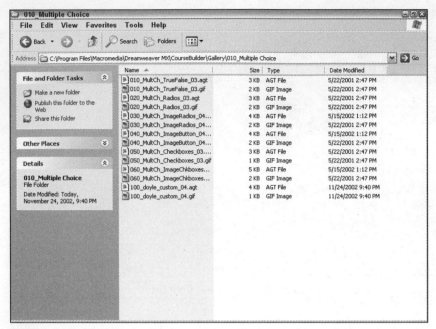

Figure C-3: The `Multiple Choice` folder within the `Gallery` folder contains the newly-added custom interaction.

Appendix D

Changing CourseBuilder Preferences

THE PREFERENCES.TXT FILE contains definitions for many of the default settings when working with CourseBuilder interactions. These settings affect your CourseBuilder working environment, and not just a specific interaction or site.

The file is stored in the directory C:\Program Files\Macromedia\Dreamweaver MX\CourseBuilder\Config.

You can edit preferences.txt using any text editor. Table D-1 describes the variables you can modify in the file.

When you change the definitions in preferences.txt, you change the definitions for all CourseBuilder development activities going forward.

TABLE D-1 VARIABLE SETTINGS THAT YOU CAN MODIFY

Variable	Description
`var PREF_scriptsUrl = "scripts"` `var PREF_imagesUrl = "images"`	Specifies the folder path where support files are copied. By default, CourseBuilder copies the images and scripts folders to your root directory. You can, however, change the default location of support files to be site-relative. See your Dreamweaver MX documentation for information about site-relative path names. *Continued*

TABLE **D-1 VARIABLE SETTINGS THAT YOU CAN MODIFY** *(Continued)*

Variable	Description
`var PREF_addFeedbackSegsToAm = "auto"`	Automatically add a feedback segment in the Action Manager when you add a new element or choice to an interaction. Specify `"true"` if you always want to add a feedback segment automatically; `"false"` if you never want to add a feedback segment automatically; and `"auto"` if you only want to add feedback if the other elements and choices already have feedback segments. By default, this setting is `"auto"`.
`var PREF_delFeedbackSegsFromAm = true`	Explore hot areas have feedback segments automatically created in the Action Manager. By setting this variable to `true`, CourseBuilder deletes the appropriate Action Manager rules if a hot area is deleted. By default, this setting is `true`.
`var PREF_newElemName = "unnamed"`	When you add a new element or choice to an interaction, this variable defines the default name for element. By default, this setting is `"unnamed"`.
`var PREF_defaultTriesLimit = 3`	Defines the default number of tries on the General tab. By default, this setting is `3`.
`var PREF_defaultTimeLimit = 60`	Defines the default number of seconds for the time limit on the General tab. By default, this setting is `60`.

Variable	Description
`var PREF_defaultJudgeBtnName = "Submit"`	Defines the default label for the *Judge Interaction* when the user clicks a button labeled setting on the General tab. By default, this setting is `"Submit"`.
`var PREF_defaultResetBtnName = "Reset"`	Defines the default label for the reset button defined on the General tab. By default, this setting is "Reset".
`var PREF_layerStyle = "left:150px; width:200px; height:115px; z-index:1; visibility:visible;";`	Layer properties when selecting the *insert layer* option on either the General tab or Property inspector for interactions.
`var PREF_backdropLayerStyle = "left:25px; top:25px; width:100px; height:100px; z-index:1; visibility:visible;";`	Layer properties when inserting a backdrop image in the Explore interaction.
`var PREF_imageAttributes = "BORDER=0"`	Image attributes for images added in the multiple-choice (Choices tab), drag-and-drop (Elements tab), or explore (Hot Areas) interactions. Format the attributes using the same format as in an HTML tag, with each attribute separated by a space.
`var PREF_autoCondNameLength = 35`	Maximum length (in characters) of a condition name in the Action Manager. By default, this setting is 35.
`var PREF_defaultSegName = ""`	The default name provided when adding a segment in the Action Manager. By default, there is no default name provided.

Index

Symbols

`.highlight` (dot, highlight) CSS class, 57

`#` (number symbol) named anchor prefix, 44

A

`.aam` files, 141

Access database. *See* Microsoft Access database, working with

Acrobat Reader (on the CD), 496

action. *See also* Action Manager; behavior

    Action Manager hierarchy, moving in, 403

    Action Manager interaction, triggering using, 391–394

    browser information, retrieving using, 69, 121, 410

    browser, opening new using, 69, 122, 168–169

    CourseBuilder, added by, 122–123

    cutting/copying/pasting, 403

    Flash movie, controlling using, 69, 121, 125

    form, validating using, 70, 122

    frameset text, setting using, 121, 201

    image, preloading using, 70, 122

    image, swapping using, 70, 122, 283–284, 300

    interaction property, setting using, 122

    JavaScript associated with, 68, 192, 193, 408–409

    JavaScript, calling using, 69, 121, 430–431, 432

    jump menu, inserting using, 69, 122

    layer, displaying/hiding using, 70, 122, 125–126

    layer text, setting using, 121, 125–126, 296–297, 393–394, 395–397

    LMS, communicating with using, 123

    plug-in existence, checking using, 69, 121

    popup menu, displaying/hiding using, 69, 70, 122

    popup message, displaying using, 70, 122, 201

    Shockwave movie, controlling using, 69, 121, 125

    sound, playing using, 69, 122

    status bar text, setting using, 121

    text, inserting using, 70, 121, 122

    timeline, controlling using, 70, 122

    Timer interaction, triggering using, 369–372

    tracking actions, 123, 486–488

    trigger, 70–73

    URL, loading using, 69, 121

Action Manager. *See also* action; Action Manager interaction

    accessing, 178

    browser type, testing, 410

    browser version, testing, 410

    bug alert, 407–409

    buttons, 402–403

    case match requirement, testing, 415

    condition, cutting/copying/pasting, 403

    condition, defining, 391–398, 401–402

    Condition Editor, 390–391, 404–405, 407–409

    condition expression, creating, 405

    condition expressions, combining, 405

    condition, moving, 403

    condition name length, maximum, 519

    condition planners, 406–407

    condition, response to, 123–124, 404

    condition testing, 404–405

    condition testing, editing JavaScript involved, 408–409

    condition testing for property of element within interaction, 406–407, 413–417

    condition testing for property of interaction as whole, 406–407, 409–413

    context, determining from active rule, 401

    control interaction, relation to, 342–343

    correctness property, testing, 410, 411, 412, 413, 414

    hierarchy, 401

    hierarchy, moving action in, 403

    interaction, as, 384–386

    interaction, relation to, 120

    interaction, testing for disabled, 410, 414

continued

521

continued

continued

continued

continued

continued

Wiley Publishing, Inc.
End–User License Agreement

READ THIS. You should carefully read these terms and conditions before opening the software packet(s) included with this book "Book". This is a license agreement "Agreement" between you and Wiley Publishing, Inc."WPI". By opening the accompanying software packet(s), you acknowledge that you have read and accept the following terms and conditions. If you do not agree and do not want to be bound by such terms and conditions, promptly return the Book and the unopened software packet(s) to the place you obtained them for a full refund.

1. **License Grant.** WPI grants to you (either an individual or entity) a nonexclusive license to use one copy of the enclosed software program(s) (collectively, the "Software" solely for your own personal or non-commercial purposes on a single computer (whether a standard computer or a workstation component of a multi-user network). The Software is in use on a computer when it is loaded into temporary memory (RAM) or installed into permanent memory (hard disk, CD-ROM, or other storage device). WPI reserves all rights not expressly granted herein.

2. **Ownership.** WPI is the owner of all right, title, and interest, including copyright, in and to the compilation of the Software recorded on the disk(s) or CD-ROM "Software Media". Copyright to the individual programs recorded on the Software Media is owned by the author or other authorized copyright owner of each program. Ownership of the Software and all proprietary rights relating thereto remain with WPI and its licensers.

3. **Restrictions On Use and Transfer.**

    (a) You may only (i) make one copy of the Software for backup or archival purposes, or (ii) transfer the Software to a single hard disk, provided that you keep the original for backup or archival purposes. You may not (i) rent or lease the Software, (ii) copy or reproduce the Software through a LAN or other network system or through any computer subscriber system or bulletin- board system, or (iii) modify, adapt, or create derivative works based on the Software.

    (b) You may not reverse engineer, decompile, or disassemble the Software. You may transfer the Software and user documentation on a permanent basis, provided that the transferee agrees to accept the terms and conditions of this Agreement and you retain no copies. If the Software is an update or has been updated, any transfer must include the most recent update and all prior versions.

4. **Restrictions on Use of Individual Programs.** You must follow the individual requirements and restrictions detailed for each individual program in the About the CD-ROM appendix of this Book. These limitations are also contained in the individual license agreements recorded on the Software Media. These limitations may include a requirement that after using the program for a specified period of time, the user must pay a registration fee or discontinue use. By opening the Software packet(s), you will be agreeing to abide by the licenses and restrictions for these individual programs that are detailed in the About the CD-ROM appendix and on the Software Media. None of the material on this Software Media or listed in this Book may ever be redistributed, in original or modified form, for commercial purposes.

5. **Limited Warranty.**

    (a) WPI warrants that the Software and Software Media are free from defects in materials and workmanship under normal use for a period of sixty (60) days from the date of purchase of this Book. If WPI receives notification within the warranty period of defects in materials or workmanship, WPI will replace the defective Software Media.

(b) WPI AND THE AUTHOR OF THE BOOK DISCLAIM ALL OTHER WARRANTIES, EXPRESS OR IMPLIED, INCLUDING WITHOUT LIMITATION IMPLIED WARRANTIES OF MERCHANTABILITY AND FITNESS FOR A PARTICULAR PURPOSE, WITH RESPECT TO THE SOFTWARE, THE PROGRAMS, THE SOURCE CODE CONTAINED THEREIN, AND/OR THE TECHNIQUES DESCRIBED IN THIS BOOK. WPI DOES NOT WARRANT THAT THE FUNCTIONS CONTAINED IN THE SOFTWARE WILL MEET YOUR REQUIREMENTS OR THAT THE OPERATION OF THE SOFTWARE WILL BE ERROR FREE. (c) This limited warranty gives you specific legal rights, andyou may have other rights that vary from jurisdiction to jurisdiction.

6. **Remedies.**

   (a) WPI's entire liability and your exclusive remedy for defects in materials and workmanship shall be limited to replacement of the Software Media, which may be returned to WPI with a copy of your receipt at the following address: Software Media Fulfillment Department, Attn.: *Dreamweaver® MX e-Learning Toolkit*, Wiley Publishing, Inc., 10475 Crosspoint Blvd., Indianapolis, IN 46256, or call 1-800-762-2974. Please allow four to six weeks for delivery. This Limited Warranty is void if failure of the Software Media has resulted from accident, abuse, or misapplication. Any replacement Software Media will be warranted for the remainder of the original warranty period or thirty (30) days, whichever is longer.

   (b) In no event shall WPI or the author be liable for any damages whatsoever (including without limitation damages for loss of business profits, business interruption, loss of business information, or any other pecuniary loss) arising from the use of or inability to use the Book or the Software, even if WPI has been advised of the possibility of such damages.

   (c) Because some jurisdictions do not allow the exclusion or limitation of liability for consequential or incidental damages, the above limitation or exclusion may not apply to you.

7. **U.S. Government Restricted Rights.** Use, duplication, or disclosure of the Software for or on behalf of the United States of America, its agencies and/or instrumentalities "U.S. Government" is subject to restrictions as stated in paragraph (c)(1)(ii) of the Rights in Technical Data and Computer Software clause of DFARS 252.227-7013, or subparagraphs (c) (1) and (2) of the Commercial Computer Software - Restricted Rights clause at FAR 52.227-19, and in similar clauses in the NASA FAR supplement, as applicable.

8. **General.** This Agreement constitutes the entire understanding of the parties and revokes and supersedes all prior agreements, oral or written, between them and may not be modified or amended except in a writing signed by both parties hereto that specifically refers to this Agreement. This Agreement shall take precedence over any other documents that may be in conflict herewith. If any one or more provisions contained in this Agreement are held by any court or tribunal to be invalid, illegal, or otherwise unenforceable, each and every other provision shall remain in full force and effect.